The mission of Circle Ten Council, Boy Scouts of America is to prepare young people to make ethical and moral choices over their lifetimes by instilling in them the values of the Scout Oath and Law.

Circle Ten Council's strategic vision is to instill ethical values in young people living in our council boundaries by: increasing the number of youth we impact, developing a program that delivers the promise, and achieving funding levels that will allow us to deliver the program. Our Board has adopted nine (9) specific goals, with annual benchmarks, for 2010 - 2015 whereby we will measure our effectiveness in reaching this strategic vision.

WHERE
CHARACTER
is CAUGHT

character caught

WHERE CHARACTER *is* CAUGHT

A Century of Stories on Service, Scouting, and Citizenship in Circle Ten Council

DAVID C. SCOTT

Photography by **JOHN K. SHIPES**
Foreword by **ROSS PEROT**

PenlandScott
PUBLISHERS

Published by PENLANDSCOTT PUBLISHERS

PenlandScott Publishers, and colophon are trademarks of
Red Honor Ventures, Ltd.

Text Copyright © 2013 by David C. Scott
Photography Copyright © 2013 by John K. Shipes
All still life photography and image enhancements used on all photographs
within this book ©2013 John K. Shipes
Copyright © 2013 Circle Ten Council, Boy Scouts of America

HARDCOVER PHOTO CREDITS:
FRONT COVER: Top left: Circle Ten Council, Top middle: Chris Fox, Top right: Thomas Alan Hord,
Center: Chris Fox, Bottom left: University of North Texas Libraries, The Portal to Texas History,
credit: Austin Presbyterian Theological Seminary, Austin, Texas, Bottom right: Circle Ten Council

BACK COVER: Lower: Rick Rembisz

LEFT INSIDE FLAP: Top: Harbin Scout Museum, Circle Ten Council, Middle: Rodney D. Carpenter
Collection, Lower: Rodney D. Carpenter Collection

RIGHT INSIDE FLAP: Top: Tim Olive, Middle: Circle Ten Council, Lower: Circle Ten Council

First Hardcover Edition 2013

10 9 8 7 6 5 4 3 2

ISBN-13: 978-098231525-5

SOFTCOVER PHOTO CREDITS:
FRONT COVER: Top: Thomas Alan Hord; Middle: Harbin Scout Museum; Lower Left: Circle Ten
Council; Lower Middle Left: Circle Ten Council; Lower Middle Right: Circle Ten Council; Lower
Right: Chris Fox

BACK COVER: Lower: Rick Rembisz

First Softcover Edition 2013

10 9 8 7 6 5 4 3 2

ISBN-13: 978-098231526-2

Many Penland Scott publications are available at special discounted rates for volume and bulk
purchases, corporate and institutional premiums, promotions, fund-raising, and educational use.
For further information, contact:

PENLANDSCOTT PUBLISHERS
P.O. Box 670324
Dallas, Texas 75367

d.scott@scottsales.com

Printed and bound in the United States of America.
Library of Congress Control Number: 2012916053

Cover and book design and layout by *LandMarc Design*
www.landmarcdesign.com

Check out more about this book at:
www.Circle10.org

Get informed and inspired at
www.PenlandScott.com

DEDICATION

For the young people of today who have been positively impacted by Scouting for the betterment of themselves and their communities, and who will do the same for those who come after.

dedication

ontents

Welcome..viii

About This Book..ix

Foreword by H. Ross Perot...x

Introduction: The Story of the Century.............................xii

Acknowledgements..xx

PART I: FOUNDING THE VISION

Chapter 1: Building Bridges (1910–1913)............................1

Chapter 2: Commissioner Richmond Stakes the Claim (1914)...........27

Chapter 3: Scouts to the Rescue (1915–1918)........................43

Chapter 4: Expanding Membership after Adversity (1918–1920)........61

Chapter 5: The Benefactor and Camp Wisdom (1920–1923)..............77

Chapter 6: Growing into Circle Ten Council (1924–1927).............95

PART II: GROWTH AND DEVELOPMENT

Chapter 7: Creating the Base (1927–1931)...........................119

Chapter 8: Surviving the Depression (1931–1936)....................137

Chapter 9: Scouting for All Boys (1937–1940).......................157

Chapter 10: A Prime Decade for Patriotism (1941–1949)..............177

Chapter 11: The Golden Age (1950–1959).............................197

PART III: SECURING THE FUTURE

Chapter 12: The Counter-Counter Revolution (1960–1972).............223

Chapter 13: Stemming the Loss (1973–1978)..........................245

Chapter 14: Turning Tides (1979–1992)..............................261

Chapter 15: Expansion (1993–1999)..................................283

Chapter 16: New Millennium, Fresh Start (2000–2009)................299

Chapter 17: The Centennial (2010–2012).............................321

Afterword by Amit Banerjee...348

Appendix A: Award Recipients.......................................350

Appendix B: Circle Ten Leadership..................................355

Notes..357

Photo Credits..366

Index..367

About the Authors..375

welcome

AS THE KEY 3 of Circle Ten Council, we offer our warm and hearty greetings to each and every Scout, Scouter, volunteer, parent, supporter, and mentor who has helped to make this great organization what it is today.

Founded 100 years ago in a well-apportioned office suite in the Commonwealth Bank building in historic downtown Dallas, prominent civic leaders sought a better way to train their youth in the art of character building and leadership development. The result was the adoption of a new program, storming the nation at the time, known as "Scouting."

When our Council was born on January 14, 1913, it consisted of merely one employee who was charged with spreading the ideals of Scouting across the city. His efforts were rewarded amply with 70 boys signing up in the first few days—all of whom wished to experience the adventures of camping and the out-of-doors. Their parents, on the other hand, appreciated Scouting for something else—the program's potential to imbue lessons that would help their sons (and now daughters) make moral and ethical decisions for a lifetime.

It is the same today.

Over the past century, Circle Ten Council has taken Scouting into North Texas and Oklahoma and given its members exciting opportunities to expand their minds and spirits by providing opportunities to learn new things, make new friends, and have new experiences, but always grounded in the tenets of the Scout Oath and Scout Law.

THE CONCEPT FOR THIS BOOK was proposed in late 2011 with the simple intention of sharing our Council's fascinating and unique relationship within our community through wonderful pictures and stories that showed our growth through the decades. And we *have* grown mightily.

Over that time, Circle Ten Council has partnered proudly with hundreds of thousands of dedicated Scouters and other volunteers who have given liberally of their time, talent, and treasure to forge legions of young people better equipped for life. Without doubt, those efforts have produced thousands of citizens ready to assume the mantle of leadership.

We three are proud and humbled to serve you as we all strive to move Scouting forward in our region. And in doing so, please know that your dedication is greatly appreciated and it will do much to develop the youth of our communities into the civic leaders they are destined to become.

ERNEST J. CAREY
President, Circle Ten Council 2012–2014

MATT M. WALKER
Council Commissioner, Circle Ten Council

PAT CURRIE
Scout Executive, Circle Ten Council

about this book

THIS BOOK IS THE CULMINATION of many months of original research and efforts to collect the best stories and images available from a variety of archives. As with many projects of this scope, it consolidates hundreds of hours of work performed by the people who made it a reality.

As there were very few physical documents available that described the Council's earliest years, the stories contained within these pages were gleaned from daily reports published in the pages of the *Dallas Morning News.*

With regard to some images in this book, the originals no longer exist and better copies could not be obtained. In these cases, every effort was made to enhance and re-invigorate the low-resolution photographs from the *Dallas Morning News'* archive.

The author has made every attempt to thoroughly research the accuracy of all statements of fact in the manuscript and hope that his efforts were completely on the mark. Any errors or omissions are unintended, and for them, apology is made in advance.

ix

W ITHOUT QUESTION, Scouting's values are America's values, and today they are stronger than ever.

International Scouting was born from the forward-looking vision of Sir Robert Baden-Powell—a man who believed that from the principles of the Knights of the Roundtable comes a better citizen. Nearly every country in the world agrees.

The Boy Scouts of America was incorporated in the United States on February 8, 1910, and once occupied a mere two rooms in a New York City office building. With the simple objective of developing better citizen-leaders from street corner boys, the Boy Scouts of America experienced sudden growth across the country.

I N ITS EARLIEST MONTHS, hundreds of inquires arrived daily asking for assistance on how to form new troops. Boys and men of all religions,

foreword

races, and creeds joined because they wanted to learn Scouting's valuable lessons on patriotism, woodsmanship, and honoring America's heritage.

From this moral training, five generations and 115 million young citizens became Scouts. Many went on to do great deeds. Eleven of the first twelve moonwalkers were Scouts, and every President of the United States since Franklin Delano Roosevelt has been either a Scout or an adult volunteer when not serving in the highest office in the land.

Of our common values, preeminent among them are devotion to faith; servant-leadership; and doing one's duty to God, country, family, and self.

To teach these values, Scouting developed an effective system to train the Scout through achievement. The Scout Oath and Scout Law are the centerpiece

to Scouting's unique proposition led by dedicated volunteers.

Through attainment of badges of rank and merit, Scouts demonstrate proficiency in subjects that hone their life skills, leading to stronger feelings of self-worth.

Through the wearing of a standard uniform, Scouts understand they are members of a team with a common goal.

Through positive association with adult volunteers and community leaders, Scouts witness strong moral examples to emulate in their own lives.

Through lessons in patriotism, Scouts develop pride in their home and nation.

Through serving others, Scouts discover that the act of giving is superior to the act of taking.

Together, these components forge the basis for building citizen-leaders of quality.

In my office, I have a bust of one of America's greatest leaders, a man who set a high bar for moral responsibility and personal integrity— President Theodore Roosevelt. Beneath that image are inscribed the seven words that inspire my life— "The doer is better than the critic."

Circle Ten Council, born in 1913 with direction over a single city, is full of doers. We have the greatest Scouts of any national assembly. We have the greatest adult leaders of any youth development organization, and we have an outstanding team of professionals and staff members that provide a solid support structure. Our many local communities have opened their collective arms and supported our Scouts by chartering our troops and providing service opportunities.

an unselfish and generous way. It also tells the story of how our Scouts responded in kind by donating their time and talents within their communities to make them better places to live.

Annually, Circle Ten Council members perform hundreds of thousands of community service hours through many troop, district, and Council projects that impact countless lives for the better.

Whether it is from sprouting trees at Camp Wisdom and then planting them throughout downtown Dallas in the 1920s, or collecting tens of thousands of bags filled with clothing for Goodwill Industries in the 1950s, or filling the North Texas food banks of today, Circle Ten Council Scouts showcase good ol' American values and exhibit leadership in action every day.

When Scouts pledge their lives to live the ideals embedded within the tenets of the Scout Oath and Scout Law, our future is secured. These basic and fundamental values promote a lifetime of selflessness through duty-driven service to others. It offers a powerful example.

By H. ROSS PEROT - Eagle Scout, 1943

Where Character Is Caught celebrates these critical partnerships. It tells the story of how local towns like Garland, Richardson, Irving, Waxahachie, Ennis, Denison, Sherman, Italy, Kaufman, Rockwall, Durant, and many others joined with Dallas after 1927 to form one of the strongest Councils in the nation.

It tells the story of how thousands of volunteers, who after toiling at their daily jobs, donated countless hours of their own free time to these youth in

I heartily applaud the great work done by our many thousands of Scouts and challenge each and every one of you to reach out to more young people today and ask them whether they have made the commitment to join the Scouting movement. If they have already joined Scouting, let them know how proud you are of their decision. If they have not, please urge them to join Scouting because, just as Circle Ten Council has proven a million times over, this world is made better, one new leader at a time.

I HEARTILY APPLAUD THE GREAT WORK DONE BY OUR MANY THOUSANDS OF SCOUTS AND CHALLENGE EACH AND EVERY ONE OF YOU TO REACH OUT TO MORE YOUNG PEOPLE TODAY. . .

The Dallas Morning News.

L. XXVIII.   DALLAS, TEXAS, SUNDAY, MARCH 16, 1913—SIXTY-FOUR PAGES IN FIVE PARTS—PART ONE—GENERAL NEWS.   NO. 1

HARRIMAN PLAN | COSTLY JEWEL COLLECTION | LOW DAY INVENTURE | PRESIDENT WILSON'S CHOICE | COLD WAVE ARRIVES | WINS IMPORTANT CASE | HAZERS FOUND OUT

THERE WAS A TIME WHEN FEW PEOPLE in America had heard of Scouting.

So it was with a farmer in the small rural community of Arlington, Texas, who was awakened one March night in 1913 by noise from his barn. It came as a shock to him to find an exhausted man dozing upright in the corner and a dozen boys bedded down in his hay, and he quickly came to what seemed to him a logical conclusion: this must be a kidnapping.

Startled from his sleep, the adult "intruder" in the barn was quick to reassure the skeptical farmer that illegal activity was not the case and he introduced himself with apologies for trespassing on the man's property. In addition to being co-founder of the Hardin School for Boys near downtown Dallas, Capt. Roy H. Hardin, known for being "a splendid exemplar of the modern school man," was Scoutmaster of Troop 4 in the newly formed Dallas Council, Boy Scouts of America.

The preceding day he had set out with his dozen Scouts for a 36-mile hike from Dallas to Fort Worth. Arlington was the mid-point on the hike, so on the evening of March 14, 1913, the boys and their adult companion bedded down for the night in a field after eating dinner and holding campfire festivities. Had the temperature not dropped suddenly during the early morning hours, they would not have taken refuge in the nearby barn where the farmer found them huddled hours later.

Having allayed the grower's concerns, Hardin explained about Boy Scouting: a citizen-building organization for youth that had launched in Dallas just a short time earlier. Much-relieved, and as dawn was near, the farmer invited the troop back to his homestead for a hearty breakfast of ham and fresh eggs before seeing them on their way to

introducti

"THE STORY OF THE CENTURY"

LADS HAVE REAL ADVENTURE.

Farmer Accuses Capt. Hardin of Kidnaping—Boy Scout Troop.

Four troops of Boy Scouts made hikes yesterday and spent all the day or some part of it in the woods and the open grounds. All returned to their homes by nightfall.

Capt. Roy Hardin, with a score or more of the students from the Hardin School for Boys, had the most adventurous time. The troop started out on Friday afternoon, camping for the night near Arlington. The marchers cooked the evening meal and ate heartily. They had a campfire and slept. In the night they were roused by the chill and took refuge in a barn. At 4 o'clock in the morning they were routed by the farmer who owned the barn, a man who had never heard of Boy Scout movements and who derided the explanations of Capt. Hardin. The scoutmaster was believed to have kidnaped the boys and was threatened with arrest, and it required persuasion by the commander and his charges to turn the determination of

Fort Worth. He was reassured that once they had reached the downtown stockyards they would head back to Dallas in an Interurban rail car.

Such were the origins of North Texas Scouting in 1913, with 400 boys hiking around Dallas in patrols of eight and troops of 24. The movement was just starting to be noticed by local businessmen who would support such an activity, and by the reading public that enjoyed a chuckle over the incident at the Arlington farm as related by a reporter from the *Dallas Morning News* in an article titled "Lads Have Real Adventure—Farmer Accuses Hardin of Kidnapping Boy Scout Troop."

Like many educators, churchmen, social workers and professionals across America, Roy Hardin seized upon Scouting because it offered him an effective framework within which to develop boys in his charge while keeping them involved in wholesome and useful activities.

ACROSS TOP LEFT and ABOVE LEFT: The *Dallas Morning News* masthead announcing the "kidnapping" of local Boy Scouts (above left). ACROSS BOTTOM LEFT: An advertisement for the Hardin School for Boys located just east of downtown Dallas at the corner of Main Street and N. Haskell Avenue. ACROSS BOTTOM RIGHT: Capt. Roy H. Hardin in 1913. BELOW: A postcard showing a spot on the Interurban rail line between Dallas and Fort Worth.

1411. Scene on Interurban, Dallas, Texas.

He was no different from hundreds of other volunteers who were beginning to flock to Scouting asserting moral and patriotic values of youthful character building. Leaders were attracted to it because something new was at its core—the detailed study of woodsmanship that would teach life's lessons.

In the late 1800s, generations of Americans lived in proximity with nature on their frontier homesteads that made excursions into the wild a normal occurrence. But as more people flocked to the cities, the sights and sounds of the natural world remained outside those borders. From that, the "Get Back to Nature" movement gained momentum and recreational camping emerged as a popular pastime rather than an uncomfortable necessity.

Camping became a key element of the Young Men's Christian Association's (YMCA) "boys' work" programs, which in that era proposed to rescue boys from their idle transgressions citing a "preventative and character-building" purpose. Camping offered "healthful recreation without temptation" and satisfied "the natural desire for a free and easy life out of doors," while at the same time developing a "manly Christian character."[1]

Some of the nation's first youth experiences with camping and organized lessons in woodsmanship came from Scottish-Canadian author, artist, naturalist, and world famous lecturer, Ernest Thompson Seton, who had achieved fame with his wildly popular, best-selling book titled *Wild Animals I Have Known*. Seton acquired a country estate in Cos Cob, Connecticut, where, in 1901, he invited local

TOP: Looking eastward down Main Street from atop the Old Red Courthouse in 1906. ABOVE: A postcard of Main Street in 1900. The Linz Building on the left became the Dallas Council's headquarters in 1926. LEFT: Constructed in 1895, Dallas' third City Hall Building was built on the current site of the Hotel Adolphus at the corner of Commerce and S. Akard Streets.

boys to spend their Easter weekend with him to live like "Indians" on his land. About 20 boys were expected, but twice that number showed up. They swam in his stream and devoured the food he provided, and then gathered around a campfire to listen to his tales of the wilderness and Native American prowess.[2]

Generations ahead of his time, Seton asserted that "if the young people of this nation can be so trained that they will grow to look upon Nature with eager interest, if they become familiar with her traditions, her kindness, her discipline, her beauty, her tragedies, [then] they will find themselves held together by a bond of sympathy that no superficial social structure can ever obliterate."[3]

But Seton's program was not the only one.

In 1905, Cincinnati, Ohio native, artist, author, and political activist, Daniel Carter Beard, founded his own organization for boys called the Sons of Daniel Boone. Using American pioneers as his exemplars of excellence, Beard's program was described monthly in the pages of *Recreation Magazine* at the request of the new editor-in-chief, who was trying to appeal to young readers.

TOP LEFT: A band of original Seton Indians camping at Ernest Thompson Seton's Cos Cob, Connecticut estate in 1904. TOP RIGHT: BSA's Chief Scout Ernest Thompson Seton in 1903. ABOVE RIGHT: BSA's National Scout Commissioner Daniel Carter Beard in 1917.

The Sons of Daniel Boone sought to "strengthen the love [that] all boys have for the out-of-doors," promoting the conservation of nature and "all that tends to healthy, wholesome manliness," its organizational constitution declared.[4]

His columns elicited interest from adults too, as some regretted not having had such an organization when they were young.[5] Dan Beard's impeccable credentials and outdoor woodsmanship skills allowed him to become a leader as well in the emerging field of outdoor work with boys.

Both of these Scouting pioneers came together in mid-1910 to help form the Boy Scouts of America (BSA), a new organization first incorporated in Washington, DC by Chicago publisher, William D. Boyce. Headquartered in the YMCA building in New York City, the fledgling BSA began work under the umbrella of the YMCA's Edgar M. Robinson in his two-room office suite at 124 E. 28th Street in Manhattan.

BSA's managing secretary, John L. Alexander, formerly of the Philadelphia YMCA, and one lone stenographer began work organizing the national Scouting movement brought over from England by Boyce in late December 1909. The publisher had obtained

TOP LEFT: An drawing by Dan Beard of a Son of Daniel Boone. LEFT: The YMCA Building at 124 E. 28th Street in New York as it appeared in 1910. TOP RIGHT: Mementos from the May 18, 1900 "Relief of Mafeking" celebrations in London, England. RIGHT: Lord Robert S.S. Baden-Powell in 1937. ACROSS RIGHT: The book that started it all – the 1899 printing of *Aids to Scouting* complete with the introductory statement claiming the proofs were smuggled through Boer lines.

Scouting materials from the English founder of the movement, Lt-Gen. Robert S. S. Baden-Powell.

The name of Baden-Powell, whose fame emanated from his direction of the successful 217-day defense of the small town of Mafeking, South Africa, beginning in 1899 during the Second Anglo-Boer War, was a watchword for heroism and valor.

Having written a small instruction manual for British army recruits called *Aids to Scouting*, English boys were buying it in droves trying to learn to "scout" like Baden-Powell. By May 1907, Baden-Powell sought to make his idea of Scouting something more.

He began working with publisher, Sir C. Arthur Pearson, to develop an experimental Scouting camp and author an instructional handbook. Pearson informed Baden-Powell that he wanted to bring it out in serial form in six parts starting in January 1908, which would help him gauge the demand for a compilation book published in time for the summer camping season.

The ever-methodical general wanted first, however, to test his scheme, and found just the place to do so—Brownsea Island—a 500-acre island in Poole Harbor off England's southern coast.[6]

Over 10 days, prototype Scouts learned the typical Scouting outdoor skills they would take back to their homes. Achieving successful results, Baden-Powell set about finishing the first installment of his handbook, called *Scouting for Boys*, which hit the newsstands on January 15—quickly selling out. Two weeks later, there would be another one, and so on for three months.

Soon Baden-Powell was receiving expressions of interest in the movement from across the British Empire and the world, including the United States.[7]

By late 1910, Scouting was in Dallas.

Men like Roy Hardin (Scoutmaster to the Scouts in the barn at the beginning) owed much to the efforts of more specialized professionals like Claude M.

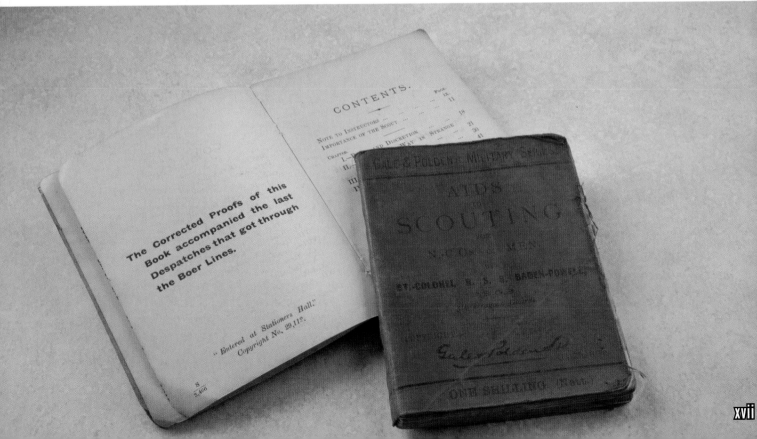

Richmond, who arrived in Dallas in October 1910 to become Boys' Work Director for the local branch of the YMCA. Since graduating in 1905 from the YMCA's training school in Chicago, Richmond had worked for the service organization in California and Florida.

Richmond was in Jacksonville during the summer of 1910 when he heard of the Scouting program that YMCAs in the northeastern United States were enthusiastically adopting as a way to develop character in an outdoor setting. Scouting seemed made to order for the YMCA, which already was welcoming thousands of boys into summer camps where a Bible was as much a standard item of equipment as a canteen. By that August, Richmond had incorporated it into his Jacksonville youth program.

Stemming from a news item published in the *Dallas Morning News* out of Fort Worth dated August 26, 1910, 27-year-old Dallas attorney Towne Young[8] wrote a letter of inquiry to the national Boy Scout organization in New York City requesting more information on the movement. Posted to Manhattan in the last days of August, Young's letter is the earliest known first-hand correspondence between national Scouting executives and someone living in Dallas proper.

In addition to a personalized form-letter response postmarked September 8, 1910, Managing

Secretary Alexander sent along promotional literature giving a fuller view of the movement. Young, officing out of room 311 in the seven-story Slaughter Building at 1017 Main and N. Griffin Streets and boarding at the YMCA, most likely turned over the enclosures to Dallas YMCA General Secretary Emerson G. Wilson at the Association's offices at 440 Commerce Street and S. Harwood. Young's simple act of forwarding this communication may have contributed to the hiring of well-known Scouting virtuoso, Claude Richmond.[9]

In late October, Richmond's role as the Scoutmaster of Dallas' Troop Number 1 based at YMCA headquarters was a critical first step in establishing a solid base for the local program. Quickly, he

reached out to the *Dallas Morning News* to announce his intentions to grow Scouting in Dallas through the launching of more troops. Its publisher, George Bannerman Dealey, made sure that his reporters covered Scouting activities, boosting local interest. And thus a powerful partnership for the movement was born locally.

Over the following years, the Dallas Council, officially formed on January 14, 1913, after opening its first headquarters in Suite 818 in the nearby Wilson Building, would expand its territory and membership to include thousands of boys and volunteers—eventually becoming the legendary Circle Ten Council of today. With time, its Scouts would spend hundreds of thousands of man-hours in giving service back to the many communities that supported it over the years and to the thousands of chartering organizations that served as its sponsors.

As words spread, businessmen and women from across the region began to give of their time and financial resources to manage the moral direction and physical growth of the local movement—giving rise to its increasing popularity and avid following.

"HONOR, DUTY, GOD AND COUNTRY—WHO SAYS THOSE WORDS ANY MORE EXCEPT THE BOY SCOUTS OF AMERICA."
—WILLIAM J. BENNETT, ORLANDO, FLORIDA, JUNE 1, 2012

Where Character is Caught is the story of how Scouting in Dallas started with a mere four members in November 1910 and grew to over 55,000 Scouts across 12 counties a century later. It is the story of the multitude of organizations that supported the movement and allowed Scouting's values to live within their halls. It is the story of the people who volunteered as its leaders and gave of themselves to make Scouting's growth a certainty. And, most important, it is the story of the legions of boys and girls that went through the program, lived the Scout Oath and Law every day of their lives, and grew to become citizen-leaders of quality.

In short, this is the story of *you*.

TOP: *Dallas Morning News* publisher George Bannerman Dealey. ACROSS BOTTOM LEFT and ACROSS BOTTOM RIGHT: The letter and envelope sent by BSA Managing Secretary John L. Alexander to Dallas lawyer Towne Young in 1910 that helped bring the Scouting movement to the city. ACROSS TOP: A piece of promotional BSA Scouting literature sent out to prospective Scoutmasters and unit organizers in 1910. ABOVE: Dallas Boy Scouts in 1913.

IN 1910, PRESIDENT THEODORE ROOSEVELT, one of my favorite people in American history, wrote in *Century Magazine,* "The greatest possible good can be the extension of a helping hand at the right moment." How right he was, as this book is a testament to that sentiment.

When Circle Ten Council's Director of Support Services, Scott Ferguson, contacted me in mid-August 2011 with the initial concept of this centennial book, I had little idea as to the eventual size of its scope or how difficult it would be to "get it right." Now, I know and I offer my humble thanks to those who made it possible.

emails and answered frequent requests for lists and documents. Lynette "Safecracker" Hendricks, Donna Pytlak, Dick Corcoran, Lyn Graham, Corina Ortiz, Espy Randolph, Gene Smith, and Linda Peoples found and allowed me to review archival papers, original documents and deeds, executive board meeting minutes, and historical images hidden away in the dark corners at 8605 Harry Hines Boulevard.

Don Burke, Scott Arrington, David M. Williams, Karen Thunert, Gary Garza, and former Council executives Rudy Gonzalez and Russell Etzenhouser all provided critical information toward my better understanding of specific points of Council policy. I thank District Executive Chris Fox for providing

acknowle

To Scout Executive Pat Currie, Council President Ernest Carey, Council Commissioner Matt M. Walker, former Council President Tom Baker, and the members of the executive board of Circle Ten Council, I offer my hearty thanks for commissioning me to complete this landmark project.

As research began, the assistance of Harbin Scout Museum Director Bob Reitz was critical to my basic understanding of the history of Dallas, Camp Wisdom, and Scouting's place in the local community. In working with me every step of the way, Bob's extensive knowledge, experience, and expertise in finding records and archival images provided many needed answers. His investigative work is second to none and this book would not have been completed without his support. *Tuesdays with Bob at Camp Wisdom* should be my next writing project.

Many Circle Ten Council staff members also provided valuable assistance. Wendy Kurten interfaced with the at-large membership through her well-timed

his wonderful photographs from Scouting events for this publication as well. Together, they are confirmation that there is a lot of talent roaming the halls of the Murchison Scouting Center.

Dan Zaccara, Scott Ferguson, Lynn Santillan, and Corina Ortiz never missed an opportunity to offer hearty "attaboys" and other encouragements at the right time when the trail to understanding was lean. Subject matter experts and collectors Joe Griffis, Mark Johnson, Calvin Grubbs, Mitch Reis, Pat Bywaters, Dr. Terry Grove, and Gene Smith all provided their time, knowledge, and "stuff" to which I offer my sincere thanks.

Appreciation goes out to Betty Ann Beckett Wilkie for granting access to her father's files, as well as to Richmond and Jim Guildart, and their cousin, Jack Boot, who provided images and stories of their grandfather, Scout Commissioner Claude Marion Richmond. Richard Johnson brought to Camp Wisdom fascinating memorabilia and stories pertaining to his father, Lemuel, who attended BSA's

1st National Jamboree in 1937. Also, I thank Jon Q. Thompson, the son of Circle Ten Eagle Scout DeWitt Thompson, who shared images of his father's awards, as well as Mrs. Arlene Mason, who provided the famous image of her family member Robert Johnsey and Babe Ruth together in 1929.

Former Council presidents Jack D. Furst, Bobby Lyle, John Stuart III, and current Council President Ernest Carey graciously granted lengthy interviews, as did former Scout Executives Billy Gamble and Ponce Duran Jr., as well as current Scout Executive Pat Currie. Additionally, Council Commissioner Matt M. Walker gave of his time to answer questions regarding his tenure as a chief volunteer.

award-winning Commercial photographer replete with future Eagle Scout William Shipes to assist with computer malfunctions.

To my good friend Bobby Higginbotham, whenever I need the use of 300 Scouts from one unit, I'm callin' you again, ole' Buddy.

I offer a hearty "thanks!" to all those in the Council who answered my call to provide images and personal stories. I wish that I could have used all submissions but limited space requirements made that impossible.

dgments

I also thank my manuscript readers and photographic commentators, Michael R. Bradle, Kevin Harrison, Charles Holmes, Curt Wilkinson, Dan Zaccara, John Copley, John K. Shipes, Tom Baker, Pat Currie, Wendy Kurten, Dick Corcoran, Scott Ferguson, Billy Gamble, and Bob Reitz, all of whom offered wonderful advice on modifying content.

Finally, to my very talented photo editor, John K. Shipes, I offer my sincere thanks for his unwavering dedication to this wonderful project, which has been a roller coaster of emotion since its inception. Using the tools of his magnificent studio, still life images were brought to vivid life. His work in the field was unmatched as well, with his making of several trips to Camp Wisdom laden with something like 900 pounds of equipment in eight specially-made cases, six miles of cables, three computers, and 2 digital 40mb Hasselblads - all used to capture three gatefold collages, a half dozen re-enactment images, and 200 interior shots. I suppose that somebody had to do it. So, it might as well have been an

Of course, I thank the talented artists at LandMarc Design and the production team there, especially editors Elizabeth Chenette and Pam Blackmon, who picked-up the ball when tragedy struck the project in April 2012, as well as LandMarc's Creative Director and President Matthew Land.

Lastly, I acknowledge and remember the dedication and devotion of my dear friend, editor, and mentor, Brendan J. Murphy, who always found the most effective words to upgrade my prose. For those who don't know, Murf was "called home" shortly after completing the edits to Part I, causing a momentary re-evaluation of the book's direction. In the end, his last piece of advice to me was right on.

"Just put as few words as needed in the right order and tell the story," he said. And that's what I tried to do.

Thanks Brother Murphy, this one's for you.

circle ten

"[Circle Ten Council] will be a place where character is caught as well as taught."

LOYS R. SESSIONS
1928 Field Executive
Circle Ten Council, BSA

council

Part I

FOUNDING THE VISION

(1910–1927)

"Your boy is probably weak, nervous and lacks self-reliance. He has been cooped-up in school for many months. He needs rest, directed play and, most of all, no doubt, he needs to come into contact with . . . men and boys of the best type. Let him go to camp, where he can recuperate and learn to take care of himself under the best adult supervision."

"A WORD TO PARENTS" DALLAS COUNCIL, BSA[1]
APRIL 27, 1913

chapter 1

BUILDING BRIDGES (1910–1913)

"When people learn the truth about the movement, it will be supported and men will flood to headquarters to act as leaders to train-up our youth into sober, industrious, and useful citizens."

CLAUDE M. RICHMOND
FIRST SCOUT COMMISSIONER
DALLAS COUNCIL, BSA
MARCH 8, 1913

TOP: Sarah Horton Cockrell was Dallas' first titan of business as she owned the town's first sawmill, gristmill, flourmill, brick manufacturing plant, and steel factory. By 1890, her partial holdings included about one quarter of the property in downtown Dallas. ABOVE: An image of the Dallas skyline in 1912 that is marked by the construction of the towering Hotel Adolphus.

W HEN CLAUDE MARION RICHMOND arrived in Dallas on October 4, 1910, aboard a Santa Fe Railroad train from Jacksonville, Florida, the city that he encountered that sunny day was well suited to the development of a network of Boy Scout troops. As the unchallenged manufacturing center on the Trinity River with a population of some 100,000 citizens, Dallas had come a long way from its origins as a settlement established in 1841 by Tennessee lawyer-turned-land speculator John Neely Bryan.

Having fallen on hard times by 1853, Bryan had sold his homestead (including the nascent town of Dallas and his Trinity River ferry concession) to Kentuckian Alexander Cockrell, operator of a brick-making concern among other enterprises that included a toll bridge to replace the Trinity River ferry company. In typical Wild West style, the Alexander Cockrell era ended dramatically in 1858 when he was shot dead in a gunfight with a local marshal. His capable wife, Sarah, however, took over operations and became one of the wealthiest capitalists in town. Bryan, on the other hand, expired in 1877 nearly destitute.[1]

This was the second bridge built over the Trinity River by the Cockrells to replace John Neely Bryan's ferry boat system. It was Dallas's first tollway.

IN 1839, *John Neely Bryan wanted to make big money. The opportunistic frontiersman from Fayetteville, Tennessee, who usually wore buckskin leggings and tanned moccasins, sought to do it in the Three Forks area of the Trinity River.*

Born on December 10, 1810, Bryan was a helper on the family farm but grew up to study law in Nashville. Upon moving to Memphis in 1833, Bryan was struck down by a rampant cholera epidemic sweeping the region. Advised to move to Arkansas and its more recuperative climate, he lived among the Cherokee Indians in the Arkansas wilderness until regaining his health, whereupon he returned to civilization in 1837 "filled with ideals and energy." That energy went into founding the town of Van Buren, Arkansas, just outside of Fort Smith, as a trading post between the native Indians and white settlers.

Upon hearing of even more fertile lands farther south into Texas, 30-year-old Bryan arrived in North Texas in November 1841 and set up a camp made of "poles, brush, and dirt at a place that today would be the foot of Main Street at the Triple Underpass."

Initially, Bryan believed that the Trinity could be a navigable river, which would allow transporting of goods via steamer and flatboat from Galveston in the Gulf of Mexico to markets in the middle of the country, thereby making his town a trade center. Unfortunately, he had competition. Bryan's settlement was not the first in the area, just the latest in a string of townships that had popped up recently.

One lay just over the Trinity to the south that was already hosting several settler families—eventually to be dubbed Hord's Ridge (now Oak Cliff). It was founded by Tennessee lawyer William Henry Hord, whose grandson, Thomas Alan Hord, would later play an important role in Dallas Scouting as one of the area's first Scoutmasters.

Another was Cedar Springs founded in February 1841 in present day Oak Lawn just three and a half miles to the northwest that had attracted a number of new families. But the largest was Farmers Branch about 10 miles to the north.

The governing land authority was established by treaty between itself and the Republic of Texas. It was the Peters Colony to the west and it held the sole ability to authorize new settlements within its boundaries. In January 1842, Bryan pleaded his case to the Colony and his claim of 640 acres was granted and "legitimized," forming the land base of the present city.

By May, the town of "Dallas" was named and advertised as a growing settlement. Always attracting controversy, the origin of the name is not clear. Several possibilities arose as to the identification of "my old friend Dallas" but consensus (and son John Neely Bryan Jr.) suggests that it was named for U.S. President James K. Polk's vice president, George Mifflin Dallas. Strangely, the two had never met, suggesting political agreement and familiarity formed purely from news reports.

Now advertising a settlement, Bryan had to ensure its safety from Indian attack. Fortunately, that was solved by treaty in 1843 by Republic of Texas President Sam Houston. Houston negotiated a 30-mile wide non-aggression corridor that stretched from the Bryan settlement to the center of present day Fort Worth. Gathering that August at Grapevine Springs in present day Coppell, Houston and the chiefs of the nine local Indian nations signed the treaty on September 29, officially ceasing all future raids into the protected area. Bryan had a secure settlement but no plan for managing growth.

The arrival of J. P. Dumas in January 1844 solved that problem as he was a city planner. Dumas laid out the downtown grid and street plan in exchange for a free lot. As designed, Dallas sat on a "one half-mile square with a block marked off for a courthouse square that still serves that purpose today." Bryan's well-built double log cabin sat south of present day Commerce Street just west of Houston Street.

Rapidly, word traveled around the region that Dallas was a "civilized" place to live and new settlers poured in monthly. In 1843, Dallas had a medical doctor. The first lawyer arrived in 1845. He was Col. John C. McCoy, the uncle of Capt. John M. McCoy—one of Dallas Scouting's first patrons, who provided his lands for troop use and patrol camping.

In 1845, the annexation of the Republic of Texas by the United States of America came up for a vote where the 32 eligible Dallas voters balloted 29 "For" and 3 "Opposed," helping to make Texas the 28th state.

For Bryan, he suffered several business failures that sent him into a cycle of heavy drinking and depression. With hope seemingly gone, he sold his entire interest in Dallas in 1853 to the couple that took his city to its next level of success—its first entrepreneurs, Alexander and Sarah Horton Cockrell—and moved away.[A]

For President:
JAMES K. POLK,
OF TENNESSEE.

For Vice President:
GEORGE M. DALLAS,
OF PENNSYLVANIA.

For ELECTORS of President & Vice-
President of the United States.
William Frick.
Albert Constable.
James Murray.
Thomas Perry.
Edward Hammond.
Benjamin C. Presstman.
William A. Spencer.
James Lloyd Martin.

support of the Baptist Church, and to endow Dallas' own Baylor Medical College.

John B. Wilson, another cattleman banker and president of the Excelsior Soap and Refining Company, located one mile north of the courthouse on the MK&T railway line, built one of the city's first high-rise commercial structures, the towering 12-story Wilson Building in 1904, at Main and Ervay Streets. Its ground floor once housed the Titche-Goettinger Department Store and the H. L. Green Variety Store, whose lunch counter would be the first in Dallas to be desegregated in the 1960s. The Dallas Boy Scout Council would move into an upper story in January 1913.[2]

Dallas was fast becoming a city filled with life's luxuries—gas lit streets, telephone lines, and indoor plumbing. The city's first opera house opened-up in 1873 the same year that local roller skaters took to the

Dallas gathered population and affluence through the late 1800s with some citizens having extraordinarily deep pockets and others having extraordinarily deep vision. Few citizens at the time embodied this "Dallas spirit" or straddled the frontier and modern eras more than Christopher Columbus Slaughter, a cattleman with about a million acres of Texas land who added finance to his activities through his National Exchange Bank located in the Slaughter Building at the corner of Main and Polydras Streets. A person of great philanthropic spirit, the former Texas Ranger lawman gave vast amounts of his wealth away in

J. B. WILSON.

RIGHT: John B. Wilson built the tallest building in Dallas when his Wilson Building was completed in 1904. FAR RIGHT: Dallas pioneer and philanthropist Christopher Columbus Slaughter claimed to be the first male child born of a marriage contracted in the newly formed Republic of Texas in 1837.

rink for the first time. Land for City Park was purchased and available for use in 1876, and the town's first bicycle (replete with iron tires) arrived in 1878.

Quickly vanishing were the frontier days that hosted legendary Dallas dentist John Henry "Doc" Holliday (who was "invited" to leave the town in 1875 after being indicted for illegal gambling and "trading gunfire")[3] as well as streets filled with horse drawn carriages, western style saloons, and Wild West vigilantism.

Now, Dallas was a "civilized" corporate center led by people obsessed with helping the city rise to its next level of success—becoming the region's central merchandising clearinghouse. To do so, civic leaders embraced the many new manufacturing technologies that were racing across the nation during this era of massive global industrialization—all requiring better-trained workers to manage the increased capabilities of their highly productive machinery.

The promise of Scouting helped make this goal become a reality as energetic boys symbolically built bridges to their futures—both as responsible employees but, more importantly, as better leaders in their vibrant and growing community.

It was within this atmosphere of social reform that Dallas YMCA management had high expectations of Richmond.

"We are extremely fortunate in securing a secretary like Mr. Richmond to take care of our Boys' Work," stated YMCA General Secretary Emerson G. White. He asserted that Richmond "will no doubt be a valuable factor in building up the work in Dallas."

By early November 1910, Richmond had organized the city's first four Scouting patrols and lectured frequently to stimulate interest and increase its membership. "The aim of the movement is to instill character into rising generations," he told a group of men that November 2, "to teach them self-reliance, independence, industry, integrity, initiative, and to make them courageous and have higher ideals."[4]

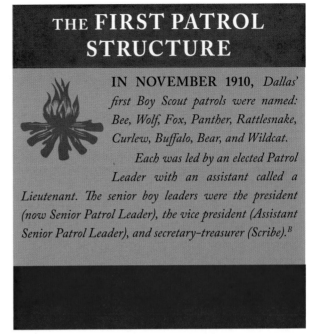

THE FIRST PATROL STRUCTURE

IN NOVEMBER 1910, *Dallas' first Boy Scout patrols were named: Bee, Wolf, Fox, Panther, Rattlesnake, Curlew, Buffalo, Bear, and Wildcat.*

Each was led by an elected Patrol Leader with an assistant called a Lieutenant. The senior boy leaders were the president (now Senior Patrol Leader), the vice president (Assistant Senior Patrol Leader), and secretary-treasurer (Scribe).[B]

The *Dallas Morning News* reported that Richmond was ready to administer the "Tenderfoot test" to any boy that desired it. To qualify, a lad had to be 12 years of age and know by memory the Scout Law, the history of the American flag, and the four

standard Scouting knots—the reef knot, the timber hitch, two half hitches, and the slip knot. The boy who could do all this could be sworn in as a Tenderfoot Scout.

The first to do so was 15-year-old Julian Forrest Nicodemus of Dallas. He joined Boy Scout Troop 1 under Scoutmaster Richmond at the downtown YMCA with his brother Chester. Known by his middle name, Forrest was the son of a local carpenter. Three years later, he would become the Assistant Scoutmaster of Troop 22 at the Oak Grove Public School at the corner of S. Harwood and Jackson Streets in downtown Dallas.[5]

Contained within the Boy Scouts of America's (BSA) organizational literature received from Dallas lawyer Towne Young two months prior were instructions on how to proceed with the official program. First and foremost,

BSA's 1910 *Official Handbook* was the version first used by Scoutmaster Claude Richmond when he began forming troops in 1910.

Scouting was to be a character-building operation used to teach and reinforce the values of doing one's duty to God, country, family, and self. The experience of outdoor camping would become the method of choice to imbue those ideals in active boys.

The first Scout outing was a hike on November 13, starting in the city's center and finishing at Marsalis Park (now the Dallas Zoo) in Oak Cliff, where they played Scouting games and matched their skills.

Richmond insisted that "all the boys take the Tenderfoot test and get their badges from him as soon as possible." He knew that the sooner his Scouts advanced, the better chance that they would stick with the program.

By late November 1910, Richmond's Dallas ranks had swollen to 70 Scouts organized in 10 patrols. The YMCA influence was still very strong: the Scouts began with Bible lessons followed by religious instruction, and only then by Scouting activities. Troop 2 was formed at the Forest Avenue Methodist Church at the corner of Forest Avenue (now Martin Luther King Jr. Boulevard south of Fair Park) and 4th Avenue with three patrols— the Cats, Ravens, and Hounds. The Colonial Hill Presbyterian Church at Forest Avenue and Wendelkin Street in Oak Cliff (now under Interstate Highway 45) quickly sponsored Troop 3. Richmond's grassroots lecturing brought in close to 100 new members in six weeks.

"I find that the interest in the movement among the boys is growing daily," he announced, "and I think that much good will be accomplished among them."[6]

Unfortunately, a few mothers began pulling their boys from the program because they believed the

CLAUDE M. RICHMOND
DALLAS' FIRST SCOUTMASTER AND SCOUT COMMISSIONER/SCOUT EXECUTIVE

CLAUDE MARION RICHMOND *was born on August 29, 1876, in the small community of Deerfield, Missouri, to John S. Richmond and his wife, Adeline. Working as a farmhand throughout his formative years, Claude learned the value of hard work at an early age.*

As a young man, he was dedicated to three main things: living his Christian faith, expanding his mind through education, and helping other people. All three came together when Richmond entered the YMCA's training school (later named George Williams College) in Chicago, Illinois, located on the city's South Side to learn how to be a Christian educator for youth.

Graduating in 1905, he left for his first appointment at the YMCA in Pasadena, California, to serve as its Boys' Work secretary. Remaining there until 1909, Richmond accepted a similar position across the country in the Jacksonville (Florida) YMCA, where he learned of the national Scouting movement. Wishing to explore the usefulness of this new program, he formed a local YMCA troop by August 1910 and sent five of his Scouts to national BSA's first two-week camp held in Silver Bay, New York, at the YMCA facility on Lake George.

Witnessing its success firsthand, he believed the out-of-doors camping program to be the key towards creating men from boys. Richmond learned more about the program and expanded Scouting's reach in Florida, thereby gaining a solid reputation as a knowledgeable Scouting instructor.

By November, Secretary Richmond was hired by the Dallas YMCA to jump-start their Scouting program. After doing so, he eventually accepted the paid position as Dallas' first Scout Commissioner (the former title of Scout Executive) in late 1912, providing him with a sufficient salary to get engaged.

Richmond married Miss Maude Toles in 1913 and moved out of his boarding room at the YMCA. After the wedding, the couple moved in with Maude's widowed mother at the now lost address of 1725 Pocahontas, just southwest of today's Old City

Park. With the birth of their daughter, Mavis, a year later they moved to a rented house of their own at 2617 Cedar Springs, now a Wells Fargo Bank branch, at the intersection of Routh Street.

After working diligently at expanding the local Scouting program for several years, he resigned as Scout Commissioner effective February 3, 1915. Richmond took work as a life insurance salesman at the Oldham and Mathis agency in Dallas. After a year, he was offered a job at the YMCA in Atlanta, Georgia, where he was employed at the Association's hospital unit on the Camp Gordon army base and experienced the birth of his second daughter, Helen.

In August 1919, he became the general secretary at the YMCA in Albany, Georgia, where he stayed until taking the position of Scout Executive in the Shreveport (Louisiana) Council in 1922. After a three-year stint, the Richmonds moved to San Antonio, Texas, where he began working as a peanut salesman. For the next two decades, he continued to work with the local YMCA until his volunteerism landed him a paid assistant's position with the Association.

Throughout his life, he remained devoted to the physical and mental growth of all children— for example, Richmond usually kept an infield's worth of baseball gloves, bats, and balls in his car trunk, just in case a pick-up game could be started.

Personally, Richmond read the Bible daily and disapproved of society's ever-changing acceptance of traditional vices like liquor and cigarettes.

"Papaw would paste sheets of white paper over those 'offensive' ads in his beloved Life Magazine *each month to 'protect' our young eyes," recalled grandson Jim Guildart. "Looking back, we all loved him dearly for what he was doing for us."*

Claude Marion Richmond died on March 1, 1965, in San Antonio from heart disease and is buried in Mission Burial Park.[C]

TOP: Claude M. Richmond in 1905. MIDDLE: Mrs. Maude Toles Richmond shortly after her marriage. BOTTOM: Claude Richmond with grandson Richmond Guildart in San Antonio around 1950.

DALLAS SCOUTING'S FIRST OVERNIGHT CAMPING TRIP

ON FEBRUARY 22, 1911, *Scout Commissioner Claude Richmond took a select group of 15 boys of Troop 1 on Dallas Scouting's first overnight trip to Kirkland Park, a few miles north of downtown now located near the intersection of Meadow Road and Greenville Avenue (formerly the Glen Lakes Stables), making local news.*

"The boys will participate in the natural sports of the woods-dweller," reported the Dallas Morning News. *"Lean-tos will be constructed and fire made without matches."*

Scouts carried a two-day supply of rations, with a blanket, a knife, fork and spoon, plus "plenty of nerve for the test of endurance that will probably come to them in their explorations."

To prevent mischief, the night will be divided into three watches with two Scout "sentries" on duty each shift.

Scene on Interurban Line, Northern Texas Traction Co., Between Fort Worth and Dallas, Texas.

troop did not spend enough time in Bible study. Other critics believed it to be military training as the lads were organized in patrols led by patrol leaders, lieutenants, and corporals.

Richmond redoubled public education, assuring parents wanting more religious instruction that all meetings would open with lengthened Bible studies. One favored text was a book by YMCA executive William D. Murray, also a member of the Boy Scouts of America's national board. *What Manner of Man Is This?* reflected on the life of Jesus Christ, and its adoption pleased many religious-minded parents—but about 50 troop members voted with their feet and left.

That December, Richmond set about creating a Scouting Council in Dallas. Financial support was essential to fund the position of Scout Commissioner and pay the rent on a permanent office. Until then, Dallas would hold the national BSA designation of "Second Class Council" (no paid executive, no office, and no budget) rather than that of "First Class Council" with all three. That would come soon enough in 1913.[7]

In 1911, Richmond launched a series of informational meetings at Dallas's Carnegie Public Library in which selected Scouts demonstrated various woodcraft skills as "illustrations of the nature of the movement," along with moving pictures taken at national BSA's Silver Bay camp.

On January 21, 1911, the *Dallas Morning News* reported that Troop 4 was to be formed within the week at the Hardin School for Boys, established in 1910 by John Alexander Hardin and his brother, Capt. Roy H. Hardin.[8]

LEFT: Some Interurban rail lines marked the future routes of the highway system between North Texas cities. Hundreds of Dallas Boy Scouts walked this road to Fort Worth many times in local Scouting's earliest years. ACROSS RIGHT: The Dallas Carnegie Library on Commerce Street was constructed in 1901 from a $50,000 grant from steel tycoon Andrew Carnegie and situated only a few yards east of the Dallas YMCA Building.

DALLAS' FIRST RECIPIENTS OF THE RANKS OF FIRST CLASS AND SECOND CLASS

IN AUGUST, *two Troop 1 boys earned the rank of First Class, a significant milestone for the Scouting movement in Dallas.*

"Under the direction of Scoutmaster C. M. Richmond," reported the Dallas Morning News, James Winn and John Booth passed "an arduous test lasting over six hours," that included a six-mile walk, the preparation of a meal, the recitation of first aid steps for 26 kinds of accidents, the identification of trees from their bark alone, and swimming 50 yards.

Scouts Winn and Booth also had to "send and receive a message by semaphore at a rate of sixteen letters per minute, read a map correctly and draw one from field notes, fell a tree using an axe, judge distance, size, numbers, [of the] height of an object within 25 percent accuracy, know basic constellations and astronomy skills, and show themselves to have lived by the Scout Oath and Law."

The test was administered at Marsalis Park about seven miles south of the downtown, making the day's hike a total of 14 miles.

Just months earlier, these same two Scouts had passed the requirements for the Second Class rank that included serving a minimum of one month as a Tenderfoot Scout, showing a knowledge of elementary first aid and bandaging, demonstrating knowledge of semaphore or Morse code, and tracking a half mile in 25 minutes or less.

Each proved that he could start a fire with just two matches, and then cook meat and potatoes using only the regulation utensil kit. Another test was to save and deposit one dollar in a savings bank. After reciting the Scout Oath with raised Scout sign and giving of the Scout salute, they were awarded the rank.[E]

TOP RIGHT: Dallas Boy Scouts opening a savings account at a local bank to demonstrate fiscal responsibility required for rank promotion. BOTTOM RIGHT: Scouts receiving a lesson in botany.

Richmond was an energetic promoter who preached that Scouting solved the "energy problem" of idle boys through plenty of outdoor exercise.

"The woods are the natural haunt of the Scouts," Richmond declared. "And under the guidance of good and competent men, they are taught to love nature."

In doing so, he convinced several church leaders to form new patrols and troops. The Church of the Incarnation at the corner of Harwood Street and McKinney Avenue, the Trinity Presbyterian Church at 901 N. Zang Street, and the Grace Methodist Church at the corner of Haskell Avenue and Junius Street in East Dallas responded first, bringing to seven the number of troops in town.

But the rapid expansion brought its own challenges with lack of sufficient funds being primary. As local Scouting had little of that commodity, in February 1911, one of Troop 1's first activities was a fundraiser. Patrols would stage a Vaudeville show in the downtown YMCA gymnasium with proceeds going toward the costs of a proposed summer camp sojourn in June.

Scout acts included "Imperial Gymnasts" performing acrobatics on a horizontal bar, a musical quartet, a re-creation of Oscar Hammerstein's "School Boys," and boy magicians. But the show's star act was "Teddy and his Teddyettes," featuring Scout Phil Lenior as Theodore Roosevelt in his days as an officer of the Rough Riders in the 1898 Spanish-American War, with music arranged by Scout George W. Saam.[9]

However, receipts proved insufficient to send the troop to the two-week summer camp as planned. That would have to be put off to another year—but Richmond and his Scouts had made their indelible mark on Dallas.

By the end of 1911, Dallas was back up to about 100 Scouts organized into four troops. By the end of 1912, that number had dropped to 70 Scouts in seven troops. A vote for the organization of the Dallas Council's official franchise within BSA's national organization took place on December 18, 1912, and local Council managers authorized the first official Scouting duties to commence in January 1913 with Claude Richmond at its helm as its first paid Scout Commissioner.

"Definite plans for the financing and management of a Boy Scout Council in Dallas were made at a meeting in [Joseph] E. Farnsworth's office last night," declared the *Dallas Morning News*. "Regular Scout work will be started soon after the holidays."

Farnsworth was elected Council president along with four vice presidents, a secretary, and a treasurer. Now Richmond, newly resigned from his post at the YMCA effective October 1, 1912, could begin his search for the Council's first headquarters and take-up the business of managing the burgeoning Scouting movement in Dallas.

Plans for membership advancement were discussed in the offices of President Farnsworth on the eighth floor of the Commonwealth Bank Building, opened just four months prior, on the southeast corner of Main and Polydras Streets, today a downtown parking lot.[10]

BORN IN MANCHESTER, *New Hampshire during the fury of the American Civil War, Joseph Easton Farnsworth's early life was full of personal tragedy. First, prior to his birth in January 1862, his parents, Simeon and Jane Farnsworth, were recuperating from the death of his brother, John, at age eighteen months. Next, his mother died when Joseph was just four months old.*

Wishing to start anew, his father moved them to Wisconsin. However, Simeon's dream of a new life died with him in 1868, leaving six-year-old Joseph an orphan. He was sent to live with his paternal grandparents (then in their 70s) in Lowell, Massachusetts, but they were unable to properly care for him. He went to live in the foster household of local grocer Enoch and Eliza Blair until age 18.

As an adult, Joseph earned a job as a newspaper reporter in Texas for the San Antonio Express *in 1882. As part of his job, he was sent to Austin as their legislative correspondent. Liking the town, Farnsworth switched papers and joined the staff of the* Austin Statesman, *while scribing articles for the* Waco Examiner.

By 1885, Farnsworth had tired of the daily writing grind and sought work as an auditor for the Southwestern Telephone & Telegraph Company (ST&T) in Austin. Founded a mere three years prior as the Texas-Arkansas franchise of the Missouri and Kansas Telephone Company, he was their general auditor within two years.

While in Austin, he met and married Miss Laura Maas in October 1890. By mid-1894, their only child, Austin M. Farnsworth, was born.

Securing further job responsibilities, Farnsworth was promoted and transferred to Dallas whereupon he began work as the 34-year-old superintendent of the North Texas division of the Southwestern Bell System.

In 1902, Farnsworth was the general manager of ST&T with the vice presidency of Bell Telephone to follow in 1905. Now moving in the highest social circles around Dallas and nearing his retirement, Farnsworth was able to devote more of his time to philanthropic causes.

Retiring from ST&T in 1912 (but keeping his vice presidency at Bell), Farnsworth threw his time into the presidency of the new local franchise of the Boy Scouts of America the following year.

"[The idea of Scouting] is to instill in [a boy] a code of morals from which it is likely he will never depart," Farnsworth said of building good citizens.

Surely his early leadership in Dallas did just that.

Bell Telephone Vice President Joseph E. Farnsworth (above) became the Dallas Council's president during a meeting held at the newly constructed Commonwealth Bank Building in December 1912.

OAK CLIFF (DALLAS) TROOP 1
ONE of CIRCLE TEN COUNCIL'S CURRENT LEGACY TROOPS

ORIGINALLY FORMED IN FEBRUARY 1913 *as Troop 25 at the James Bowie Elementary School on N. Lancaster Avenue, co-Scoutmasters Kenneth Capers and William A. Middleton led 20 Scouts in the Crow, Black Bear, and Owl Patrols. (Assistant Scoutmaster Claude Campbell would join the unit on November 9, 1913.)*

On May 9, 1913, Thomas Alan Hord became the Scoutmaster of Troop 27 at the Reagan Elementary School at 9th and Llewellyn Streets, just prior to the Shriners Parade through downtown Dallas a week later. Over the coming months, Hord requested and received assistance in his Scouting program from both Capers and Middleton.

Sometime after March 1914, Troop 27 was folded into Troop 25 with the meeting place being changed to the Reagan School and Hord becoming the unit's sole Scoutmaster under the new number. Operating this way until mid-1916, the troop was temporarily disbanded due to lack of interest.

By February 1920, Hord restarted Troop 25 and operated it under the newly vacant designation of Dallas Troop 1. For the next 42 years, he remained its leader, celebrating his golden anniversary in Scouting in 1963.

Today, Troop 1 is chartered by the Holy Spirit Catholic Church in Duncanville and operated under the direction of Scoutmaster Jim Scott.[F]

TOP LEFT: Troop 25 Scoutmaster Thomas A. Hord relaxing outside of his homemade tent on a campout in 1915. LEFT: The Crow Patrol of Troop 1 on their summer trip to the Colorado River near San Saba, Texas in 1921. ABOVE: Members of Troop 1 at their 90th Anniversary celebration in 2003. ACROSS: Dallas Council Scouting supporter and local retail department store magnate Edward Titche.

On January 14, 1913, Scout Commissioner Richmond was given official instructions by the Council's recently formed executive board to "begin active Scouting work at once." From his new office in room 818 of the Wilson Building, he was intent on expanding the local program. With the assistance of board members, some of whom were the city's most affluent and influential Dallas businessmen, he launched an even more aggressive lecture and recruiting tour at any school or institution that would welcome him.[11]

A typical endorsement came from insurance agent George M. Stuart, Scoutmaster of Troop 5 chartered by the Church of the Incarnation in February 1911.

"I regard [Scouting] as the greatest boy movement of the century," he said. "The laws are highly moral

THE UNCLE OF A FUTURE COUNCIL PRESIDENT

IN APRIL 1913, *Scout Commissioner Claude Richmond visited nearby Wills Point, Texas to help that community start a Boy Scout troop. After delivering a stirring speech in the high school auditorium, 20 lads were "sworn in" prompting "two hours of tugging at the first test with their Scoutmaster, [Baptist minister] E. L. Brandon."*

Three patrols were formed replete with patrol leaders at their helm. One was 18-year-old Buck Jim Wynne, the uncle of future Circle Ten Council President Angus G. Wynne Jr. and his cousin, future Circle Ten Executive Board Member Toddie Lee Wynne Jr.[G]

and I believe the movement will help train-up a cleaner and manlier citizenship."

Stuart went on to serve on the Council's executive board as its chairman of the Finance Committee.[12]

Despite his prestigious backing, Richmond and his fellow Council managers worked hard to raise funds. In March 1913, they initiated a campaign to raise $2,500 for annual expenses. As budgeted, Richmond was to be paid $125 a month while the rest was to go toward office rent and operational costs. In the funding effort, five teams of three businessmen each solicited colleagues in "promoting the work of the Boy Scouts of America among the Dallas youth."

Men of means like Alex Sanger (the father of future Council President Eli L. Sanger) and Edward Titche, both owners of local department stores, contributed $5 each—even in those days not a large

—Photo by Voorhees & DeVoe.
Edward Titche.

sum, but a positive gesture of approval. Donations also came from Dallas Mayor William Meredith Holland and Judge Quentin D. Corley (to be the Council's second president in late 1914).

Corley was a man of great character and resolve. He had lost one arm and both hands in a train accident as a youth but refused to be defeated emotionally. He drove around Dallas in a specially modified automobile of his own design, steering with a prosthetic hook grasping a ring on the steering wheel. As a former Dallas justice of the peace now serving as the county judge, Corley eventually would be elected as the Dallas Council's first representative to the BSA National Council in 1916.

With the arrival of official BSA literature and clothing in downtown stores, Scouting was "rapidly perfecting" in Dallas. The Scout *Handbook* was available at Smith & Lamar, "the South's Largest Book Store," in the southeast corner of 1308 Commerce Street at S. Field[13] and Scout staves could be purchased from A.G. Spalding and Bros. at 1503 Commerce Street (now the valet parking lot for the downtown Neiman Marcus department store). The first shipment of 100 uniforms had arrived earlier in March 1913 and was available for sale at Burk & Company outfitters in the northwest corner of 1005 Main at N. Griffin Street. By June 1914, that company would be out of business and turn over their

Scouting concession to longtime Dallas outfitter E. M. Kahn and Company.[14]

Up until then, however, local Scouts simply had worn clothing of appropriate ruggedness and warmth that allowed them to be active and complete all requirements given them by the Scout Commissioner.

Now attired like true Boy Scouts, the boys were prepared fully to perform their most important civic project to date: crowd control for the Shriners Imperial Conclave Parade.[15]

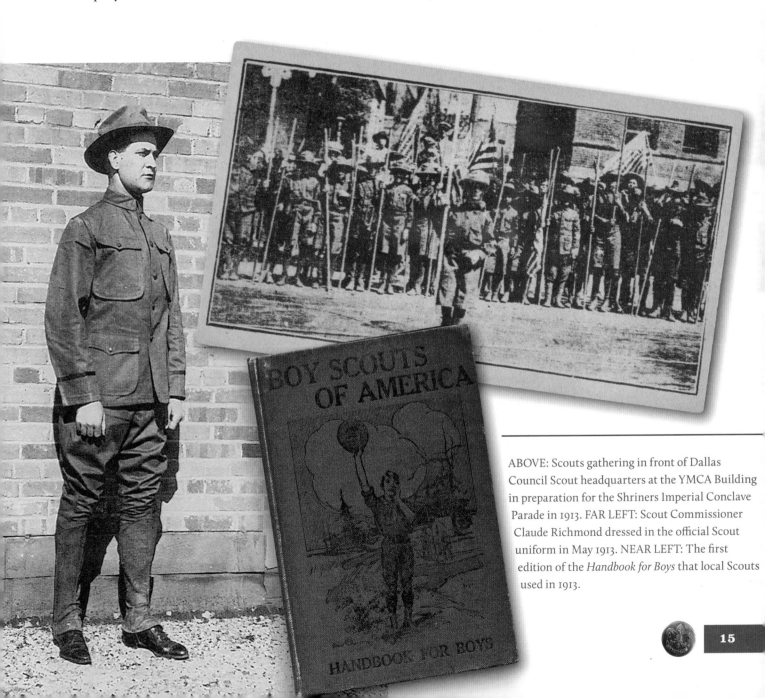

ABOVE: Scouts gathering in front of Dallas Council Scout headquarters at the YMCA Building in preparation for the Shriners Imperial Conclave Parade in 1913. FAR LEFT: Scout Commissioner Claude Richmond dressed in the official Scout uniform in May 1913. NEAR LEFT: The first edition of the *Handbook for Boys* that local Scouts used in 1913.

15

On May 13, 1913, the 39th annual Shriners convention was held in Dallas. Some 37,000 members poured through Union Station and into the streets of the city, swelling to 80,000 spectators who witnessed the parade. Dallas Boy Scouts and their adult leaders were called on to maintain order—following a clean-up and beautification of the city in preparation for the influx of visitors.[16]

On parade day, 350 Dallas Scouts from most of the city's 30 troops assembled alongside police officers on the route throughout the downtown area. Each Scout carried a six-foot walking stave and donned a white sleeve band on his left arm—both marks of being deputized to "keep back the crowd [and] make the street clear for the drilling of the Shrine teams."

The Scouts were instructed to "be courteous but firm" with the crowds in their charge but lacked authority to make arrests. In case of need, any one of them could report unruly behavior to the police or their Scoutmaster.

Pleased with the Council's first big service project, Mayor Holland sent Commissioner Richmond a letter of thanks.

"They are a band of little gentlemen," he declared of the Scouts. "It is highly commendable work."

Police Chief J.W. Ryan added, "I consider the services of Scoutmasters and the Scouts as very valuable in assisting the police to keep the crowds under such perfect control."

TOP: The medal presented to Members of the Shrine attending the Imperial Conclave in 1913. ABOVE: The participation medal for members of Dallas' Hella Shrine at the Imperial Conclave in 1913. RIGHT: The Dallas Council Scouts marching in a parade down Commerce Street in 1913. ACROSS TOP RIGHT: The only known photo of the Dallas Boy Scout Band, Drum & Bugle Corps (Troop 1) in May 1913.

With this service project completed, the boys could concentrate on preparing for their first Council summer camp coming up in June.[17]

UPON RETURNING FROM the summer camp, Richmond checked-in on a new troop that he had formed in the spring—the *new* Dallas Troop 1. When he accepted the commissionership in 1912, he had not only

resigned his position with the YMCA, but also stepped down as the Scoutmaster of the original Troop 1. Since no one else stepped up to serve as its leader, it folded by 1913. The new Troop 1 became the Dallas Boy Scout Band, Drum & Bugle Corps under the direction of Jackson W. M. Vidler, a sign company owner and former Scoutmaster from Tulsa, Oklahoma.

Vidler began with a dozen boys who formed a Bugle Corps only—a relatively easy step as every Dallas troop already had an assigned bugler to blow *Taps* at bedtime or *Reveille* at dawn. To be added at a later date were three snare drummers, a bass drummer, and a group of fifers. Two of the initial members were Richard Kimmons and Arthur Gorman—soon to be the first and seventh Eagle Scouts in the Dallas Council. Practices were held at the Dallas Central High School.

The Council reasoned that a Bugle Corps would draw new members to its ranks through public performances, a factual certainty that had already occurred after their performance at the Shriner's parade the previous May. The Corps had garnered the reputation as being "one of the sights of the town" as well as having earned $50 to purchase

THE **SCOUTMASTER RACE**

ON JULY 19, 1913, *Commissioner Claude Richmond and nine Scoutmasters departed downtown Dallas in a "fast hike" competition bound for Fort Worth some 34 miles to the west. Donning heavy shoes and walking staves, the racers negotiated the gathered crowd of Scouts that witnessed its start. The first man to complete the distance without running would be declared the winner.*

Of the four men that finished, Scoutmasters Thomas Hord of Troop 27 and Kenneth Capers of Troop 25, both in Oak Cliff, placed first and second. To Hord went a signet ring and Capers received a "fine watch fob."[1]

IN APRIL 1913, the Council's executive board was advised of a possible location for a summer camp on a tract of land about eight miles west of the city on Stewart's Lake (owned by a local farmer) near the town of Irving. In a meeting at the Elite Restaurant at 1215 Main Street (believed to be the location of John Neely Bryan's original campsite before the construction of Dealey Plaza), Farnsworth threw his full support behind preparing the location to make it happen.

But although the Scouts had the farmer's permission to use the site, it would not be ready for use on such short notice for the two-week camp in June as it rested in a flood plain and needed much brush clearing and clean-up. So three other sites were considered: one on private land at Goose Lake about 10 miles northwest of Wills Point, Texas and slightly south of present day Lake Tawakoni; a second at Moore's Park about six miles from Glen Rose; and the third at Bee Mountain about 20 miles south of Cleburne at Horseshoe Bend on the Brazos River (now known as Kimball Bend).

Richmond spent much of April inspecting the sites, keeping in mind the physical requirements of 150 Scouts, a handful of Scoutmasters, and their wives, as ladies were to be accommodated in a separate part of camp. Goose Lake was the victor with the Scout's cost, (which included food, gear, transportation, and supervision for the two-week camp), coming in at $6.50.

"Each patrol will be in [the] charge of a certified and experienced Scoutmaster, who will be responsible for the boys all the time," reported the Dallas Morning News. "Stated times will be set apart for swimming, baseball, trapping, fishing, boating, and exploration."

For accommodations, one hundred mothers manufactured the tents so their boys could concentrate on "the enjoyment of fresh air, nature, and clean thoughts."

As scheduled, most of the Scouts would ride a Texas and Pacific Special rail train to Wills Point, but Glenn D. Addington, the enterprising patrol leader of Troop 15 at the Dallas Central High School, intended to organize a hiking party to trek the 57 miles from Dallas.

Unfortunately, by the end of May, the owner of the Goose Lake site reneged on the deal and forced the sudden change to the Bee Mountain site that ran along a 15-mile bend in the horseshoe formed by the Brazos River. It was a dramatic location that featured "great hills covered at the crest with large rugged limestone rocks with cedars above and below."

The Bee Mountain site was situated on a part of the river that was deep enough for swimming instruction and boating lessons. Each attending Scoutmaster advised a patrol of seven Scouts, all of whom had to pass a cooking test over an open fire before being accepted to attend camp.

The test covered the ability to "fry meat, potatoes and onions, boil potatoes, corn and beans, and stew dried fruit and tomatoes." Rye bread would be supplied for meals but the Scouts would make their own corn bread in lidded cast iron pots, also known as "Dutch ovens."

To help Scoutmasters teach first aid, Dallas physician Scurry Terrill was recruited to instruct the men at a preparatory dinner banquet in the Oriental Hotel. Not long before, Dr. Terrill had attended to President Theodore Roosevelt after he had been shot in the chest by a would-be assassin while on his "Bull Moose" presidential campaign in Milwaukee, Wisconsin.

On the morning of June 10, 75 teenage boys lined up behind the Dallas Boy Scout Bugle Corps and marched through the city to the Interurban rail train that would take them to Fort Worth and then on to Cleburne. Once there, the Scouts shouldered their packs and set off on a two-day, 20-mile hike south to the Bee Mountain campsite.

The bulk of their equipment and supplies followed them on wagons provided by civic-minded Glen Rose merchants who met them at the station.

"It is a hilly country, really mountainous, with plenty of cedar and oak for shade and great boulders for play," reported the Dallas Morning News. "Bedticking will be filled with soft cedar. There is ample dry wood for fires. Produce and vegetables from the rich farm lands will be available and all about."

Most of all, there was plenty of fresh water for playing and swimming in. A $1 prize was offered to the Scout who came up with a name for the camp. By June 11, "Camp Tejas" on Squaw Creek at Bee Mountain was in full session. "The place could not have been better," reported a delighted Scout, "and we expect to have the time of our lives."

Activities included fire building, open-fire cooking, first aid skills, axe work, and knot tying. At its conclusion on June 21, setting apart a few episodes of fighting and swearing among some boys, Commissioner Richmond declared it to have been a "fine camp."[H]

ACROSS: Like the Scouts of today, 1913 Boy Scouts took specific equipment on camping trips. In addition to staples like rope, a sleeping blanket, water bottle, hat, and bugle they frequently left with a baseball glove and ball, Handbook for Boys, facial cold cream, ironstone china plates, silverware, manicure kit, needle and thread, and the Holy Bible —all toted around in a large burlap feed sack carried over each Scout's shoulder.

their own instruments. Their next performance was scheduled for the Texas State Fair in Dallas that October.

The Boy Scout Band portion was formed in June under the direction of musical director Paul Harris. He was in charge of two patrols being prepared to lead the big State Fair parade that would be attended by 1,000 Scouts.

"Scouts from over a hundred Texas towns will be invited to Dallas on that day," reported the *Dallas Morning News*.[18]

THE DALLAS COUNCIL held its first annual meeting and banquet on July 8, 1913, at the Southland Hotel at 400 N. Olive Street. About a hundred men attended. Richmond reported on new troops, patrols, and Scouts recruited since he had taken the job the previous January. He led discussions on funding requirements and the purchase of a permanent Council Scout camp, and talked up the coming Scoutmaster's endurance hike to Fort Worth and Scout message relay to Waco.

Although Richmond had shown himself to be a highly capable leader, funding remained a key requirement. He told the Council that without increased financial support, the "office will be closed." However, good things were happening: Scouts were giving up swearing and cigarettes, finding new

reverence for God, respecting property, befriending animals, earning their own money, and keeping clean in body, mind, and spirit. He closed his presentation saying, "Anyone desiring to mail a check for the work can mail it to J. Howard Ardrey, treasurer of the Dallas Council, 818 Wilson Building."

One result of this meeting was another Vaudeville show fund-

Two Artists for Boy Scouts' Vaudeville

J. Howard Ardrey.

TOP LEFT: Two Scout leaders perform in the Council's vaudeville show to raise funds for summer camp. LEFT: The Council's treasurer, J. Howard Ardrey, was a crucial player in the founding of the Dallas Federal Reserve Bank as well as being a vice president in the Dallas offices of the National Bank of Commerce of New York.

raiser—this one led by the Bugle Corps. Future Eagle Scouts Kimmons and Gorman performed military calls. Future Eagle Scout Tom C. Clark was featured alongside another future Eagle Scout, Commissioner Richmond, who gave a closing talk to the audience detailing the importance of Scouting to the community. This would be the only time in which four of the first nine Dallas Council Eagle Scouts of 1914 would perform together on stage.[19]

AS THE SCOUTMASTER *of one of the earliest troops in Texas, Thomas "Fred" Mercer fought against naysayers who believed Scouting to be a militaristic movement that produced miniature soldiers.*

"School teachers, Sunday school teachers, they all fought us," he recalled. "We couldn't even find a hall to meet in, so we met in barns, outhouses, and fields."

Receiving its official BSA charter dated May 28, 1912, Troop 1 was in full operation by the summer of 1913, when several exciting activities were planned. One was the Texas State Scout camp organized by the Texas Scoutmasters' Association being held at Bee Mountain on the Brazos River south of Cleburne in late August.

Another was the Texas State reunion of Civil War veterans being held in nearby Greenville on August 7th and 8th. Invited to attend by the city's organizers, Troop 1 Scouts served as aides-de-camp to the elderly warriors. From the Scouts' dedicated service that day, a resolution was adopted by the members of the Sterling Price Camp of Civil War Veterans No. 31:

RESOLVED: The Boy Scouts under the leadership of Fred Mercer captured the old Rebs—fairly took them by storm. They are manly little fellows and deserve all praise for their devotion to duty. May they prosper and fulfill the promise of their early boyhood.

In 1923, Scoutmaster Mercer moved to Dallas and Royse City's Troop 1 dissolved without his leadership. [1]

In 1939, it was restarted in Circle Ten Council under Scoutmaster J. R. Coolidge and his assistant, S. C. Cooper. Sponsored by the local Methodist Church, membership in the new Troop 312 quickly tripled from eight Scouts in May to 27 just a few weeks later.

Today, its 25 Scouts thrive under the under the direction and leadership of Scoutmaster Cody Stevenson and his seven assistants. [1]

TOP: Royse City's Troop 1 before departing for the Civil War veterans' reunion in Greenville, Texas in 1912. ABOVE: Troop 1's original BSA charter – the oldest one in existence in Circle Ten Council. BELOW: The current members of Troop 312 led by Scoutmaster Cody Stevenson.

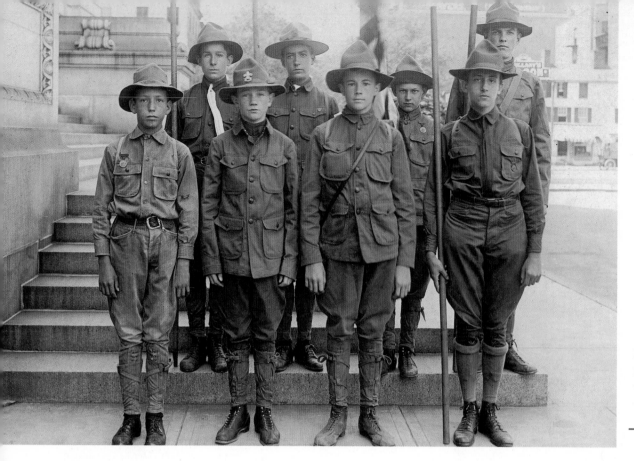

LEFT: An image of the lucky patrol inspected by President Woodrow Wilson in the movie, *The Making of a Scout.*

IN LATE SUMMER and early autumn, attention focused on the upcoming State Fair of Texas held each October since 1886 on the 277-acre Fair Park fairgrounds about a mile east of downtown. On Scout Day, October 25, Scouts from the region paraded the grounds in full uniform to the cadences of the Dallas Boy Scout Band, Drum & Bugle Corps.

Wishing to underscore the service aspect of Scouting, the Dallas Council set up a booth at the Fair to record daily good turns performed by Scouts and Scoutmasters. So that there would be a plentiful supply of these, Scouts responded to questions by visitors, took care of lost children, and ran errands as their good turns.

The Dallas Chamber of Commerce recruited the boys to help out-of-town visitors with the "utmost consideration," for instance guiding them to their rooming house or hotels in town.

All in all, Scout Day allowed the Dallas Scouts to show the community what they could do.

Richmond himself presented a lecture titled "Fifty Common Birds of Farm and Orchard," followed by the screening of a new motion picture in national release, "The Making of a Scout." One observer found it "replete with dramatic power, beauty, and interest." A small entrance fee was requested to raise funds for the Council.[20] The result was that thousands of Fair visitors were exposed to Scouting for the first time with very positive results.

AS THE YEAR closed, one particular challenge remained for the Dallas Council: securing a permanent campground. Many troops went on day hikes and overnight expeditions, but organizing local long-term camping was still problematic. There was no shortage of land offered by supporters for one-off campouts, but the Council needed a piece of land that it could improve and enhance with essential facilities.

Farnsworth set out some requirements: at least 10 acres no farther than 10 miles from Dallas, close

AT THE 1913 STATE FAIR OF TEXAS, *Scouts demonstrated a variety of skills to the public. They showed the Litter Drill for handling the sick and injured (as shown in BSA's Scoutmaster Handbook published that year), staged a water-boiling contest, signaled with flags, tied knots, and showed 23 uses for a six-foot walking stave, (one of which pertained to crowd control). One troop engaged in barrel boxing, where the young pugilists fought each other from inside large casks. Others raced while engaged in the "fireman's lift" rescue carry, while another unit competed in flinging the assegai—an African spear—the greatest distance.*

Signalers sent messages to Dallas Mayor William Holland at City Hall a mile or so away in downtown Dallas using semaphore, wig-wag, and American Morse atop Scout-built, wooden towers.

Scouts also demonstrated the Silvester method of resuscitating the drowned, invented by British physician Henry R. Silvester in 1858.

Using this technique, victims were placed on their backs, their arms pressed to their chests to expel air from their lungs, then raised above their heads to allow the entry of air.

With 1,000 Scouts and 300 Scoutmasters from over a hundred Texas towns pouring into the State Fair, Scout Day shaped up as an exciting event. State Fair President J. J. Eckford allocated camping sites near the fairgrounds with federally supplied tents "so that expenses of the out-of-town Scouts will be as small as possible."

Dallas Scout Band members, with two private lessons a week and a number of semi-weekly full band rehearsals under their belts, were ready to provide marching tunes and concert numbers to lead the parade. Although the boys had acquired their own instruments, Council President Farnsworth donated $50—about $1,100 today—to purchase a dozen new French bugles.[K]

BELOW: Scouts of Troop 1 at the 1913 State Fair of Texas. BELOW MIDDLE: Dallas Scouts perform the Litter Drill at the Fair.

LITTER DRILL

ABOVE: Since 1886, millions of Texas citizens have made their way to Fair Park in East Dallas to attend the multi-week festivities. Over the century, it has served as the host of many Scouting functions.

enough to an Interurban rail station to allow access by troops on foot. There must be a lake nearby and open lands to build a baseball field and athletic grounds. He suggested each troop, with the aid of a carpenter, build its own cabin to store equipment and that the Council build a pavilion at the center of camp to enhance the experience.

Farnsworth suggested that logs for construction could be brought in at a relatively low cost, "and the work be done in a manner to give it the appearance of a Western scout's cabin of the early days." Last, a flagpole should be raised to "float the banner of the Boy Scouts of America."

Richmond said several tracts of land were under consideration and "one will be selected within two months."

Should it be purchased with funds solicited from local businessmen, the Scouts would be expected to contribute $2 to $3 per year in dues to support the camp and Scouting headquarters operations,

thereby living the principle of "paying your own way." With a budget of $2,500 set for 1914, Scout dues would pay half that cost.

"With such a site, Dallas next year could have a camp running for the entire summer," Richmond declared.

By late September, one piece of land had risen to the top of the list: Stewart's Lake, eight miles west of Dallas, two miles southeast of Irving. It was close enough that troops hiking there and back for an overnighter could start on the old boundary loop of Oak Cliff and make the trip in one morning. Those wishing to travel by rail could take the Texas and Pacific train to the nearby community of Eagle Ford and back for a fee of 25¢.[21]

Richmond announced in November that a generous local donor was prepared to bear the costs of either building an amphitheater at the camp or furnishing "certain equipment."

BELOW: The unfinished cabin of Oak Cliff's Troop 25 at the Stewart's Lake campsite in 1914. ACROSS: The only image of the Stewart's Lake campsite known to exist .

On January 10, 1914, almost a year to the day after the Council began operations, Farnsworth announced the purchase of a 46-acre tract of land surrounding Stewart's Lake from the farmer who owned it as the Council's first permanent campsite.

"Here in the open air, under the trees, the opportunity would be afforded for the development of those virtues" suggested in the Scout Oath and Scout Law, Farnsworth declared. "The Boy Scouts of Dallas have one of the best camp sites in the country" with troop-built log cabins high on a knoll overlooking the lake below.

Detailed instructions for building log cabins were provided in the Boy Scout *Handbook,* and numerous troops embarked upon constructing them at Stewart's Lake. By spring, five troops were ready to roof their cabins, providing all local Scoutmasters with an opportunity to get together in fellowship on the weekends that they did not camp with their units.

To communicate between the camp and downtown Dallas, Scouts resorted to the wireless technology of the times—semaphore and lighted Morse code. They also built their own boats for the lake. In the future, the Council would provide a mess hall and sleeping cabins for guests. And at the center of the property would be a performance pergola for the Dallas Council Boy Scout Band.

WITH 500 TOTAL MEMBERS, THE COUNCIL WAS ON A GROWTH PATH AND SCOUTING WAS NOW WELL ESTABLISHED IN DALLAS.[22]

THE BRIDGE BUILDING TO THE FUTURE HAD BEGUN.

chapter 2

COMMISSIONER RICHMOND STAKES THE CLAIM (1914)

"I, personally, see in this movement wonderful possibilities for Dallas. I hope that it will gain the general recognition to which it is entitled."

Joseph E. Farnsworth
First President
Dallas Council, BSA
January 10, 1914

BELOW: The Dallas skyline as it appeared in 1914. ACROSS NEAR RIGHT: A Boy Scout assisting a decorated Union veteran at the 1913 Gettysburg Reunion in Pennsylvania. ACROSS FAR RIGHT: A Boy Scout serves as a valet for two Confederate Gettysburg veterans attending the Reunion .

ON A NATIONAL LEVEL IN EARLY 1914, the Boy Scouts of America began to gain members rapidly—due mostly to positive coverage of their good turn helping aging Civil War veterans at the 50th Reunion of the Battle of Gettysburg in Pennsylvania the previous July 1913. Boy Scouts worked as medics and aides-de-camp, and provided information to the returning veterans. The event helped consolidate the position of the Boy Scouts as the premier youth-building organization of the United States. Although the country was still three years away from entering World War I, the Scout uniform, in that era distinctly military in style, was attractive to youths as well.

Nationally, BSA counted some 200,000 total members as 1914 opened, up 50 percent from the 130,000 total Scouts one year before.

In Dallas, Scout Commissioner Claude Richmond worked on building local membership having started some 30 new troops in 1913 sponsored by churches, public and private schools, professional associations, and large downtown department stores. He launched a new recruiting drive in January 1914 and signed-up two new units within a fortnight. The first was located at the Sam Houston Public School in the northwest corner of Dickason Avenue and Throckmorton Street

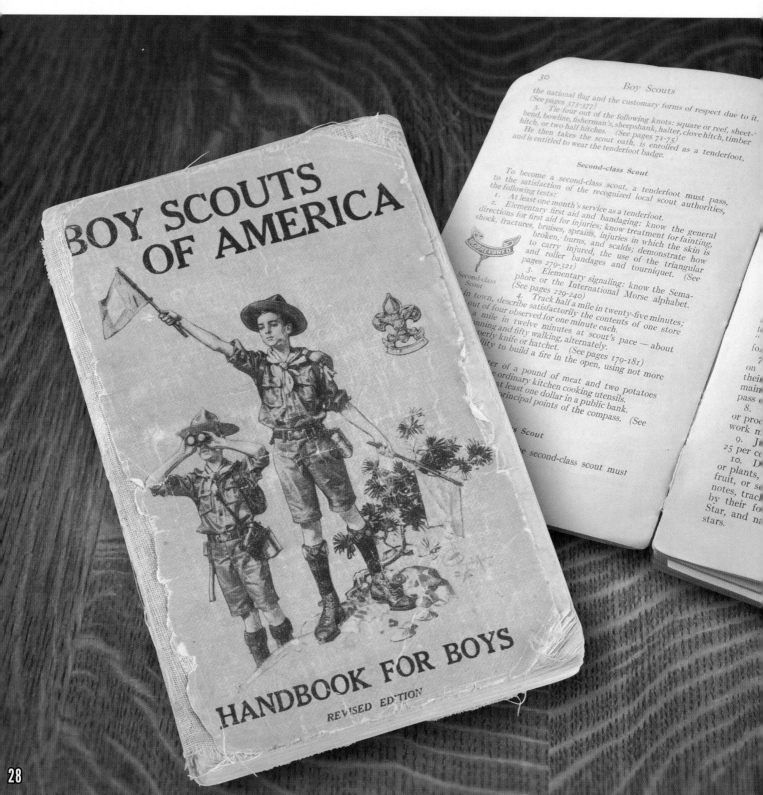

in Oak Lawn under Scoutmaster E. L. Shepherd, while the second met at the First Baptist Church of Dallas under the leadership of Pastor Benjamin Oscar Herring.[1]

Additional troops were started at the Titche-Goettinger department store, housed out of the ground floor of the Wilson Building, the Austin Public School at 3308 Gaston Avenue, the Oak Cliff Presbyterian Church at 9th Street and Patton Avenue under Scoutmaster Thomas Hord, and a unit re-started at the Oak Grove Public School in downtown Dallas.

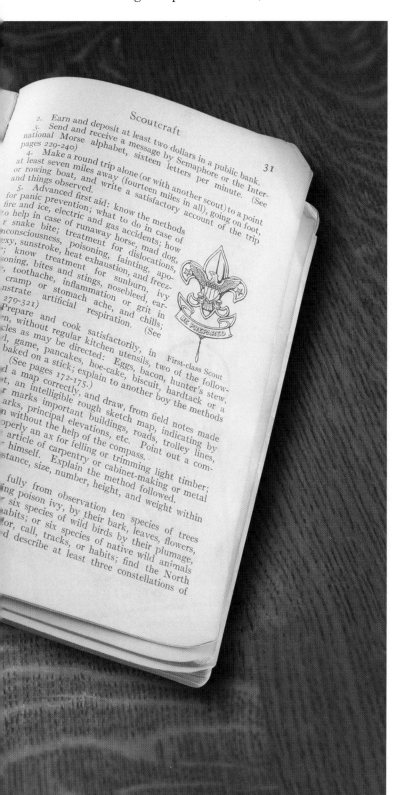

As the Boy Scouts of America gained national popularity, its *Handbook for Boys* sold more than several hundred thousand copies. This Revised Edition with an oil cloth cover was the version used by local Scouts and leaders in 1914.

Scouts were making strides in rank advancement. First Class Scout Arthur Gorman of the Troop 1 Band, Drum & Bugle Corps was continuing to earn merit badges, closing in on his goal of Eagle. His most recent accomplishment was passing the Scout Cook test—similar to today's Cooking merit badge. Since official merit badge pamphlets had not yet been invented, the requirements were published in BSA's *Handbook for Boys*.

Young cook Arthur had to build a fireplace out of stone, sod or logs, light a fire and in the open, cook camp stew, two vegetables, an omelet, and rice pudding. Then he had to mix bread dough and cook a loaf in the camp oven, make tea, coffee, and cocoa, carve meat properly, and serve it in a "civilized" fashion.[2]

Troop 1 Scouts Clyde Smith and Patrol Leader Prince Harris (the son of Musical Director Paul Harris) and DeWitt Harris of Troop 21 at the William B. Travis Public School on West McKinney Avenue earned the rank of Second Class. A few weeks later, Fred L. Sliney of Troop 21 became Dallas' 17th First Class Scout.

According to the *Dallas Morning News*, "[Sliney] will try for the Eagle Scout test next" as the latest boy to enter the race to become Dallas' first Eagle Scout.

Going into April, First Class Scouts Winguit A. Turner of the Davy Crockett Public School's Troop 18 located on Alcalde Street south of Worth Street in East Dallas, and Arthur Gorman were neck-and-neck in earning the 21 merit badges required for the

Lynnwood Bradshaw.

William C. Geller.

Scouts Eugene Bradshaw (left), Lynwood Bradshaw (middle), and William C. Geller (right) were three of the Dallas Council boys working to become the Council's first Eagle Scout.

ABOVE: (left) Members of Troop 25 under the direction of Scoutmaster Thomas A. Hord cook over a campfire while on an overnight trip. (middle) Troop 25 Assistant Scoutmasters Kenneth Capers (2nd from left) and Bob Addison (2nd from right) pose with the Black Bear Patrol. (right)Troop 25 Scouts and leaders at their cabin constructed at the Stewart's Lake campsite.

Eagle rank. Behind them were Eugene Bradshaw of Troop 15 at the Dallas Central High School and 16-year-old Richard Thomas Kimmons of Troop 1.

Turner began to increase his lead by earning Pioneering, followed by Painting, Camping, and Gardening, giving him a total of 15 merit badges. Watching from the vantage point of the Scout Commissioner's seat, an excited Richmond suggested that as the race heated up, there could be five Eagle Scouts in town by the end of the summer.

Kimmons answered by acquiring First Aid to Animals and a few other badges. His full tally included Civics, Camping, Art, Lifesaving, Public Health, Personal Health, Swimming, Bugling,

Firemanship, Pioneering, Painting, Handicraft, Gardening, Cooking, Beekeeping, and Interpreting. Turner was at 17 badges, Gorman at 15, and Eugene Bradshaw and newcomer Douglas Barnhurst at 10 each.

On May 23, 1914, Richmond announced that Dallas had not one but *two* Eagle Scouts. The first was Richard Kimmons, who gained his final badges just hours ahead of Winguit Turner. They were the second and third Eagle Scouts west of the Mississippi as fewer than 100 Eagle awards had been earned nationally by that point. The first Eagle in Texas, William Elmo Merrem, was the nation's 37th.[3]

INVOLVEMENT IN THE SCOUTING COMMUNITY EACHES LEADERSHIP SKILLS THAT YOUNG PEOPLE WILL CARRY FORWARD IN THEIR LIVES AND I AM A STRONG BELIEVER THAT THE EARNING OF THE RANK OF EAGLE SCOUT WILL POSITIVELY IMPACT ONE'S DESIRE TO ACHIEVE FUTURE GOALS.

—JAY YOUNG PRESIDENT & CEO, KING OPERATING CORPORATION

DALLAS' FIRST EAGLE SCOUT CLASS—1914

NO.	NAME	BIRTH DATE	BIRTH PLACE	DEATH DATE	DEATH PLACE
1	RICHARD THOMAS KIMMONS	18 JUL 1897	SULPHER SPRINGS, TX	28 DEC 1962	BUTTE, CA
2	WINGUIT ALFRED TURNER	22 JUL 1899	GA	27 DEC 1976	TALLAHASSEE, FL
3	SAMUEL WILLIAM CLARK JR.	16 MAY 1901	COVINGTON, TX	24 JAN 1991	DALLAS, TX
4	HENRY HARRIS JACOBY	1 DEC 1897	DALLAS, TX	10 JUL 1974	DALLAS, TX COCHRAN CHAPEL CEMETERY
5	BRYAN T. BILLUPS	27 JAN 1898	WAXAHACHIE, TX	1 AUG 1962	DALLAS, TX RESTLAND FUNERAL HOME
6	CLAUDE EDWARD PIMLOTT	12 MAY 1901	MO	4 JAN 1973	WICHITA COUNTY, TX
7	ARTHUR GORMAN	25 AUG 1899	WEATHERFORD, TX	27 MAY 1918	DALLAS, TX (BURIED IN WEATHERFORD, TX)
8	CLAUDE MARION RICHMOND	29 AUG 1876	VERNON COUNTY, MO	1 MAR 1965	SAN ANTONIO, TX
9	THOMAS CAMPBELL CLARK	23 SEP 1899	DALLAS, TX	13 JUN 1977	NEW YORK CITY, NY

BELOW: The Dallas Council's second Eagle Scout Winguit R. Turner. FAR BELOW: The 1914 Eagle Scout card for future U.S. Supreme Court Associate Justice Tom C. Clark (far below right).

As Dallas' first Eagle Scout, Kimmons received a prize of $125 (about $2,700 today) awarded by the Council along with a pledge by the president of Southern Methodist University, Robert Stewart Hyer, for a four-year scholarship to the institution. SMU, founded in 1911 and opened for classes on September 22, 1915, had 456 co-educational students, 37 faculty members, and five buildings that hosted study in three academic units: the School of Theology, the School of Music, and the College of Liberal Arts. But as it turned out, Kimmons could not claim his educational reward because his father, a traveling sales-man, moved the family to the Texas Panhandle immediately after Richard graduated from Dallas Central High School.

BORN ON JULY 18, 1897 *in Sulpher Springs, Texas, to Illinois native James M. Kimmons and his wife, the former Maude Byers of Indiana, Richard was their second son. By 1910, the family was living in the Routh Street area of Dallas where the brothers attended the William B. Travis* Public School. *Both 13-year-old Richard and 15-year-old Byron Kimmons lost no time in joining Claude M. Richmond's Troop 1 at the downtown Dallas YMCA in November 1910.*

With Troop 1's demise two years later as Scoutmaster Richmond began his work as the Council's first paid Scout Commissioner, Richard was a founding member of the new Troop 1, now re-started in 1913 as the Dallas Scout Bugle Corps. Elected its president, his parents opened the doors to their home as a weekly practice location. By mid-September 1913, Kimmons was a First Class Scout and by May 1914, he was the Dallas Council's first Eagle Scout award recipient.

Although still living in Dallas in 1916, father James Kimmons, a traveling salesman for a surgical supply distribution company, moved his family to Hereford, Texas in Deaf Smith County. Richard remained there until 1924 when he moved to nearby Amarillo, where he took employment with the Pacific and Santa Fe Railroad.

By the following year, he had quit that job and was working as a clerk at the Amarillo Daily News. *By 1926, he began a short stint at the J. P. Mathis Real Estate Company as a salesman, a post that he held until taking work in 1930 as a debt collector at an Amarillo furniture company. At the time, he was 26-years-old, unmarried, and still living with his mother as his father had passed away. Those living arrangements would change with his move to Bloomsburg, Pennsylvania, where he met his future wife, Mary Alice Stackhouse, a schoolteacher from nearby Shickshinny. The couple married in Shickshinny in 1940 and moved to Amityville on Long Island, New York, through*

This vintage Eagle Scout medal manufactured by the Thomas H. Foley Company was the same style and design earned by Richard Kimmons (top) and the rest of the Council's Eagle Scouts in 1914.

the duration of World War II.

In 1945, they moved to Orange County, California, where the Kimmons' resided for 11 years. In 1956, they moved to Paradise, California, where Richard worked as a distributor for Simplified Tax Records, Inc.

Richard Thomas Kimmons died without heirs at age 65 on December 28, 1962, in Butte, California. He was buried in his wife's family's plot in Shickshinny alongside her three sisters and parents. *His beloved wife, Mary, joined him in death on New Year's Day 1999.[A]*

BORN IN WEATHERFORD, TEXAS, *in August 1899 to local blacksmith Oscar H. Gorman and his wife, Alice, Arthur was the youngest of six children. By 1910, Oscar had died and Alice had moved the family to 3205 Swiss Avenue in Dallas since better job prospects awaited.*

In March 1913, shortly after Arthur turned 12, he joined the Coyote Patrol of Troop 15 at the Dallas Central High School under Scoutmaster and Principal Walter S. S. Gray. Taking the leadership position of "corporal" or assistant patrol leader, he transferred to the Troop 1 Bugle Corps in May, now under the direction of R. S. Bradford. Elected treasurer of the unit, bugler Gorman began a noteworthy Scouting career.

Within a week, Gorman was one of three Scouts to earn the rank of Second Class after being examined by Scout Commissioner Claude Richmond at nearby Forest Park (south of Fair Park between Grand Avenue and Martin Luther King Jr. Boulevard). By August, he had earned the rank of First Class, and at 13 years old, was the youngest Scout in Texas to have done so. The Dallas Morning News *announced his "enviable record" in its* August 3 front-page headline. By the end of September, he was the Dallas Council's seventh Eagle Scout.

He graduated from Dallas Central High School in December 1917 but, sadly, his life would end tragically.

Riding horses with friends in Anna, Texas just north of McKinney, Gorman ran into a low hanging branch while at full gallop and was knocked to the ground—fracturing his skull. Rushed quickly via Interurban rail car to Dallas, he passed away at St. Paul's Sanitarium (now the St. Paul Medical Center) on Bryan Street on May 27, 1918, leaving behind a legacy of achievement.[B]

BELOW: The Dallas Central High School as it appeared in better times. It now sits boarded up and abandoned on Bryan Street across from the DART rail station. BELOW RIGHT: First Class Scout Arthur Gorman in 1914. ACROSS TOP: The Oak Cliff Presbyterian Church sponsored Troop 25 and eventually Troop 3 in 1923.

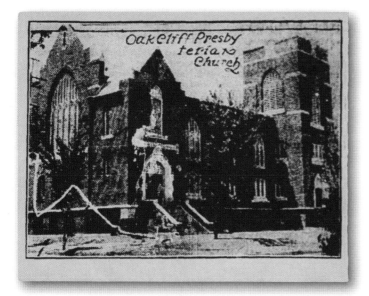

But to maintain such a pace of growth and expand membership, the Council needed ever more funding and Richmond was intent upon bringing it in. At its second annual meeting, the Council re-elected Farnsworth as its president and established a solid slate of vice presidents: insurance firm owner George M. Stuart, Dallas County Judge Quentin D. Corley, merchandiser Edward Titche, and Superintendent of Dallas Schools James Albert Brooks. The owner of the Jester & Company Insurance Agency, L. I. Jester, became treasurer, and William A. Middleton, the co-Scoutmaster of Troop 25 at the Oak Cliff Presbyterian Church, took the position of secretary.

Farnsworth appointed a capable finance subcommittee. Sitting on it were: Frederic F. Sliney, an executive at John Moody's Rating Agency (and father of First Class Scout Fred J. Sliney); Dallas lawyer Curtis Hancock (and later first chairman of the Texas State Highway Commission); founder of the Maloney Hat Company, W. P. Maloney; Judge Corley; George Stuart; and Commissioner Richmond.

The Executive Board approved a budget of $2,500, proposing to raise the money in a three-week campaign with one-third coming from the parents of Scouts and the rest from members of the community. Farnsworth drafted a letter of appeal to the fathers of the boys for a donation of $5 each, assuring them that all monies raised would "go toward the support of the local office and the salary of the Scout Commissioner, who devotes all of his time to the movement."

The budget included the Commissioner's $1,800 annual salary, monthly office rent of $15 for Suite 624 in the Wilson Building, printed matter projected to cost $50, and miscellaneous expenses of $470. Presumably, Dallas with its 120,000 citizens would have little difficulty supporting the fledgling movement at that very modest level of cost.

Farnsworth informed potential donors that only a year earlier when Scout work was organized, there

BONNIE AND CLYDE IN VICKERY, TEXAS

THE NEARBY COMMUNITY *of Vickery was a six-mile hike to the northeast from downtown Dallas—a favorite destination for visiting Scout troops to participate in "baseball games, swimming, and some fishing." Although the town had their own Scouting "council" totaling a single troop, they merged into Circle Ten in 1927 to utilize its professional Scouting staff. Not long after, the community gained a reputation for its other well-known visitors—the infamous Texas outlaws Bonnie and Clyde. Whenever passing through the area, they chose the Vickery Gas Station at the southeast corner of today's Greenville Avenue and Park Lane (later the Filling Station restaurant) to refuel their getaway cars.[c]*

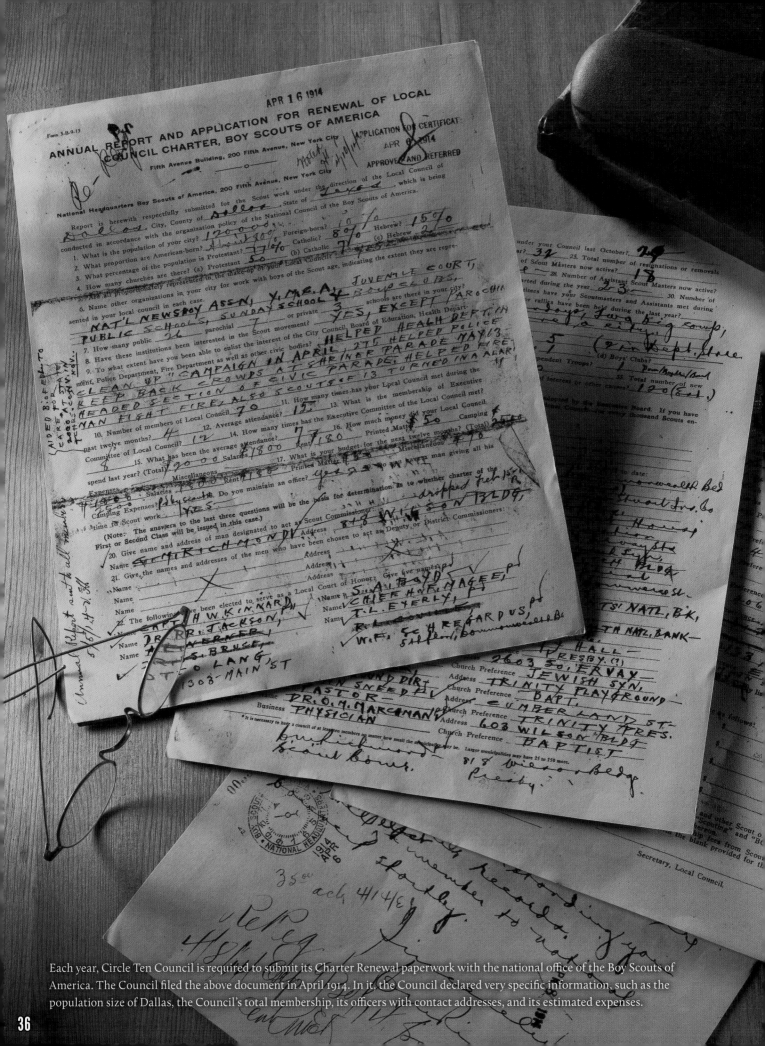

Each year, Circle Ten Council is required to submit its Charter Renewal paperwork with the national office of the Boy Scouts of America. The Council filed the above document in April 1914. In it, the Council declared very specific information, such as the population size of Dallas, the Council's total membership, its officers with contact addresses, and its estimated expenses.

had only been one Scoutmaster. But, "today there are more than 500 Scouts in twenty-three troops and twenty-three active Scoutmasters" due to Richmond's outstanding efforts. Current chartering organizations included 15 public schools, six churches, the Sanger Brothers department store, and the Titche-Goettinger department store.

The Council sought business commitments of $2.50 a month. Companies that "contributed liberally" to the goal were Linz Brothers jewelers, Burk & Company, Owl Drug Company, Briggs-Weaver Company, and the Brown Cracker and Candy Company. (Interestingly, a decade or so later, Brown Cracker's most infamous employee named Clyde Barrow would quit his $1 a day job at the factory at 603 Munger Avenue in today's West End Marketplace to eventually start a career robbing banks with his partner and girlfriend Bonnie Parker.)[4]

Real estate agent Lloyd Nash, officing out of his boarding room at the YMCA Building at 1310 Main Street, made a unique proposition to potential clients by offering to make a donation to the Council whenever they presented him with a "Boy Scout Card," which had been handed out previously by Scouts advertising Nash's homes and lots for sale.

"The Dallas Division of the Boy Scouts of America has done a great work during the short time that it has been organized," he stated in promotional literature. "For every adult who goes to see WESTWOOD and presents me or my representative [with] a card furnished for that purpose [and] properly filled out, I will give the Scout 25¢ and $2.50 to the organization for each $200 lot sold through the Boy Scouts. This means that every Boy Scout who is active and in good standing has an opportunity to make a little spending money for himself and greatly help his association."[5]

Despite such efforts, the fundraising campaign fell short by $600, a problem that would have to be addressed later.

With the arrival of autumn, Farnsworth called his final Council meeting as its president at the Oriental Hotel at 1400 Commerce Street at N. Akard, now the location of AT&T's Whitacre Tower. The agenda included filling board vacancies as well as formally designating Stewart's Lake as the Council's "official" campsite *despite* its situation on lowlands and tendency to flood.

Board elections confirmed Judge Corley as the Council's second president, filling the last month of Farnsworth's unexpired term. Elsewhere, well-known Dallas florist Otto Lang was elected first vice president, A. R. Phillips became second vice president replacing

The Oriental was Dallas first luxury hotel built at a cost of $500,000 ($12.3 million today). Making it unique for the times, it included many modern day conveniences like electricity, gas, and elevators along with other amenities such as a barber shop, a grand dining room, first floor cigar stand, and second floor bridal parlor. Opened in 1893 by Thomas William Field, it was known locally as "Field's Folly" as much of his personal wealth was spent in constructing the hotel that eventually bankrupted him.

HENRY HARRIS JACOBY
FROM TENDERFOOT TO EAGLE SCOUT OVER THE SUMMER

HENRY JACOBY'S EARNING *of the Eagle rank was a legendary and record-setting accomplishment—it took a total of 97 days. As the fourth of five children born to Dallas constable and future real estate agent Henry Hibbler Jacoby and wife, the former Laura Jane Harris, on December 1, 1897, young Henry was accustomed to competition and was a certified overachiever.*

Joining Troop 1's Bugle Corps at the Dallas Central High School in late May 1914, Henry began working immediately toward his goal of Eagle Scout after reading about Richard Kimmons' and Winguit Turner's earning of the rank only days before. Devoted to purpose, he began his meteoric ascent and earned the First Class rank by July 22—along with seven merit badges.

Working throughout the summer that included winning races in the Scout swimming competition held at the local Gill Well Sanitarium (mineral bathhouse and natatorium) at 3305 Maple Avenue near Turtle Creek Boulevard in today's Reverchon Park, Jacoby earned the Eagle rank in late August, being the Council's fourth to date. In October, he entered and won the gold medal for efficiency and proficiency in Scouting skills in the Dallas Boy Scout competition held at Fair Park.

Graduating high school, Jacoby won the 6th annual Phi Kappa Medal from the Forensic Society for oratory for speaking on the topic of "The Criminal." Another oration was at the Dallas Council's First Annual Reunion in 1917, where he keynoted the dinner in front of 70 local Scouting alumni.

Marrying Margaret Cameron Miller in Dallas on July 23, 1933, the couple remained in town where they raised two sons and a daughter: Henry, Daniel, and Caroline. Jacoby served in World War II and when discharged, he began a career as an insurance agent.

Henry Harris Jacoby died a widower from a heart attack on July 10, 1974. He is buried in the family plot along with his parents, siblings, wife, and son, Daniel, in the Cochran Chapel Cemetery in Dallas at the Cochran Chapel Methodist Church at 9027 Midway Road, just south of Northwest Highway.[D]

Judge Corley, and Edward Titche remained as third vice president. Scoutmaster William Middleton succeeded outgoing Dallas School Superintendent James Brooks as fourth vice president. Henry Hibbler Jacoby (father of Eagle Scout Henry Harris Jacoby) and Justin Ford Kimball, the incoming Dallas public school superintendent, were elected to the Council's board.

Corley's first order of business was to speak to the Scouts on the topic of "Overcoming Difficulties." Having overcome some severe handicaps from an early age, Corley spoke with much authority.

Soon Corley, Richmond, and two First Class Scouts, Haron Dobey and John Trieller, would travel to nearby Garland and advise their citizens on the Scouting movement and how to form their own council. However, one Scout troop was already in the town.[6]

Back in Dallas, Richmond struggled to fill the many vacancies within the Scoutmaster ranks as a number of men had left town or resigned their Scoutmaster commissions.

To make matters worse, as 1914 closed Richmond and Corley faced that budget shortfall of $600, no insignificant sum in those days. Their solution was to hold a Scout Round-Up at the Fair Park Coliseum, where they invited the Scouts to "do a good turn to the local Council [in] helping them to raise money to close the year out of debt."

Richmond sent each Scout's family a letter urging them to report to Fair Park on December 11 to partake in music by the local 25-piece Woodman Band and watch "free motion pictures by the Texas Film Corporation." The event would conclude with a short talk by Finance Committee Chairman Eli L. Sanger on how to go door-to-door and solicit funds. Sanger planned to send out 150 to 200 pairs of Scouts the following day to canvas local neighborhoods for contributions; the team that brought in the most would claim a prize of $7.50, with prizes of $5.00 and $2.50 for second and third place.

Scouts who could not afford uniforms would wear an armband with "BSA" on it, while all other Scouts bore a letter of purpose written by Commissioner Richmond "authorizing them to receive money for the association." They would ask for donations from a nickel to 25¢. "Loyalty and unity of purpose will win the day for our Scout movement," Sanger told them.

Before the evening ended, future U.S. District Judge William H. Atwell spoke to the boys and related his first experience with Dallas Boy Scouts at a recent civic event.

"The bugle corps came along and I watched them pass a corner where two old men were in a buggy watching the parade," Atwell said. "As the horse became frightened, I noted with pleasure how the boys went about quieting the horse and preventing a panic. Since then I have been interested in the movement [and] am glad to know the boys are receiving this training in decency and manliness."[7]

On January 2, 1915, Commissioner Richmond again moved the Council's operations to larger quarters, this time into Room 7 in the Dallas Terminal Railway and Union Depot building (now the Greyhound Bus

Judge William H. Atwell, an early supporter of Scouting in Dallas, was an influential member of Dallas society. Not only was he a distinguished jurist, he served also as the Commissioner of the Dallas Zoo in its formative years. Under his leadership, the Zoo moved from its cramped quarters in (Old) City Park to Fair Park in 1910, and eventually in 1912 to its current site in Oak Cliff's Marsalis Park.

Depot) across from *Dallas Morning News* offices. Making the move that much sweeter, the holidays had produced a crop of rank advancements suggesting Scouting was increasing in popularity in Dallas. More advancement tests were scheduled for the following weekend—a fitting end to the Claude Richmond era in Dallas Scouting as he had decided to go into another line of work—life insurance. The higher paycheck and predictable working hours made the move across town more palatable.

At the Council's annual meeting held on January 20, 1915, Scout Executive Richmond tendered his resignation effective February 3, which the Executive Board reluctantly accepted. Four days later, Richmond gave his final State of the Council

Report citing a total membership of 597 Scouts in more than 20 local troops.

During his two years at the helm, he witnessed the designation of nine Eagle Scouts, 34 First Class Scouts, and 85 Second Class Scouts. He had formed more than 30 troops that had held 543 meetings attended by 6,782 boys, who had gone on 95 hikes and attended three, week-long summer camps (two held in 1913). The Council's budget was balanced, he noted with pride.

Richmond had left the Council in excellent shape for future growth provided that another visionary take the helm as Dallas Scout Commissioner. President Corley appointed four deputy Scout

ACROSS: Always happy to put on a themed campout, Scoutmaster Thomas A. Hord of Oak Cliff's Troop 25 dresses in pirate garb on an early campout. ABOVE: Troop 25 gathers for a patrol photograph on an outing. RIGHT: A Troop 25 Scout repairs the sole of his boot.

Commissioners to tend to the four regions of the Dallas Council for the time being. J. S. Bowling would serve North Dallas that included Oak Lawn and Highland Park. C. E. Fisher would work East Dallas that included Fair Park, while W. L. Bishop would serve South Dallas. James A. Glidewell was assigned Oak Cliff. From them, the new executive would be chosen.

ON FEBRUARY 20, PRESIDENT CORLEY MADE HIS DECISION, LAUNCHING THE BRIEF JAMES GLIDEWELL ERA OF THE DALLAS COUNCIL.[8]

chapter 3

DALLAS—Where Men are Looking Forward

JEFFERSON HOTEL · TERMINAL · COURT HOUSE · CRIMINAL COURTS BUILDING · COTTON EXCHANGE · WESTERN INDEMNITY BUILDING · WALDORF HOTEL · LINZ BUILDING · SOUTHLAND HOTEL · INSURANCE BUILDING · ORIENTAL HOTEL · ADOLPHUS ANNEX · ADOLPHUS HOTEL · AM. EXCH. NAT'L BANK BUILDING · S.W. LIFE BUILDING · SOUTHLAND LIFE INS. BUILDING · INTERURBAN BUILDING

SCOUTS TO THE RESCUE
(1915–1918)

"Not a slacker Scout in Dallas."

ROBERT C. McDOWELL
SCOUT EXECUTIVE
DALLAS COUNCIL, BSA
MAY 12, 1917

ABOVE: A pin was given to anyone participating in the sale of Liberty Loan bonds. This pin was awarded during the first sale in June 1917. RIGHT: The bicycle riding Scout messenger was a common sight in downtown Dallas during World War I.

ON FEBRUARY 15, 1915, 25-year-old Scout Commissioner James Arthur Glidewell settled into his official quarters in Room 7 of the Dallas Chamber of Commerce offices in the two-story Terminal Railway and Union Depot Building at 808 Commerce Street. He had just been given charge of an organization that his predecessor, Claude Richmond, had put on solid footing but still needed to be built up.[1]

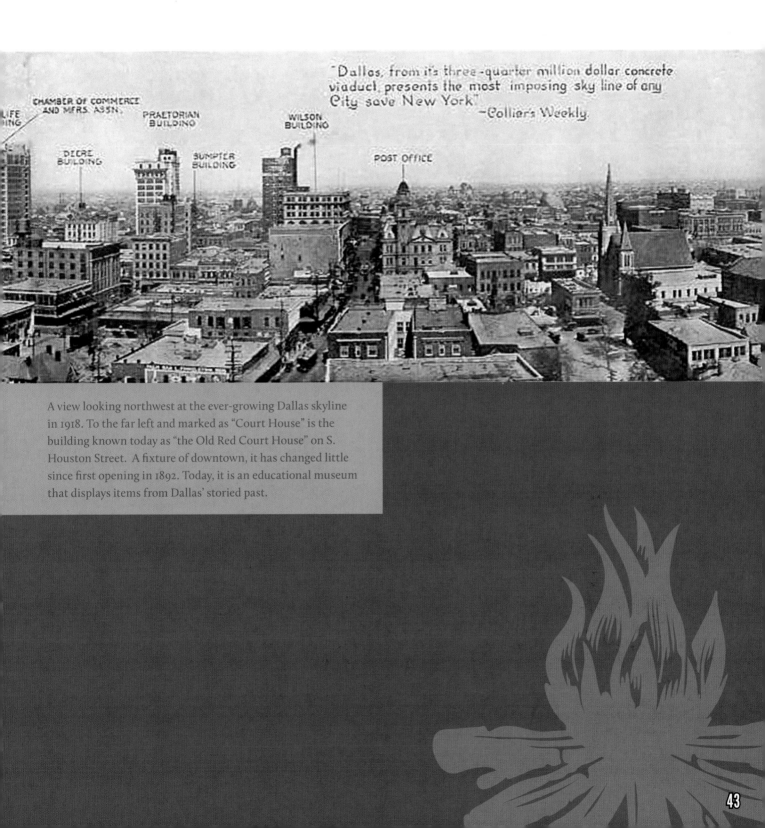

"Dallas, from its three-quarter million dollar concrete viaduct, presents the most imposing sky line of any City save New York"
—Collier's Weekly.

CHAMBER OF COMMERCE AND MFRS. ASSN.

PRAETORIAN BUILDING

WILSON BUILDING

DECRE BUILDING

SUMPTER BUILDING

POST OFFICE

A view looking northwest at the ever-growing Dallas skyline in 1918. To the far left and marked as "Court House" is the building known today as "the Old Red Court House" on S. Houston Street. A fixture of downtown, it has changed little since first opening in 1892. Today, it is an educational museum that displays items from Dallas' storied past.

BORN ON NOVEMBER 5, 1889 in Cooper, Texas, James Arthur Glidewell was the son of James H. Glidewell, a North Texas cotton sharecropper, and his wife, Lula. Moving with his family from county to county along Texas' border with the Indian Territory in the future state of Oklahoma, he lived a hard life looking for agricultural opportunities.

In 1907, at the age of 17, Glidewell moved from Delta County to Fort Worth and found work chopping cotton in a local processing factory. Marrying Miss Edith Rupard that year, they moved to Dallas two years later, in 1909, where Edith gave birth to their first child, Ruth. They later had four more children, James Jr., Richard, Charles, and Jane.

Interested in working with young people, Glidewell joined the newly formed Troop 12 in Oak Cliff in June 1914 as its Scoutmaster and led them to summer camp that year. After their return, he resigned the position (and left Dallas) to find work. Unsuccessful, Glidewell returned in October and re-joined the Council as Deputy Scout Commissioner before being named Scout Commissioner upon the resignation of Claude M. Richmond in February 1915.

Eventually leaving the Scouting profession eight months later in October, Glidewell took a job in the local Western Union Telegraph office and began working as a telegraph engineer. After suffering the death of his daughter Ruth, who was hit by "an automobile truck" in December 1920, he moved his family eastward to Texarkana and became a salesman for a rubber company.

Settling back in Dallas by 1930, the Glidewells made their home at 809 Cristler Avenue in the Hollywood Heights section of East Dallas near Samuel Park. He re-established himself at Western Union, becoming a supervisor.

James Arthur Glidewell died on December 11, 1964, from heart disease and is buried at the Grove Hill Memorial Park at 4118 Samuel Boulevard.[A]

Immediately, Glidewell appointed Dr. George W. Keeley, president of the newly formed Texas Scoutmasters' Association based in Dallas, a society consisting of Scoutmasters from all over the state, to the volunteer position of Deputy Scout Commissioner with duties that included "partial supervision over the general Scout movement in Dallas."

Aware of his predecessor's successes, Glidewell continued many programs such as aggressive recruiting, more Council-sponsored hikes, Council-wide service projects like taking a bird census for the Bureau of Biological Survey in the U.S. Agriculture Department, delivering food to needy families at Thanksgiving, and organizing guest lectures on a range of Scouting topics.[2]

By mid-1915, Glidewell's diligence had produced an increase in membership of 100 Scouts bringing total enrollment to around 700. But within a year, when BSA nationally was adding 15,000 new Scouts a month to its rolls, Dallas Council membership again would plunge to just a meager total of 100 Scouts

due to a lack of full-time management and effective recruitment. A tight budget didn't help either as Glidewell was only a part-time Council employee. Council President Quentin D. Corley hoped the membership woes would end once Glidewell started working full-time on September 1.

Historically, when new members did join, they did so due to the offering of a unique camping experience. One of the most frequented destinations for Scouting hikes and overnighters was Bachman's Dam on the west end of present day Bachman Lake directly north of Love Field. It was superior to the Stewart's Lake campsite in two ways. First, it was not in a flood plain and did not get washed out as the other did. Second, it was conveniently located for easy access by troops from the city via Interurban rail.

Recognizing these advantages, the executive board voted to rid itself of the Stewart's Lake property and fund construction of a bungalow 24 by 40 feet at Bachman's Dam on three acres purchased from the city at a cost of $600 (about $12,800 today). As designed by Woerner & Cole Architects in Suite 513 of the Sumpter Building at 1604 Main Street, it could house as many as 300 Scouts at a time.[3]

The first floor would serve as a boathouse with assembly and changing areas to get into swimsuits. The second floor would house the kitchen, dining room, and "quarters for Scout leaders." During inclement weather, the bungalow would serve as a bunkhouse with a screened-in area and a wood-burning stove to provide "nourishing food for the boys." Each troop would build its own canoe using materials provided by the Council, and then they would receive instruction in handling the vessels, which were considered "tricky" to operate. Council managers believed that by June 1916, the

ACROSS: A depiction of a Scout performing a service to the community by documenting eggs in a nest during a bird census.

A THANKSGIVING DAY 'GOOD TURN'

LEFT: A patrol of Scouts performing a Good Turn by delivering food to the needy during the Thanksgiving season. ABOVE: Looking northward at Bachman's Dam, a favorite camping location for early Dallas Boy Scouts. Today, the cars on Northwest Highway travel behind the treeline.

45

Bachman's Dam camp would be Dallas Scouting's new official summer campsite after the renovation.[4]

Unfortunately, due to changing Council leadership and funding challenges, the Bachman's Dam development project was tabled and not revisited until 1922.

The Council held its annual meeting October 6, 1915, elected new officers, and named a new commissioner; Glidewell had tendered his resignation because his full-time salary was inadequate to cover his living expenses. As the Council was not in a position to increase his compensation, another job took precedence and he started to travel out of town more frequently "making it impossible to retain his office [of Scout Commissioner]."

Reluctantly, Glidewell departed, leaving the position open for a new appointment. Deputy Scout Commissioner Dr. George Wesley Keeley was given the temporary assignment pending the hiring of a full-time executive by new Council President Otto Henry Lang, the Dallas Commissioner of Streets and Public Property as well as an architect and partner in the firm of Lang & Witchell in Southwestern Life Insurance Building on Main Street (and not to be confused with well-known Dallas florist, botanist, and Scouting volunteer, Otto Lang at 3515 Ross Avenue and Villars Street).

When Glidewell did return to Dallas and begin working at the

local Western Union telegraph office in town by late October 1915, he re-joined Troop 12 as its Scoutmaster. It soon merged into the newly re-started Troop 7 at the Colonial Hill School at the southeast corner of Wendelkin Street and Pennsylvania Avenue, now long since torn down and resting under Interstate Highway 45 South. On October 26, 1916, the new Troop 12 was reorganized at the Oak Cliff Christian Church at E. 10th and Crawford Streets under Scoutmasters Fred Harris and L. N. Hays.

Having engaged Keeley on a part-time basis and banked the profits from the Stewart's Lake property sale, the Council had sufficient funds to operate for the next six months without worries. But in April, President Lang set in motion an aggressive campaign to raise enough money to operate comfortably for the next two years with an "expert" full-time Scout Commissioner at the helm.[5]

LEFT: Dr. George W. Keeley at the time he served as the Dallas Council's Scout Commissioner. RIGHT: Otto H. Lang in 1916 when he was the Council's president.

At Lang's order, the 30-day fund-raising campaign fell under the day-to-day direction of H. M. Butler, the special national field director of the Boy Scouts of America in New York City, called into Dallas for this purpose. The first three weeks would be "devoted to a general public explanation of the movement, so that the citizens of Dallas will have a broad understanding of the policies of the organization." Then 20 teams of Scouts would be sent out to collect pledges over two whirlwind days—May 15 and 16. The goal was $7,000—the equivalent of $140,000 today.[6]

The *Dallas Morning News* publicized the Council's intentions and explained the need for the funding, as did local preachers during their sermons on Sunday May 14. Support for the Council was on the rise—it was becoming known for helping other local organizations such as the police department during the Elks Lodge and Knights of Pythias parades in downtown Dallas. In addition to general crowd control, two young Scouts exceeded expectations and apprehended a purse snatcher along the route.

The Council raised $5,000 on the first day prompting the executive board to declare the bar raised to $10,000. That goal was not achieved but the campaign produced $8,500 that secured the immediate financial future.

Now, Lang could bring in a "well paid" Scout Commissioner and he sent a telegram to BSA's national headquarters in New York for help in identifying the right man for the job. The nearby pro-Scouting communities of Vickery and Garland took notice. As their budgets did not allow for a full-time executive, they expressed interest in merging with the Dallas Council.[7]

Despite these moves by the Council, by late May 1916 the lack of strong executive leadership was

In 1915, the official BSA membership card was printed on three pieces of cardboard stock and held together by a metal rivet in the lower right corner. Featuring the iconic image of a Boy Scout signaling in flag semaphore by famed artist Joseph C. Leyendecker, this design was featured on the cover of the second edition of the *Handbook for Boys*.

evident as membership had collapsed to a handful of Scouts in only *five* troops. The surviving units included Keeley's own Troop 2, and ink company salesman George Cunningham's Troop 3. Troop 4 at the McKinney Avenue Baptist Church still was led by Reverend J. H. Moore, while Troop 18 was under the direction of Scoutmaster Charles T. Neu, and Troop 19 was assigned to Scoutmaster R. P. Griffin. Then, Keeley was instructed by President Lang to recruit Troop 3 up to a total of 32 members and re-form them into the new drum and bugle corps (as the first one had long since dissolved) and then rename it Troop 1.

This work marked the end of Dr. Keeley's tenure in office and any more recruitment efforts were left for the new Scout Commissioner.

In New York, National Field Work Director Samuel A. Moffitt started interviewing potential

Scout Executive Robert C. McDowell was in charge of the Dallas Council's participation in the nation's war effort. McDowell's son, Robert Emmett McDowell, grew to become a well-known author of pulp fiction magazines.

On July 29, Moffitt wrote to former Council President Corley to inform him that Robert Chester McDowell, previously the head of Scouting in Louisville, Kentucky, had been named the Dallas Council's Scout Executive—the first to bear that title as "Scout Commissioner" now denoted a district's highest-ranking *volunteer*. Having spent the previous three years building up the Kentucky Scouting program with public speaking events and grassroots efforts, McDowell was just the kind of man that Lang wanted. Building membership was to be his number-one job.[9]

Upon his arrival in mid-August, 1916, McDowell led a Council of only seven troops (though three more were being formed). Lang wanted fast results but McDowell declined to force "unnatural growth"—meaning the signing-up of Scoutmasters simply to increase membership numbers. McDowell insisted on recruiting the best Scoutmasters and training them to do effective Scouting work, which would bring in new recruits.

"I plan to give the boys everything that a boy can want that is clean and reasonable for him to have," McDowell declared. "I will also try to impress upon them that anything worth having is worth working for."

executives. After speaking with 15 candidates by early July 1916, Moffitt sent a telegram to President Lang indicating, "several good men that I would [have] gladly recommended turned me down." Moffitt noted that the minimum salary that could be offered on an annual basis was $1,800. Lang was prepared to offer $2,000.[8]

Meanwhile, Dallas Scouts were kept busy doing community service, in particular helping local public health service officials roll out an anti-malaria campaign. Scouts canvassed affected areas and destroyed mosquito-breeding habitats. Dallas Scouts also took on clean-up projects such as the removal of a "wagon load" of tin cans from an unkempt backyard in Vickery Place.

Scout Tom Jones performed 54 inspections, finding 24 "unsanitary" yards and eventually cleaning up five of them.

Scout Executive McDowell established new headquarters at 1214 Main Street at N. Field, former home to the Beeman Shoe Company. The second floor housed McDowell's office and contained a practice room for the re-organized Drum & Bugle Corps, now under the direction of Frank P. Margolin.[10] Those needing to speak to McDowell in the office could ring him up on the phone at the number, "Bell Main 2132."[11]

LEFT: Frank P. Margolin was the director of the third iteration of the Dallas Boy Scout Band & Bugle Corps when it was re-started as Troop 1 in 1916. MIDDLE: The Rosemont Christian Church in Oak Cliff sponsored Troop 9 starting in 1916. RIGHT: Twelve-year-old bugler Clardy Young of Troop 1 was the victor of the Messenger Race during the Scout Field Day, where he was the first contestant to speedily navigate his bike through the streets of downtown Dallas and deliver a missive to the Mayor.

On September 19, 1916, McDowell asked the *Dallas Morning News* to print an announcement aimed at recruiting a specific type of Scouting volunteer: business executives, especially those based in Oak Cliff.

By October 1, Oak Cliff led the Dallas Council in new troop recruitment, mainly due to its unique *adult* troop. Soon, it took the name of the Oak Cliff Scoutmasters' Club and began forming local youth units in Oak Cliff starting with Troop 1, a designation already in use by Dallas' new Drum & Bugle Corps.

Troops 1 and 2 were formed at Oak Cliff's Christ Church located at 9th Street and N. Marsalis Avenue, while Troop 3 started at the Brooklyn Avenue Methodist Church at the corner of S. Montreal and W. Brooklyn Avenues. Troop 4 was based at the Oak Cliff Methodist Church at Jefferson Boulevard and S. Marsalis Avenue under Scoutmaster D. Caldwell. Troops 5 and 11 were formed at the Tyler Street Avenue Methodist Church at the Sunset Avenue intersection, while Troops 6 and 10 began at the Central Baptist Church located at 10th Street and N. Beckley Avenue. Troops 7 and 8 were formed at the Calvary Baptist Church at S. Windomere Avenue at W. 12th Street, and Troop 9 was chartered by the Rosemont Christian Church located at 1304 S. Hampton.[12]

To create a Council event for boys to look forward to, McDowell proposed the first "Scout Field Day Program" to be held on New Year's Day 1917. Scouts would compete in events ranging from a message-carrying race to a bugling contest to log-splitting to potato-sack races.

ADULT TROOP ZERO

IN SEPTEMBER 1916, *a number of enthusiastic Oak Cliff men formed Boy Scout Troop Zero, the nation's first adult male Scouting unit to cultivate future Scoutmasters and troop leaders. They elected L. E. McGee as their Scoutmaster with Ralph Malone as his assistant. H. E. Moore was elected scribe. John W. George led the Fox Patrol with former Scout Commissioner James A. Glidewell and Curtis Hancock as members.*

Immediately, Troop Zero planned a series of outings and hikes during which they completed requirements for the Tenderfoot rank.

"The troop will also have the duties and responsibilities of a district council," Scout Executive Robert McDowell reported, "and will push for the organization of ten troops in Oak Cliff with the hope of getting them organized in time to participate in the municipal parade on the opening day of the State Fair of Texas on October 14."

He informed the Dallas Morning News *that Troop Zero was a legitimate Scouting unit because national BSA regulations had no age limit on "youth" membership.*

"Troop Number Zero conforms to the rules of the Boy Scouts of America," McDowell said, adding that he intended to launch a similar unit in nearby East Dallas. That never happened.[B]

Council President Otto H. Lang and his architecture firm was responsible for designing some of the landmark buildings in the Dallas area. They included the Sanger Brothers department store in 1910, the 16-story Southwestern Life Insurance Building in 1911, the 29-story Magnolia Oil Building in 1921, and the Highland Park High School Building in 1922.

"Chief Judge" Otto H. Lang officiated and prizes were awarded to the winner in each event based on a tally of troop and individual scores.

"Field Street between Commerce and Main Streets was the undisputed property of the Dallas Boy Scouts for two hours yesterday," reported the *Dallas Morning News*. Three thousand people looked on.[13]

But in early 1917 international events were pushing the United States into the European war that had been in progress since August 1914. Tensions between the United States and Germany had surged with the sinking of the British passenger ship *RMS Lusitania* on May 15, 1915, by a German U-boat. Of the 1,195 victims, 128 were Americans. Despite this, President Woodrow Wilson was reluctant to enter the war and embraced a policy of U.S. isolationism. But pressure on Wilson for action increased steadily—from

In 1917, after the United States had entered the war raging in Europe, President Woodrow Wilson delivered an address in Washington, DC on June 14 to the citizens of the country. Orated on Flag Day, he reminded Americans that their duty was to the defense of the country and that "woe be to the man or group of men that seek to stand in our way."

former President Theodore Roosevelt, among others—and in April 1917 Congress passed a joint resolution declaring war on Germany. The Boy Scouts of America earlier had adopted a position allowing each member to choose the position he believed in—neutrality or preparation for war.

But with the declaration of war, Chief Scout Executive James E. West decided to place the full force of his legions of Scouts behind the country's war effort. At the call of President Wilson, the Boy Scouts began an historic service project that would weave the movement into the very fabric of the nation.

One of Scout Executive McDowell's first orders to the Council was for each Scout to plant a family garden to free up foodstuffs that were needed by the military heading overseas under the "Every Scout to Feed a Soldier" campaign.

McDowell put his own spin on the project with the local slogan: "Not a slacker Scout in Dallas." A slacker was defined as any Scout "who fails to grow a garden or otherwise do his bit." He expected 100 percent participation, and peer pressure helped. At one troop's meeting shortly after the declaration, four boys lacked gardens but "pledged themselves to get in line at once after being reprimanded by the other boys."

McDowell pleaded with local men to become Scoutmasters.

"Any man who is not eligible for military service because of physical defect or dependents or . . . on account of his age . . . can do a great work by getting into the Scout movement now," he said. "We want this kind of man and we want clean men who will have a good influence on the boys under their tutor." Scout Executive McDowell was concerned because 158 new Scouts had joined up in the previous two weeks and Scoutmasters were in short supply. His revised mission was to sign up 100 new men to lead them.[14]

With a total membership of 300 boys, there were at least 300 "Feed a Soldier" gardens growing in Dallas. Those producing beans were especially valuable as legumes were a staple in the military food supply and had a long shelf life. They had their own slogan—"Bean, Beans, Beans."

Another Dallas Scouting service project was to help the Marine Corps (the nation's "first line of defense") recruit in the area. In a letter to Scout Executive McDowell, the Marines expressed their desire for the Dallas Scouts to serve as their bicycle-riding messengers "especially in the distribution of printed matter." This kind of project became a common sight in Dallas as hundreds of Scouts put up weekly posters in downtown storefronts advertising national needs. Posters promoting "Liberty Loan" campaigns to fund the war effort were especially commonplace.

Starting in June 1917 at the request of President Wilson and Treasury Secretary William G. McAdoo, Boy Scouts across the nation began selling subscriptions for Liberty Loan Bonds in local drives. Some 300,000 Scouts placed 10 million copies of an 18 x 24-inch three-color poster in storefronts asking: "Have you bought your Bond?"[15]

Secretary McAdoo named Dallas as the center of one of the 17 national zones and Treasury officials took up headquarters in Suite 506 of the Wilson Building. Upon receiving a letter from BSA Chief Scout Executive James E. West in New York City instructing the Council "to begin work immediately," McDowell called his 38 Scoutmasters

ABOVE: The Boy Scout War Service Gardening Medal was awarded nationally in 1917 and 1918. But due to the strenuousness of the requirements, only 214 were ever awarded. For example, the Scout had to start and work his own garden in addition to convincing nine others to do the same. He had to spend over 100 hours tending to it over a minimum of sixty days and submit a written plan for approval by his Scoutmaster and the United States Department of Agriculture. However, every Dallas Boy Scout attempted to earn it.

together and assigned each an area to canvas beginning June 11 under the slogan "Every Scout to Save a Soldier."

Any Scout who sold 10 subscriptions to at least 10 different people received a handsome round medal with his name engraved on the back of it or on the pin bar. Repeating the achievement in a new campaign brought an additional pin bar linked by two small chains to the bar below for uniform wear.

On the morning of June 10, 250 Scouts and 300 interested citizens gathered in Dallas' City Park

One of the food projects performed by Boy Scouts nationally was the planting of Boy Scout Farms that grew mass quantities of food like beans and corn.

Have you bought YOUR BOND ?

ADOLPH TREIDLER

Liberty L

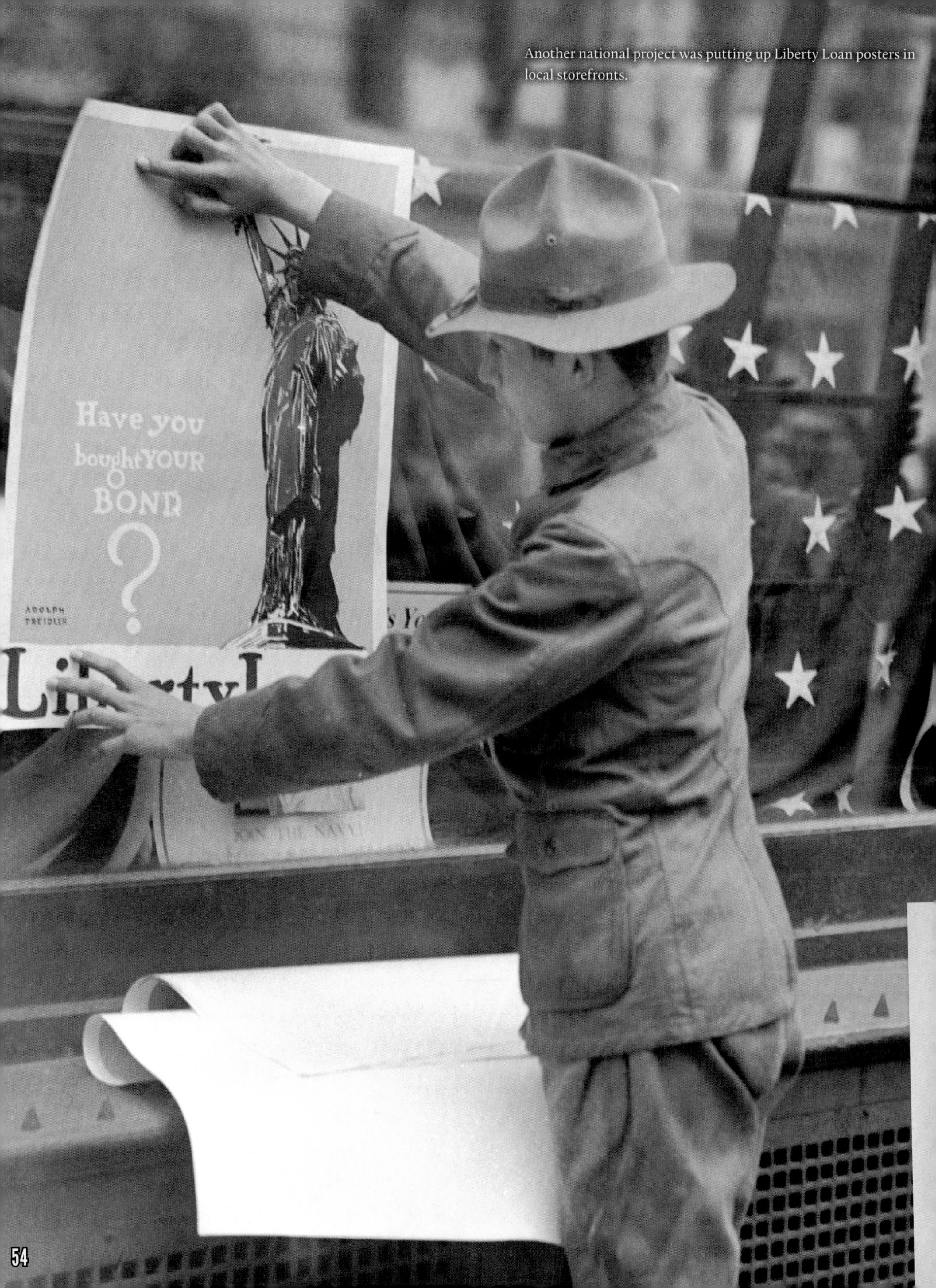

GROWTH IN THE NUMBER OF DISTRICTS

IN EARLY 1917, *the number of districts in the Dallas Council was increased from the original number of four to five due to increased membership. At the time, over 300 Scouts in about 20 troops were registered.*[C]

(now known as Old City Park south of Interstate 30 at S. Harwood Street) for motivational speeches intended to fuel their desire for national service the following day. Dallas was divided into five canvassing districts corresponding to the five existing Scouting districts of Oak Cliff, North Dallas, East Dallas, Central Dallas, and South Dallas, each under the direction of a member of the local Liberty Loan committee based at the

Dallas Federal Reserve Bank at 1105 ½ Main Street at N. Griffin.

On day one the Scouts sold $5,350 in bonds to 106 purchasers. Scout Ingram Lee, a member of Dallas' Troop 4 (as Oak Cliff's Troop 4 had folded earlier) who was the nephew of the future Dallas Council Scout Executive Walter Sanders Lee, earned the distinction of selling the city's first bond shortly after 9 o'clock a.m. Clarenton Davis of Troop 27 was the high individual seller of the day grossing 10 sales for a total of $900.[16]

Another local Scout, Jimmie Sanders, sold $1,000 worth of bonds to 10 separate people on day three, while Andrew White and Oscar Hodnett took second and third places. All three earned the right to wear the round Liberty Loan Medal.

When the drive concluded three days later on June 14, the Council had tallied $50,150 in sales averaging $275 sold per Scout seller in the city.

BELOW: In assistance of the local police force during the war, Boy Scouts were sometimes seen directing traffic in busy downtown Dallas streets. RIGHT: With the creation of the Federal Reserve system in 1913, each of the 12 member banks distributed the nation's currency.

Nationally, the Boy Scout organization logged over $15 million in sales.

Dallas' performance ranked the third best nationally behind New York City and Seattle. A very pleased Scout Executive rewarded his salesmen with a 10-day summer camp experience on Lake Worth near Fort Worth—aptly dubbed "Camp Liberty."

Upon conclusion of the camp, McDowell laid out an aggressive Council growth strategy under the slogan, "A Thousand Boy Scouts in Dallas by October 1." But he ended 400 members shy.[17]

Nationally, the Second Liberty Loan campaign began on October 25, 1917, this time pitting indiviual councils in each state against the other. The highest-selling council claimed the prestigious Treasury Secretary McAdoo Prize. By the end of day one, Dallas Scout Charles Witchell of Troop 28 (also the son of Council President Lang's architectural firm partner Frank O. Witchell) had turned in 64 bonds sold, while fellow troopmate, John McCoy, the grandson of Dallas' first lawyer, Col. John M. McCoy, sold a staggeringly large $25,000 bond (the largest single sale to date) to local businessman W. H. Wolfe.[18]

"Dallas Scouts have just as good a chance to win the prize . . . as any other city, although several [other councils] have gained a good start," McDowell declared. "The assistance of businessmen and firms buying bonds in large amounts is necessary, of course."

The Dallas Scout Executive reminded *Dallas Morning News* readers: "A Scout can always be procured at headquarters by telephone and we will appreciate the co-operation." In response, Security

FIRST LOCAL COURSE ON SCOUTMASTER TRAINING

BEGINNING IN FEBRUARY 1917, *Scout Executive Robert McDowell created a training program called "Scoutmaster's School" for leaders that taught 16 different Scout skills over eight sessions. With the object of "acquainting the Scoutmasters with the various phases of the [Scouting] work," McDowell instructed his new recruits on topics ranging from "the weekly meeting" to techniques in Scout discipline and advancing the out-of-doors program. Additional lessons on merit badge counseling and "the psychology of Scouting" rounded out the course. Graduates of four sessions earned a "Class B" certificate. Those who completed all eight received the "Class A" certificate.[D]*

The Liberty Loan medal was presented to each Boy Scout that sold a minimum number of subscriptions and minimum dollar total. A bar was presented after those requirements were met in subsequent campaigns. The maximum number of bars that a Scout could earn was four.

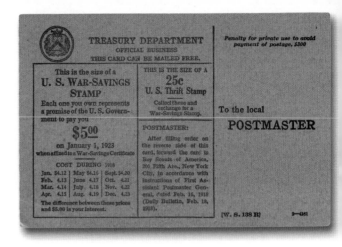

National Bank purchased $400,000 worth of bonds through Troop 4 based at the McKinney Avenue Baptist Church.

Ultimately, Louria F. Lewis of Troop 39, son of local dry goods store credit manager Louria H. Lewis, turned in the most individual sales at 101 subscriptions, while Troop 4 logged the most total sales coming in at $410,000.

At the end of the second campaign, the Dallas Council tallied sales of $1.1 million in Liberty bonds. Unfortunately for the Council, New York City Scouts had sold $32 million in bonds, St. Louis Scouts $6 million, and St. Paul, Minnesota Scouts $4 million.

When the Council gathered for its annual meeting on December 28, 1917, its members elected Eli L. Sanger president. Named vice presidents were William H. Atwell (the future U.S. District Court Chief Justice and commissioner of the Dallas Zoo), newspaperman Charles Seay, former Council President Otto

H. Lang, and *Dallas Morning News* Publisher George B. Dealey.

Post Office official Henry B. Goodnight was the new secretary, oil refiner Carl Ferris became treasurer, and Dr. George W. Keeley was elected Scout Commissioner.

Scout Executive McDowell reported an increase of membership by December 31, 1917, to 643 Scouts compared with a total of 174 at the end of 1916. Organized troops had increased to 35 from seven and the platoon of Scoutmasters and their assistants increased to 78 from 37.[19]

Fund-raising was a top priority in 1918. Starting on January 29, McDowell and his executive board launched a campaign to raise $10,000 "for the promotion of the Boy Scout movement." But the Council also sought to recruit 300 men into the new Scout Leader's Reserve Corps—a pool of trained and registered substitute Scoutmasters to assist or fill-in when needed—to help commissioned Scoutmasters lead their troops. Led by Troop 4 Scoutmaster Walter

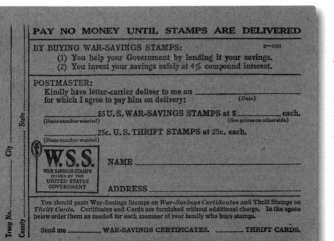

LEFT and TOP RIGHT: Locally, red postcards advertising the War Savings Stamps program were mailed to each household. Like the Liberty Loan Bond program, all monies were used to fund the American war effort. ABOVE: Participation pins were worn to promote the money raising campaigns lasting the duration of the war. TOP LEFT: The U.S. Government issued this *Manual* that described the objectives of each loan campaign.

· ELI SANGER.

THE FIRST FIRE BY FRICTION EXPERT

IN MARCH 1917, *15-year-old John Allen Boyle, a member of the troop sponsored by the Munger Place Methodist Church at Greenville Avenue and Bryan Street in old East Dallas, became the first local Scout to "make fire by rubbing two sticks together after the fashion of the Indians" on a campout.*[E]

Sanders Lee, members of the Reserve Corps had to be "men of good character aged twenty-one or over" and be able to dedicate about "three hours a week" to the program. Or as noted in the Council's new organ, *The Dallas Scout* newspaper, this level of volunteerism had "easy hours, good pay."[20]

As for the Dallas Council's funding efforts, volunteers were asked to make a total of 50 phone calls to potential donors over two days starting on February 11, 1918. At its culmination, Council President Sanger declared the results to be "over the top,"

TOP LEFT: Council President Eli L. Sanger was the son of Philip Sanger, one of the original Sanger Brothers that came to Dallas and opened the first local department store in 1872. He also was one of the first men in Dallas to own an automobile. ABOVE RIGHT: The Munger Place Methodist Church (at the intersection of N. Munger Boulevard, Bryan Street, and Greenville Avenue) is located in Old East Dallas. This area was developed for commercial homes in 1905 by cotton gin manufacturer Roy Munger. Envisioned to attract the elite of Dallas society, it was the first subdivision in the city – just a mere carriage ride from the downtown area. Homes were required to be at least two-stories tall and cost no less than $2,000 ($49,300 today) to build. ACROSS TOP RIGHT: The Coliseum at Fair Park where the first Scout Stupenda was held.

having exceeded the $10,000 goal. With a fresh $10,470 in the bank, the Council could continue operations. The *Dallas Morning News* reported that "it is hoped that the amount will be sufficiently oversubscribed to make possible the financing of the Scout farm camp" the coming summer.

Late February 1918 brought a victory banquet at the new and luxurious 22-story Hotel Adolphus constructed by Milwaukee beer baron Adolphus Busch in downtown Dallas at 1321 Commerce Street at N. Akard. Guests received a copy of the current *Boy Scout Diary* setting forth upcoming Council events. Scouts attending the event (all from Troop 4) included Ralph Brown and Jerude Buvens, who demonstrated first-aid bandaging, and Charles Henning and Ingram Lee who showed semaphore signaling. Houston Boyd proved his proficiency in Morse code. Additionally, Scout Buvens related the history of the American flag and Allan Boyle made fire with a bow and drill.

By mid-March, Walter Lee's solid leadership of the Reserve Corps resulted in his appointment as the Dallas Council's Assistant Scout Executive. One of his first assignments was to help organize the "Scout Stupenda," a demonstration of Scouting skills to be presented at the Fair Park Coliseum in East Dallas. These included simple first-aid techniques, calisthenics to keep in shape, tent pitching, bridge building, fire by friction, and wall scaling.

Troop 4 of Dallas, now led by Scoutmaster Harrison Holman McGill after the departure of Lee, stole the show by building a 14-foot tower out of lashed-together six-foot staves to be used for flag signaling—this in the remarkable space of 12 minutes.[21]

Unfortunately, Scout Executive McDowell did not witness this landmark Scouting event as he had resigned with immediate effect on April 2 and accepted the leadership of the Scouting council back in Lexington, Kentucky.

McDowell left the Dallas Council with close to 800 Scouts and more than $10,000 in the bank. With gratuity, the Council presented him with a parting gift of "a handsome gold-headed umbrella with his name inscribed thereon."

BUT IN THE MEANTIME, MANAGEMENT LOST NO TIME NAMING HIS REPLACEMENT: FORMER DALLAS SCOUTMASTER AND CURRENT ASSISTANT SCOUT EXECUTIVE WALTER LEE—THOUGH LEE WAS TO HAVE BUT A BRIEF AND TRAGIC TENURE AT THE TOP.[22]

chapter 4

EXPANDING MEMBERSHIP AFTER ADVERSITY (1918–1920)

"We are going to preach the gospel of the 'out-of-doors' for boys and train them for a citizenship that is really worthwhile."

James P. Fitch
National Field Commissioner
Southwest Division (Region 9), BSA
Dallas, Texas
November 7, 1919

THIRTY-FIVE-YEAR-OLD WALTER SANDERS LEE was an on-again, off-again citizen of Dallas. Born in Newton, Georgia, in 1882, he was the sixth child of William Bell Lee and his wife, Lavinia Butler. William Lee, a local merchant, eventually turned to farming and seized the opportunity to move his family to better soil in Sparta, Georgia. Walter, however, grew weary of the hard farming life and followed two of his brothers to Dallas, where he briefly found employment with a local life insurance company.

By 1915 Lee was a regular volunteer with the Dallas Scouts but as the United States headed toward war, he enrolled in an officers training course at Leon Springs Military Reservation near San Antonio. However, his aspirations were disappointed when his commission was denied due to a minor physical defect. Determined unfit for military service, Lee returned to Dallas and rejoined Scouting in February 1917, serving as the Scoutmaster of Troop 4 at the McKinney Avenue Baptist Church in the Oak Lawn area of Dallas and eventually taking the leadership of the Council as its fifth Scout Executive overall.[1]

For several years, the Dallas Morning News *ran a monthly column dedicated to promoting the Scouting movement called, "Lessons for Boy Scouts." It featured instruction on woodmanship, first aid, and other Scouting skills.*

Upon assumption of his duties, one of Lee's first assignments was to address the upcoming Council-wide event—the "Scout Stupenda." Receiving organizational help from volunteer Walter Scott Barcus, Lee successfully managed the program, a precursor to the Scout Circuses and Scout Shows to come. In between performances, Scout Executive Lee explained to the crowd about the "scope and nature of the work with boys." Featuring demonstrations of Scout skills performed by individual patrols and troops, the consensus was that the Stupenda was "very entertaining."[2]

From the confines of the Council's new offices in the Busch Building at 1501 Main Street at N. Akard Street, the next pressing matter to which Lee had to turn his attention was organizing the Council's Third Liberty Loan bond campaign scheduled to begin on April 27, 1918. Within the Eleventh Federal Reserve District that included Texas and Oklahoma, the Dallas Scouts maintained their leadership role in the community with sales of $600,000 in the latest bond drive.

TOP: A Scout stands on the platform of a signaling tower, much like the ones that were built during the Scout Stupenda under time constraints. ABOVE: Pins from the Third Loan (across middle right) Fourth Loan and Victory (Fifth) Loan campaigns. NEAR RIGHT: Future Region 9 Director James P. Fitch assists a Scout tie an arm sling during a first-aid demonstration. FAR RIGHT: Scouts assisting each other to get over a wall during a demonstration of teamwork.

✦ THE ARM SLING ✦✦✦

Scout Stanley Marcus of Troop 28 headed by 20-year-old Scoutmaster Harrison Holman McGill was the top seller in Dallas in both number of customers and gross receipts—in retrospect not a great surprise as Marcus would later gain fame as the second generation manager of his family's internationally recognized retail business, Neiman-Marcus.

The next milestone was the Council's annual summer camp, set for late June near Big Sandy in East Texas. It sat two miles north of the town of Winona in Smith County on 1,000 acres of orchard owned by farmer Elmer C. Butterfield. By mid-May, 156 Scouts had signed up for the trip, which would unfold "under strict supervision of the Scoutmasters." For good reason, this outing would be called "Camp Service."

LEFT: Built in 1913 by beer baron Adolphus Busch to accompany his nearby Hotel Adolphus, the 17-story Busch (Kirby) Building housed the Dallas Council's headquarters during the year 1918. It was the first Dallas high-rise to be converted from office space to apartments in the 1980s. TOP RIGHT: Boy Scout super salesman Stanley Marcus at age 18. He would later manage the operations of his family's upscale specialty retail department store business, Neiman-Marcus Company (above), which was founded in 1907 by his father, aunt, and uncle.

Part of the deal between the Council and Farmer Butterfield was that the Scouts would carry out a service project—specifically, picking peaches—railroad carloads of peaches. Due to a labor shortage in the area, Butterfield faced the real possibility of watching his fruit rot on their branches without their help. By the end of their first week in camp on June 30, the Dallas Scouts, who were paid at a rate of 20¢ an hour, had picked 10 train carloads of peaches. Those wages covered the agreed upon fee for use of the land for the camp.

Realizing that more unpicked peaches awaited, Scout Executive Lee assured the farmer that camp would not break until the orchard had been cleared, which would take another week.[3]

As for the rest of camp life, it was reported, "the food served is well cooked and wholesome and the appetite of the boys usually [is] keen whenever the mess call is blown." Although some boys came down with an unidentified illness, the mess hall was "the most popular feature of the camp." By July 10, working seven hour days (and many volunteering to work overtime), the Scouts had picked clean 600 of the 1,000 acres, filling up to two train carloads a day.

By the time they were done, the Scouts had picked a total of *50* railroad carloads of peaches, or *two full trainloads*. The fruit's importance could not be

underestimated, as once the peaches were processed for any food value, their pits were crushed to make filters for the gas masks of the American soldiers fighting overseas.[4]

When the Scouts got home in mid-July, they went back to work selling War Service Stamps in their

TOP RIGHT : During the summer camp experience known as "Camp Service," injured Scouts had access to a fully stocked first-aid kit. RIGHT: This is the only group photograph known to exist from Camp Service. Featuring Troop 4 under the direction of Scoutmaster and future Council Scout Executive Harrison Holman McGill, it was published in the *Dallas Morning News*.

"spare time." As an added incentive, they could earn a distinction known as the Ace Medal, presented to any Scout who booked sales to 25 different people with total monies collected amounting to a minimum of $250.

By July 31, 1918, only Scoutmaster R. H. Lively of Oak Cliff's Troop 9, and Scouts Frank Ford of Troop 28 and Giroud Bivens of Troop 4 had earned Ace Medals.

President Wilson authorized the Fourth Liberty Loan campaign for September. As in the three preceding campaigns, the president asked the Scouts to mobilize, but this time as messengers, orderlies, and helpers for local Liberty Loan committees. Each troop was assigned a specific day of service with each Scout receiving a card to log their service hours. Based upon hours worked, Scouts could earn the standard, round Liberty Loan campaign medal or an additional service bar.

BOTTOM LEFT: The recipient of this Ace Award medal for sales of War Savings Stamps earned the bronze and silver palms. The bronze palm represented an extra $100 in sales, while the silver palm denoted an additional $1,000 in subscriptions. BOTTOM RIGHT: The descriptive *Manual* for the Fourth Liberty Loan campaign.

CLAUDE A. MAST
DALLAS' TENTH EAGLE SCOUT

IN DECEMBER 1918, *the "Eagle drought" ended—the Dallas Council presented its first Eagle Scout rank in four years to 14-year-old Claude Albert Mast, the son of Frank A. Mast and wife, Elfrieda, after he earned merit badge number 21.*

Born on September 11, 1904, in Davenport, Iowa, Claude's family moved to Texas when his father was promoted to assistant manager at the local Pittsburgh Plate Glass Company in Dallas. Shortly after arriving, Claude joined Troop 28 under the direction of Scoutmaster Harrison H. McGill, formerly of Dallas' Troop 4 in Oak Lawn.

Having earned merit badges in Pioneering, Handicraft, Craftsmanship in Wood, Firemanship, Lifesaving, Safety First, Carpentry, First Aid to Animals, and Swimming, First Class Scout Mast reported to "Camp Service" in August 1918 to earn the remaining merit badges required for Eagle Scout. Two weeks later at the Council Court of Honor ceremony, he was awarded seven more—Cycling, Camping, Civics, Pathfinding, Cooking, Signaling, and Machinery.

By November, Claude had earned Athletics, Astronomy, Electricity, Ornithology, Photography, Printing, and Surveying. First Aid and Automobiling badges would be awarded on December 23, 1918, at the Court of Honor, along with the rank of Eagle Scout— Dallas' tenth to date.

Claude went on to graduate from Crozier Technical High School in May 1921 and remained in Dallas after graduation. Eventually marrying his wife, Nelwyn, around 1931, they moved south to Brenham, Texas, where he took work as a salesman at the Brenham Cotton Mill.

After a career in textiles, the couple retired back to Dallas where Claude Albert Mast died on May 10, 1988, at age 83.[A]

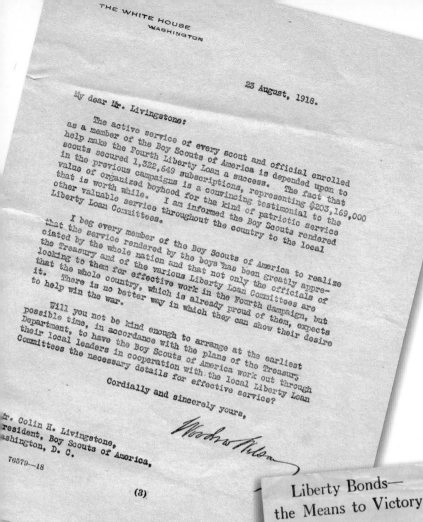

THE WHITE HOUSE
WASHINGTON

23 August, 1918.

My dear Mr. Livingstone:

The active service of every scout and official enrolled as a member of the Boy Scouts of America is depended upon to help make the Fourth Liberty Loan a success. The fact that scouts secured 1,322,649 subscriptions, representing $203,169,000 in the previous campaigns is a convincing testimonial to the value of organized boyhood for the kind of patriotic service that is worth while. I am informed the Boy Scouts rendered other valuable service throughout the country to the local Liberty Loan Committees.

I beg every member of the Boy Scouts of America to realize that the service rendered by the boys has been greatly appreciated by the whole nation and that not only the officials of the Treasury and of the various Liberty Loan Committees are looking to them for effective work in the Fourth Campaign, but that the whole country, which is already proud of them, expects it. There is no better way in which they can show their desire to help win the war.

Will you not be kind enough to arrange at the earliest possible time, in accordance with the plans of the Treasury Department, to have the Boy Scouts of America work out through their local leaders in cooperation with the local Liberty Loan Committees the necessary details for effective service?

Cordially and sincerely yours,

Woodrow Wilson

Mr. Colin H. Livingstone,
President, Boy Scouts of America,
Washington, D. C.

76579—18

(3)

Liberty Bonds— the Means to Victory

BUYING Liberty Bonds is patriotism, the strongest support of our fighting men, *your* direct help to winning the war—but buying them is also business—for they mean the return of your original investment with interest. They mean present security for the Nation, but they mean as well future security for the purchaser and his family.

> "SCOUTING HAS THE ABILITY TO CHANGE THE LIVES OF YOUNG MEN AND WOMEN. IT CAN GIVE THEM CONFIDENCE, TEACH THEM LIFELONG SKILLS, AND DEVELOP LEADERSHIP TRAITS THEY MAY HAVE NEVER KNOWN TO EXIST."
>
> –CURTIS C. FARMER
> VICE CHAIRMAN, COMERICA BANK

Dallas School Superintendent Justin Ford Kimball authorized Scouts to take one day off from school during campaign week to perform their national service.

Upon completion of the Fourth campaign, Scout Executive Lee reported that the Council had a membership of 500 Scouts. He expressed his belief that exposure to the community through service activities would eventually bolster the Council's membership to between 1,500 and 3,000 Scouts.[5]

But Lee was not to see those objectives reached as the end of the war in Europe also brought a worldwide epidemic of a virulent strain of Spanish Influenza that claimed millions of lives. In late November, the Scout Executive came down with what soon revealed itself to be the deadly Spanish flu. Attended by his devoted brother, J. E. Lee, and former Scout Executive Dr. George W. Keeley, Lee succumbed on December 7, 1918, due to complications from pneumonia.

BOY SCOUT EXECUTIVE
WHO DIED YESTERDAY.

WALTER S. LEE.

Dallas Council Scouts were prominent at Walter Lee's funeral services. All available members marched in his funeral procession from Loudermilks Chapel at the corner of Harwood and Main Streets down McKinney Avenue to Routh Street and to the McKinney Avenue Baptist Church,[6] the home of his beloved Troop 4 where he had performed his Scoutmaster duties years earlier. After services, the Scouts escorted Lee's body to its final resting place at the Oakland Cemetery, now on Malcolm X Boulevard south of Fair Park. His pallbearers were made up of several Council Scoutmasters, among them his eventual full-time successor, Walter Barcus.[7]

But until that decision was made by the council's executive board, the interim post of Scout Executive was filled by the 21-year-old Troop 28 Scoutmaster Harrison H. McGill, a reporter with the *Dallas Evening Journal* newspaper and president of the Dallas Junior Chamber of Commerce (Jaycees). McGill was the Scout Executive for 32 days—holding it from December 7, 1918, through January 7, 1919.

Under Lee, Council membership had rebounded to over 600 very active Scouts, who participated in

ACROSS TOP: This letter from President Woodrow Wilson was sent to national BSA President Colin R. Livingstone congratulating the Boy Scout organization on the thousands of service hours performed during the Fourth Liberty Loan campaign. ACROSS BOTTOM: A flyer promoting the purchase of Liberty bonds. ABOVE: Although Walter S. Lee was the first Dallas Scout Executive to die while in office, his legacy lived on for decades. His grandnephew, Ingram Lee Jr., earned the Eagle Scout rank from University Park's Troop 70 in 1940 (the unit's 8th overall), while great-grandnephew, Ingram Lee III, earned his Eagle badge with Troop 70 in 1972. RIGHT: Built at the corner of Routh Street in 1906, the McKinney Avenue Baptist Church was the location of Lee's funeral services. Years later, it would become the Hard Rock Café and be demolished on January 20, 2008.

BORN ON AUGUST 5, 1897, *in Corsicana, Texas, as the oldest child of Dallas Railway postal clerk Harrison Hugh McGill and his wife, the former Mary Ruth Holman of Mexia, Texas, young Harrison and his sister, Maelan, grew-up in several parts of Dallas. Their first local home was of modest size in the downtown area on Harwood Street. Their second, at 3712 Euclid Avenue in Highland Park, was greatly enlarged. Harrison graduated Highland Park Academy in June 1915 with a keen interest in journalism.*

With the passing of his mother just after Christmas 1916, he took work at the Dallas Evening Journal *newspaper as a "cub" reporter, where his appreciation for the ideals of Scouting took hold as he covered those stories. Gradually becoming move involved with the movement, McGill served as an Assistant Scoutmaster (eventually Scoutmaster) of Troop 4 at the McKinney Avenue Baptist Church with future Scout Executive Walter Sanders Lee. This led to his staffing of the "Camp Liberty" summer encampment on Lake Worth in 1917 as its director of play.*

Soon he was the Scoutmaster of Troop 28, where he mentored Claude Mast to the rank of Eagle Scout.

In September 1917, McGill was elected to the Wimachtendienk honor camper society (today's Order of the Arrow) and onto the Council's executive board that December. Following the death of his grandmother at his home in April 1918, he was accepted into the U.S. Army's tank corps. Deciding not to enter the military, he helped found the Dallas Junior Chamber of Commerce (Jaycees) on November 22, 1918, and was elected their first president at age 21. With the unexpected death of Walter Lee in December 1918, McGill accepted the office of Interim Scout Executive, thus becoming the Council's sixth chief manager.

By 1920, McGill was on a different path in life and took work as a salesman for the Texas Homebuilder's Company, which led to the formation of the McKnight and McGill Company with fellow Jaycee, Rufus N. McKnight. Serving as real estate agents that offered both insurance and investment advice, they officed out of Suite 327 at the Western Indemnity Building at 1000 Main Street.

Now living at 4802 Gaston Avenue, McGill left the partnership and began working as an editor with the Associated Press (AP) wire news service in 1922. Satisfied with his new-found job security, he married Miss Mary Kate Watkins of Tehucana, Texas, on June 18, 1924, in New York City, as she had moved there three years earlier after working as a schoolteacher at the Forest Avenue High School in Dallas, now the James Madison High School. They never had children.

The couple moved to Oklahoma City, Oklahoma, for two year stint as McGill took the night editor's post in the local AP office. By 1926, the McGill's were living in Kansas City, Missouri with Harrison continuing his career in journalism.

On April 28, 1942, Mary died due to the ravages of cervical cancer. Some years later, fifty-three-year-old Harrison McGill married 32-year-old Dorothy R. Robinett in Kansas City on August 5, 1950. She passed away a short time later.

Afterward, Harrison Holman McGill moved back to his home state and died in Houston on March 20, 1961, having retired from the AP.[B]

local and national service projects. He left a memorable legacy of achievement.

On January 8, 1919, the Council met in the seventh floor café of the Sanger Brothers department store at the northwest corner of Main and N. Lamar Steets, now the El Centro Community College, and chose Walter Scott Barcus as the new Scout Executive. He would start the following week on January 15.[8]

Scout Executive Barcus had two main objectives that moved toward the same goal as he took hold of Scouting in Dallas. The first was to recruit more men into the leadership ranks—with the goal by mid-June being 1,500 new "associate members" of the Council as either donors or Scoutmasters. The second was to plan a memorable summer camp both to retain current members and attract new recruits.

But as the summer days rolled into July, the desired number of associate members had not been realized, prompting Council President Eli L. Sanger to send a letter to the 80 chief executives of the largest firms in Dallas asking them to do two things: donate $1 a year to the National Council in New York as a sign of good faith to the movement at large, then "secure" those individuals as local Scouting supporters by asking each company head to canvass his own employees for new donors. Once again, the Dallas citizenry came to the full aid of Scouting when asked.[9]

Barcus then turned his attention to the upcoming Council summer camp, which focused on advancing the boys in rank and honing their Scouting skills. "Camp Advancement" would be the first Dallas summer camp to teach all *60* merit badges offered by the Boy Scouts of America.

WALTER SCOTT BARCUS
DALLAS COUNCIL'S SEVENTH CHIEF EXECUTIVE

BORN ON NOVEMBER 12, *1886, in Walker County, Texas, as the third child of local farmer William Franklin Barcus and his wife, Katie, Walter spent much of his early years either in the classroom or in the fields.*

By 1900, the family had moved to Eagle Ford just west of the town of Dallas, and eventually southeast to Athens in nearby Henderson County by 1910. Soon, Barcus moved to Amarillo, Texas, and took a degree at the Hereford Christian College. Returning to Athens, he married Miss Naomi Armstrong on April 2, 1911, and their daughter, Naomi, was born the following year.

Wishing for a career change, Barcus moved his growing family northwest to Dallas where he took a job as a clerk in the U.S. Post Office. Making their home at 1331 S. Henderson Avenue, (now an industrial building parking lot south of Interstate Highway 30 in East Dallas) Barcus joined the Masonic Lodge and obtained the degree of Master Mason. It was during the May 1913 Shriners Imperial Conclave and parade through downtown

Dallas that he had his first exposure to Scouting.

A short time later, he left for a stint to study at the University of Illinois courtesy of the Masonic Lodge. However, Barcus soon returned to town and to his postal duties. By 1918, he was a dedicated Scouting Council volunteer now under the direction of Scout Executive Walter S. Lee, and took over for him on January 8, 1919, after Lee's untimely death.

Offered the job of Scout Executive for the Tyler (Texas) Council in September 1921, Barcus left for his new assignment. In February 1924, Barcus moved again and became the Scout Executive of the small West Texas town of Colorado City near Abilene.

By 1929, Walter and Naomi had moved to Austin to be closer to their daughter attending the University of Texas nursing school, when they divorced. A short time later in 1931, he married his second wife, 31-year-old Miss Eva Dee Mitchell.

The couple moved to Midland where he worked as a civil service training coordinator during World War II. Eventually, they settled

in San Antonio where Walter took ill and died on November 12, 1970, from a blockage of the main artery to his lung, known as a pulmonary embolus. Both he and Eva are buried in the San Geronimo Cemetery in Seguin, Texas.[C]

The camp was to take place in Johnson County on the 1,045-acre ranch that once had been owned by a nephew of the first president of Texas, General Sam Houston. It was ripe with stories of buried gold treasures deposited there by Spanish explorers centuries before. But with only a week to go until departure, the owner refused the Council access, so the location was changed to the friendly shores of Lake Worth near Fort Worth, where it had been held two years prior. The usual summer activities were held on the lake like swimming and boating, along with lots of "practical instruction in Scoutcraft." Lasting a full two weeks, camp festivities included a Boy Scout track meet held on July 4 "in the blazing hot July weather."[10]

BELOW: Scouts participated in a variety of activities when on campouts ranging from basic camp maintenance and trash cleaning (far below right) to games involving skills like signaling from one team to another at a distance (near below) using the flag semaphore alphabet (below left).

Camp Advancement closed on July 14 with 75 Scouts riding the Interurban rail line back to downtown Dallas from Fort Worth. Council reports reveal that "450 individual tests were passed, [with] 20 Second and 20 First Class badges awarded, and 104 merit badges granted." The litany of skills taught and passed included, "first aid, signaling, tracking, use of knife and hatchet, fire building, cooking, boxing the compass, swimming, hiking, map drawing and reading, judging distance, size and number, observation of trees, birds and animals, and astronomy." Some merit badges earned were Athletics, Bee Keeping, Civics, Camping, Firemanship, First Aid, First Aid to Animals, Lifesaving, Masonry, Pathfinding, Personal Health,

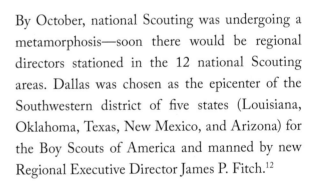

Pioneering, Public Health, Safety First, Signaling, and Swimming.

But in spite of these exciting events, the "most enjoyable feature of camp was the twice daily swim in the municipal bathing beach," which was especially helpful to the many boys who did not know how to swim at the beginning of the summer. By the end of the encampment, only a few Scouts had failed to pass the swim test.[11]

By October, national Scouting was undergoing a metamorphosis—soon there would be regional directors stationed in the 12 national Scouting areas. Dallas was chosen as the epicenter of the Southwestern district of five states (Louisiana, Oklahoma, Texas, New Mexico, and Arizona) for the Boy Scouts of America and manned by new Regional Executive Director James P. Fitch.[12]

Fitch had been a longtime Scouter having begun his professional Scouting career in 1915 as a Chicago council camp director.

Moving up through the administrative ranks, he was asked by Chief Scout Executive James E. West to expand the movement within the Southwestern

In 1923, James P. Fitch (left), the director of BSA's Region 9 —symbolized by the American bison (middle)— moved area operations into the newly constructed Magnolia Oil Building (top right) on Commerce Street next to the Hotel Adolphus.

Official Organ of The Dallas Council B. S. A.

DALLAS, TEXAS, APRIL, 1919.

VOL. 1.

NO. 8

SOME CAMP DOPE.

We are not prepared to give the location of the Summer Camp, but we can do the next best thing. We can tell you when it will be and how much it will cost.

The camp will not be earlier than June 15 and will cost each Scout attending $10, which must be deposited with the Scout Executive before June 1, 1919.

We will not do any manual labor, such as peach-picking, etc., and neither will we loaf the whole two weeks of the camp. It will be a camp of instruction and progress. Several of the older Scouts as well as the Scoutmasters will act as instructors and we expect to have all the tenderfoot Scouts to come back second class, the second class to come back first class, the first class —well, Life, Star or Eagle. Remember the Ten Iron Men.

SUMMER CAMP NEWS!!!

SPECIAL—EXTRA

Cook Engaged.

It is with great pleasure that we announce that we have engaged a cook, a good one, for the Summer Camp, and he says he knows how to cook "turtle soup." We know he is all right, but we have a substitute on tap, and guarantee to fire him the first time we are handed a bum feed.
—D.S.C.

Thass all for this time.

MISSING !!!

We are in receipt of information from the Scout Executive of Atlanta, Georgia, that Scout Hubert F. Lee, of Troop 31, of that city, has run away to "see the west," and it is thought that he is now in either Dallas or Fort Worth. Hubert is eighteen years of age, and five feet, five inches tall. When he left Atlanta he wore a Scout hat, army breeches, spiral leggins, dark blue coat with a light blue check; not certain about what kind of shirt he wore.

If, by any chance Hubert reads this article, he will kindly telegraph his father his whereabouts. If he should desire transportation home his father will be glad to send it.

Any Scout who knows anything of Hubert will confer a favor upon his father and this office by notifying Mr. Barcus immediately.

BIG HIKE.

Last Saturday and Sunday representatives from nearly all the troops in Dallas took part in the biggest overnight hike that we have ever had.

Assistant Scoutmasters Jack Berry and Clayton Kerr left for the camp Friday night and found it all right. Then Saturday morning Assistant Scoutmaster Ingram Lee brought out some fifty-six fellows and came into camp about noon. At 3 o'clock inspection was held and Troop 6 received the distinction of having the best troop camp in the place. The individual prize went to Davis and Whitley of Troop 28, who built a lean-to which was very creditable. The patrol distinction went to Troop 1, Vickery, who were housed in small dog tents and had a neat and water-proof camp. After the inspection, which was conducted by Assistant Scoutmasters and Eagle Scout Mast, swimming call was sounded and we all enjoyed a swim for about twenty minutes. The water was fine, though rather cold, but the pool was the best that can be had. Ask anyone that was there and he will tell you. At dark after supper we had a treasure hunt on the hill. A can of beans was offered for first prize, but the winner never claimed the prize; we still have it at headquarters. Then after the hunt the Scout Executive in company with Mr. Hord and Scoutmasters Taylor and McConn came and camped with us. They inspected the camp and found it in good condition. The next morning after breakfast some of the boys started for Blue Cut and were followed all day by bunches. Mr. Taylor was the last to leave camp. Some of the fellows took another good swim before they left. Troop 21 led in number with 12 present, 14 second with 11 members, and Troop 10 with 10 members.

We hope everyone had a good time day again we will take another hike.

A new map with definite direction reach the camp site will be placed in ters within a few days and anyone who been out there can get all information from Berry or C. P. Perr.

One scout executive, one deputy commissioner, two scoutmasters, three assistant scoutmasters, one eagle scout and sixty-seven scouts attended. How' that?

P. S.—We didn't find any wildcats, but we did find a perfectly good gray wolf. The fact that he was dead didn't hurt, for it made him STRONGER than ever—we know.

states. Arriving in town from a Scouting recruitment trip to Galveston, Fitch believed Dallas to be the best place to headquarter his Regional operations.

For several years, he worked out of the Dallas Council's offices at 108 ½ Field Street as well as from Suite 423 in the Dallas County State Bank Building at 1614 Main Street (now part of the Neiman-Marcus retail store building). In 1923, he moved Region 9 operations into Suite 603 in the 29-story Magnolia Oil Building at 1401 Commerce Street at S. Akard Street. The building, designed by former Council President Otto H. Lang to be the tallest structure west of the Mississippi River, was owned by local drugstore magnate Z. E. Marvin.

"This is really the beginning of the movement to develop what I believe to be one of the most promising fields in the country," Fitch declared, "one that will give us as large an organization as any of the Northern and Eastern cities have."[13]

As the Dallas Council, once again, looked toward new funding, they were chosen to be given capital by the Welfare Council, a precursor to the present day United Way, which donated money to local community

ACROSS: One of the few copies known to exist of the Dallas Council's first newsletters, *The Dallas Scout.* As Circle Ten Council developed, the newsletter became known as the *Circle Ten Scouter,* the *Circler,* and finally the *Full Circle.* Today, email is the method of choice for disseminating Council and district information. RIGHT: For many years, E.M. Kahn & Co. was the only official outfitting franchise for BSA uniforms in Dallas. Eventually, Dad and Lads would assume that mantle along with the J.C. Penney Co., the Dallas Scoutfitter, and finally, BSA's National Scout Shops.

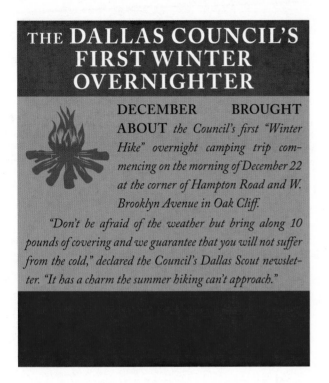

organizations that promoted civic service among the poverty stricken. In exchange, the Scouts would hang posters and hand out leaflets promoting whatever cause the Welfare Council needed to advertise at the time.

As declared by Welfare Council Chairman L. H. Lewis, membership dues in the Boy Scouts cost virtually nothing—"about 2¢ a month"—and the Scouts developed among their members "the habit of clean living, clean thinking, and unselfishness." But by the end of 1920, the Dallas Council had withdrawn from the Welfare Council as the latter had changed their funding requirements.[14]

But even without their financial aid, the Dallas Council still engaged their Scouts in a variety of community-driven service projects performed at their own expense that endeared themselves to the city and its citizenry. One was giving assistance during the fireworks or *pyrotechnic* display at the

annual State Fair. Another was filing a report with the city that included hand-drawn maps indicating the "exact locations" of dead trees that needed to be cut down. A third was participating in a "Salvage Clean-Up Conservation Week" event that collected and removed backyard junk from one's own property. A fourth was standing at the doors of the larger local churches and distributing pamphlets promoting the "proposition to build homes for delinquent children in Dallas," as well as reminding people to vote in the election on the following Tuesday.[15]

As the year 1919 closed, the Dallas Council had a total of 658 Scouts in 26 troops that neared "the largest number ever enrolled under the Dallas Boy Scout Council." Financially, the executive board spent $3,600 of the annual budget ($45,000 today) to promote and support the local program.[16]

On January 1, 1920, the fifth president of the Dallas Council took over for the outgoing Eli Sanger. He was a man who had fought in two wars that included the Spanish American War of 1898 as a major in the 3rd Cavalry Regiment that assaulted San Juan Hill with the 1st Volunteer Cavalry under Colonel Theodore Roosevelt. (Of course, Roosevelt would later go on to become the president of the United States as well as the first and only Chief Scout Citizen of the Boy Scouts of America.)

Council President Major Leigh Hill French was the father of three sons and touted as "knowing what boys wanted" in terms of out-of-doors activity. Having only arrived in Dallas the prior year, Major French already was well known on the local social scene as an executive of the General Petroleum Company of California—eventually to become Mobil Oil in 1959. Unfortunately, his tenure as Council president would be short lived as he resigned from the position by August 16, 1920, and headed for California and new work responsibilities. First vice president Charles L. Sanger, the first cousin to former Dallas Council President Eli Sanger, took over.[17]

But in the meantime, the national Scouting movement had turned 10 years old in February 1920 and to celebrate, the national office planned a "Good Turn Week" observance where local councils preformed acts of service within their communities.

In Dallas, Lawrence Kahn, the owner of BSA's current local official uniformer, E. M. Kahn & Company, offered a loving-cup to be awarded to the most efficient troop—with efficiency meaning service to the community as well as proficiency in Scout skills and drills when competing against other troops—beginning with the Good Turn Week activities. The winning troop would keep the trophy for three months, whereupon the scores would be reset and the contest would start over. Should a troop win it three consecutive times, then the trophy would become theirs permanently and a new one would be offered.

In early July 1920, the first victor was Troop 1 of Vickery, Texas, who displayed it proudly in the window of the downtown Vickery drugstore. Unfortunately, on July 15, burglars smashed the glass and stole it. However, upon realizing it was highly recognizable and unable to be sold, they dumped the cup near the White Rock area, where it was found in the weeds by two small children whose father alerted a thankful Scout headquarters.

But perhaps the most fortuitous event to happen to local scouting that year was a fateful meeting at a small lake on a 137-acre tract of land owned by a local doctor named Payton L. Campbell, when "Old Man" Wisdom trampled through Campbell's tree line to face the young hooligans who kept disturbing the peace.[18]

LITTLE DID THEY KNOW AT THE TIME THAT THIS SINGULAR VISIT WOULD HAVE HISTORIC REPERCUSSIONS FOR THE DALLAS COUNCIL.

chapter 5

THE BENEFACTOR AND CAMP WISDOM (1920–1923)

"Cement sidewalks and flower beds may appeal to girls and grown folk, but boys need the space to do something even if it does stir things around some."

JOHN SHELBY "DADDY" WISDOM
JULY 9, 1922

JOHN SHELBY WISDOM had a reputation for being a grouch. His sour temperament was well known, which allowed him to live a relatively solitary life on his farm with his wife, Hattie, of 43 years and her son, Madison Pinkney "Pink" Wright. Patrolling his acreage with a pair of dogs replete with more bark than bite, Mr. Wisdom lived with his family in a log-cabin-style homestead that he and Pink had built.

BELOW: A view looking northwest at the ever-expanding Dallas skyline in 1920. LEFT: John Shelby "Daddy" Wisdom walking with his dog, Woodrow, along the dirt road near his homestead on Cedar Ridge. The land behind him eventually would house the camp's dining hall, swimming pool, and the assistant camp ranger's quarters.

As late as 1920, John S. Wisdom was no fan of Scouting and "did not approve of the boys running wild in the woods" biographer George M. Haas wrote in *Daddy Wisdom: Boy Scout Benefactor,* "they should be doing something useful." So, when Old Man Wisdom saw the smoke rising above the tree line on a neighboring farm on Sunday, February 22, 1920, he and his dogs went to see what the delinquent boys were doing. His neighbor, Dr. Payton L. Campbell and his wife, Clara, as it turned out, were big Scouting *supporters.*

Campbell was a former staff member of the University of Dallas Medical Center and later a member of the Health Officers Association of the State of Texas specializing in smallpox eradication. Soon he would be operating a general medical practice out of Suites 415 – 416 in the Wilson Building in downtown Dallas.

But on that chilly day in February, the good doctor's property line of the so-called "Camp Campbell" was merely an obstacle to be ignored as Wisdom spied Scout Executive Walter Barcus

DADDY WISDOM

OLD MAN WISDOM *was not a native of Texas, but as the saying goes, he got here "as fast as he could." According to his elder brother Bill, John Shelby was born near Mulberry, Arkansas (or perhaps in Hardin County, Tennessee), around 1846, where his father, Alfred Henry Wisdom, was a schoolteacher and farmer. With his eight siblings, Wisdom lived a hard, rugged life helping his family bring in crops. When the Civil War broke out, Alfred and son Bill joined the Confederate Army, leaving the family to fend for itself with little money and many privations.*

During the war their small farm suffered invasion by Union forces that drove off their oxen, looted their house, and stole their supply of foodstuffs hidden in a box under the floor of a deserted barn under a pile of dung.

Union commanders offered to spare them further harm if they pledged to cease helping the Rebels, but the Wisdoms refused and their home was burned to the ground. They

lost everything including their precious family Bible. John Wisdom's mother died in 1863 and she was soon followed by his father of what was called "bendy fever," possibly meaning dysentery, on a battlefield near Paris, Texas. Bill survived the war but did not return home immediately to his siblings.

Relatives cared for the Wisdom children, and at 17, traveling in the company of two local men, John headed west through Indian Territory into what is today Oklahoma and North Texas. Finding work on a ranch as a hired hand he was asked to help drive a herd of cattle to Dallas with their cowboys. Upon reaching the Trinity River near the frontier community of Eagle Ford a few miles west of the Dallas township, the drive stopped to let the cattle graze during a surprise rain shower. Riding off to explore the area, Wisdom's horse slipped in the fresh mud and fell on him, crushing his leg. Painfully crawling the several miles back to camp by evening, he was taken to medical facilities in the nearby community of Hord's Ridge to recuperate and never left the area.

After recovering, Wisdom became acquainted with a 12-year-old boy who played the fiddle. A lover of traditional hoe down tunes performed at parties and square dances, he struck up a friendship with the mother of the musician. He married her, Hattie Roberts Wright, in 1880.

The Wisdoms moved to Aledo, just west of Fort Worth, where they bought 96 acres of wooded land. With his sun-baked and wrinkled skin, Wisdom was known as a "true woodsman," who made a living chopping and selling cords of firewood in town.

But that wasn't enough work to keep him there, and in 1892 he filed a quitclaim deed giving up title to his land and moved closer to Dallas. In 1901 he bought 158 acres of land on Cedar Ridge from Joseph Morris Kuhen Sr. and wife, Mary, for $400. Wisdom bought another 37½ acres in the same parcel for $100, putting together a 200-acre homestead. In 1923, he would deed the land to the Dallas Council, Boy Scouts of America as their first permanent Scout camp.[A]

In 1922, Troop 1 Scoutmaster Thomas A. Hord (kneeling on the far left) re-created the scene upon which Daddy Wisdom stumbled on that fateful day in February 1920 that resulted in the Council's first long-term Scout camp.

and Scoutmaster Thomas Hord of Troop 1 standing in a ring of 50 Boy Scouts with heads bowed in thoughtful reverence—a sight that changed the course of Council history.[1]

"As he came nearer, he heard murmurs, then he heard the boys . . . pray to the heavenly Father," wrote biographer Haas, "giving thanks for the woods, the streams, the birds, the boys' friends, the boys' parents, and asking His help to be better Scouts."

As a man who had only killed one bird in his life and who thought of himself as the local protector of animals, Wisdom was particularly moved. The service closed with the *Scoutmaster's Benediction:* "And now may the Heavenly Scoutmaster of all good Scouts be with each of us until we meet again, and may we follow the trail that leads to Him."

The boys scurried back to camp to prepare their noon meal and John Wisdom began to make peace with Scouting.

Walking through the tree line, he approached Barcus.

"Did those boys do that every campout?" he asked.

"Yes," Barcus replied. "The twelfth point of the Scout Law says that a Scout is reverent."

Not knowing Scouts had "a law" to live by, Wisdom pelted the executive with more questions. Barcus ran through the Scout Law's twelve points, the Scoutmaster's aims, and those of the Scout ranks.

"Well, Son, I didn't know," Wisdom drawled, his rugged features softening. "I've done you all an injustice. I thought all you boys done was to run wild out here. But now I know different. And Son, the Scouts will always be welcome to camp on my land anytime they get good and ready. Yes, siree."[2]

From that day on he was "Daddy Wisdom, Boy Scout Benefactor."

By the end of September 1920, the Dallas Council had embarked on an energetic fundraising campaign as Council leaders launched their annual funding drive on Tuesday, December 7, in hopes of raising $18,000 in a

OAK LEAF TRAINING'S EARLIEST PRECURSOR

IN DECEMBER 1920, *the opening of the new "Scout Commission School" for instruction of "troop non-commissioned officers" was announced in the* Dallas Morning News. *Under the management of the Council's director of field service, C. P. Kerr, the two-day-a-week sessions lasting a full four weeks were developed for both "employed boys" and "school boys."*

The curriculum featured detailed instruction in the duties of a patrol leader as well as other parts of Scout work that included the "ten phases of instruction" centering on the Scout Oath and Law; Scout notes, badge and slogan; the American flag; and forms of respect. Additionally, "instruction in service, games, authority, and camping [was] given."

There were two "instruction hikes" in the field for patrol leaders—one with full packs for 20 miles and one of 15 miles with camp cooking and model camp demonstrations at their ends.

Graduated students were recognized at the Councilwide Court of Honor in February 1921 held in Dallas Judge E. B. Muse's courtroom.[B]

one-day canvas. President Charles L. Sanger expressed his confidence in their ability to raise the funds.

"The Boy Scout movement takes thousands of boys in the dangerous stage and teaches them the principles of right living, justice, and equality in such a manner that they adopt them as their own standards," President Sanger declared in a statement.

By Wednesday, Sanger reported that some $12,000 had been raised and the remainder would be collected behind the scenes in "a quiet manner until the objective has been obtained."[3]

With the final third of the target amount successfully raised by that Christmas, Barcus refocused on training the boys, especially the patrol leaders. Lessons covered general Scout work and patrol leader duties, resembling in many respects the classes taught today in the Council's Oak Leaf and National Youth Leader Training courses. Barcus knew that 1,600 local boys turned Scouting age every year and the Council needed to attract them to the program for it to expand and survive. Emphasis on camping fun and community service would be their recipe for success.

Starting in 1921, Scouts took part in a large-scale tree census by counting each one on the street border between sidewalks and curbs throughout the city and its suburbs. The Dallas Forestry Department needed the data for its five-year beautification program, which would include tree plantings in

Fidelity Petroleum and was no longer available for use by the Scouts. Its loss hit the Council hard as the location had become the principal campgrounds for 75 percent of local Scouts, since it was situated just 12 miles from downtown Dallas and five miles from Oak Cliff. Realizing that borrowing other private property would leave the Scouts subject to future disappointments, Council executives started looking for land they could purchase as their next acquisition, since it had been several years since they had divested themselves of the Stewart's Lake site and done nothing with the Bachman's Dam site. Having its own camp would enhance the Council's image of being a well-funded organization.

Some argued that owning suitable land close to Dallas could boost membership to 3,000 Scouts, given the popularity of camping. One local Scoutmaster who endorsed this hypothesis was Dallas Rotarian and lumber company representative, Hubert E. Ratliff.[5]

Ratliff was a strong promoter of Scouting in the Dallas Rotary Club, a fraternal society of businessmen dedicated to philanthropy within their communities. By November, Ratliff had replaced the outgoing Scout Executive Walter Barcus, who accepted the same position in nearby Tyler, Texas.

Because the Council was not immediately in a position to purchase the Campbell property, Ratliff sought the city's permission to utilize the land surrounding Love Field, formerly a World War I air training station complete with barracks, near the area that the Council had first identified for expected use as a summer camp in 1916. The requested site was 700 feet south of the old

areas with scant cover. In May, 18 troops of Scouts denoted the location and species of each tree on 411 miles of city streets. Eventually, trees grown at Camp Wisdom would be planted around Dallas.[4]

In November 1921, the Council faced some complications with respect to its most convenient and popular local camping destination—Camp Campbell had come under the ownership of

---

ACROSS: Hubert E. Ratliff as he appeared as the Dallas Council's Scout Executive in 1921. ABOVE: Former Dallas Scout Executive Walter Scott Barcus during a visit to Camp Wisdom in 1929.

THE UNIT NUMBER of "Troop 8" long has been a successful designation within Circle Ten Council. Originating with some of the earliest units formed by Scout Commissioner Claude Richmond, the original Troop 8 was formed most likely between May 8 and May 12, 1913, just in time to serve the city during the Shriners Imperial Conclave parade. At the time, the boys were led by Scoutmasters T. R. Campbell and Robert C. Tapp. Although little is known about Campbell, Robert Tapp was well known around town.

A native of Oak Park, Illinois, Tapp came to Dallas in 1912 as the former athletic director of DePauw University in Greencastle, Indiana. Additionally, he served as that school's football coach beginning in 1910. Now in Dallas, Tapp was the football coach at Dallas Central High School on Bryan Street north of the city.

Presumably, his tenure as Scoutmaster was short lived as the troop had folded by May 1916. At the time, there were only five Dallas troops left in operation and none was designated as "8."

However, on September 19, 1916, new

Troops 8 and 4 were founded in Oak Cliff. The former being chartered by the Calvary Baptist Church at Windomere and W. 12th Streets, while the latter was at the Oak Cliff Methodist Church at Marsalis and Jefferson Streets, as their new sanctuary building had been recently completed.

Oak Cliff Methodist's Troop 4 folded by February 1917, as the number reappeared in Dallas at the McKinney Avenue Baptist Church with Walter S. Lee as its Scoutmaster. Troop 8 at Calvary Baptist suffered a similar fate and had an eventual resurrection some years later.

By May 1922, the Troop 8 number was renewed when Dr. G. M. Gibson, the pastor at the Oak Cliff Methodist Church agreed to sponsor a new Boy Scout unit. (The following

year, a Girl Scout unit also met there.)

And for the past 50+ years, Troop 8 has operated under the direction of Clarence W. "Tom" Bohanan Jr., who also was a youth in the unit in the 1930s. Without doubt, he is one of the Council's legacy Scoutmasters being Circle Ten's longest tenured troop leader to date—and this being in the 90-year-old unit that he grew up in.[c]

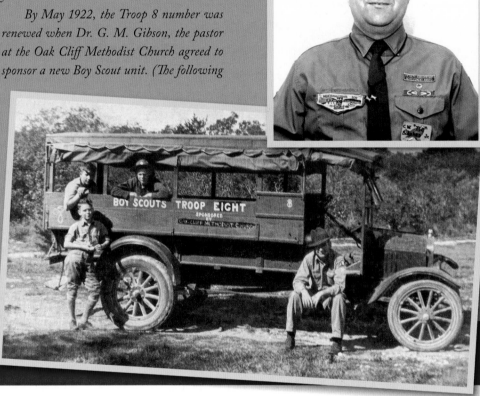

Bachman's Dam location. The dam structure itself was completed in 1902 to hold water from Bachman Creek, creating a 1 billion gallon water reservoir for the growing city's needs.[6] With the site being close to Love Field and the Interurban rail line, it was readily accessible for weekend camping.

The barracks were "equipped with electric lights, hot and cold water, and heat" making it attractive

for use as a summer camp. The Council had access to the lake at the dam and like years earlier planned to install "motor boats, small boats, and row boats for the older boys." Blueprints for a swimming pool were drafted as city ordinance prohibited swimming in the city's drinking supply.

A paid cook would be on site to help prepare meals "at a very small cost," but Scouts could cook their

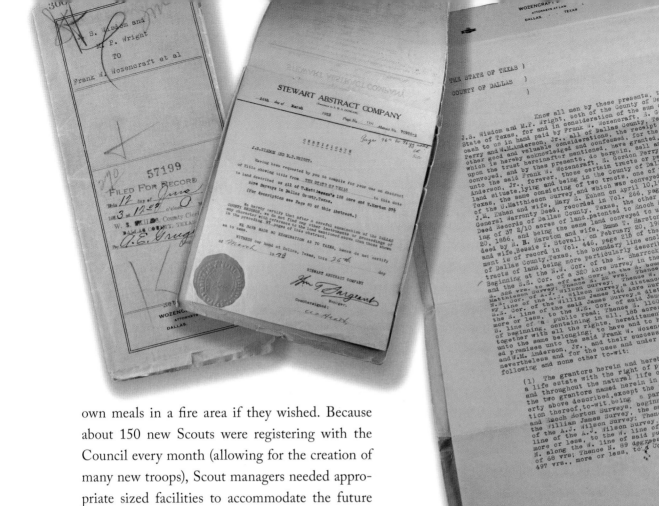

own meals in a fire area if they wished. Because about 150 new Scouts were registering with the Council every month (allowing for the creation of many new troops), Scout managers needed appropriate sized facilities to accommodate the future camping requirements of a thousand boys a month.[7]

Dallas' rapid growth caught the attention of Chief Scout Executive James E. West, who came to Texas to visit Dallas and the other Councils in the region. During his visit he inspected the Love Field site. West, always hard to satisfy, expressed his desire that local Scouting "make still greater progress in the future."

With the school year coming to a close, the Council held its annual Court of Honor in May. No Scouts earned Eagle, Life, or Star honors, but 27 boys earned the rank of Second Class, and 16 earned First Class. Numerous merit badges were awarded to a total of 69 recipients out of 700 total youth members. Future Council President Walter

ACROSS: As a youth in Troop 8 in 1934, current Scoutmaster Tom Bohanon (top) remembers riding in the official Troop truck (below) to and from Scouting trips. ABOVE: The deed (right) with cover (left) and land abstract document (middle) pertaining to Daddy Wisdom's donation of his land to the Dallas Council in 1923. RIGHT: This magnificent oil painting of Daddy Wisdom wearing the Eagle Scout medal is the only one of its kind known to exist. It resides in the Harbin Scout Museum at Camp Wisdom.

E. Kingsbury described the evening as "a wonderful showing."[8]

In August 1922, Scout Executive Ratliff announced a surprise: a "magnificent gift" from Daddy Wisdom—his entire property essentially was deeded to the Dallas Council at a symbolic sales price of $100. To express the council's profound gratitude, the executive board bestowed upon him the rank of Eagle Scout.

"The 200 acres deeded to the Scouts is of a rough and rugged nature, where the boys will get the full benefit of the real camping-out features," reported the *Dallas Morning News.* "The Scouts are at present building a dam, which will make a lake of ten to fifteen acres." Today this is Lake Wozencraft— named in honor of the

FRANK W. WOZENCRAFT.

ABOVE: Daddy Wisdom hands a young visitor a cat in 1923. RIGHT: Future Council President Frank W. Wozencraft spent 4 years at the helm of the Council that ended on December 31, 1926. BOTTOM RIGHT and ACROSS TOP LEFT: Similar to the troop cabins built at the Stewart's Lake campsite, other local troops like Troop 1 in Italy, Texas, and Troop 1 in the community of Whitesboro, Texas, constructed their own cabins at local campsites in the 1920s before coming under the management of Circle Ten Council.

lean-framed gentleman, Frank W. Wozencraft, once the 26-year-old "Boy Mayor of Dallas," who would later be tapped as the Council's president following the term of Walter E. Kingsbury.

Daddy Wisdom appreciated all that the Scouting movement could do to help local boys grow into men. And with boys spending so much time in school, he believed

TOP RIGHT: Camp Wisdom's first Museum as seen in 1923. ABOVE: One of the first land bridges constructed at Camp Wisdom using Scout labor. BELOW: The Technical Club of Dallas, a fraternal club of local engineers, helps supervise the construction of the dam at Lake Wozencraft in 1923.

THE **FIRST WINTER CAMP—DECEMBER 1922**

SCHEDULED TO BEGIN *the Friday and Saturday after Thanksgiving on December 1 and 2 of 1922, 250 members of the Dallas Boy Scouts met at Camp Wisdom under the direction of Interim Scout Executive Jack R. Berry.*

"The Scouts will leave Dallas Friday morning and will spend [all day] standing tests for merit badges in Cooking, Pioneering, and Camping," announced Berry. Before leaving for home the following day, the boys feasted at Daddy Wisdom's first annual winter camp barbeque.[D]

they needed time working in the field learning agriculture, gaining farming knowledge from local experts, and using their hands to build their character as well. In those ways, Scouts cleared the land, erected their own troop log cabins, and tended to their three-acre garden for the benefit of the Council and their own troops.

At the time of Wisdom's gift, those three acres were planted with watermelons that the Scouts could sell to "derive a revenue for their troop treasuries." In addition to the troop cabins, a single 40-foot long cabin would be erected to serve as the Council's first museum, along with a blacksmith forge and a carpenter's shop. The drilling of a 70-foot-deep well to supply water to the camp had to start immediately under the direction of local engineers in the Technical Club of Dallas.[9]

Ratliff brought 50 members of the Club out to Camp Wisdom to survey it and create a detailed topographical map that included the marking of standing trees and other vegetation. The Club, led by its president, O. H. Koch, regularly held its lunchtime meetings at the Mecca Café at 1801 Main Street. (The present Mecca Café sits two miles north of the John D. Murchison Scouting Center on Harry Hines Boulevard.)

Based on those maps, the Council laid out future campsites and buildings, walkways, the swimming beach, clubhouse, and of course Lake Wozencraft, retained by a dam 125 feet long by 30 feet high.

As the work on the dam proceeded, Technical Club members let Scouts help, which gave them valuable work experience and the opportunity to earn merit badges in Automobiling, Mining, Surveying, Botany, Forestry, Architecture, Blacksmithing, Chemistry, Cement, Electricity, Machinery, Masonry, and Plumbing.[10]

FIRST SCOUTING IN **OKLAHOMA**

BOY SCOUTING *received an early start in Oklahoma being brought to the state from England by Episcopal minister John Forbes Mitchell. Assigned to a parish in Pawhuska, Oklahoma, in 1909, the Englishman had witnessed the advent of the movement back home in England and made the founding of a United States Boy Scout troop one of his first initiatives. Possibly receiving the first English Scouting troop charter in the country, Mitchell imported the Scout handbook, Scouting for Boys, and began teaching the program to 19 enthusiastic lads.*

In February 1910, the Boy Scouts of America was incorporated in Washington, DC and by June 1, its first office was opened in New York City. From there, the teachings of Scouting bounded across the country in rapid fashion.

FIRST SCOUTING IN DURANT, OKLAHOMA

AS THE SCOUTING MOVE-MENT *made its way across Oklahoma, communities began organizing local franchises. For example, BSA's Durant Council, was first chartered in 1921. But because the financing from a single town rarely provided sufficient funds for such an enterprise, many of these "city councils" merged with other townships and formed larger area councils. As was the case for the Durant Council that lasted only two years until merging into the new Southwest Oklahoma Council in 1923. It included the area from Durant in Bryan County eastward to the Arkansas border.*

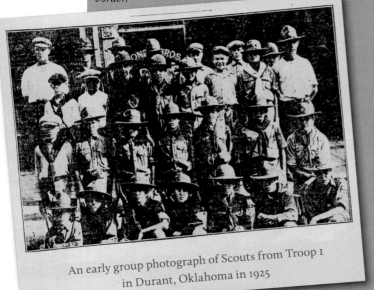

An early group photograph of Scouts from Troop 1 in Durant, Oklahoma in 1925

By 1926, the Southwest Oklahoma Council was split-up for better manageability and the Kiamichi Area Council was formed from the combination with the city of Hugo in Choctaw County, Oklahoma. This lasted until 1930 when the Lone Star Area Council (that was formed when the Kiamichi Area Council reached over its southern border and combined with Paris, Texas) and combined with Collin County.

Bryan County pulled out of Lone Star Area Council in 1940 and combined with Cooke County in Texas and the Denison Council to form the Red River Valley Council—eventually merging (temporarily) into Circle Ten in 1947.

In late 1922, the Dallas Council was on an upswing and Executive Board Member Wozencraft wanted to capitalize on this success. At the time, 34 volunteer Scoutmasters were the only adults directly involved in the program; hundreds of executives and Scouting fathers made little contribution. Recognizing that the Council needed their participation, Wozencraft created an association to financially support the program through a $10 annual membership called the "Good Old Scouts of Dallas." Recalled President Kingsbury: "What better [a] Good Turn can the businessmen of Dallas do, than to lend encouragement to such a program."

A weeklong membership drive in September coincided with the Council's annual budget recruitment campaign, somewhat diluting the impact of the Good Old Scout drive. The results fell short of what the Council had sought, netting only a meager $7,000. The disappointment was sharpened by news of the Fort Worth Council's $40,000 take.

"I hope that the business institutions and individuals of Dallas will reconsider the important work of character building done by the Scout organizations," fumed Kingsbury, "and forward their support to this campaign."[11]

But by mid-September 1922, the Good Old Scouts concept and the budget fund drive had both been abandoned, the latter re-scheduled for March 1923. Under review, the Good Old Scouts campaign failed because it had been run "by *men*," not boys, Wozencraft concluded in his report to National Headquarters for the annual recharter of the Council. Future campaigns would involve Scouts to maintain authenticity.

SCOUTING UNOFFI-CIALLY CAME to Denison with the arrival of five Boy Scouts hiking in from nearby Sherman on September 12, 1911. Under the direction of Scoutmaster H. E. Crate, the former physical director at the Sherman YMCA, the Scouts' appearance made local news reports. Only passing through Denison, they trekked northward to the Red River "to perfect their Scout practice in order to stand an examination for the [rank of] Second Class.

Speculation suggests that a local Denison troop or two probably sprang-up in the weeks following but facts reveal that the Denison Council was formed officially on February 27, 1913, after a visit from Dallas Scout Commissioner Claude Richmond. Operating as an independent council until March 10, 1924, tight financial straits led it to merge with the independent Sherman Council on March 19, 1924, forming the Grayson County Council.

In 1930, the Grayson Council added Fannin County, Texas and Bryan County, Oklahoma to its territory becoming the Texas-Oklahoma (T-O) Council. Sherman pulled-out in 1933 due to management dis-agreements and Denison abandoned it on July 28, 1936, as their community was failing to support Scouting financially.

After a three-month analysis, Denison, once again, re-formed as an independent council on October 10, 1936. By the follow-ing year, council managers courted executives from Oklahoma's Chickasaw Council based in Ardmore to the north, eventually ending with Denison merging into it by February 1938.

Denison's first adult leader training school was held on March 23, 1939, at the American Legion Hall under the direction of executive Major Wiles of Ardmore. Chickasaw Council had an annual budget of $1,800 of which $300 was to be raised from the Denison district under the direction of fundraising chairman E. N. Berglund.

In May 1940, Denison wished to break away and form their own organization—again called the Denison Council, Boy Scouts of America—and made application for a char-ter from the Region 9 office under the direction of James P. Fitch in Dallas. Believing the city to be too small to run a singular operation,

Fitch negotiated the formation of the Red River Valley Council at the Hotel Denison on September 8, 1940, under Organizing Chairman R. K. Ownby. This council would include Denison plus Cooke County, Texas, to the west and Bryan County, Oklahoma, to the north.

The first elected officers were Council President Dr. Charles N. Hess of Durant, Oklahoma, Vice President W. L. Ashburn, National Council Representative R. K. Ownby of Denison, Treasurer Henry Etter, Scout Commissioner W. T. Hall, and executive board members C. J. Corcoran, T. T. Montgomery, Bassett Watson, and Frank Dyer.

The first Red River Valley Council Scout Circus was held on November 16, 1941, at the Munson Football Stadium with 424 boys tak-ing part in the festivities. Under Chairman W. T. Adams, troops performed 14 events "depicting all phases of Boy Scout work." Of the Scouts, 179 attended from Durant. Other camping events took place at Camp Grayson near Pottsboro, Texas.

On October 17, 1947, the Red River Valley Council became part of Circle Ten under a merger agreement.[E]

The Council's $18,625 budget included a $5,000 sal-ary for the Scout Executive and $1,500 for office staff, an $875 recharter fee for National Headquarters, $1,300 for transportation and camping expenses, and $200 for "publicity and propaganda." Camp Wisdom was to receive $7,500 in improvements with $300 allotted for new equipment, and the Council autho-rized $500 to buy a truck to tote Scouts to and from the property. But as the campaign had netted just $8,792, the Council ran a deficit and had to borrow needed operating cash to be paid back following the next financial solicitation campaign.[12]

As the Dallas Council licked its wounds from the failed fund-raising campaigns of the past, it received some good news in the form of a new Eagle Scout scholarship. In September 1922, Scout Executive Ratliff announced that the board of regents at the University of Texas in Austin were so impressed with the quality of boys earning Scouting's highest rank that they planned to grant all Texas Eagle Scouts free tuition to the University valued at $50 a student.

"Recognizing the splendid training in the Boy Scouts' organization," Ratliff announced, "all

TOP LEFT: Eagle Scout William Joor Jr. of Troop 1 in Cockrell Hill at the time he accepted his scholarship to the University of Texas. TOP RIGHT: Scoutmaster Thomas A. Hord (left) and former Dallas Council Scout Executive Jack R. Berry (right) showing off a fish caught at summer camp during 1925. BOTTOM RIGHT: Dallas Council Scout Executive Clinton B. Harris upon his arrival from Oklahoma. BOTTOM LEFT: Dallas Council Scout Commissioner William E. Joor Sr.

Scouts who receive the rank of Eagle Scout will be exempted from matriculation fees."

The first Dallas Scout to be so rewarded was 18-year-old William E. Joor Jr. of Troop 1 in Cockrell Hill. Young Joor was the son of local civil engineer William E. Joor Sr., the Council's second Scout Commissioner after the retirement of Dr. George Keeley.

But the fund-raising failures had taken their toll on Ratliff, who resigned on November 1, 1927. He joined the real estate firm of Bucker & Jones specializing in Oak Cliff properties.[13]

The job of Interim Scout Executive fell to 21-year-old Jack R. Berry, a former member of Troop 1 in Vickery and current Council field executive. The plan was for Berry to hold the position for incoming Ardmore, Oklahoma, Scout Executive Clinton B. Harris, who was to take the job on a contingency basis while running the new fund raising campaign.

Howard W. Wester upon his arrival in Dallas to take over the job of Scout Executive in 1923.

Unfortunately, tragedy intervened. Within a month of his arrival in Dallas in February 1923, Harris died of pneumonia in late March.

The Scouting movement was well represented at his funeral in the Grove Hill Cemetery at 4118 Samuel Boulevard.[14] His pallbearers were 12 Scouts from Troop 1 in Dallas (the former Troop 25 and now the only Council troop with that number) under the direction of Scoutmaster Thomas Hord. A bald eagle was released into the skies by the Eagle Patrol of Ardmore, Oklahoma, to the sound of a lone Boy Scout blowing *Taps* on a bugle.[15]

Once again, the Council was without an executive. Berry was recalled on a second interim basis. His first job was to execute the Council's long-delayed fund-raising campaign.

On March 27, the four-day drive for $20,000 began, kick-started by 150 businessmen who pledged substantial sums at a previous meeting at the Oriental Hotel. Roy R. Munger, the official Cadillac distributor for Texas, put up a $1,000 donation urging 100 men of similar means to contribute respectable offerings of $100 to support the budget and Camp Wisdom improvements.

His donation was quickly followed by two $500 contributions from the Dallas Telephone Company and Smith Brothers Construction Company, specialists in large civic building projects.

"Subscriptions are coming in faster than we expected," reported Council Finance Chairman E. Gordon Perry. "Although the campaign does not officially open until March 26, the response of the business men is decidedly gratifying."

The Dallas Optimist Club contributed another $2,000 while the Council's own executive board raised $4,080.[16]

By the end of the first day, $10,091 in subscriptions was reported with three days to go. At the end of day two, $15,738 in pledges had been recorded and, as a bonus, the Utility Drafting Company promised to do all of Camp Wisdom's blueprints gratis.

After three days, $20,272 had been collected, prompting Council leaders to raise the target to $25,000.

By the end of the campaign, the Dallas Council had raised $25,913, which included $250 from Mrs. John B. Wilson, the widow of the owner of the Wilson Building that had been the location of the Council's first headquarters. Her contribution almost equaled the entire sum of rent the Council paid as a tenant in 1913 and 1914.[17]

Led by Region 9 Director James P. Fitch, the Council scoured the Southland to identify its new Scout Executive, who came in the person of Howard Winfrey Wester, a former field staff member of Region 6 and a former chief executive of the Birmingham and Mobile (Alabama) Councils.

Wester had joined the movement in 1912 in Fortuna, California, later serving as a Scoutmaster in Prescott, Arizona, before moving to Birmingham. Council President Frank Wozencraft expressed great satisfaction at the hire, promising that "things will start moving rapidly."

One of Wester's first achievements after arriving in May 1923 was to convince city officials to allow the Dallas Boy Scouts to assume the leadership of the city for 24 hours in an event called "Mayor for the Day." As expected, local officials were pleased to promote the movement in this way, allowing 23 Scouts to receive the single day commission.[18]

Commented the *Dallas Morning News*: "Two dozen clear eyed American boys, who as Boy Scouts have won the plumes of knighthood in the sternest school of modern society."[19]

As 1923 closed, the Dallas Council, now operating from its most recent headquarters at the Dallas Chamber of Commerce Building at 1101 Commerce Street at S. Griffin (the current location of the 1.5 acre Belo Garden Park) had membership of 460 Scouts as compared to 286 Scouts at the end of 1922. Now, there were 17 local troops under the direction of 18 Scoutmasters and six assistants.

The Council had granted ranks to 175 Tenderfoot Scouts, 41 Second Class Scouts, 23 First Class, 10 Life Scouts, nine Star Scouts, and one Eagle Scout. Some 55 boys had earned a total of 285 merit badges with Public Health, First Aid to Animals, Carpentry, and Personal Health being the most popular.

LOUIS MATTHEWS
A LIFESAVING HERO

IN SEPTEMBER 1922, *15-year-old Louis Frederick Matthews saved the life of another at a pier on Lake Worth near Fort Worth. Matthews, a First Class Scout in Troop 17 sponsored by the St. John's Methodist Church located at the intersection of Beacon and East Side Streets in East Dallas, dived into the water to rescue eight-year-old Lee Gordon, who was fishing at the end of the pier and was swept into the lake by high waves.*

Grasping the boy's torso, Matthews swam the lad back to the pier, where he was pulled out by a nearby fisherman. Amazingly, this was the third person that the Scout had rescued from downing within the past year—some months earlier he had saved two small girls from the 10-foot-deep pool into which they had fallen.

Receiving his Eagle Award in 1923, Matthews continued to participate in Scouting for many years. As an adult, he took up the mantle of Scoutmaster for Troop 112 at the Edgecliff Christian Church in the Trinity Heights Boy Scout District of Circle Ten, as well as taking a Council leadership role in training adult volunteers.[F]

LOUIS MATTHEWS.

ABOVE: The Dallas Council called the Dallas Chamber of Commerce its home for only a few months at the end of 1922, as they moved quickly to more permanent quarters in the Dallas Board of Education Administration Building in early 1923. At the time, the Chamber Building also served as the home of the Dallas Federal Reserve Bank. ACROSS TOP: Circle Ten Council's charter renewal form filed with BSA's National office for the year ending June 1923. ACROSS BOTTOM RIGHT: The President Harding Round-Up ribbon was presented by BSA's National office to troops that increased their membership by a minimum of 10% in 1923.

for Renewal of Charter
Local Council

irst CLASS
second

Scouts of America
ary 8, 1910. Chartered by Congress June 15, 1916

CIL, Boy Scouts of America,
Avenue, New York City, N. Y.

DO NOT WRITE HERE
Fee $ _____
Quota _____
Mag. _____
Supplies _____
Total _____

ation is hereby made for renewal of charter of the ____Dallas____ ____Texas____
jurisdiction over ____the City of Dallas____   City, Town, or County   State
of the ____First____ class, for the year 1923, in accordance with the provisions of the Constitution
policy and regulations of the Boy Scouts of America. This application for renewal of charter was officially
the local council at a regular meeting held on ____April 4th____, 192__3__, at which meeting the Council
accepted its obligation to loyally co-operate with the National Council and its representatives in promoting
of the Boy Scouts of America during the period of the charter for which application is made.

required under the Federal Charter and the By-Laws of the National Council, reports are herewith sub-
ering the activities under the direction of this Council during the year ending December 31st, 1922, including
the extent of the work, financial statement of receipts and expenditures, camping activities, Court of Honor
d detailed outline of our local organization for the coming year.

This Council has accepted its quota of $ ____800 00____ * for the year 1923, and agrees to pay it to the Treasurer
National Council as follows:

Enclosed herewith. ✓

In ____ equal payments of $ ____ each, during the months of ____

ouncil charter fee amounting to $ ____75 00____ is transmitted herewith.
This amount should not include charter fee.

In accordance with Article V, Section 3, of the Constitution and Article I, Section 1 of the By-Laws, the fol-
ng have been elected as our representatives on the National Council, the undersigned hereby certifying to such
ion ____Frank W. Wozencraft____ Address ____Magnolia Bldg.____
        (One additional representative for each 1,000 Scouts registered.)

Signed ____Sign by F. Woz____
                (President of Local Council)
Title: ____

Sign By Hord
Scout Executive (Scout Commissioner, if 2nd class council)

Date ____

— 1 —

Twenty-two Scoutmasters and assistants had gone through Council training sessions approved by the Texas Department of Education. Though there was no formal Council training for patrol leaders, Council-sponsored instruction was given to troop guides. Nine troops made overnight hikes during the year, and the Council provided a winter camping experience after Christmas at Camp Wisdom, with its land and buildings now valued at $20,000.

The Council had raised $23,000 from 1,019 contributors over the year allowing for debts of $3,500 to be carried into the next year's budget. However, Council executives expected to pay those debts off in full by expanding the camping program and increasing membership.[20]

DALLAS SCOUTING WAS ON AN UPSWING.

chapter 6

GROWING INTO CIRCLE TEN COUNCIL
(1924–1927)

*"Boys should never lose their love of the fields and the streams,
the mountains and the plains, the open places, and the forests.
That love will be a priceless possession as years lengthen out."*

CALVIN COOLIDGE
30TH PRESIDENT OF THE UNITED STATES
JULY 25, 1924

*Daddy Wisdom (in hat and suspenders) hosting one of his
annual barbeques that was held at the close of each Winter
Camp experience at Camp Wisdom between Christmas and
New Year's Day.*

THE 1924 SCOUTING YEAR OPENED a few days after Daddy Wisdom's annual barbeque for the 200 Scouts that had just finished their five-day Winter Camp outing between Christmas and New Year's Day. Held near the spot where the Old Man's log cabin had burned to the ground in 1923, Wisdom was beaming with pride as he snuck a peek back every so often at the new house that "his boys had built for him." He was filled with joy, a feeling that only intensified when his camp was teeming with activity or new buildings were going up.

The new mess hall (with non-attached kitchen area to diminish any potential fire hazard) was the largest edifice in camp. With the three completed bunkhouses of rustic design that slept 16 Scouts each, it formed a semicircle that "swung into the woods." The next big project was an administration building that would be ready by April 15.

LEFT: Two images of Daddy Wisdom's house that the Dallas Council Scouts built for him starting in 1923 after his cabin burned to the ground, leaving only the stone chimney (across bottom). A short time later, the Council purchased a fire tank with a carriage for the camp and deputized the Scouts as the Camp Wisdom Fire Brigade during each summer camp session (below). ACROSS TOP: Assistant Scoutmaster Don Birdsong and First Class Scout Ryan Johnson work on knot tying while sitting on the 3-step concrete porch of Daddy Wisdom's house that still remains on property.

All buildings would have chimneys made from native stone with "broad, old fashioned fireplaces on the interior." Running water was pumped to each structure from a 500-foot-deep well.[1] While in camp, Scouts tackled many projects that included bridge construction and other tasks overseen by Camp Director Thomas Hord, who also was a local engineer. The bridges were mostly 10 to 15 feet in length, with some strong enough to support a crossing automobile. The Council soon purchased an "auto truck [to] comfortably seat twenty-five boys to be used to carry [them] and their supplies to Camp Wisdom during the summer encampment and week-ends." Of course, the truck was operated only by "experienced" drivers. But after the boy-centric Winter Camp session ended, it would be the men who would have the fun.[2]

On Saturday, January 19, 1924, twenty-three Dallas Scoutmasters met at Camp Wisdom for an overnight training event led by Scout Executive Howard Wester. They were divided into two patrols and sent on a hike through the dense underbrush and plentiful cedar trees to "ascertain

LEFT: The cabin of Camp Wisdom's Ranger R.F. "Pop" Churchill in 1928. MIDDLE LEFT: Scouts from Troop 1 in Oak Cliff finish the masonry work of the chimney on the roof of Camp Wisdom's Administration Building in 1924. On the right hand side, Scoutmaster Thomas A. Hord, an engineer by trade, examines their work. BOTTOM: Eager Scouts await lunch in the dining hall during summer camp at Camp Wisdom. Unlike the campers of today, these boys ate from ironstone pottery dishes and handblown water glasses. This building, the last remaining structure from the 1920s, was torn down in July 2012.

which patrol was the best versed in woodcraft [with] each to bring back and identify a number of woods to be found in the forest." After judging, they were off to a different part of camp to receive instruction on proper fire-building techniques with an emphasis on the Hawaiian style of pit cooking without the use of utensils or stoves. As described:

A pit was dug, after which a fire was kindled and a number of stones were heated. The stones were placed in the bottom of the pit and covered with lettuce, cabbage leaves, and other greens. A pork roast with potatoes and other vegetables were placed on top of the greens and the pit was closed by covering it with wet sacks and dirt. The Scoutmasters then left the camp for their hike and when they returned they found a savory, thoroughly cooked meal awaiting them.[3]

TOP: The first truck purchased by the Dallas Council to transport Scouts to and from Camp Wisdom. RIGHT and BELOW: Scoutmasters receiving adult leader training at Camp Wisdom.

Finally, a patrol competition was held to determine which unit could start a fire in the shortest amount of time "using the old Indian method of fire by friction." Scoutmaster J. L. Leslie of Troop 12 at the Colonial Hill Presbyterian Church established the Camp Wisdom record of 45 seconds, which was posted on the camp bulletin board until bested. Other instruction included training in nature lore, axe handling, and knot work.

The only thing missing was a camp logo. Within a few days, the Council adopted the "Camp Wisdom Owl" as the camp's totem, an obvious choice since the owl symbolized strong mental acuity as "the bird of wisdom." As a memento, all summer campers were issued a red felt logo patch with the owl perched inside a red "C" as well as a sweater emblazoned with the totem. It was understood that the clothing remained Council property to be used by future Scouts. For repeat campers, each received a red felt bar bearing the current year to be worn below the "Owl C" patch earned in a previous year.[4]

With the end of the winter season, Scout Executive Wester began pressing for more adult involvement in the program. Answering the call was one of the largest religious congregations in Oak Cliff, the Cliff Temple Baptist Church, founded in 1898 by 26 churchgoers who had defected from the First Baptist Church of Oak Cliff. Eventually merging with the Memorial Baptist Church to become Central Baptist Church of Oak Cliff, it was led by Dr. W. A. Hewitt until 1918. Afterward, Dr. Wallace Bassett took the reins and initiated its name change to Cliff Temple Baptist Church.[5]

Under Bassett's leadership, church membership surged to over 5,000 members, among them Wester. With his call for new service to Scouting, about 500 Cliff Temple men quickly formed into Troop 48, the first all-adult unit in Oak Cliff since Troop Zero had morphed into the Oak Cliff Scoutmasters' Association (a predecessor of today's district roundtables) years earlier.

The adult unit's purpose was "to interest and train leaders of the city in Scout work." And being the single largest troop in the Council, their participation was sure to be noticed and meaningful.

Scoutmaster Preston Sneed and Assistant Scoutmaster W. C. Barnes led the planning with assistance from several patrol leaders. Prominent among these were George A. McGregor, a building and loan vice president who had endowed Baylor College; Baptist missionary Granville S. Hopkins; and Major A. C. Burnett, a veteran of the World War I. Rounding out the leadership was Troop Scribe William W. Duncan, a billing manager; and District Commissioner W. A. Perryman. Troop 48 was first to use the Council truck to transport several score of men to Camp Wisdom for a February property inspection.[6]

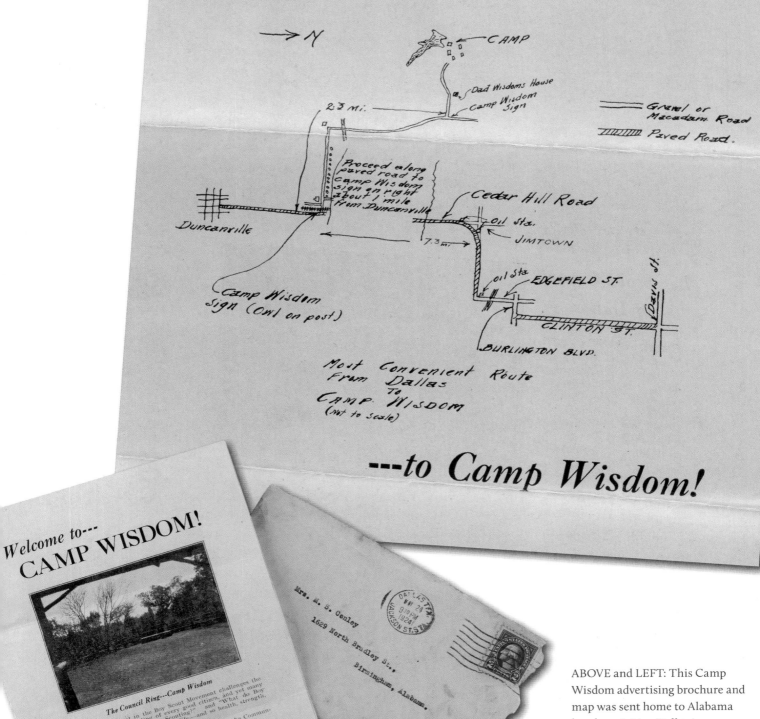

Follow This Trail

→ N

CAMP

Dad Wisdoms House
Camp Wisdom Sign

2.3 mi.

Gravel or Macadam Road
Paved Road.

Proceed along paved road to Camp Wisdom sign on right about 1 mile from Duncanville

Cedar Hill Road

Oil Sta.

Duncanville

JIMTOWN

7.3 mi.

Oil Sta. EDGEFIELD ST.

Davis St.

Camp Wisdom Sign (Owl on post)

CLINTON ST.

BURLINGTON BLVD.

Most Convenient Route
From Dallas
To
CAMP WISDOM
(not to scale)

---to Camp Wisdom!

Welcome to---
CAMP WISDOM!

The Council Ring---Camp Wisdom

THE World Interest in the Boy Scout Movement challenges the intelligent understanding of every good citizen, and yet many people still ask "What is Scouting?" and "What do Boy Scouts do? Scouting means out-door life,-- and so health, strength, happiness, and practical education.

The Dallas Council of Boy Scouts is a member of the Community Council, and such is distinctly YOUR organization.

Boy Scouting has grown tremendously within the past few years—until today, in Dallas, there are over 1000 boys active and eager in receiving the lessons of Scoutcraft.

You are cordially invited to visit Camp Wisdom.

Dallas Council
BOY SCOUTS of AMERICA
Educational Building   Royal and Akard Streets
Phone X-8318

Mrs. M. S. Conley
1629 North Bradley St.,
Birmingham, Alabama.

DALLAS TEX
MAY 20
9:00 PM
1924
JACKSON ST. STA.

ABOVE and LEFT: This Camp Wisdom advertising brochure and map was sent home to Alabama by a boy visiting Dallas in 1924. ACROSS TOP LEFT: The patches awarded to a Scout who attended summer camp at Camp Wisdom from 1928 through 1932.

WALTER CARROLL DOUGHTY *was born on September 8, 1907, in Marlin, Texas, as the son of State Superintendent of Public Schools, Walter F. Doughty, and his wife, Ettie.*

Relocated to Dallas by 1923, young Walter joined the Dallas Council's Troop 17 at St. John's Methodist Church located in East Dallas. Operating under the direction of Scoutmaster R. H. Taylor and his assistants Fred Kanmacher, Theodore Bison, and Hugh Berry (the brother of the interim Scout Executive at the time), the troop was well known for its former members becoming cadets in the ROTC. Walter distinguished himself by earning both junior and senior ROTC levels of Red Cross lifesaving certifications as well as the rank of Eagle Scout on January 28, 1924—becoming the Dallas Council's 14th boy to do so.

After graduating high school, Doughty entered the University of Texas at Austin in 1925 and served in the ROTC program attaining the rank of captain. He graduated in May 1928 with an associate of applied science degree (AAS) and moved into his parents' home in Hillsboro.

While there, Doughty married Miss Hazel Marguerite Webb in 1932 and the couple moved to 4515 Live Oak Street in Dallas where he took work. By 1937, they had purchased a house at 6348 Lakeshore Drive in an affluent part of town and began moving in higher social circles.

After the outbreak of World War II, Doughty joined the U.S. Army in the 3rd Base Section located in the Southwest Pacific and, while training in Australia, attained the rank of captain by September 1942. Quickly promoted to lieutenant colonel, tragedy struck.

On July 31, 1944, the military transport plane in which he was flying crashed into the Pacific Ocean after leaving its Hawaiian airbase. Lt Col. Walter C. Doughty perished along with a Navy admiral and sixteen others. Declared Lost-at-Sea, his body was eventually recovered and buried at the National Memorial Cemetery of the Pacific in Honolulu, Hawaii on February 28, 1949.

St. Johns Methodist Church

BELOW LEFT: Eagle Scout Walter Doughty at the time of his ceremony. BELOW RIGHT: At the time of Doughty's elevation to the rank of Eagle Scout, Troop 17's Scoutmaster R. H. Taylor (right side of photo) ran the unit out of the St. John's Methodist Church at 5601East Side Avenue at S. Beacon Street. It is now an elegant private home (above).

Eagle Scout Badges to Be Awarded Soon

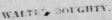

WALTER DOUGHTY.

"SCOUTING PROVIDES A SERVICE THAT WE NEED MORE THAN EVER IN OUR SOCIETY TODAY; NAMELY TRAINING YOUTH TO DEVELOP PRINCIPLES OF CHARACTER, HONOR, TRUST AND LEADERSHIP."

—TOM BAKER, PRESIDENT, CIRCLE TEN COUNCIL 2008–2010

By summer 1924 there were 30 troops in Dallas and one new 14-year-old Eagle Scout from Troop 9 named William Nelson Rees—Dallas' youngest to date. For Rees and his Oak Cliff troop located at the Rosemont Christian Church, Camp Wisdom was a short five-mile hike from their meeting place.

It is unclear if his troop was present on Monday, April 21 when tragedy struck. Around 11 o'clock in the morning at Camp Wisdom as Scouts were spending the day preparing the property for its summer season, 14-year-old Scout Harold Frederick Gardner drowned in 25 feet of water in Lake Wozencraft.

Gardner, on a work break, was swimming with his troop and dived to the bottom. When he failed to surface within a minute, his swimming buddy called for help. Assistant Scout Executive Caleb M. Moss dove in but could not find the boy. Scoutmaster Hines searched the bottom—again in vain. Only after 40 minutes was Gardner's body recovered.

"Harold was a good swimmer," recalled his father. "The cool water in the lake likely caused him to have cramps."

Young Gardner "was an energetic boy [who had] recently drawn a plan for a new Oak Cliff viaduct for streetcars and vehicular traffic and submitted it to County Judge Arch C. Allen urging something to be done to improve that phase of the traffic problem."

Harold was an academically distinguished student at the Oran M. Roberts Elementary School on Grand Avenue near Fair Park in East Dallas, and a promising artist. His funeral was well attended by his fellow Scouts and of course by local Scouting leadership. Despite the tragedy, Camp Wisdom's opening loomed in just a few weeks.

In memory of Harold, Richard S. Haseltine, the manager of the Culbertson Corporation, as well as the vice president of the Rotary Club of Dallas and father of future lifesaving hero Richard G. Haseltine, donated an Old Town brand canoe to be deployed for any future water rescue on the lake. And ever since then, each Circle Ten Council summer camp includes both swimming and lifesaving instruction, as well as lessons on operating small watercraft.[7]

As the May 31 opening day approached, about half of the 1,100 registered Council Scouts awaited their turn at camp over the following five weeks.

it was known to the Indians several centuries ago, when they roamed the virgin forests."[9]

When asked why he did it, the oilman referred to a story from his impoverished youth when a kindly shoemaker presented him with some peanuts and a peppermint as a Christmas present.

"This is just a dividend on a sack of peanuts and a stick of candy," he replied.[10]

In the fall, Camp Wisdom hosted 70 Scouts for a 10-day camp. Scouting skills took center stage for instruction: woodcraft, trailing, fire building, architecture, engineering, geology, forestry, and chemistry.

The highlight of the camp was the selection of Wisdom's first "Honor Camper," anticipating by over a decade local adoption of the Order of the Arrow, Scouting's national honor society. From the five patrols participating in the 1924 camp came five candidates for Most Efficient Scout. The victor was Ivan Irwin, who received his Eagle rank with four others at the Council Court of Honor held a week later on September 5.

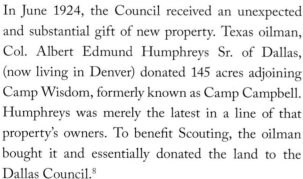

In June 1924, the Council received an unexpected and substantial gift of new property. Texas oilman, Col. Albert Edmund Humphreys Sr. of Dallas, (now living in Denver) donated 145 acres adjoining Camp Wisdom, formerly known as Camp Campbell. Humphreys was merely the latest in a line of that property's owners. To benefit Scouting, the oilman bought it and essentially donated the land to the Dallas Council.[8]

Scout Commissioner Thomas Hord, the Council's lead volunteer commented: "There is room on the land for every troop of the Dallas Council organization to construct its own cabin [but] an opportunity will be afforded for teaching Scoutcraft, as

IN 1915, *Dr. Payton L. Campbell paid a sum of $2,600 to John Catton and his wife for 145 acres of land on Cedar Ridge, southwest of Dallas. But for several years, he failed to pay the taxes due on the property. The county sued him for back assessments in court in 1917, winning the case. Ordered by the court to sell the land to the highest bidder in a public auction to* be "held at the courthouse door," *the acreage was purchased for $1,000 by the Fidelity Petroleum Company in December 1920.*

In December 1921, Fidelity Petroleum sold the land to George S. Hoagland, who turned around and sold it to Frank R. Bowles, a land trustee for the Stewart Abstract Company in June 1922. Bowles, who took over payments of the mortgage note, was approached by the lawyer of oil-man Albert E. Humphreys. Humphreys had made his fortune some years earlier in the Mexia Oil Fields and bought the note from Bowles in June 1924. The oilman quickly paid off the outstanding $7,000 debt in full.

Solicited by Dallas Council President Frank W. Wozencraft to help buy the Campbell land, Humphreys "sold" the 145 cedar-lined acres to the Council for "One Dollar cash [paid] to me in hand." The addition of Camp Humphreys made the total size of the combined Scout property about 345 acres.[A]

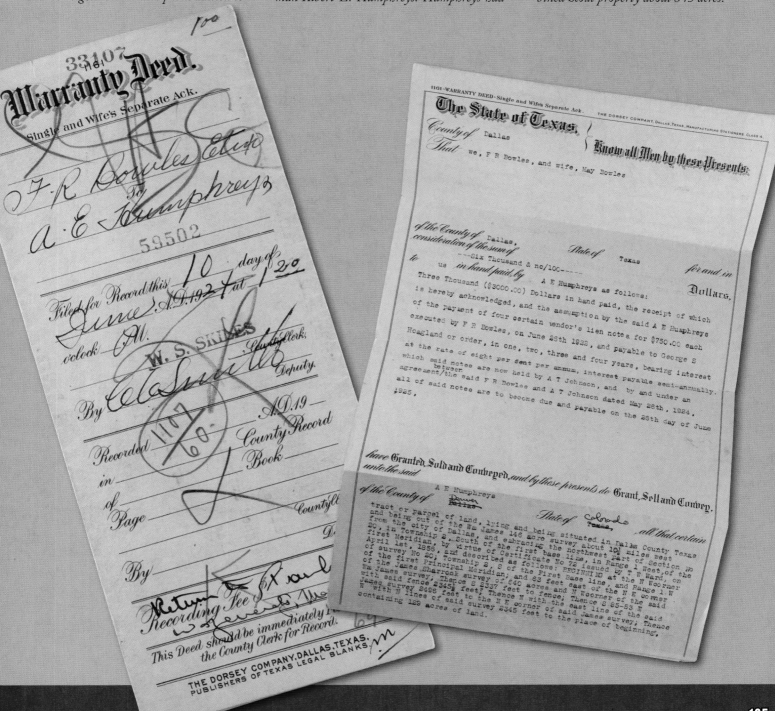

THE DALLAS MORNING NEWS *headline of March 20, 1924, read "[Businessmen] Decide to Form Scout Council in Grayson." The previous day, many local citizens had gathered in a "well-attended" luncheon at the posh Binkley Hotel in downtown Sherman, Texas, (now the site of a branch of Chase Bank) to discuss the formation of the Sherman Scout Council. Although there had been individual Scout units in Sherman since September 1911, the city had no formal BSA council franchise.*

"Definite decision [has been made] to go into the organization of a County Council in Boy Scout work in co-operation with other communities in the county," reported the Dallas Morning News. *Speeches in favor of formation included A. L. Shuman, the advertising manager of the* Fort Worth Star Telegram *newspaper and member of Fort Worth's Scout council. Other testimonials came from Denison bank cashier D. J. Brennan, furniture storeowner Frank Jennings, and Denison Mayor Will Hibbard.*

Mayor Hibbard informed the crowd that the Denison Council had been formed recently with "financial assistance pledged on a pro rata basis." However, the city had hosted Scouting units since the visit of Dallas Council Scout Executive Claude Richmond to the area in late February 1913.

The Sherman Council's executive committee was elected and began discussing its budget for the whole of Grayson County, in a one-year partnership with the Denison Council. Expenses included splitting the county's national chartering fee, executive salaries, and travel expenses.

"All other expenses will be borne by the local council," reported the Dallas Morning News, *"including the expense of such summer camps as are decided upon."*

Grayson County's first Scout executive was Fort Worth native H. L. McLean with George L. Hamilton elected president of the countywide council. Its headquarters would reside in Denison with monthly meetings to alternate between Sherman and Denison.[B]

The Honor Court also brought recognition to Troop 33's Richard G. Haseltine, who had saved a girl from drowning in a swimming pool while on a family vacation to the East Coast. After retrieving the child from the bottom, he performed the Silvester method of resuscitation—forcing the water from her lungs by pressing her arms to her chest then raising them above her head to bring in air. Haseltine credited his training to skills learned at Camp Wisdom earlier that summer. [11]

As the 1925 summer camp concluded, Col. Humphreys presented the Council with a $10,000 check for improvements to the newly consolidated camp. The oilman convinced the county to match his gift with the funds supporting the construction of a 50-foot x 100-foot pool with a new deep well to supply it. Digging began immediately so that it would be ready for 300 campers signed-up for the September camp.[12]

That November the baton of leadership was again handed off when the new Dallas Scout Executive, Oscar Avery Kitterman, newly arrived from the Ardmore (Oklahoma) Council.

Outgoing Scout Executive Wester's accomplishments were many, particularly in light of the disorganization into which he had stepped in 1923. In the last year of his leadership, membership had risen to 842 Scouts in 31 troops directed by 54 Scoutmasters and their assistants. Of the Scouts, 428 were registered Tenderfoots, 203 were Second Class Scouts, 45 First Class, 51 Star Scouts, 14 Life, and 9 Eagle Scouts.

Having received $38,000 in contributions from more than 600

donors in 1925, frugal Council managers had spent only about 60 percent of the total, leaving a generous reserve. Most spending arose from improvements to the expanded camp—some $17,000 worth. An additional $2,300 was spent on the Council vehicle. Executive salaries came in at about $8,000.

In the transition, Kitterman sought larger office space and moved Council headquarters from Suite 406 in Dallas City Hall at 106 S. Harwood Street to the seven-story Linz Building at 1608 Main Street and Lane Street, now demolished with a newer building and an entrance to Main Street Alley in its place.

Also, he named new heads of Council committees. *Dallas Dispatch* newspaper publisher Charles H. Newell headed training; Charles H. Seidenglanz, general manager of the Ruud-Humphrey Water Heater Company led camping, Scoutmaster Thomas Hord took charge of publicity, national political lecturer John W. Slayton worked on the reading program, Dr. William M. Anderson, the pastor of the First Presbyterian Church, handled church relations, and Dallas architect Harre M. Bernet and railroad terminal freight manager George R. Angell co-managed the Court of Honor.[13]

Early 1926 brought an adult training course for the Council's committee members, Scoutmasters and assistants, interested fathers, and citizens

ACROSS: Troop 1 in the Grayson County Council in 1924. RIGHT: Eagle Scout Daniel C. Deffenbach in 1928.

UNTIL THE LATE 1920s, *all Eagle Scout records at BSA's national headquarters were known to be notoriously inaccurate. For example, according to those records both Harry M. Wingren and Don William Freeman of Denison were presented the Eagle rank in years 1914 and 1915, respectively. However, local archival records reveal that Wingren was born on October 18, 1908, making him no more than six years old when "earning" his Eagle Scout award, while Freeman was a lad of about the same age in 1915. The first true recipient was 15-year-old Daniel Coleman Deffebach in 1924.*

Born on April 22, 1910, to lumber merchant Charles Levi Deffebach of Colorado and his wife, the former Lillian Lane of Virginia, he was their only child. Dan graduated Denison High School in 1927 and moved to Sherman to take a degree in Chemistry in 1931 at Austin College.

Remaining a bachelor for most of his life, he married Mary Ann Carpenter at age 58 in November 1968. Their son Dan Jr. was born in 1970 in Rusk County east of Tyler.

After Dan Senior's Eagle award, there were at least four more Eagle presentations made by the year 1928 as records indicate "four scholarships were given by the University of Texas to four members of the [1928 Senior] class that had attained the rank of Eagle Scout in the Boy Scouts of Denison." Those lucky Scouts were 1925 Eagle recipient W. Doak Blassingame, 1927 Eagle Scouts Jesse Thompson and Tillman McDaniel, and 1928 Eagle Scout Wilbur Green.[C]

JAMES W. "BILL" THOMPSON
WAXAHACHIE'S SECOND EAGLE SCOUT

ON MAY 4, 1924, *the* Dallas Morning News *announced the elevation of 15-year-old James William "Bill" Thompson to the rank of Eagle Scout becoming Waxahachie's second overall. The medal was presented by Scout Executive Loys R. Sessions, the future Circle Ten field executive and Camp Wisdom director, along with 12 "merit-badged" Scouts.*

Bill was born in Waxahachie in 1908 as the fourth of five sons to Tennessee native David Henry Thompson and his Texas-born wife, the former Mary Nettia Timmons. David was the owner of the Thompson Grain Company founded in 1882 and passed away in 1934 as Waxahachie's longest-tenured businessman at 52 years of service to the community.

Bill joined Scouting at an early age and advanced quickly. Born into a family of means, he became the first North Texas Scout to attend a World Jamboree, traveling to the 1924 event in Ermelunden, Denmark, with the 48 Scouts that made up the United States contingent. Sailing from New York Harbor on July 26 bound for England aboard the ship Leviathan, *they arrived in London for a short training camp and sightseeing tour before departing for Denmark and meeting up with 4,500 international Scouts. He returned to the United States on September 18.*

Thompson remained in Texas his entire life that included an enlistment in the U.S. Army. Arriving at Camp Wolters outside the town of Mineral Wells, Texas, in Palo Pinto County in February 1942, Thompson began serving during in World War II as a 34-year-old warrant officer for the duration of the conflict.[D]

LEFT: Waxahachie Eagle Scout J. W. Thompson as he appeared in the *Dallas Morning News* upon the announcement of his notable achievement. BELOW: His official rank card was signed by Scout Executive Loys R. Sessions. ABOVE RIGHT: Oscar A. Kitterman while performing the duties of the Dallas Council Scout Executive in 1926.

of Dallas over 21-years of age. The course aimed to show the local business community of Scouting's importance.

Two new course positions were added: Harre Burnet as "morale officer" and Thomas Hord as Council photographer. Participants were organized into nine patrols; the Panthers, Foxes, Jaybirds, Roosters, Wolves, Lions, Hounds, Tomcats, and Beavers. At the end of the eight-week course, Scout leaders were recognized at a banquet and performed a show in the guise of Boy Scouts. Their certificates were not immediately presented because a second course was to begin without delay.

In May, the 110 graduates of round two combined with the 76 members of the first course; all received their certificates in a Court of Honor ceremony held

DADDY WISDOM REUNITES WITH HIS BROTHER

IN MAY 1925, Scout Executive Wester asked 100 Scouts to volunteer at a reunion of Civil War veterans in downtown Dallas.

Organizers asked the boys to "assist in entertaining and escorting" the veterans, among whom was an aged gentleman by the name of Bill Wisdom. Chatting with a local businessman in a Dallas café, the old soldier asked for help in locating a death record, explaining that his brother had died in Dallas 36 years before.

Intrigued, the businessman asked his brother's name.

"John Shelby Wisdom," he answered.

The businessman's eyes gleamed as he made the connection with Daddy Wisdom. He quickly phoned Scoutmaster Thomas Hord.

"What is Daddy Wisdom's other name?" he asked.

"His initials are J. S. and I think the other name is John," came the answer.

Returning to the old soldier, the host (name unknown) told him that the next day they could visit a man who might know more about what had become of the brother. In the morning, they left for camp. Arriving on property, the car rolled up to Daddy Wisdom walking along the dirt road. The businessman got out of the car and walked over to Daddy.

"Mr. Wisdom," the businessman said. "I have a man out in my car who might have known you when you were a boy; I want you to come out and meet him."

The old veteran got out of the car and shook hands with Daddy.

"I'm looking for a man named John Shelby Wisdom," he said.

"Well, I guess I'm your man," replied Daddy Wisdom. "What did you say your name was?"

"Wisdom," answered Bill Wisdom, as he began scrutinizing Daddy Wisdom. "Did you have a brother named Bill?"

"Why yes."

"Did you have a brother named Tom?"

"Why, yes."

Both men were "trembling" but the questions continued.

"Well, you don't look much like my brother," Bill Wisdom said. "But if you are, you have a scar on your side and arm."

Daddy rolled back his sleeve to reveal the powder burn suffered as a boy. Upon this, Bill Wisdom threw his arms around his brother's neck. "I will never be a doubting-Thomas anymore!"

As they exchanged details of the many years since they had last seen each other, Bill tried to convince Daddy to return to Arkansas with him. But he refused.

"I'm glad I saw you again, Bill," said Daddy, "but my home is here with the boys. I want to die here with them."

But Daddy Wisdom did visit his childhood home that fall, accompanied by a select group of Dallas Council Eagle Scouts.[E]

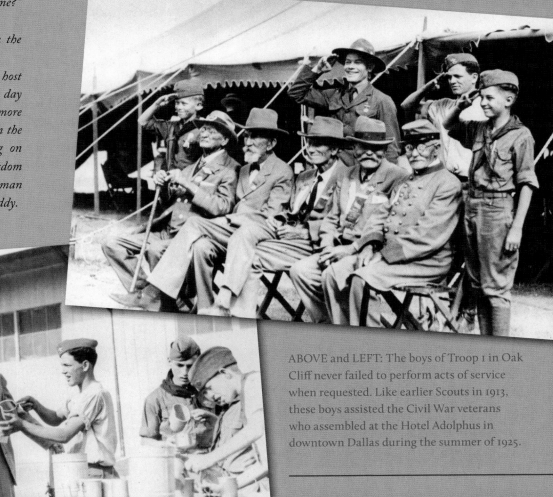

ABOVE and LEFT: The boys of Troop 1 in Oak Cliff never failed to perform acts of service when requested. Like earlier Scouts in 1913, these boys assisted the Civil War veterans who assembled at the Hotel Adolphus in downtown Dallas during the summer of 1925.

ABOVE: With the gift of $10,000 by Col. Albert E. Humphreys, Camp Wisdom got its first swimming pool in 1925 replete with a two-story diving platform. ACROSS: Scout perform a flag ceremony at Camp Wisdom in 1926.

CAMP WISDOM'S FARM

BEGINNING IN 1924, *Council managers sought to fortify the mess hall's meals with food harvested from camp plantings that included 800 fruit trees and several vegetable sections. The next year brought in cotton production as a cash crop as well as expanded vegetable gardens.*[F]

at First Methodist Church attended by 1,200 people. Dallas Eagle Scouts performed a candle ceremony.

As a bonus, 15-year-old William Nicols Jr. of Troop 6 at the Tyler Street Methodist Church under Scoutmaster Lex Buchanan and Fred Hester of Troop 4 (now designating the youth unit at the Cliff Temple Baptist Church in Oak Cliff) each received the Eagle Scout rank.[14]

At the Councilwide Court of Honor, Elmer Scott, Council board member and Dallas Health Department administrator, challenged the Scouts "not [to] be satisfied with achievement but to strive more vigorously for higher attainment in Scouting service." As a result of the new influx of leaders, 12 new troops were formed to work with 350 newly enrolled Scouts.

With membership expanding, the Council's five districts each had new identification—colored neckerchiefs: black for North Dallas; orange for Highland Park; red for Oak Cliff; purple for East Dallas; and blue for South Dallas. Kitterman proposed that henceforth each district hold its own courts of honor as needed. Additionally, each one would host individual district training courses for its local leaders.[15]

More sweeping developments were about to expand the Council's geographical scope and prestige. BSA's National Council concluded that the Dallas Council had excellent prospects for survival given its strong membership, financial support, and facilities. And other nearby city-run organizations that were not so fortunate—towns like Vickery and Richardson—were going to be placed under management of the Dallas Council by the national BSA officials.

TOP LEFT: Founded in February 1923 at the Oak Cliff Presbyterian Church, Troop 3 has been Scouting ever since. ACROSS: Several suites in Dallas City Hall served as the Dallas Council's headquarters from mid-1925 to the summer of 1926. LEFT: After vacating City Hall, the Council took up offices in the Linz Brothers Building at 1608 Main Street. Eventually occupying successive suites on three separate floors, the Dallas Council moved out into larger and more modern quarters after a four year tenure in 1930. ABOVE: Eagle Scout William Nichols Jr earned his rank in 1925 at the Tyler Street Methodist Church in Oak Cliff (above).

What resulted was the Dallas Council's expansion to six surrounding counties in June 1927 that included Rockwall, Kaufman, Henderson, Van Zandt, and parts of Ellis, giving the expanded Council a total of 57 troops, with expectation of expanding to 90 troops within two years. Even with such anticipated growth, Kitterman set a target of 175 total troops under his watch.

Camp Wisdom opened its gates to all Dallas Council units, helping to take the annual budget to $10,000. To fund it, the Council set up a Boy Scout Foundation with annual dues of $10 for subscribers. An initial recruitment campaign was scheduled for the first week of October.

The Foundation was to be "strictly a financing body and the Council will supervise the program of Scout activities," promotions declared. The initial drive amount was set at $25,000, which would be increased if needed.

By September, however, national BSA headquarters added another four counties to the Dallas

LEFT: Daddy Wisdom (left) poses with local Scouting supporter Elmer Scott (right), the organizer of the community-wide social service agency known as the Civic Federation of Dallas.

Council that included Johnson, Rains, Navarro, Hill, and the rest of Ellis County, now totaling ten counties that *encircled* the city of Dallas.

"A large part of the Dallas trade territory who have not heretofore had an opportunity to enjoy Scouting in the way that Dallas boys have enjoyed it will be given an adequate opportunity," declared Council President Harry E. Hobson.

But he noted that in order to do so, the Circle Ten Foundation would have to serve "as an integral part of the enlarged activities of Scouting in this area of Texas."[16]

JOHN M. "DON" CLARDY JR.
DALLAS COUNCIL'S FIRST HEROISM AWARD RECIPIENT

IN OCTOBER 1925, 13-year-old First Class Scout Don Clardy Jr. of Troop 15 in Cockrell Hill set aside his own safety and rushed into a burning two-story house to rescue an infant girl who was trapped inside. Using only methods learned from his Scout training that included instruction from both Firemanship and First Aid merit badges, young Don turned certain tragedy into an heroic event.

"I was on the school grounds when I heard a woman screaming," Clardy recalled. "I saw smoke and fire coming out of all the doors and windows, [so] I ran to the house and saw the woman on the porch screaming that her baby was in the house."

Knowing that he had to go in, Clardy dropped to the ground, covered his face with a neckerchief, and started crawling.

"I did not know where the baby was and did not find her in the first room. I could hardly breathe," he told the Dallas Morning News. "I crawled into the next room and there I heard the baby whimpering. The smoke was almost as thick as mud in the room but I finally got to the bed where she was lying."

Quickly, he grabbed little Maple Pearl Jordan and dragged her beside him as they made their way to the outside air. Realizing she had slipped into unconsciousness, he performed artificial respiration and revived her lifeless body.

"I just did what we had been taught to do in my Boy Scout training," he said. "Any other Boy Scout could and would have done the same thing if they had been where I was. One point of our Scout Law is, 'A Scout is brave,' and part of our Scout Oath binds us to help other people at all times."

For his valor, BSA's National Court of Honor presented him with the 74th overall Gold Honor medal and Dallas' first for the saving of a life at the risk of his own.

As an adult, Don went on to become a field executive with Circle Ten Council intent upon growing the local organization in North Texas.

After many years of dedicated service to the movement, John McDonald "Don" Clardy

Jr. passed away on July 11, 1982, and was buried next to his wife, Lucille, in the Garden of Mt. Vernon section of the Restland Funeral Home on Greenville Avenue in North Dallas.[G]

IN THE MEANTIME, SEPTEMBER 15, 1927, MARKED THE BEGINNING OF OPERATIONS IN THE NEWLY RENAMED CIRCLE TEN COUNCIL AND A BRIGHT FUTURE LAY AHEAD.

Part II

GROWTH AND DEVELOPMENT
(1928–1959)

"HE'S A SCOUT"

He may not be 12-years-old,
He may be thin or stout,
But if he can smile,
And do things worthwhile,
I want you to know he's a Scout.

He may not have passed his Eagle tests,
Or his mother won't let him out,
But if he can grin,
He'll be sure to win,
And prove that he's a Scout.

When he helps an old lady across the street,
The boys may sit-up and shout,
But if he will do it,
And go right on through it,
He's proving himself a Scout.

He thinks of those jeers,
When the enemy's "knocked-out,"
But he just forgets them,
And goes in and helps them,
He has proven himself a Scout.[1]

By Lloyd Rigby
12-year-old Boy Scout
Circle Ten Council, Wilmer, Texas
October 6, 1930

chapter 7

CREATING THE BASE (1927–1931)

"The best camping for the best Scouts and leaders."

HARRY E. HOBSON
PRESIDENT (1927) CIRCLE TEN COUNCIL

AS THE SCOUTING MOVEMENT flourished across the country, few councils could boast the same growth as was seen in Dallas' Circle Ten Council. Successful management had resulted in handsome membership increases and positive press.

The *Dallas Morning News* had printed an interview with local juvenile county judge F. H. Alexander suggesting that Scouting's lessons had lowered the crime rate.

"The fact that there are no Scouts among juvenile offenders is convincing proof that Scouting prevents lawlessness and fosters good citizenship and upright living," said the judge. "In most cases, the delinquent boy is not only without the wise leadership and character-building activities of the Scouts, but he has lost interest in his home, the church, the school, and all other agencies that exert a restraining and refining influence."

ACROSS: *Camp Wisdom summer camp staff members outside their tent during the 1930 season.* BELOW: *The 19-story Dallas Medical Arts Building at 1713 Pacific Avenue stood within the city's growing skyline beginning in 1923. Although being the tallest reinforced concrete building in the world at the time and containing a staggering eight elevators, it was demolished in 1977.*

Texas Governor Daniel J. Moody concurred and added, "Scouting *is* a positive deterrent to crime."[2]

In September 1927, Council President Harry E. Hobson reaffirmed Circle Ten's claim of providing "the best camping for the best Scouts and leaders" in the nation's best-funded Scouting territory. To remain so, he called for a minimum of $30,000 to be raised for both the annual budget and for improving Camp Wisdom. Unlike others in the past, this campaign had a unique twist—a western theme.

Meeting in the Hotel Adolphus on September 19, fifty Council managers hashed out the details.

THE CIRCLE TEN RANCH

FOR THE 1927 FUND-RAISING CAMPAIGN, *Council managers "formed" the Circle Ten Ranch as a fun way to solicit donations.*

Six "superintendents of the Ranch" were in charge of Dallas' enlarged six districts. L. O. Donald, the first president of the Oak Cliff Chamber of Commerce, roamed "Hell Hole Hollow"(Oak Cliff), while 19-year-old Scouting alumnus John J. Garrity patrolled "Gun Shy Pass" (South Dallas). "Dead Man's Curve" (Highland Park) was under the direction of beer and flour distributor Kurt K. Meisenbach, with "Bumble Bee Point" (North Dallas) being supervised by the pastor of the Westminster Presbyterian Church, Dr. T. O. Perrin.

Finally, the co-owner of local printers Vogel & Stellmacher, Herbert Stellmacher, moseyed around "Red Devil Hills" (East Dallas), while the manager of the Fulton Bag and Cotton Company, Dave Ellison, wandered within "Powder River Flats" (East Dallas).

Under each superintendent were three "foremen" in charge of the "Hereford," "Brahma," and "Longhorn" outfits. Each foreman had a crew of eight "ropers," eight "branders," and eight "wranglers" that acted as door-to-door solicitors. Total manpower equaled 602 men and no person was off limits to approach—including President Calvin Coolidge, whose two sons were Boy Scouts in Washington, DC.

In a letter written by "Chief Hired Hand" (Council President) George R. Angell to "Silent Cal" Coolidge—a reference to the President's nickname for using minimal words to convey paragraphs of thought—Angell hoped for a response from the nation's chief executive, albeit unlikely. He wrote in character:

Dere Mister President,

I has seen yer picshur in the paipers with a 4-gallun hatt and etc, and as I am in need of a fust-class cow hand I take my pen in hand to offer you a job as sech.

We is having a roundup here in Dallas October 3rd in which thar will be considable ropin' and brandin' and etc of mavericks for the Boy Scout foundashun.

I fele shore you wood like the job as they is a furst class bunch in the outfit with good grub throwed in. The wages is a dollar a day, and we provides you with good hosses but you kin bring that cay use I seen you with in the paipers ef you want.

Pleze let me no rite soon as they is plenty of boys hankerin to get hired.

Yurs very trooly,

[signature]

GEORGE R. ANGELL
CHIEF HIRED HAND OF THE CIRCLE TEN RANCH

Ps. They aint no use bringin' eny artillery as they quit shootin' republicans in Texas day before yestiddy when one of them give ten dollars to the Boy Scout Foundation.

On October 3, six luncheons were held at the three posh Dallas hotels: the Baker, the Adolphus, and the Jefferson, that netted the Council a little over $9,000 in several hours. Afterward, 200 men hit the streets and began canvassing the area during the two-day funding drive.

In a symbolic gesture, the widow of former Dallas Scout Executive Clinton B. Harris was the first woman to contribute funds to the campaign. She felt compelled to do so to "further the work in which her husband had died and be as a memorial to him." Her $10 check was delivered to Joe Burt at Scout headquarters in Suite 603 in the Linz Building on the campaign's first day.[4]

The Circle Ten *Ranch* would be headed by "Big Boss" Charles H. Newell, the Council's finance chairman. Joe Burt would be his fundraising assistant. They set a goal to raise $45,000 within a three-month timeframe, aided by district managers who would oversee the many door-to-door solicitors. They succeeded.

Daddy Wisdom riding in his New Year's gift from the Council in 1928—a horse and buggy.

The Council reached its goal by December placing it on good financial footing for the next twelve months. To celebrate, Circle Ten managers presented Daddy Wisdom with a new horse and buggy on New Year's Day 1928.[3]

In March 1928, the County Health Department closed Camp Wisdom citing "unsafe" conditions—putting the summer camping season in jeopardy. However, with dedication to purpose and flush with new funds collected from the recent campaign, the mess hall received immediate renovations and was ready for use by opening day in June.

Always prepared, Assistant Scout Executive and Camp Director Albert H. Watts made sure the first week's group of 80 campers brought with them canvas tents and cots to sleep in as there were no bunkhouses permitted for occupation. Thus, many Scouts experienced the joys of long-term *tent* camping for the first time rather than living in cabins. Although most Scouts appreciated this new style of living, they loved the instruction in camp gadget creation, nature study, swimming, lifesaving, and "rustic construction" more.[4]

As in previous years, the favorite camp activity was lifesaving taught to youthful staff members but in

Daddy Wisdom surrounded by a group of young campers in 1927.

THE FIRST PRESENTATION OF AN EAGLE PALM

IN 1927, *BSA's national office adopted the Eagle palm as a recognition of Scouting achievement as an Eagle Scout. To earn the bronze palm, an Eagle had to complete an additional five merit badges beyond the 21 required for the rank. The gold palm followed after a total of 10 additional merit badges were earned and the silver palm was given after 15 additional.*

Christopher C. Isbell of Hillsboro was one of the first Scouts in the Council to earn the bronze palm, which was presented on January 26, 1928, in SMU's McFarlin Auditorium by BSA's Chief Scout Executive James E. West. He was in Dallas for the Region 9 meeting. Also present at that ceremony were representatives of 49 of the Region's 58 total councils, which was a territorial showing that West regarded as "remarkable." In fact, he considered Circle Ten's adult participation as being "the best in the nation." The next day, West visited Daddy Wisdom at his camp.[B]

ACROSS FAR LEFT: Daddy Wisdom (right) and Chief Scout Executive James E. West (left) posing together in January 1928—the only photo of its kind known to exist. It was taken by Circle Ten Council Eagle Scout DeWitt Thompson. ACROSS LEFT: Assistant Scoutmaster Mark Johnson of Troop 1001 at the Trinity Bible Church in Richardson regales Scouts with the story of the Ghost Tree at Camp Wisdom (above left). TOP: Staff members pose for a photo during the 1929 summer sessions at Camp Wisdom. ABOVE: Scouts from Troop 60 at Camp Wisdom in 1929.

THE **WHITE SHARKS** OF TAHKODAH

by Robert Reitz,
Curator, Harbin Scout Museum

THE WHITE SHARKS OF TAHKODAH *was one of the early Scout honor organizations to be adopted in Circle Ten Council. Begun in the summer of 1925 at north central Arkansas' Camp Tahkodah by Waxahachie Scout Executive Loys R. Sessions, he believed it to be a way for its members "to blaze a new trail for the strong to follow."*

From tradition, Chief Tahkodah was the Quapaw Indian leader who refused to go to the reservation with his tribe. His "spirit" was said to roam about the camp and light the campfire with a mysterious flaming arrow.

When the Dallas and Waxahachie Councils merged to help form Circle Ten in 1927, Sessions eventually became the camp director for Camp Wisdom's summer season in 1928. In doing so, he brought with him the traditions of the White Sharks to augment the Wisdom Honor Camper program already in place.

Each week the staff voted for the Scout who best represented the ideals of the Scout Oath and Scout Law. That chosen Scout received a large green and white felt patch with the figure of a white shark with the word "Tahkodah" on it and a membership certificate (this one belonged to Daddy Wisdom). Each year thereafter, the members reunited for a barbecue banquet at Camp Wisdom on December 26.

The order was disbanded on December 26, 1936, whereupon the competing Wisdom Guide honor program, symbolized by a small medal suspended beneath several hanging bars, became the Council's sole honor camper recognition. It, too, was abandoned in 1937 when the Order of the Arrow, BSA's eventual national honor society, was adopted by Council leadership at his camp.[B]

ABOVE TOP: Swimming was a big attraction for local Scouts during summer camp sessions as instructors taught the latest Red Cross lifesaving techniques. ABOVE: The Scouts who passed their Red Cross certification for lifesaving during a 1928 summer session at Camp Wisdom. ACROSS TOP RIGHT: The certificate presented to Honor Camper Frank Young of Dallas' Troop 50—one of the last local boys to earn that distinction prior to the Council's adoption of the Order of the Arrow honor camper society in 1937.

1928 it was taught to Red Cross certifications by professionals. New and junior Scouts tested under Raymond Gokey, the director of lifesaving for the Dallas County chapter of the Red Cross, while the senior campers tested with one of the assistant camp directors and future Scoutmaster of Troop 70 in University Park, George M. Haas. Learning under the slogan, "Every Scout a Life Saver," Gokey believed this year's lot of Scouts to the "best trained" in Council history.[5]

Sadly in mid-session, tragedy struck. Camp Director Watts collapsed on property, as the victim of acute appendicitis. Rushed to Baylor Hospital east of downtown, he died a few hours later. Being a native of Madison, Indiana, no family members were present to fill out his death certificate. The task was performed by Scout Executive Oscar Kitterman. Assistant Camp Director and Council Field Executive Loys R. Sessions assumed Watts' duties for the remainder of the summer.[6]

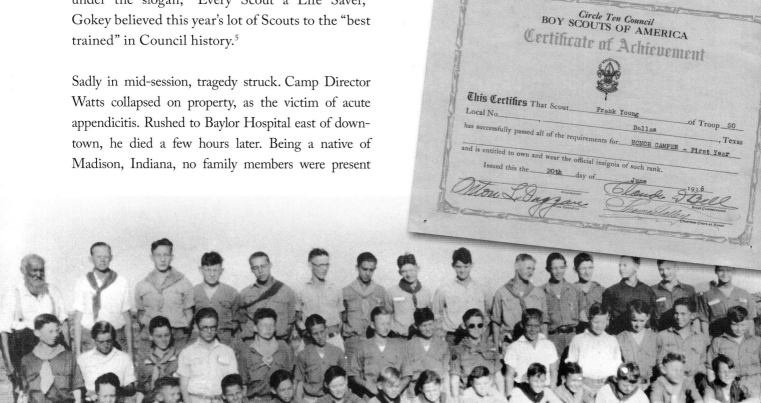

ABOVE MIDDLE: A photo of the 1928 Council Honor Campers during their trip to New Mexico. LEFT: Lifesaving assistant instructors DeWitt Thompson (left) and George M. Haas (right) in 1928. ABOVE: Camp Director Loys R. Sessions paddles across Lake Wozencraft at Camp Wisdom during the 1928 summer season.

As in years before, the Wisdom Honor Campers were elected. In August after camp closed, 41 of the 49 honorees went on a Council-funded trip to Carlsbad, New Mexico. For one week, they toured that state via bus and visited a number of caverns and other Native American sites and ruins.

In May 1930, Scout Executive Oscar Kitterman resigned his post to accept the same position in the Greater Boston Area Council.

"It has taken three or four years to develop the necessary manpower to accomplish great things," he

BABE RUTH SPEAKS to CIRCLE TEN COUNCIL

IN APRIL 1929, *Circle Ten Council was running a large debt. To help pay it down, Council managers decided to hold a fund-raising dinner for local donors and businessmen. The drawing card was the nation's best-known and most-beloved sports hero—New York Yankees slugger, Babe Ruth. Scout Executive Oscar Kitterman believed that if anyone could hit a financial home run for Circle Ten Scouting, it was the Bambino.*

As luck would have it, "the Babe" agreed to appear when a simple phone call was made to him in New York City. "Sure I'll do it," said Ruth over the long distance line. "I'll do it if you'll promise to have some kids there."

The noon fund-raiser was held at the Baker Hotel, similar to the annual Friends of Scouting banquets held today. The 700-room, 18-story Baker Hotel (eventually demolished in 1980) had been built on the site of the razed Oriental Hotel in 1925. The location now holds the Whitacre Tower at One AT&T Plaza.

Reported in the Dallas Morning News *under the headline "Babe is Scout Pinch Hitter: Commends 'Big Boys' for Work in Interest of Youths," Ruth's "highly inspirational talk" impacted the big hitters of Dallas business. Taking the podium, he drew hearty laughs*

when looking over the large audience of men and quipping, "Boy Scouts grow big in this town!"

"Seriously, you men are doing one of the finest pieces of work you could possibly do," he said. "There is nothing finer in the world and nothing more worthwhile than a boy."

At his request, many Boy Scouts were present to hear his address.

"As for you boys, I want every one of you to remember two things, that you should be grateful and [to] show in all of your deeds that you appreciate these things being done for you," he advised. "I also want each of you to do whatever you do with your whole heart and soul. If you play baseball, be the best baseball player that you can possibly be. If you are a doctor, try to be the best doctor you know how to be. No matter what you are, play the game hard and you can't help succeeding."

The Council collected $12,600 in pledges that day, making a good start toward the campaign's $55,000 goal.

After the luncheon concluded, a Dallas Morning News *photographer asked Ruth for permission to take his picture. Looking around, the slugger asked a 13-year-old Scout from Oak Cliff named Robert W. Johnsey to join him (top right)—certainly one of the lad's greatest moments in life.*[C]

said. "The greatest source of comfort which I have as I leave this program is that the volunteers will carry on in a vigorous and satisfactory manner."

During Kitterman's four-year tenure as the head of the Dallas Council, Scout membership had increased from 842 Scouts in 31 troops at the end of 1925 to 3,188 Scouts in 147 troops under the direction of 308 Scoutmasters and their assistants in 1930. The addition of 25 more local Commissioners rounded out the new grassroots level recruiting team. Financially, the Council maintained a budget in excess of $62,000 that included support for a vigorous summer camping program with buildings and assets valued at $26,000 and land at $60,000.[7] His leadership and vision resulted in the funding of a $10,000 water pump system, a dam for Lake Wozencraft, and a new $16,000 swimming pool.

As for the Council's indebtedness, $11,000 was owed to the Republic National Bank and another $3,000 to the Mercantile Bank in notes that covered previously underfunded budgets. Another $2,716 in unpaid bills sat in the payables folder. To the positive, $7,500 was tallied as unpaid pledge income, which put the overdrawn bank account to the negative by $518.98.[8] But within two months, debt would be reduced by $5,000 resulting from "careful management, careful collection, and reduction of expenses."[9]

ACROSS TOP: Babe Ruth (left) posing with Circle Ten Scout Robert W. Johnsey after the slugger's speech to Council leaders at the famed Baker Hotel (across left) on Commerce Street. TOP LEFT: Norman Hargraves relaxes in the Honor Camper cabin during a 1931 summer camp session at Camp Wisdom. TOP RIGHT: A member of Dallas' Troop 1 flips a pancake on a campout. RIGHT: Scouts from Troop 60 under the direction of Scoutmaster George M. Haas pose for a photo before eating dinner on a campout in 1930.

1928 TEXAS STATE FAIR LOST AND FOUND SERVICE

ON OCTOBER 13, 1928, *the* Dallas Morning News *headline announced, "242 Lost Children Found by Scouts at Fair on Friday." Under the direction of Troop 2 Scoutmaster R. G. Howard and Assistant Scoutmaster A. L. Stone, a team of Scouts scoured the grounds at the request of frantic parents.*

"The radio loudspeaker kept booming its announcements of 'losts,'" reported the newspaper, whereupon lads from Troops 50, 46, and 2 emerged from their five-tent encampment and roamed the fairgrounds. Other volunteers included Kurt. K. Meisenbach, who would become the eventual namesake of Camp Meisenbach at the future Clements Scout Ranch; William G. Burnett, the treasurer for Texas Power and Light; and Herbert Stellmacher, the proprietor of Stellmacher & Clark publishing company.

One memorable "find" involved a seven-year-old girl who announced, "Please find my momma and papa. I lost them and I knew this is the place to get them back again."

Another situation involved a couple that had lost their three-year-old son. They believed the tot to have been kidnapped as he was "so cute, we know they stole him." But to their good fortune, the "cute one" was found quickly on the grounds.

In a third case, Scouts found a "lost" boy who was caught smoking a cigarette in the automobile section.[D]

ABOVE: Eagle Scout DeWitt Thompson poses for a picture on a bridge near Balance Rock at Camp Wisdom. LEFT: Troop 1 Scoutmaster Thomas Hord with his Scouts on a campout in 1930.

AKE WOZENCRAFT, CAMP WISDOM

TOP: Camp Wisdom staff member DeWitt Thompson writes a letter home to his mother during the 1930 summer sessions.
ABOVE: The serene Lake Wozencraft in 1930.

Kitterman's tenure was successful not only because he was an effective leader but also because he was the beneficiary of a great period of national economic growth under the pro-business fiscal policies of President Calvin Coolidge.

By the time of Kitterman's resignation in May 1930, President Herbert Hoover was presiding over the nation's worst economic disaster—the Great Depression.

This was the economy into which the new Circle Ten Council Scout Executive Orton Lorraine Duggan

A "GOOD TURN" WITH CAMP WISDOM PEACHES

IN JULY 1929, *the 1,400-tree orchard at Camp Wisdom was awash in large, juicy Elberta peaches—a luxury food. As part of Circle Ten Council's service to the community, the peaches were donated to orphanages, to the elderly and infirm in Dallas' nursing homes, to the Salvation Army, and to hundreds of working mothers in the poorer districts of town.*

To institute this program, local florist and Scouting supporter Otto Lang of the Lang Floral and Nursery Company planted the trees on property in 1924 as his own "good turn" to the Boy Scouts.

"Mr. Lang has taken care of the these trees, with the assistance of Daddy Wisdom and the Boy Scouts, cultivating the orchard, spraying the trees, and otherwise seeing that the fruit they bore was sound and that proper use was made of it when it ripened," reported the Dallas Morning News.

When ready for picking, a small army of Scouts gathered at camp and filled bushel after bushel of baskets furnished by the Ben E. Keith Produce Company and the Texas Produce Company. Recipients included the "Little Mexico" community in East Dallas.

"When word went out that a 'whole truckload' of ripened peaches was at the [Methodist] Mexican Mission at Wichita and Highland Streets," reported the newspaper, "hundreds of children to whom a big juicy Elberta is a treat came with pails, pans, bags, and whatever they could get. Many mothers said these were the first peaches their children had tasted this year."[E]

Scouting was making a tangible difference within the Dallas community.

found himself when arriving in Dallas in early September 1930.

Duggan, the former chief executive at the Denver (Colorado) Council, was offered the job after a national search by Region 9 Director James P. Fitch, who had been performing the duties of the Scout Executive since July and had begun fiscally economizing due to decreasing donations. Fitch's most dramatic decision was to move Council headquarters from the "cramped, shabby, and obsolete" offices in the Linz Building into a larger suite in the Santa Fe Building at the intersection of Commerce and Jackson Streets. Even sweeter, Fitch negotiated a $20 per month decrease in rent and month-to-month lease terms should Duggan wish to move again.[10]

Fitch also pared down budgetary expenses from September through December. Some office staff was eliminated and field executives took over their own secretarial work. Pre-printed letterhead stocks were used even if out of date. District donation quotas were raised and misplaced donor leads were located and prospected.

ABOVE: A summer camp staff member standing on Balance Rock at Camp Wisdom. TOP RIGHT: A view of Lake Wozencraft. RIGHT MIDDLE: Scouts gathered around a campfire in the original Council Ring. RIGHT: Scouts at Camp Wisdom donning their "Owl logo" and "White Shark" patches on their shirts.

GROUP OF HAPPY CAMPERS AT CAMP WISDOM

Scout Executive Duggan arrived on September 6, 1930, to a welcoming Council. His official reception was held on September 8 at the First Methodist Church at the corner of S. Ross Avenue and Harwood Street. Hosted by the former Dallas mayor, Council president, and toastmaster, Frank P. Holland, the evening featured local dignitaries, Scout Commissioners, and selected Scouts. One of the young men who spoke at the event was Circle Ten Council's newest Eagle Scout from Troop 32, 13-year-old Billy Clements, who had attained the rank in a mere 17 months after joining.

Many years later, young Billy would grow to become Texas' most important man as a two-term governor. He also would serve as the Council's president from 1968 to 1970 and be a financial benefactor that would assemble a massive 3,300 acres of cedar-rich land for Circle Ten Council outside Athens, Texas known as the Clements Scout Ranch.

"I recall Mr. Duggan came from Dallas to Colorado and in my speech I told him that we in Dallas did not have Pecos cantaloupes or Greeley Irish potatoes," Gov. Clements recalled years later. "That was a long time ago and these are still fond memories."

Also presented that evening was the Council's first Scoutmaster's Key award to the 10-year tenured leader of Troop 34, Rufus A. McClung.

The Scoutmaster's Key was a "first-of-its-kind to be awarded in Circle Ten Council" as it recognized significant contributions to Scouting made by an individual Scoutmaster.

The following year in 1931, BSA's National Council introduced the Silver Beaver award that acknowledged *any* volunteer's extraordinary service to a council, greatly reducing the significance of the Scoutmaster's Key.[11]

In January 1931, Daddy Wisdom was ill and required admittance to nearby Methodist Hospital. Sensing something wrong, Daddy's Irish terrier, Woodrow, hid under his bed and refused to eat, drink, or come out. He died while Wisdom was in the hospital. Daddy's other dog,

ABOVE LEFT: New Scout Executive Orton Duggan as he looked upon his arrival in Dallas in 1930. TOP: Circle Ten Council's logo in 1930. BOTTOM LEFT: The Santa Fe Building at 1122 Jackson Street that hosted the Council's 18th headquarters from 1930–1935.

WILLIAM P. "BILL" CLEMENTS JR.

By Robert Reitz,
Curator, Harbin Scout Museum

WILLIAM PERRY "BILL" CLEMENTS JR. *was born on April 13, 1917, in Dallas as the second child of William P. Clements Sr and his wife, Evelyn. Graduating Highland Park High School in 1934, he was elected Most Popular Boy and Class President.*

Awarded his Eagle Scout rank in 1930, Clements was elected a member of the White Sharks of Tahkodah, Circle Ten Council's newest Honor Scout organization as well as being a member of Camp Wisdom's camp staff during the summer of 1931.

In 1947, Clements founded Southeastern Drilling Inc. (SEDCO), soon to become the world's largest oil drilling contracting company. That business prowess garnered him attention from politicians in the federal government earning him an assignment as deputy secretary of the U.S. Department of Defense in 1973, where he ultimately served under two presidents. With his taste for political achievement whetted, he was elected governor of Texas in 1978 and served again as governor in 1986.

As a life-long student of Texas history, he founded the William P. Clements Center for Southwest Studies at Southern Methodist University and the Fort Burgwin Research Center near Taos, New Mexico.

As head of the Circle Ten Council camping committee, he helped create the Clements Scout Ranch near Athens, Texas, in Henderson County, which opened in 1966. He also served as the Council's president from 1968 to 1970.

Clements received the Council's first Distinguished Eagle Scout award from BSA's national office in 1969 as well as the Silver Buffalo award for extraordinary service to youth in 1980.

After an exceptional career of achievement, Gov. William P. Clements Jr. passed away on May 29, 2011, at age 94 and is buried at the Sparkman-Hillcrest Funeral Home on W. Northwest Highway.

Babe the Spitz, was old, toothless, and being taken care of by a neighbor when she escaped and tried to make it back to camp. She, too, died before arriving back at the house. Both dogs remained "faithful to the last."

Daddy, knowing that he was dying, wished to pass away in the home "built by his boys." His doctors obliged and released him.[12]

On March 7, Daddy's health continued to deteriorate and he left camp for the final time. Unconscious when he arrived at the hospital, two Council Eagle Scouts were posted on a 24-hour watch outside his hospital door. On March 8, the *Dallas Morning*

News announced, "Death Takes Away Benefactor and Friend of Dallas Scouting."

That Sunday, John Wisdom's body lay in state in Camp Wisdom's administration building, "where a guard of Scouts was maintained through the night."[13]

John Shelby Wisdom was buried in nearby Wheatland Cemetery, escorted by six Eagle Scout pallbearers. As described in the *Dallas Morning News*, "*Taps* was blown for Daddy Wisdom in his earthly life and we will soon carry him to the grave where he will sleep, with these flowers over him, until that final day. But he has left an indelible

ACROSS LEFT: An iconic image of Daddy Wisdom taken about 1929. BELOW: Daddy Wisdom's funeral was a landmark event in Dallas Scouting history. The open casket memorial service was held on the concrete porch of his house laden with many flower bouquets given by appreciative Scouts and their families. RIGHT: Daddy Wisdom's gravesite at nearby Wheatland Cemetery was visited regularly by local Scouts. TOP RIGHT: The official inventory of Daddy Wisdom's possessions as filed with the county in 1931.

CIRCLE TEN LEADS TEXAS COUNCILS IN SMASHING THE RACIAL BARRIER

IN JANUARY 1931, *Circle Ten Council consummated one of its most significant organizational decisions by adding an "Interracial Committee" to the executive organization. From the earliest days of the movement in America, African American boys have been a part of Scouting. Elizabeth City, North Carolina, chartered a Negro troop in 1911. Another was present in Nashville, Tennessee, in 1913. By 1923, Port Arthur on the Texas Gulf Coast had a troop of Black Scouts.*

In fact, by 1926 a national Scouting survey revealed a total of 248 Black-only units that served 4,923 members. Dallas led Region 9 in fully breaking the color barrier.

According to the 1930 federal census, Circle Ten's territory had 5,843 black boys of Scouting age who could be recruited. By year's end, the Council had formed one African American troop made up of 37 Scouts along with 74 Hispanic boys who were members of other units.

In April 1932, under the Council's diversity initiative, a troop of "Explorador" Scouts was installed at the Methodist Mexican Mission at 2502 Highland Street in East Dallas. Since these boys lived in "Little Mexico," they were difficult to recruit for English-only speaking leaders. However, the Council brought in volunteers to explain the program to both them and their parents in Spanish, generating interest.

"The boys are taught by acts [of good deeds] and not by words," recalled the Rev. Felix Segovia of the Methodist Mexican Mission, "and against acts there are not arguments."[F]

example to this and all future generations of Dallas boys and men. It is an example of willingness to share what he got from the world."[14]

The next day, a Council committee was formed to create a memorial to honor its great benefactor, which included the preservation of his home and personal effects. One of Daddy's most-prized possessions was his large Seth Thomas clock that had been in his family for over 100 years.

The fund for a Wisdom Monument was approved by the Council's executive board and they began collecting offerings on June 6, 1931—the opening of the first summer camp without Daddy

present—where Scouts could make $1 donations. The plan called for an archway to be erected at the entrance of Camp Wisdom through which all Scouts and leaders would pass upon arrival. A bust of Daddy Wisdom would be at its center.

Before the start of the 1932 summer camp, the welded metal "Wisdom" sign with plaques on either side of the cedar pole gateway were dedicated. Today, the plaques and a bust of Daddy Wisdom reside in the Harbin Museum on property, now situated behind the "Wisdom Memorial Archway."[15]

THE DEATH OF DADDY WISDOM SYMBOLICALLY CLOSED SCOUTING'S INFANCY IN DALLAS. CIRCLE TEN COUNCIL HAD COME OF AGE.

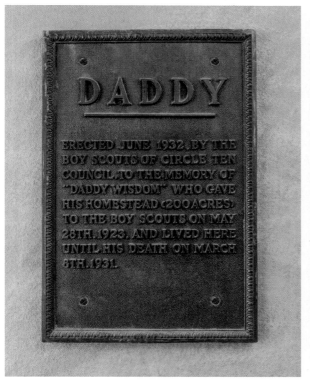

ACROSS TOP: A father and son salute the memory of Daddy Wisdom at the entrance to camp. LEFT: Scouts line the entrance road that passed in front of Daddy Wisdom's house in 1932. ABOVE and ABOVE RIGHT: The two plaques that were once attached to the right and left upright poles of the Camp Wisdom gateway. They now reside in the Harbin Scout Museum.

chapter 8

SURVIVING THE DEPRESSION
(1931–1936)

"Out of this group of Boy Scouts, the citizens of today expect the real leaders of the next generation. A rededication to the Scout Oath . . . will bring out the qualities of leadership needed in the world of tomorrow."

James V. Allred
33rd Governor of Texas
February 9, 1936

RIGHT: The Eagle Scout portrait of polar explorer Paul Allman Siple in 1923. FAR RIGHT:
Paul Siple at Fair Park upon his arrival in Dallas to speak to Scouts at Camp Wisdom in 1931

DURING THE SUMMER OF 1931, Camp Wisdom was abuzz with excitement as the nation's most renowned Eagle Scout, Paul Siple—affectionately known across the country as "Boy Scout No. 1"—was to visit. Famous for being BSA's choice to accompany Polar explorer Admiral Richard E. Byrd on his first Antarctic expedition in 1928, at 19, Siple stood on the precipice of his life's work. Within a decade, he would become a celebrated polar explorer in his own right, who would coin the term "wind chill factor" relating to the actual temperature hitting the skin during winter.

A former Sea Scout from Erie, Pennsylvania, Siple was a hero to all boys due to his fascinating exploits and clean image. His visit occurred on July 4, when he delivered several inspirational talks to Dallas' Scouts, their friends, families, and patrons.[1]

Met by a group of fellow Eagle Scouts at the front entrance of camp on the east side, the young explorer walked to the small, newly revamped mess hall nestled in the trees behind the swimming pool for lunch and his first oration.

A second session followed at 2 o'clock, where he regaled his audience with stories from his polar conquests that ended with how Scouts could positively impact their own communities as well.

THE DALLAS GAS COMPANY'S ADULT TROOP

AS CIRCLE TEN COUNCIL *continued its commitment to BSA's Ten-Year plan for growing its national membership, Council managers sought better ways to organize its district leadership now based only in higher populated areas.*

As designed years earlier, these district committees developed only city-based units rather than rural-based units. The solution was to form district committees charged with growing the movement across entire counties. This way, smaller rural units would receive much-needed Council resources to fuel their expansion across these mildly populated yet highly pro-Scouting areas.

On the unit level, chartering organizations now could place two members from their institution onto the local district committee. The committee was authorized to elect its own leadership, run its own courts of honor, finance its local program, and promote its own Scouting work.

Results would be reported to the Council on a regular basis (which included both gains and losses) so managers could more easily track changing membership totals. Some unique new troops caught the attention of Council officials like Troop 80 formed at the Dallas Gas Company—it was made-up completely of men, similar to Oak Cliff's landmark Troop Zero and Cliff Temple's Troop 48.*

Formed in February 1933 to train the gas employees in the principles of Scoutmastership, starting new troops, and bettering recruitment, members were placed in five patrols and "took special training" under the supervision of Scout Executive Orton Duggan. Scoutmaster C. A. Holtmann and Assistant Scoutmaster Ben A. Newberry led the unit. D. W. Bright was senior patrol leader with G. B. Hillyer as scribe. The patrol leaders were C. I. Langdon, J. A. Martin, F. G. Robinson, John P. Viglini, and W. G. Nash.*

After completion of the training course on March 7, Scout Commissioner (and former Council President) George R. Angell and Scout Executive Duggan inducted the graduates in the Dallas Gas Company's auditorium. Council President Leslie B. Denning, the founder of the Dallas Gas Company, served as chairman of the troop's advisory committee and handed out the adult leader commission certificates alongside Scoutmaster Holtmann and Assistant Scoutmaster Newberry.[A]

"There are plenty of things boys can do at home just as important as discovering the South Pole," said Siple. "Probably a little more so."

After finishing, Sea Scout Siple was made an honorary member of the Council's local fraternity of service-oriented Eagle Scouts called the "Tipi Huya," which translated to "House of Eagles" in a local American Indian tongue. As members, Eagles earned "honor points" when giving service to the community. This organization was another precursor to BSA's current society of honor campers, the Order of the Arrow.[2]

At the end of 1931, Council managers bestowed BSA's highest honor upon noteworthy Council Scouters—the newly created Silver Beaver award that was given to any volunteer upon recommendation of the Council's executive board (right).

Circle Ten's first presentation of Silver Beavers was made at the Council's annual meeting in January 1932. Held at the downtown Young Women's Christian Association (YWCA) at 1709 Jackson Street at Prather Street (now a downtown parking lot), BSA's national personnel director, Harold F. Pote, gave the keynote address. The first two awards were made posthumously to Daddy Wisdom and to Col. Albert E. Humphreys—the two land donors of Camp Wisdom.

Daddy, of course, had died the previous year from illness and Col. Humphreys in 1927 under tragic circumstances. On May 8, 1927, Humphreys allegedly shot himself accidentally while examining his guns for an upcoming hunting and fishing trip. Known as the "King of the Wildcatters" in the

BY MID-1932, *a total of 153 Circle Ten Scouts had earned the rank of Eagle, of which 83 hailed from Dallas County. One of the most successful was George M. Jones Jr., a recipient of 80 of the 96 total merit badges available at the time (below). His accomplishment made front-page news.*

"An almost encyclopedic spread of information is included in this Dallas Scout's list of badges, which range from agriculture to zoology," reported the Dallas Morning News. *"All have been won in a period of less than six and a half years [with] young Jones having joined the Scouts October 13, 1926, when he was thirteen-years-old." It would be many years before his feat would be bested.*

Born the son of local dentist, Dr. George Miller Jones Sr., young George was an overachiever who graduated Dallas' Woodrow Wilson High School in 1931. While studying premedicine at Southern Methodist University, Jones served as an Assistant Scoutmaster in Troop 56 at the Greenville Avenue Christian Church. He was elected to the Beta Beta Beta society, the national biology fraternity, and Sigma Theta, the national science fraternity.

After taking his medical degree (as well as a master of arts degree), Jones practiced medicine at the University of Michigan Hospital before coming back to Dallas and rejoining Scouting, where he worked on the Council's executive board as its health and safety officer.[B]

ACROSS LEFT: During national BSA's Ten-Year membership recruitment program beginning in 1932, the training of new Scoutmasters was paramount. Circle Ten Council held a special training session at the Dallas Gas Company headquarters (lower middle) at the request of Council President Leslie B. Denning (lower right). Upon graduation, Scoutmasters and their assistants were awarded with a pin and a position patch. The lower patch was awarded to Scoutmasters, while the upper was for their assistants. TOP: The 1931 Silver Beaver medal.

THE GREAT DEPRESSION

was well underway by April 1932 when a group of concerned citizens formed Troop 42 in Whitewright, Texas. Located 18 miles southeast of Sherman, the town was full of local boys who flocked to Scouting to escape the economic chaos engulfing the country at the time.

In June 1935, Council Field Executive Ben Burget and District Scout Commissioner L. C. Arnold met with a committee of Whitewright's civic leaders to arrange for the troop to transfer its independent charter designation into the Texas-Oklahoma (T-O) Council. The committee was made-up of 41-year-old store cashier Willis L. Stowers, 34-year-old rural mail carrier Benjamin W. Newman, and 46-year-old hardware salesman C. J. Meador.

The latter two gentlemen each were fathers of a Scout-age boy. Meador's 14-year-old son, Jack, had earned the rank of Eagle Scout the previous year in 1934. (Interestingly, Jack's own future son, Joe Mickey Meador, would follow the family tradition and earn the Eagle rank in Troop 42 on July 30, 1962.)

Burget arranged for the troop to be sponsored by the American Legion post in town with their meeting place to be in the log cabin behind the Legion Hall near today's Whitewright Elementary School. As a result, Troop 42 attracted excellent adult leaders and Scouts who lived the Scouting program throughout the year. They sent boys to Camp Grayson each summer and traveled frequently to local high school cafeterias for "intertroop Boy Scout meets." For some of these events, Scouts made their way in from Sherman, Van Alstine, Bells, and other regional locales.

The unit continued to function without stoppage throughout the Depression, World War II, the Korean War, and the Vietnam War. Through 2011, Troop 42 has produced over 40 Eagle Scouts—with more to come. And it continues to serve Circle Ten Council proudly as it builds the character of local North Texas youth.[C]

petroleum industry from oil discoveries made in Wyoming, Oklahoma, and Mexia, Texas, Humphreys was a man who "got ahead on sheer nerve, application to duty, and astuteness in business affairs."

The next Silver Beaver went to former Council President Frank Wozencraft followed by presentations to insurance agent George Hedden Bird, former Council President George Robinson Angell, oil executive Frank V. Faulkner, Archie Wood, electronics engineer Thomas E. Craig of McKinney, and Episcopal clergyman Walter Howard Meyers of Hillsboro.[3]

By May 1932, Troop 71 had been founded at the John S. Bradfield Elementary School in western Highland Park under Scoutmaster Marshall Diggs and assistant Leslie Hill. What made it special was the reason it was founded—it was Dallas' first Cubbing pack—and it had just graduated the Council's first Cub Scouts into Boy Scouting.[4]

Formally launched by national BSA managers as an "experimental program" for nine to 11-year-old boys in 1928, Cub packs were formed in each of BSA's 12 regions. Cub Pack 3071

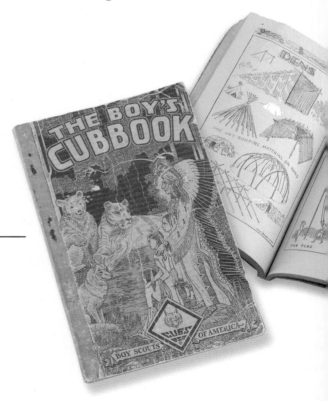

RIGHT: Upon approval to create BSA's experimental Cubbing program in 1930, rank handbooks were produced to aid leaders in delivering the lessons to their young Scouts. This Wolf Level *Cubbook* was used by first year Scouts.

GEORGE HEDDEN BIRD (right) was born in Jersey City, New Jersey, on November 2, 1868, as the son of John Bird and his wife, Elizabeth Woodruff Hedden. By the time he was 12, his father had died and the family had settled in Morristown, New Jersey, where he received public schooling and showed an interest in accounting. Meeting Miss Myrtle L. Haden, the couple married in her hometown of Honey Grove, Texas, on April 20, 1896. The newlyweds briefly lived in the Bronx, New York, where George worked as a solicitor for a trust company. After they moved back to North Texas, their daughter Mary Haden Bird was born in 1902 followed by son John William Bird in 1907.

With a background in finance and a growing family to care for, Bird joined forces with CPA Charles H. Schoolar and founded Schoolar and Bird, Corporate Audit Company in 1906. He served as its secretary-treasury.

Shortly after America entered World War I, Bird joined the American Red Cross on October 21, 1918, and served on the Balkan Commission. His work took him into a number of war-torn European countries that included Serbia, Romania, Albania, Greece, and Montenegro. Obtaining the rank of major, he was decorated in 1919 for his service during the relief effort in Armenia. Bird received the Order of Prince Danilo I of the third class by King Nicholas of Montenegro along with awards from the Kings of Serbia and Romania.

Following the death of Myrtle in 1920, Bird was a temporary widower. He married the former Ms. Julia Shay on February 17, 1921, and two daughters followed, Jeanne and Barbara.

As his accounting firm grew, Bird came into contact with a number of Dallas' elite and powerful. Among them was the vice president of Magnolia Petroleum, Frank V. Faulkner. The affable Faulkner was a strong supporter of Scouting and served on Circle Ten's executive board. Intrigued, Bird began working with Troop 30 and volunteered as the chairman of Camp Wisdom's camping committee, provided that Faulkner would serve as his co-chairman.

For nearly 25 years, the two partners "visited the camp every Wednesday" to assess its needs and take in its beauty.

"With Faulkner's money and my ideas," Bird once said, "we should make Camp Wisdom into something long remembered by Boy Scouts of this area."

When Faulkner died in 1951, Bird continued to visit thr camp but brought along daughters Jeanne and Barbara. By then, Jeanne had married Arkansas native Thomas A. O'Dwyer, who would eventually serve as Circle Ten's president from 1979 to 1980. Bird's grandson Thomas R. O'Dwyer would later serve as North Trail District's last chairman in 2011.

In 1961, an aging George Bird was bestowed with the title of Circle Ten's "Chief Scout," (the first was former Council Presdient George R. Angell) being the last man to hold that honorary position. In honor of Bird's 90th birthday in 1958 and his contributions to local Scouting, the Council dedicated to him a granite monument (below, right) and a flagpole in Camp Wisdom's assembly area.

As a living memorial to the pair, the Bird-Faulkner College Scholarship was established by 1961 from funds gifted by Frank Faulkner's estate into the Circle Ten Foundation. Two of the early recipients were Troop 543 Eagle Scout Robert Reitz of Oak Cliff and Troop 153 Eagle Scout Lee Smith of Dallas. Reitz attended the University of Texas in Austin, while Smith attended Harvard College in Cambridge, Massachusetts. Currently, Reitz, a Circle Ten Silver Beaver recipient, is the curator of the Harbin Scout Museum at Camp Wisdom, while Smith serves as the vice president in the Administration and Legal Affairs department at the University of Texas.

George Hedden Bird died in Dallas on August 18, 1964, from arteriosclerosis and is buried at the Calvary Hill Cemetery a few miles north of the John D. Murchison Scouting Center.[D]

THIS FLAG POLE ERECTED BY SCOUTS AND FRIENDS OF FORMER SCOUTMASTER GEORGE H. BIRD, IN GRATEFUL RECOGNITION OF THREE DEVOTED SCOUTERS:
GEORGE H. BIRD
JOHN S. "DADDY" WISDOM
FRANK V. FAULKNER
WHOSE VISION, INTEREST IN BOYS, ZEAL AND PERSONAL EFFORTS HAVE CONTRIBUTED SO MUCH TO THE THOUSANDS OF SCOUTS WHO HAVE CAMPED AT CAMP WISDOM
NOVEMBER 2, 1958

CIRCLE TEN COUNCIL PRESIDENT GEORGE R. ANGELL EARNS THE EAGLE SCOUT AWARD

IN 1933, *Circle Ten Council's former president, George Robinson Angell, earned the rank of Eagle Scout as an adult— the Council's first president to do so. Reported on the front page of the* Dallas Morning News *only weeks before as being two merit badges shy of the required 21 (those being Swimming and Lifesaving) the Rock Island Railroad division freight agent believed he had to lead by example and finish his quest to earn them. With confidence built from passing the First Aid merit badge test under the instruction of Scout Executive Orton Duggan, Angell soon earned both.*

1933 Eagle Scout George Angell later moved to Fort Worth as the railroad's assistant general freight agent but remained involved with Dallas Scouting.[E]

at the Bradfield School was Circle Ten Council's first in 1930. It wasn't until May 25, 1933, when the "experimental" label was removed from Cubbing and the program was mainstreamed nationally.[5]

After joining Cub Scouts, the nine-year-old boy would work on the Bobcat entrance requirements that included the Cub Scout Promise, the Cub Scout sign, and handshake. After passing, he worked on the rank of Wolf Cub. For that, the Cub had to repeat the Pledge of Allegiance from memory, understand basic U.S. flag regulations, and know the origins of Cubbing.

BELOW: Sandra Davila works with Scout Miguel Velasco on backpacking skills at the Sailers Point campsite at Camp Wisdom.

At age 10, the Cub worked on the Bear rank that included having knowledge of the history of the American flag and being able to identify international countries that had an operating Cub Scout program. After turning 11, the Cub worked on the Lion requirements and had to demonstrate "advanced flag courtesies, pass the Boy Scout Tenderfoot requirements concerning the U.S. flag, and show some knowledge of world geography or current events."

After earning any or all of those three ranks, the Cub worked on the 24 "elective activities" that resulted in the earning of either a gold or silver arrow point to be worn on his uniform shirt below his rank. Electives included things like Secret Codes, Electricity, Garden, Things that Go, and Bachelor Cooking.

By the end of 1930, there were 5,102 Cub Scouts across the nation within 243 packs in 93 councils. Locally, 16 boys were Circle Ten Council Cubs and

CIRCLE TEN'S 15,000TH REGISTERED SCOUT

ANOTHER HIGH POINT *for Circle Ten Council came in March 1934 when the 15,000th registered Boy Scout, George T. Connell, received his membership card from the hand of Council registrar, J. A. Yeager (below). Twelve-year-old George, a Cub Scout in Pack 3071 at the Bradfield Elementary School, was excited to join Scouting and participate in its adventurous activities.*

Ultimately graduating Highland Park High School in 1940, he eloped with his sweetheart shortly after receiving his diploma and enrolled at Southern Methodist University's School of Engineering. After the start of World War II, Connell joined the U.S. Air Force and served as a flight instructor throughout the conflict, developing a passion for flying that continued for the remainder of his life.

He founded the Connell Construction Company in 1947 and built local business parks like Stemmons North, Northlake, Beltline 35, and the Mary Kay Cosmetics Complex. He was a longtime member of the Dallas Salesmanship Club and served as the chairman for the PGA's Byron Nelson Golf Classic in 1973. He remained a faithful member of the Highland Park United Methodist Church and drove for Meals on Wheels as one of his many services to the community until his passing on March 16, 2006.[F]

CIRCLE TEN COUNCIL'S FIRST CUB SCOUTS TO CROSS-OVER INTO BOY SCOUTS

IN MAY 1932, *Thomas W. Shoop (below, left) and William Chunn Ballow (below, right) of Cub Scout Pack 3071 were the first Council Cubs to cross-over into Boy Scouts. Chunn Ballow was born in 1920 and went on to attend the University of Texas at Austin, pledging Phi Kappa Psi fraternity and moving around Texas on various work assignments. After settling in McKinney and eventually retiring to Grapevine, Ballow was a member of the Tarantula Train Railway Board and died in that town in January 2001.*

Thomas Shoop graduated the University of Missouri at Columbia, Missouri in 1940 after pledging the Kappa Alpha fraternity. After retirement, he moved to Plano, Texas, then to Colorado Springs, Colorado, and back to North Texas into the small town of Keller by 1994. He married in 1997 at age 77 to his 68-year-old bride, Mary Campbell. He passed away 21 months later in Dallas in February 1999.[G]

214 were about to join Scouting and form 10 new dens within four new Cub packs in 1931.

By the end of 1932, the Council had 10 packs with 296 Cubs and 47 registered adult Den Leaders or "Cubbers." One hundred and two Lion Cubs had "separated" or *crossed-over* from their packs to join Boy Scouting. The first two Cubs from Pack 3071

TOP: The Lion Level *Cubbook* was used by third year Cub Scouts. The square patches (Bear Cub on left, Wolf Cub patches at middle, right) represented the program over the years. ABOVE: Den mothers work with their Cubs at a Scout Exposition in 1939.

IF CIRCLE TEN COUNCIL *ever had a youth member that was a poster child for the benefits of Scouting, it was DeWitt Peyton Thompson.*

Born on October 11, 1911, in Denison, Texas, to DeWitt K. Thompson and his wife, the former Mae Roger Peyton, young DeWitt only had eight years with his father—the man had died by 1920. Living off family savings, mother and son moved to 4222 Swiss Avenue in Dallas where DeWitt attended the Terrill School a few doors away (now the Banc of Texas parking lot). Attaining the academic honor roll in 1926 but suffering from a "physical breakdown," out of pure desperation, Mae signed him up for Scouting as she believed its outdoor program to be the only way to "cure" him.

Joining Troop 60 under the direction of Scoutmaster George M. Haas, Thompson flourished and ran quickly through the ranks. He received the Eagle Award from Chief Scout Executive James E. West, himself, at the Council Court of Honor held in McFarlin Auditorium on the campus of Southern Methodist University (SMU) on January 26, 1928 (right, below right, below middle). Thompson was the Council's 54th Eagle Scout to date. As a Scout, he was an active staffer during summer sessions at Camp Wisdom and even gained election as a Wisdom Honor Camper as well as into the Tipi Huya, the honor society of local Eagle Scouts.

Graduating the Terrill School in June 1929, Thompson attended the World Jamboree held that summer in Birkenhead, England, in August.

Receiving a scholarship to SMU, he became the Assistant Scoutmaster of Troop 32 at the Highland Park Methodist Church, the same unit in which future Texas Governor William P. Clements Jr. was a member.

In 1933, Thompson was chosen to lead the Council's nine-person contingent to the World Jamboree in Hungary, thus becoming Circle Ten Council's first member to attend two World Jamborees (below left).

Graduating SMU in 1934, he left to become a field executive in the New Jersey Council located in North Bergen. By 1940, he had taken the position of Assistant Scout Executive in Shreveport, Louisiana, where he married Miss Leah Christine Quinn on June 15, 1940, producing a son, Jon, and daughter, Mollie. Remaining there for the next seven years, Thompson accepted the Scout Executive position in Pensacola, Florida. He stayed there until the early 1950s, when he accepted the same position in Anniston, Alabama.

Thompson migrated to Lubbock, Texas, and served as the South Plains Council's Scout Executive from 1965–1967, and after the passing of his first wife in 1963, he married Nelda Marie Snow on August 12, 1966.

Scout Executive DeWitt Peyton Thompson died in Lubbock on April 16, 1987, having spent his lifetime giving back more to Scouting than it had given to him.[H]

TOP: An early Cub Scout uniform. ABOVE: Boys of all ages participated in summer activities at Camp Wisdom, especially in the swimming pool. ACROSS TOP: In 1935, the national BSA organization celebrated the membership of its 5 millionth Scout. To celebrate, it printed a special edition of the *Handbook for Boys* and presented a copy to President Franklin D. Roosevelt. ACROSS BOTTOM: The Santa Fe Building in Dallas.

IN EARLY APRIL 1933, *150 adult Scouting leaders assembled at Circle Ten Council's headquarters in the Santa Fe Building (below) at 1114 Commerce Street for the first University of Scouting. Taking place over several sessions, courses educated new leaders on the art and skills of Scouting. The first session included classroom study, while the second took the form of an "all-night bivouac at Camp Wisdom."*

Council President Leslie B. Denning, served as the course director. Council bookkeeper Y. B. Yeager served as registrar. The dean was Dallas School Superintendent Dr. Justin F. Kimball, who also served as an inspirational speaker along with Dallas YMCA Executive W. G. Echols and attorney Earl Parker. The Heads of Departments included Troop 1 Scoutmaster Thomas Hord, Lloyd O'Neal, former Circle Ten Council President George R. Angell, Ford Automotive Assistant District Manager Ralph C. Buddington, Troop 1 alumnus and Eagle Scout Norman Hargrave, and Scout Executive Orton Duggan. Duggan also served as "administrator of the school."

"Practical demonstrations of various portions of Scout work and administration makes up a large portion of the school work," reported the Dallas Morning News.[1]

that crossed-over into Boy Scout Troop 71 were Thomas W. Shoop and W. Chunn Ballow.[6]

In 1936, Texas celebrated its state centennial with a large extravaganza and exposition at Fair Park in East Dallas. Region 9 Director James P. Fitch conferred with BSA's national director, Dr. Arthur A. Schuck, on the Council's participation. Fitch believed that 60,000 Scouts and Cubs could take part.

Texas Governor James V. Allred attended the celebration and delivered a speech entitled "A Centennial of Scouting" and shared the Centennial Exposition's auditorium stage with 16 former

A STAR SCOUT SAVES HIS SISTER

IN OCTOBER 1933, *four-year-old Nadine Nicholson of Terrell, Texas, in Kaufman County fell through a window at her home. Witnessing the accident, her 16-year-old brother, Star Scout Drue Edward Nicholson Jr. (below, left) used his Scout training to quiet her and stop the bleeding. Quickly, he fashioned a bandage and lightly pressed it to her head wound knowing that a roughly applied compress would imbed the glass fragments. Thirteen stitches were required to close the laceration.* [J]

Scouts who had distinguished themselves as adults. The nation's largest Boy Scout band that contained a staggering 267 pieces based in Springfield, Missouri performed as well.

Since Dallas hosted the Centennial, the Council offered facilities at Camp Wisdom for all visiting Scout units. Beginning on June 27, troops and packs visited from across the southwest, as well as Texas-based units. [7]

On June 16, the Fair Park gates opened and thousands of visitors rushed in—30,000 to start. Featured attractions were the legendary midway rides and carnival barkers that separated exposition-goers from their money. The public marriage of the

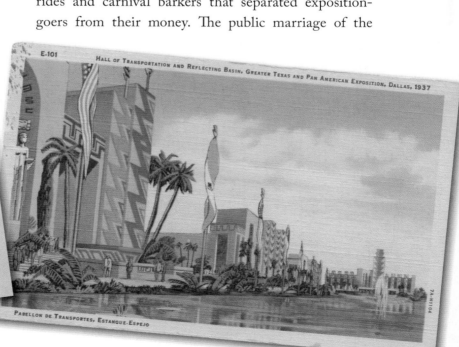

Hilton Siamese twins in the Cotton Bowl was particularly popular. However, other events were more serious such as the national folk festival that depicted 400 years of state history called the *Cavalcade of Texas*.

Its theme song titled *My Cowboy Love Song* was composed by the world famous Texas-born composer, David Wendell Guion, and was performed daily during the show's six-month run.

As exhibitors, Circle Ten Scouts displayed their skills in areas of "handicraft, camping gadgets, natural history collections, and first aid carts with uniformed Scouts on hand to explain the material." Even BSA's national office sent display material since it was an opportune event to advertise the Scouting program.

In addition to displays, Scouts performed a daily flag ceremony each evening with a Scout bugler blowing *Taps* and others firing a cannon as the sun set. It did not hurt that former Council president, Fred F. Florence, was the president of the Centennial Exposition Corporation in charge of producing the event.[8] The reviews of the Exposition were glowing.

One Scout leader crowed, "This $25,000,000 show is the greatest educational project ever conceived in Texas and will never be duplicated within the lifetime of the youngest child now living." Another claimed, "every pupil in Texas should have a chance to attend."

Circle Ten's own grand display (not dedicated until July 19) was located in a separate

ACROSS TOP: Members of Troop 1's Imperial Patrol in 1935. ACROSS LEFT and ACROSS BOTTOM LEFT: In 1936 and 1937, Dallas hosted Texas's Centennial celebrations as well as the Pan American World's Fair at Fair Park. Among the items for sale were special stamps sold in booklets and postcards that depicted the events and buildings. BELOW LEFT: One of the structures raised at the time was the Federal Building that, today, stands behind the 52-foot-tall icon of the Texas State Fair, Big Tex. BELOW RIGHT: Council President Fred F. Florence was also the chairman of the Centennial Exposition Corporation that put on the multi-year festivities.

locale between the Magnolia Building on the Fair Park grounds (built in 1936 by the oil company that would become ExxonMobil) and the Grand Avenue entrance. It depicted the Scout's trail from a nine-year-old Cub Scout through Eagle Scout. The underlying that Scouting was message was forge boys who were the place to trained for leadership."9 "thoroughly

"The whole exhibit is of a rustic nature, for in the great-out-of-doors Scouts get their thrill of romance and adventure," reported the *Dallas Morning News.* "There are ten living trees, a miniature lake, cooking gadgets, fireplaces, a signal tower, Indian lore, and relics including an Indian teepee made by the Scouts."

Manning the teepee was Eagle Scout Al Avery, president of the Tipi Huya. Much of Al's time was spent hitting a rhythmic beat on an Indian tom-tom drum in full Scout uniform, complete with a regulation BSA tie.

This exhibit included a large bronze plaque emblazoned with the words from the Declaration of Independence that was presented to the Council's Scouts by local candy salesman George D. Wiley. Also, Will R. Wilson presented Admiral Byrd's 1934 Antarctic expedition outboard motor to Henry Shull of Troop 1, as he had won it in a national contest on airplane knowledge. The motor was turned over to Council Scout Commissioner and local attorney, Claude D. Bell Sr. for safekeeping and put on public display in Council headquarters.10

After closing on November 29, the 1936 Centennial Exposition had attracted over 6.3 million visitors and created over 10,000 local jobs—helping stave off the local effects of the Depression. Dallas' investment in new buildings and structures were quickly used again as 2 million more visitors made their way to the Great Texas & Pan American Exposition—a World's Fair—that ran in Fair Park from June through October 1937. Many of these buildings are still standing and being used today.

In honor of the Texas Centennial, the Wisdom Honor Campers made their way to the 8,000-foot-high El Capitan peak within the Guadalupe Mountains National Park, at the time believed to be the state's highest (it is actually the eighth). The group planted a Texas flag provided by the Centennial committee at its summit.

ABOVE LEFT: Tipi Huya President Al Avery mans the organization's exhibit at the 1936 Texas Centennial celebration. ABOVE RIGHT: A 1930s sash once belonging to a Circle Ten Eagle Scout now in the permanent collection of the Harbin Scout Museum. ACROSS TOP: The program given out at the farewell dinner of Scout Executive Orton L. Duggan in 1936. ACROSS BOTTOM: Scouts from Troop 32 prepare to deliver Christmas toys to needy families in Highland Park.

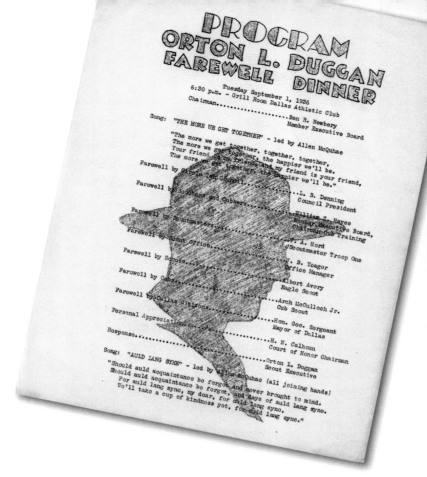

CHRISTMAS SERVICE PROJECTS

CIRCLE TEN COUNCIL'S units have long served the community. In November 1931, the Community Chest (similar to today's United Way) requested Council assistance in distributing promotional literature connected with its annual Christmas funding drive. Over 1,000 Scouts answered the call and went door-to-door handing out 260,000 pieces of Chest literature in two hours.

As the Chest had not the manpower (boy-power) to perform such a large task on its own, Scouting again came to the rescue and confirmed its positive impact within Dallas.

Another Christmas service project that was performed involved the Scouts of Troop 32 (below) sponsored by the Highland Park Methodist Church. They repaired broken toys for "Santa Claus" that had been collected year-round in their Sunday school classes. Many donations were rehabilitated simply with hammer and paint—an effort that resulted in local families having a Merry Christmas during the depths of the Great Depression.[K]

Led by Scoutmaster Thomas Hord, the Scouts rested the day before the ascent at the ruins of old Butterfield Fort in the Guadalupe Pass (also in the National Park) that had been a main stop on the Pony Express. A trail guide met the group (along with Scout Executive Duggan and Dallas Mayor George Sergeant) as they left for the peak and led them to the top.[11]

The climb effectively marked the end to Orton Duggan's tenure as Circle Ten Council's Scout Executive. Upon returning, he tendered his resignation effective September 15. Accepting the post as the chief executive of the Knoxville (Tennessee) Council, Duggan returned home to be near his elderly mother. His father had died recently and Duggan was named the executor of his estate. Council board member Neth Leachman led the search committee to find his replacement, while Claude Bell led the farewell committee.

IN FEBRUARY 1934, *Troop 1 Scoutmaster Thomas Hord had the distinct honor of being the first local Scoutmaster to lead two generations of Scouts in one family—Illinois-born Theodore E. Lynn Sr. and son Ted Jr. In a recognition ceremony held at the troop's meeting place at the First Baptist Church in Oak Cliff, the Lynns were asked to join the rest of the troop to hear President Franklin D. Roosevelt's national radio address to the Boy Scouts of America in honor of Scouting's 24th anniversary.*

Ted the elder, a traveling salesman for a local hardware company, joined Hord's troop as a boy in the mid-1910s after his father, a member of the Dallas Shrine, witnessed the service of the Dallas Council Scouts at the 1913 Shriners Imperial Conclave and parade. His son, Ted Jr., joined Troop 1 in 1934. Although neither achieved the rank of Eagle Scout both performed distinguished service to the country as adults.

As direct descendants of Revolutionary War veteran Andrew Lynn Jr. of the Pennsylvania Militia, the Lynns believed heartily in military service. Ted the elder enlisted in World War I while Ted Jr. joined the U.S. Marine Corps in World War II fighting in the battles of Midway Island and Guadalcanal.

During the Korean War in September 1950, Ted Jr. was a member of the 1st Marine Regiment during the Inchon Landing, serving as a "radioman." Cited for "gallantry in action against an enemy of the United States" and being wounded in action, he received two Silver Stars and the Purple Heart.

Theodore E. Lynn Jr. died in 1988 and is buried at Restland Cemetery in North Dallas along with his parents.[L]

"He is a Christian gentleman and he carries his spirit into his work that would win success in anyone," proclaimed Council President Leslie B. Denning. "His leaving is a distinct loss to Dallas and the boys of Circle Ten Council. We wish him continued success."[12]

During Duggan's tenure as Scout Executive, membership numbers increased 30 percent from 2,667 Scouts in January 1931 when he arrived to 3,792 at his departure. He had recruited 17 Cub packs that totaled 689 new youngsters, six Negro troops, and Hispanic Troop 100 sponsored by the Presbyterian

ACROSS FAR LEFT: Scoutmaster Thomas Hord (left) with Theodore Lynn Sr (right) and son, Ted Jr. (middle) in 1934. ABOVE: Troop 162 sponsored by the B. F. Darrell School. TOP: Troop 100, sponsored by the Presbyterian Mexican Mission, was the second Hispanic troop to be formed in Dallas around 1935. ABOVE RIGHT: Council President Milton Brown.

ACROSS TOP: Happy summer campers at Camp Wisdom in 1936. ACROSS BOTTOM: DeWitt Thompson (left), Norman Hargrave (middle), and an unidentified staff member in their cabin during the 1931 summer sessions at Camp Wisdom. ABOVE: Camp Wisdom summer campers working on a leatherwork project in 1931.

Mexican Mission. Today, the location of that former Mission sits just north of the American Airlines Center at 1803 Payne Street at the corner of N. Akard, now a Victory Park parking lot.

As a Depression era Scout Executive, Duggan understood that Circle Ten had to remain financially solvent with fewer resources. He slashed expenses and fired staff (including reducing three field directors, now known as district executives,

down to one) and successfully increased the monetary intake through new donations and, with the help of Council treasurer and Mercantile National Bank Vice President Milton Brown, paid the outstanding debt from $25,000 down to $9,000.

Upon his departure, every bill prior to August 1, 1936, was paid, leaving $6,000 in cash in the bank. The Council was moving toward financial independence and ready for its next Scout Executive.

THAT MAN WOULD ARRIVE IN THE PERSON OF FORT WAYNE, INDIANA, NATIVE LOYS L. HOTCHKISS AND UNDER HIM CIRCLE TEN COUNCIL WOULD ENTER ITS GOLDEN AGE OF EXPANSION.[13]

chapter 9

SCOUTING FOR ALL BOYS (1937–1940)

"The rewards that men can gain in taking part in the character building of the younger generation are beyond estimation."

MILTON BROWN
PRESIDENT, CIRCLE TEN COUNCIL (1940–45)
FEBRUARY 7, 1938

WITH 1936 NEARING A CLOSE, Dallas attorney and chairman of Circle Ten Council's executive search committee, Neth Leachman, had large shoes to fill with the departure of Scout Executive Orton L. Duggan. With nominations being passed back and forth among its members and recommendations coming in from Region 9 Director James P. Fitch, in mid-October, the final decision was made in the upper-story Director's Room of the Mercantile National Bank.[1]

The Council found their man in longtime Scout Executive Loys Leon Hotchkiss, a person of gentle nature who had been involved with Scouting since joining the organization at the tender age of 13-years in 1911. As an adult, "Hotch" had served as both a Scoutmaster and a volunteer Scout Commissioner.

He and wife Martha, a former Camp Fire Girl, had been high school sweethearts and were very comfortable with "talking shop" at home about Scouting. Now blessed with an eight-year-old

Circle Ten Scout Executive Loys L. Hotchkiss.

One of the service projects performed by Council Scouts during the Great Depression era was a door-to-door polio awareness campaign. Unknown by many at the time, President Franklin D. Roosevelt had been stricken with the disease years before.

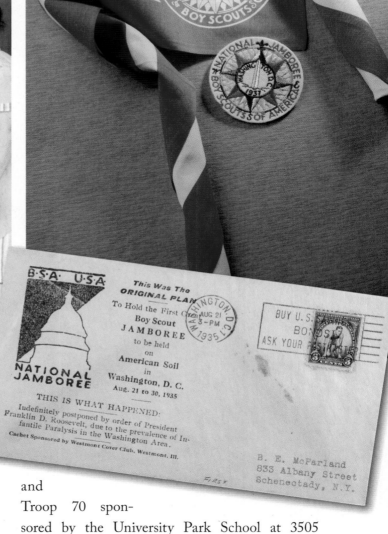

daughter, Nancy, and a six-year-old son, Bob, the Hotchkisses were pleased to start their new life in Dallas. Of particular interest to him were the Scout Circuses, merit badge exhibitions, and other large Council-wide activities such as camporees and service projects.[2]

Arriving in October 1936, he had little time to prepare for the Council's upcoming service project in November—the Community Chest's Smile Day clothes collection drive. Like in years past, Scouts canvassed the city collecting worn but usable clothes for needy Dallas families.

Although most local troops worked this project, some units added additional ones to their Christmas docket of activities Units like Troop 55 located at the East Dallas Christian Church at 629 N. Peak Street and

Troop 70 sponsored by the University Park School at 3505 Amherst Avenue each collected and delivered "baskets of food and clothing to poor families." The members of Troop 29 from the Temple Emanu-El synagogue at S. Harwood Street and South Boulevard, (the third location for Dallas' oldest Jewish house of worship and now resting under Interstate Highway 45 South), collected a "truck full of toys" for children and residents on Park Row, South Boulevard, and Forest Avenue

ACROSS BOTTOM LEFT: When national BSA turned 25-years-old in 1935, Chief Scout Executive James E. West planned for a grand National Jamboree of Scouts to be held in Washington, DC at the invitation of President Franklin D. Roosevelt. However, an outbreak of polio caused the event to be cancelled. ACROSS TOP LEFT and ABOVE: Rescheduled for 1937, many Dallas area Scouts participated in the event such as future Eagle Scout Lem Johnson III from University Park. Displayed are some of the actual items taken by him to the 1937 National Jamboree.

between Cleveland and Meadow. As reported by the *Dallas Morning News*, "The toys were delivered to the fire station on Forest Avenue for distribution to underprivileged children for Christmas presents."[3]

As the first National Jamboree planned for 1935 was cancelled due to a polio outbreak, in 1937 the Council began preparations for the re-scheduled event that would take place in June and July in Washington, DC. With Circle Ten managers expecting 100 Scouts to make the trip to the nation's capitol, the first two local Scouts chosen made the front page of the *Dallas Morning News* on January 2. They were Mike Mahoney and James A. Tucek, both of Troop 87 at St. Edward's Catholic Church at 4001 Elm Street

in East Dallas. Mahoney was a student of the Crozier Technical High School (the current name of the Dallas Central High School) and a Life Scout. Tucek attended St. Joseph's High School and edited the troop's newspaper.[4]

Other early registrants were Eagle Scout Edward Overbeck (the senior patrol leader of Troop 23 under the direction of his Scoutmaster father) and Eagle Scout Forrest Greene Jr. of Troop 57 in Arlington, Texas. Not only was Forrest scheduled to attend the National Jamboree but he also was preparing to head overseas for the 1937 World Jamboree being held in Holland.

Another Jamboree participant was young Lemuel Homer Johnson III of N. Fitzhugh Avenue in

TOWN OF DAWSON, NAVARRO CO., TEXAS

The yellowed card found in one of my mother's carefully maintained scrapbooks is a reminder of an era long passed that speaks of pride in accomplishment, of good times, of having little that meant much, of camaraderie, and of honor.

This is to certify that Carl Matthews Became a

SECOND CLASS SCOUT
April 8, 1939

Signed: L. L. Hotchkiss, Scout Executive

705 Dallas Gas Bldg   Dallas, Texas

My hometown of Dawson, Texas, had been without a Boy Scout Troop for a decade after a failed attempt by someone to form a troop in the 1920s. But Ralph Glenn Akers, the Davis twins, Sparton Duke, and other older boys in Dawson still had remnants of some old uniforms and a Boy Scout Handbook. In the Depression years of the 1930s, 12-year-old boys had little to occupy their time other than school, home chores, and church.

Although I don't know how it happened—maybe someone in Circle Ten Council approached someone in our little town to organize a new troop. Regardless, Conrad "Sonny Boy" Newton Jr. and Rev. R. Glenn Commander, pastor of the Dawson Baptist Church, became Scout Leaders and the initial meetings were held in fall 1938.

Our newspaper, the Dawson Herald published by Mr. F. H. Butler each Thursday probably carried an announcement that a troop would be formed and that 12-year-old boys could join. I suspect other announcements were made at school and at the local churches. The meeting place was to be the large vacant room over the bank. I remember that the troop met on Monday evenings and was very well attended.

Scouts included Gene Allen Holt, Reuben Travis Connor, Sambo Akers, Hugh Lewis Womack, Douglas Bankston, Jimmy Cornelius, A. M. & Walter Hulen, and others whose names have been forgotten.

Brother Commander and Sonny Boy Newton made Scouting a serious business. Meetings began with the recitation of the Scout Oath and motto, along with the Pledge of Allegiance. The Scout Oath was filled with fine moral ambitions and each young Scout wanted to follow the path the Oath blazed.

We all had to memorize the Scout Oath and motto and know how to give the Scout salute in order to earn the Tenderfoot rank. Next, we worked toward becoming Second Class Scouts, which demanded further memory work in addition to learning several basic skills such as trailing, signals, and cooking.

I recall one Second Class requirement was to learn various ways to tie a rope knot, specifically the square knot and the sheepshank. Once a Scout demonstrated proficiency in tying these required knots in front of an adult leader, he initialed the completion of that requirement on the Scout's advancement card that listed all of the requirements.

Other requirements like "tracking and reading signs" necessitated completion in the out-of-doors. Around September the Dawson Boy Scouts scheduled an overnight hike to a wooded area near Spring Hill on some land owned by Will Matthews.

Each Scout was responsible for his own needs but no one had a Scout uniform, a tent, or a sleeping bag. So, we slept under the stars on old quilts that our mothers permitted us to use. Our food was whatever the family could spare. My mother prepared an "amplecy" of corn bread, sausage and ham, biscuits and jelly. They were all homemade items with nothing from the store.

Jimmy Cornelius and A. M. Hulen had some "store boughten" items that had real class like canned french fries and canned fruit. At the time, I had never eaten canned french fries but canned fruit was available at our house on a few occasions. I was thrilled when the boys shared them with me.

The hike from the Scout meeting place over the bank to the Spring Hill area was exciting. We did not look like "real" Boy Scouts because we had no uniforms or Scout hats. But we were Scouts, and presented ourselves that way as we paraded in an orderly manner through town.

One or two of the boys had secured Scout neckerchiefs, complete with regulation slides that bore the Boy Scouts of America's emblem. Douglas Bankston wore some World War I "nickers" and a heavy World War I woolen shirt. His legs were wrapped with matching strips of cloth.

When we reached our destination, the first order of business was to prepare for the night. Each Scout unrolled his quilt and placed it neatly and orderly on the ground. When accommodations for sleeping were completed, it was time to prepare the evening meal, which everyone was ready for. That was the time for laughing, joking, sharing stories, and for camaraderie.

Scouts were to be "clean" and our leaders made sure we left no unsightly trash to violate nature's beauty. When the sun faded out and darkness moved into the woods, we lit the campfire held within a ring of large stones. We gathered additional wood and placed it nearby to keep the fire going during the night hours.

That evening, Sonny Boy and Brother Commander gave us our instructions. They reminded us of our obligations as Boy Scouts to our country, to our community, to our parents, and to ourselves. It was a good learning experience for our young minds. Afterward, Brother Commander taught us some songs that were appropriate to sing around a campfire.

One was . . .

"There's a long, long nail . . . a winding
Up through the sole of my shoe,
And it's wound its way into my foot
A mile or two . . . !

There's a long, long road before me
And what I'm thinking about . . .
Is to set me down in some nice spot,
And pull that darn nail out!

The campfire session ended with the recitation of the Scout Oath—with all of us standing tall and straight, and exhibiting the three finger Scout sign. Then we went to bed around the fire ring.

In the morning, we did not need an alarm clock to remind us when to arise because as daybreak neared, the temperature began to drop and we began to shiver. Fresh logs were added to the campfire and we lost no time gathering around the warm flames with quilts wrapped around our shaking bodies. Daylight's rays were welcomed.

For breakfast, someone back in town had donated ham and eggs, and Brother Commander prepared a hearty breakfast for his hungry Scouts.

As an activity to earn Second Class, we had to follow a trail blazed with markings made by another Scout. Having received instruction at a previous Scout meeting, we were excited to try it. One by one we started and followed the trail to its end. When each completed the quest, the adults placed the date and his initials on the Scout's advancement card. Most of us completed the requirement for Second Class in only a few months.

Back at home, another activity during the wintertime was boxing. A boxing area was marked on the floor of the meeting room and each week we had several matches. One week I was paired with Reuben Travis Connor. Before the bout, Brother Commander reminded me that Reuben was heavier and taller than I, but that I was faster. When the bell sounded, I may have torn into him with 65 pounds of "faster" but he beat the tar out of me with "heavier and taller" in all three rounds.

Later, Reuben and I did our 14-mile hike for the rank of First Class. Early one Saturday morning, we hiked from Dawson to the town of Hubbard and back. We traveled along the railroad track that sat adjacent to the "old Hiway 31." Unexpectedly, we saw Sonny Boy Newton in his car. Not realizing that we were Scouting, he stopped, backed up, and offered us a ride back to town. We told him what we were doing and he waved back at us and went on his way. At the next Scout meeting, Sonny Boy initialed "Item 5—Fourteen Mile Hike" on our advancement cards and wrote the date, April 15, 1939. It went along with "Item 11—Nature," and "Item 12—Oath & Law" initialed previously on March 11.

My family moved away from Dawson the following summer and within a few years most of the members of Troop 253 had joined the armed forces that served in World War II. Sonny Boy was in the China-Burma area and returned to be president of the Dawson Bank. Brother Commander left Dawson to become a pastor of several churches in Texas and New Mexico. He died in 2007. And what became of all the members of Troop 253? I couldn't say. That would probably require writing a large book, but those were some of the greatest days of my life.

Carl W. Matthews Jr. is the patriarch of three generations of Circle Ten Boy Scouts and makes his home in Cedar Hill, Texas

THE CIRCLE TEN COUNCIL CONTINGENT TO THE 1937 NATIONAL JAMBOREE

ON JUNE 21, 1937, sixty-six Circle Ten Scouts and eight leaders were divided into two groups of 33 boys and four adults each that made-up the membership of National Jamboree Troops 18 and 19. Scoutmasters Rufus McClung of Troop 34, D. W. Bright of Troop 45, and Bill Flowers, led the first unit. Scoutmasters R. E. McHenry of Troop 30, Anson van Slyke of Troop 66, and J. E. Johnson of Troop 70 led the second. Additional men who escorted the contingent were Troop 1 Scoutmaster Thomas Hord of Oak Cliff, Region 9 Director James R. Fitch, and C. C. Boren of Troop 204 in Ennis. With them, they brought their gateway to be raised at the campsite.

With "packs on backs and prepared for everything," the 77-member contingent left Dallas' Union Terminal train station for the two-day train ride to New York City. After some sightseeing that included the Empire State Building, Coney Island, and the Statue of Liberty,

they departed for a tour of Philadelphia's Independence Hall and other sites before leaving for the District of Columbia. However, their interest briefly turned to a pair of boys that had hiked on their own to the Jamboree—from South America.

Arriving a week earlier from Venezuela were South American Boy Scouts Rafael Petit and Juan Carmona, who had completed their 800-mile journey to Washington by walking the entire way from their hometown of Caracas. The two teenage boys had left their country on January 11, 1935, and covered 25 miles a day for two years to make it to the American Jamboree on time.

At the opening parade held on June 30, President Franklin D. Roosevelt rode in an open-air automobile with Chief Scout Executive James E. West and National Scout Commissioner Daniel Carter Beard—all escorted by a group of Eagle Scouts.

"We are a people in transition. We are continuously working out a civilization. You share it. You will improve it," said Roosevelt. "That is the undimmed glory of youth. That is the challenge of our time."

While there, the Scouts from Regions 8 and 9 performed the "Texas Under the Stars" arena show for the 25,000 attendees that included President Roosevelt, himself. The show included chariot races, a rodeo, a cyclone, and a Kansas land rush, all performed by the boys from Texas, Oklahoma, Kansas, Nebraska, New Mexico, and Missouri.

"Costumed pioneers in wagons and astride horses will race for choice land sites and a frontier village will be leveled by a tornado, followed by a first aid demonstration on the victims," reported the Dallas Morning News. "Elaborate lighting and sounds effects have been arranged."

The regional display was staged in a "huge pavilion built near the base of the Washington Monument."

In the Texas camp, chuck wagons from Fort Worth, Sweetwater, and San Angelo "provided color" along with oil drums cut in half and suspended by ropes as hammocks. For their museum display, the contingent brought along hundreds of Horned toads, non-poisonous snakes in

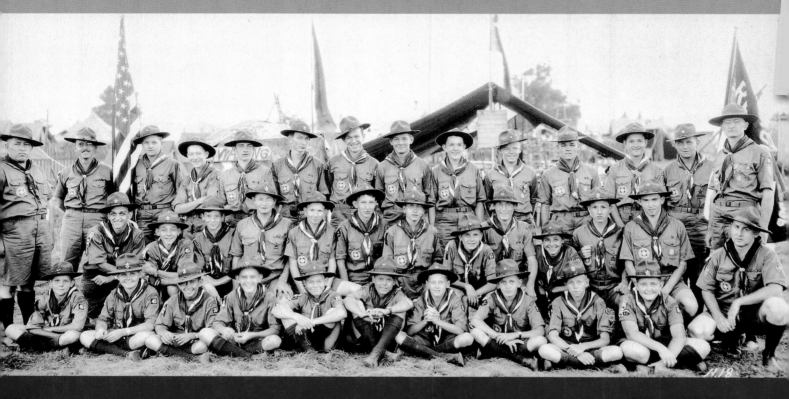

glass cases, dead rattlesnakes packed in alcohol, and native plant material.

Local day trips included excursions to George Washington's home and grave at Mount Vernon in nearby Alexandria, Virginia, the Naval Academy at Annapolis, Maryland, and the Capitol building. At the end of the Jamboree, half of the 2,800 Texas Scouts left for St. Louis, while the others traveled to New York City on special trains. Unlike other Scouting excursions, it was reported that many Scouts had actually gained weight during the trip as food was tasty and plentiful.

"All we know now is that this Jamboree has exceeded all expectations," exclaimed a relieved Chief Scout Executive West. "It most certainly has been less of a headache than we expected."[1]

ACROSS BOTTOM LEFT and FAR BELOW: These wonderful images of the two Circle Ten Council contingent troops reside in the photographic collection of the Harbin Scout Museum. BELOW LEFT: President Franklin D. Roosevelt presenting an Eagle medal to his Scout escort in the Jamboree parade. Seated beside him are Chief Scout Executive James E. West (middle) and National Scout Commissioner Daniel Carter Beard (right). BELOW: Circle Ten Scouts traveled to Washington, DC via special train that donned the temporary graffiti scribbled on it by enthusiastic Dallas Scouts.

University Park. "Lem" was a freshman student at North Dallas High School, where he participated in the band and the ROTC program.

Like in the cancelled 1935 event, national BSA planners divided the Jamboree site into 25 villages located on the Mount Vernon Memorial Highway. Jamboree organizers promoted the trading of items as a way to build camaraderie among Scouts from different regions, much like today, but in 1937 the trading items were different—sometimes living.

For Lem, his prime swapping objects were live lizards or Texas "horned toads," so named for their blunt snout, rounded body, and spines on their back. It is not currently known what he got in exchange for his lizards, but the story of another Scout's swap does exist.

When trading at the Jamboree, Washington state Scout Parker Ward traded a neckerchief slide for a horned toad, but on this occasion, it probably turned out better for Parker. Upon consummation of the deal, his new pet gave birth to 19 babies, making it a 20-for-1 swap.[5] No record exists as to what his mother said when he brought them home.

In a similar trading coup, the young Harold J. Lankford of Edwardsville, Illinois, traded a now forgotten knick-knack for a live baby alligator from a Florida boy. On the train ride home it bit the finger of the Scout sitting next to him who was teasing it.

In 1939, Harold earned his Eagle award and moved to Texas. He eventually became a successful insurance agent in Dallas as well as the proud father and grandfather to four Circle Ten Eagle Scouts.[6]

As 1937 came to a close, Scout Executive Hotchkiss had increased the number of troops from 160 to 175. Scout membership had grown over 11 percent to about 3,500 Scouts from 3,123 when he began. The number of registered Scouters had

Dallas Scouts Register First for '37 Jamboree At Washington in June

LEFT: Scouts Mike Mahoney (top) and James A. Turek (bottom) were the first two boys to sign up to participate in the 1937 National Jamboree from Dallas. ABOVE: This is the official Jamboree participation card issued Lem Johnson III by the Boy Scouts of America. RIGHT: This registration card belonged to Assistant Scoutmaster Sandy Fletcher of Troop 309 in Plano, Texas.

AS 1937 CAME TO A CLOSE, *a new Council program was beginning—the Order of the Arrow or "Brotherhood of Cheerful Service"—BSA's official national honor society. Dating back to the Treasure Island summer camp held in the Philadelphia Area Council in 1915, current members wore a white sash with a red arrow over their right shoulder.*

Arrowmen were elected for membership by their fellow Scouts on an annual ballot based upon the service that they would perform once initiated through a fourfold Ordeal; the eating of scant food to demonstrate temperance, the keeping of silence to promote inward reflection, the performance of arduous labor to show a willingness serve others, and sleeping alone under the stars to symbolically demonstrate one's bravery.

Although Scout Executive Hotchkiss had already received national BSA permission to start a lodge in June 1937, Circle Ten Scouts only truly became aware of the Order when seeing many "white sash-wearing Scouts" at the 1937 National Jamboree in Washington, DC. The Council finance report even had a line item for "Order of Arrow" as early as November 1, 1937.

Early Circle Ten members of the Mikanakawa Lodge (the name of the Council's Order of the Arrow franchise) were Eagle Scout members John Mier, Charles Blaha, Eugene Dougherty along with Cecil Cameron of Dallas, Red Lanier, and brothers Fred and Bill Haynes of Plano. Fred Haynes was elected as Mikanakawa's first Lodge Chief in 1937 and Cecil Cameron was his successor in 1938. The first annual Mikanakawa Lodge banquet was held in the Oak Cliff YMCA in 1938.

One of the earliest and best-loved Mikanakawa Lodge service projects was the annual pilgrimage to the grave of Daddy Wisdom at nearby Wheatland Cemetery. First led by Lodge Chief Cameron in 1938, Scouts, Cubs, leaders, families, and friends met at the gravesite and placed wreaths made from branches of Daddy's "perfect cedar trees" on his grave. Then a history of Camp Wisdom was recounted. After the ceremony, everyone headed for camp and partook in late afternoon activities and a tour followed by a barbeque, just like the ones that Daddy threw for the boys after his Christmas winter camps.[B]

ABOVE: The Wisdom Honor Camper program began winding down in 1937 after the adoption of BSA's soon-to-be national honor society, the Order of the Arrow (OA). One of the last recipients of the Honor Camper recognition was Eagle Scout John Leedom of University Park's Troop 32 (above), who eventually became a Texas State Senator. One of his fellow troopmates was future Texas Governor William P. "Bill" Clements Jr. FAR LEFT: Membership in the OA was symbolized by the white sash bearing a red arrow. The red felt arrow sewn to the sash (left) was one of the earliest versions, followed some years later by the flocked red arrow on the sash (middle). The red triangle was added to represent the highest level of membership in the OA—the Vigil Honor (right). TOP: Along with the sash, a membership patch was issued for uniform wear. The first Mikanakawa Lodge 101 patch was in the shape of an arrowhead bearing the owl as its totem and the 3 "W's" representing "the Brotherhood of Cheerful Service." LEFT: These early OA membership cards belonged to Circle Ten Council Scout Eddie Reitz (top) and Lem Johnson III (bottom).

HOMER C. JONES— GARLAND'S FIRST ORDER OF THE ARROW MEMBER

ABOVE: A 1937 patrol of Scouts from which several would earn the Eagle rank in the 1940s.

HOMER COLE JONES *was born on October 16, 1923, in the small town of Electra, Texas, near Wichita Falls to Homer D. Jones and wife, Mary. The elder Jones worked as a salesman in a dry goods store until he moved his family to Garland in the early 1930s.*

Enrolled as a Lone Scout in January 1938, young Homer was an extremely enthusiastic Scout, so much so that his work helped inspire growth of the local program through his aggressive merit badge work.

"[His] example as a Scout has contributed to the interest in Scouting in the community to the point that a Scout leaders' training school is now under way with fourteen men enrolled," declared the Dallas Morning News.

By mid-March, Homer had earned the rank of Tenderfoot and joined Troop 111 at the First Presbyterian Church in downtown Garland under the direction of Scoutmaster C. E. Fuller.

On August 4, 14-year-old Homer Jones received the rank of Eagle Scout (along with his 38th merit badge) at the Court of Honor held in the Nicholson Memorial Hall at the northeast corner of Garland's city square—becoming the city's second Eagle Scout after the 1929 presentation to David Loving Tisinger Sr. of Garland's Troop 1.

As Troop 111's senior patrol leader, his excellent leadership prompted his election into the Order of the Arrow—Garland's first inductee—on July 20, 1939, at Camp Wisdom.

When World War II broke out, Homer joined the U.S. Army Air Corps and gained the rank of 1st Lieutenant. Afterward, he entered the Baylor University College of Dentistry where he earned his degree and later began his practice.

Marrying Barbara Jean Coates, they had two children, Don Homer and Sheryn, and moved to north to Bonham, Texas by 1952. While there, Homer served as a local Scoutmaster.

Dr. Homer Cole Jones passed away on October 9, 1997, and is buried near his parents in Bonham's Willow Wild Cemetery.[D]

[image caption:] Garland Boy to Get Highest Scout Rank
HOMER COLE JONES.

expanded by 33 percent to 1,149 with an additional 750 Cubs and 90 Cubbers working in a total of 18 packs. Also the new Senior Scout Explorer program had begun in Circle Ten with an initial six crews. The Council also proudly had 64 African American Scouts in eight troops along with 21 Hispanic Scouts in two troops.

To maintain such progress, Hotchkiss recognized that Circle Ten needed to perform better in publicizing its community work, declaring it as "not organized" in the 1937 Charter Renewal to the National Council. He also noted that Circle Ten needed some "reorganizing," (assessing it as being only "fair" when meeting its goals), and thought Cubbing needed more attention. However, he was satisfied with the goal of "enlarging membership in 1937."[7]

Within the advancement arena, 37 boys earned the Lion Cub rank and crossed-over into Scouting. There were 117 Eagle Scouts enrolled who earned a collective 48 bronze palms, 29 gold palms, and 10 silver palms. The number of merit badges awarded in 1937 stood at 1,469 with the most popular being Public Health (71), Swimming (68), First Aid (65), Civics (60), Cooking (57), Bird Study (56), and Safety (50). The least popular badges completed by only one Scout each included Architecture, Foundry Practice, Soil Management, Textiles, and Fruit Culture.

FRED E. HAYNES JR.—MIKANAKAWA LODGE'S FIRST CHIEF

By Robert Reitz, Curator, Harbin Scout Museum

FRED ELMER HAYNES JR. *was the oldest child born to farm loan inspector Fred E. Haynes Sr. and his wife, Louise. Spending much of his early years in the community of Plano, he joined the Lone Scouting program as a Tenderfoot on July 3, 1931, as there were no units in his immediate area. Working through the ranks on his own, he eventually joined Troop 309 and earned the Eagle Scout medal at age 13 on February 8, 1935, at Fair Park on BSA's 25th anniversary. The celebration was attended by 2,000 local Scouts and dignitaries that included Texas Governor James V. Allred.*

As a young person, he was an accomplished whittler having won 4th place in a national competition, as well as the Marksman designation in the Junior National Rifle Association. Fred was the president of his sophomore class at Plano High School, where he played football in the position of center from 1934 through 1936. He also ran track.

He attended Camp Wisdom from 1932 to 1937 and was elected an Honor Camper, completing all four parts of the Wisdom Guide program that included "Veteran," which meant serving as a camp staff member. When Circle Ten Council adopted the Order of the Arrow program during the late summer of 1937, Fred was chosen as the first Lodge Chief of the newly formed Mikanakawa Lodge.

After graduating high school, Fred continued his studies at Southern Methodist University, where he was a Senior Honor student, lettered in track, and presided over Alpha Phi Omega, Scouting's collegiate service fraternity.

Fred soon joined the Marine Corps obtaining the rank of lieutenant, where he served as a member of Combat Team 28 in the taking of Mount Suribachi at the Battle of Iwo Jima in 1944 during World War II.

As a colonel, he commanded a combat team during the Vietnam War and acted as the top operations officer of all Marine forces in that conflict during 1967. Promoted to brigadier general, he commanded both the 2nd and 3rd Marine Divisions and retired a major general.

He was the first Marine Corps officer elected to the Council of Foreign Relations and was Chairman Emeritus of the American Turkish Council. For his work in encouraging Turkish Scouting, he was awarded the Silver Beaver medal by the Transatlantic Council in 1961.

With James A. Warren, General Haynes co-authored the 2008 book, The Lions of Iwo Jima—The Story of Combat Team 28 and the Bloodiest Battle in Marine Corps History. *He was the last living officer involved in the planning and coordination of that attack.*

Major General Fred E. Haynes Jr. passed away in New York City on March 10, 2010. His wife Bonnie said that of all of his accomplishments, none were more important to him than his Scouting successes.

BELOW: Scout Fred Haynes in 1934. FAR LEFT and LOWER LEFT: Haynes' Scouting experiences included the 1937 National Jamboree and several years at Camp Wisdom as seen by the patches on the back of his merit badge sash. He also completed the Wisdom Guide program and earned all five parts of the medal. TOP LEFT: This is one of Haynes' early Mikanakawa Lodge membership cards (top) as well as his Eagle Scout card (bottom).

WHILE VISITING TREASURE ISLAND *outside Philadelphia, Pennsylvania during the 1915 sum-*

mer camp season, Waco Council Scout Executive Nat Hayes was inducted into a new Scouting honor society founded by Scout Executives E. Urner Goodman and Carroll A. Edson. Hayes was charged with taking word of the Order of the Arrow society, then known as the Wimachtendienk (wo-mok-ten-dink) or "Brotherhood," back home to the Waco Council in Central Texas. It would gain national popularity through similar word of mouth exposure.

> **BOY SCOUT EXECUTIVES FORM CHAPTER OF WO-MOK-TUM-YANK.**
>
> A chapter of the Wo-mok-tum-yank was installed last night at Boy Scout headquarters under the direction of Nat Hayes, scout executive of Waco. The Wo-mok-tum-yank is composed of scout leaders and officials, scoutmasters and assistants and one representative from each troop of eight members.
>
> The order is fostered with the idea of instilling the higher ideals of scouting into the organization and has been successful in the East. The Dallas chapter is the first to be organized in Texas.
>
> The following have been granted membership: Otto Lang, Herbert L. Crate, W. A. Zischang, Henry B. Goodnight, C. C. Carpenter, Alan Hord, J. H. Taylor, E. J. Blaine, Harrison McGill, T. N. Crawford, Albert Walker, Allan Boyle, Dale Sedgwick, Dr. G. W. Keeley and Ingram Lee.
>
> Those who were given offices in the chapter were T. A. Hord, H. B. Goodnight, Harrison McGill and C. C. Carpenter.

By September 1917, a chapter of the "Wo-mok-tum-yank," as denoted in the Dallas Morning News *(above)*, was installed in Dallas and comprised of "Scout leaders and officials, Scoutmasters and assistants, and one representative from each troop of [at least] eight members."

"The order is fostered with the idea of instilling the higher ideals of Scouting into the organization and has been successful in the East," reported the Dallas Morning News. "The Dallas chapter is the first to be organized in Texas."

The first inductees in 1917 were Council President Otto H. Lang, Herbert L. Crate, W. A. Zischang, Henry B. Goodnight, C. C. Carpenter, Troop 25 Scoutmaster Thomas A. Hord, J. H. Taylor, E. J. Blaine, future interim Scout Executive Harrison Holman McGill, T. A. Crawford, Albert Walker, Allan Boyle, Dale Sedgwick, former Scout Commissioner Dr. George W. Keeley, and Troop 4 Scout Ingram Lee, the nephew of Scout Executive Walter Sanders Lee. The chapter's elected officers were Hord, Goodnight, McGill, and Carpenter.[C]

T. A. Hord

No Scouts earned awards for Sheep Farming, Nut Culture, Stalking, or Taxidermy.[8] Financially, the $26,536 budget was sufficient to fully meet expenses and not put the Council deeper into debt.

On February 25 and 26, 1938, Circle Ten Council's first-ever Boy Scout Merit Badge Show took place in the Agricultural Building at Fair Park. Dallas Mayor George Sprague, donning the Scout neckerchief, extended the official invitation to the community.

To garner even more attention, Hotchkiss convinced local radio station WFAA to broadcast a 30-minute show—or advertisement—on the happenings at the exposition.

"WFAA's portable pack transmitter, W5XAJ, will be brought into use as WFAA announcers Hal Thompson and Earl Kalusche wander among the thirty-five different booths, which have been arranged representing the many different fields in which Boy Scout may earn merit badges," reported the *Dallas*

Morning News. "Numerous interviews with Boy Scouts at the various booths will feature the broadcast." As a bonus, multiple airings were arranged throughout the length of the event.

Both Boy and Cub Scouts sold more than 15,000 tickets by canvassing their neighborhoods in the weeks prior to the Show, with Cub Pack 3071 at Highland Park's John S. Bradfield Elementary School selling the most. Individually, the champion sellers were Bradfield Cub Scouts Forest Muire and Ben Bradford.[9]

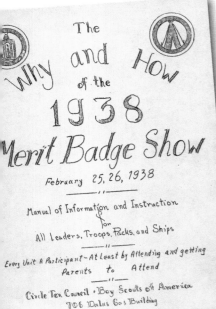

The
Why and How
of the
1938
Merit Badge Show

February 25, 26, 1938

Manual of Information and Instruction
for
All Leaders, Troops, Packs, and Ships

Every Unit A Participant - At Least by Attending and getting
Parents to Attend

Circle Ten Council • Boy Scouts of America
706 Dallas Gas Building
Dallas, Texas

LEFT: Scout Executive Loys Hotchkiss created the Scout Show concept in Dallas beginning with the first Merit Badge Show held in February 1938. BELOW: It consisted of Scouting units hosting a small booth in the Agriculture Building at Fair Park. ACROSS TOP LEFT: A promotional image for local Scouting published in the *Dallas Morning News* in 1938. ACROSS LOWER LEFT: Rows of tents (and one teepee) during a campout in 1938 by University Park's Troop 70.

WINTER CAMP AT CAMP WISDOM

HOUSED IN TENTS *at Camp Wisdom from December 27 through 29, 1937, twenty First Class Scouts representing a dozen local troops continued the tradition of the Council's annual Winter Camp, first begun by Daddy Wisdom over a decade earlier.*

Headed by Acting Camp Director E. F. Gatheman and F. M. Arnold, the boys participated in "a possum hunt, a treasure hunt, mystery hikes, a sham battle, games, athletic stunts, and other out-of-doors activities. Winter Camp continues today as a 5-day advancement program held between Christmas and New Year's Day sponsored by the Council's Mikanakawa Lodge of the Order of the Arrow."[E]

SCOUTING SAVES LIVES

IN SEPTEMBER 1938, *nine-year-old Bobby R. Watts impaled his leg on a picket fence post in his backyard after falling. Coming to the rescue were 13-year-old Boy Scout Bobby Godden and friend, 14-year-old Scout Howard Lennon, both of S. Briscoe Street in Oak Cliff. Seeing great loss of blood, the Scouts quickly grabbed a kitchen towel from inside Watts' home and wrapped it securely around the wound. Taken to Dallas Methodist Hospital, young Bobbie underwent a blood transfusion provided by George Fenley, an employee at the Dallas Morning News, saving his life.*

The two boy heroes were students at Sunset High School in 1941 with Godden being a member of Troop 4, at the time chartered by the Rosemont Dad's Club at the Rosemont School in Oak Cliff. Lennon was a member of Troop 10, sponsored by the Lida Hooe School at 2419 Gladstone Drive in Oak Cliff.

In October, Circle Ten representative, F. V. Folsom, Rosemont Dad's Club President Dr. Fred Schultz, Scoutmaster Fred Pennington, and Scout Executive L. L. Hotchkiss presented Godden with a bronze medal for saving another's life.

The victim, young Bobby R. Watts, went on to graduate Sunset High School in 1946.[F]

Present that day were Boy Scout bands from across the region as well as executives from a half dozen nearby states. There was an airplane flown in from Love Field for the Aviation merit badge. There was a large replica of a battleship in the center of the Agriculture Building for demonstrations in the Seamanship and other water-related badges. There were even live snakes in the reptile area. Each exhibit booth was judged and scored for the "best-in-show" award. Others awards were given for excellence in presentation.

Scenes from the first Merit Badge Show put on by Circle Ten Council in February 1938. Oak Cliff's Troop 2 (below) demonstrated indoor archery skills, while Cub Pack 3070 in University Park (far below left) demonstrated leatherwork and Troop 70 in University Park taught lessons on Dog Care (far below right).

TOP: At the Merit Badge Show, Dallas Troop 72 put on a fingerprinting merit badge exhibit and Oak Cliff's Troop 6 (above) used rats to teach lessons for the Public Health merit badge.

A BLIND SCOUTMASTER ORGANIZES A TROOP

IT WAS DIFFICULT TO TELL *that James A. Richardson was blind (below). As Scoutmaster of the troop sponsored by the Forest Avenue Baptist Church at Oakland* and Peabody Streets, he was known to many in the Dallas area as the "genial owner of the candy-tobacco-magazine concession in the Railway Terminal Annex." But, he also was adept at running a troop of active boys.

The Dallas Morning News *article subtitled, "Can't See Youngsters but Watches over Them, and Even Rescues One from Drowning," alluded to his sixth sense of being the protector of his Scouts.*

"We almost had a boy ready for the Court of Honor next week but he failed to pass his swimming test," *recalled Richardson in July 1940.* "He had to swim a certain distance but started to go down before he finished it. I was 'watching' him, though, and pulled him out in time."

As a boy, Richardson was a product of a quality Scouting program in Austin, Texas, at the State School for the Blind. Years later, he reportedly "never forgot that he was a boy" and when the church needed a Scoutmaster, he stepped up to the job and a dozen boys followed. His only regret was, "I need a good Eagle Scout who will come in and work with us."G

BY NOVEMBER 1938, the Circle Ten Council's first chairman of the Boy Scout Circus was Frank L. McNeny, a local real estate broker and former general director of the 1937 Greater Texas & Pan American Exposition. Arranging for the event to take place in the Livestock Arena at Fair Park on December 9 and 10, McNeny planned for participation by 5,000 Scouts, Cubs, and leaders performing many exciting acts (sans clowns) in a Ziegfield Follies–type revue that glorified the American boy rather than Ziegfield's formula of honoring East Asian themes.

The show opened with a mass march of Scouts in civilian clothes "thieving, fighting, teasing girls, tincupping" followed by Uncle Sam, who shakes his head in disbelief at the "poorly behaving" boys. Uncle Sam motions to a Scoutmaster to come from the grandstand to assist. He carries with him the Boy Scout Handbook and shows it to the ruffian lads. They follow the Scoutmaster across the arena into a colossal super-structure dubbed "the melting pot." When Uncle Sam climbs to the top and gives it a stir, a hundred bugles blow and out step "5,000 Scouts in mass march behind their Troop flags and ring the arena."

Next, a troop of Scouts acting as firemen enter the arena and erect a house in less than a minute, then a gas explosion starts a fire. A fire truck rolls up and the Scouts begin a water bucket brigade to bring in water to extinguish the flame. Actors jump from windows and are saved by the enterprising Scouts, all completed in five minutes, followed by a dozen more troops who demonstrate different types of campsites with tents rapidly erected in multiple configurations. Red torches serve

as campfires. Then the bugle blows again and all assemble at the central campfire to sing c Scouting amp songs. The arena goes dark and the tents are quickly torn down—all completed in another five minutes.

More acts followed that entertained the amazed crowd. Scouts started fires with flint and steel, others made ropes, cracked whips, and flew a hundred model airplanes at one time in the arena. But the most impressive part of the show were the feats of Scout engineering where Troops erected log cabins, bridges, lean-tos, and towers "reaching high into the rafters" in less than four minutes

The Circus resulted in 140 new boys joining and seven new troops being formed on the first day after the show. Another 1,000 boys signed-up over the next three months— a membership increase of 20 percent—as a direct result of the incredible Circle Ten Council Scout Circus. As the event's popularity increased, future events were held in the Cotton Bowl.[H]

As the Merit Badge Show developed into the Scout Circus in the Livestock Arena at Fair Park (below right) it grew large enough eventually to take place in the Cotton Bowl (far below). Scouts sold tickets to the public for a commission (right) and as is Scouting tradition, a patch was issued to hand out to participants at each annual event (across far left).

Boy Scout
CIRCUS

Presented by

CIRCLE TEN COUNCIL
Boy Scouts of America

at the

LIVE STOCK ARENA
Fair Park, Dallas
7:30 P. M.

December 9th and 10th

In all, there were 106 crafts, sciences, and trades with manned booths. Scouts demonstrated skills in fire-manship, pioneering, leather work and woodcraft, health, safety, machinery, and a number of others.

A "red-cheeked" Scout worked in the blacksmith-ing booth. Others repaired china, wove baskets, mended clothes with needle and thread, made bis-cuits, bound books, showed lifesaving methods, and "waved flags from lookout posts" built with six-foot spars and lashings for the 5,000 visitors.[10]

The Show was so much of a success, that the next one was planned for 1939. But by then, a new concept would take center stage to rival it—the Scout Circus.

Following the lead of the East Texas Boy Scouts in Tyler whose Scout Circus had been a rousing success for two years running, Circle Ten leaders decided to do the same, partially as a public relations event and partially as a fund-raiser for the Council. Although Council managers had proposed the concept at an executive board meeting in August 1935, the recent successes in Tyler made it even more appealing.

Tyler's May 1938 Circus had attracted 3,000 Scout performers hailing from 17 nearby counties to the East Texas Fair Grounds in a show of flag-waving patriotism and good old-fashioned performance fun.[11]

One of the initiatives that Council President Leslie B. Denning supported was the aggres-sive recruitment of African American boys into the program. By 1940, Circle Ten had 20 Negro troops in operation with 302 Scouts. As the boys were advancing, the first Negro Scout Court of Honor was held on Scouting's birthday, February 8, 1940, at the Munger Avenue Baptist Church at 3919 Munger Avenue near N. Haskell Avenue, the home of Troop 163. The attendees heard the annual radio address by President Franklin D. Roosevelt along with a greeting by Chief Scout Executive James E. West.[12]

To expand the African American Scouting pro-gram, more funds were needed. This resulted in the Council's first drive for $2,000 to employ Circle Ten's first African American district field executive dedicated solely to promoting the movement within the African American community. With a dinner

A SCOUT IS TRUSTWORTHY

ON JANUARY 6, 1940, *Scouting's values were on display. Hispanic Boy Scout Mike Rodriguez, a sixth grade student at the Cumberland Hill School and a member of Dallas' Troop 100 at the Presbyterian Mexican Mission, found $100 in cash in a discarded envelope in a crate behind the A&P grocery store. Without hesitation, he took it to the manager inside. To reward his honesty, his troop awarded him their highest acco-lade, a special red, white, and blue ribbon with an honor bar (right). Additionally, the store hired him to work on Saturdays. Humbled, Rodriguez told his well wishers that he simply was living the Scout Oath and "just being trustworthy."*[I]

"FOR MORE THAN 100 YEARS, THE BOY SCOUTS OF AMERICA'S PROVEN APPROACH TO INSTILLING VALUES IN YOUNG BOYS AND YOUNG MEN AND WOMEN HAVE PRODUCED BETTER CITIZENS FOR OUR COMMUNITIES, BETTER FATHERS AND MOTHERS, AND GREAT LEADERS FOR OUR TOWNS AND OUR NATION. I KNOW THIS TO BE TRUE FROM MY OWN SCOUTING EXPERIENCE AS A YOUTH, AS WELL AS FROM THE SCOUTING EXPERIENCE MY SONS RECEIVED."

—REX W. TILLERSON, CHAIRMAN AND CEO, EXXON MOBIL CORPORATION

kicked off at the Morgan branch of the YWCA at 1709 Jackson Street on S. Ervay in Dallas, C. F. Stark, chairman of the finance drive, reported that a recent survey revealed that there were 826 eligible African American boys in eight Negro schools who wished to become Scouts. Some 120 Council volunteers assisted in the recruiting process.

A meeting at the Negro Chamber of Commerce at 814½ N. Good Street reported that after a week, $1,016 had been raised toward the goal. Speakers that evening were a Mr. Hulen and Scout Executive Hotchkiss. The drive succeeded and on July 1, the new position of field executive for the Council's newest district—the Silver Palm District— was created.[13]

In early May, 125 African American Boy Scouts spent the weekend at the Silver Palm District's first camporee at Wahoo Lake (now renamed Lakeview Park Pond) located north of Scyene Road about two miles southeast of Fair Park in East Dallas.

The Council also maintained a camp in the African American community of Bear Creek just west of downtown Irving, probably one of the first Council-sponsored and supported camps of this type in the nation, certainly one of the first in Texas.

Other camps for Negro Scouts were held in the Prairie View area, now the location of the University of Texas Southwestern Medical Center at Harry Hines Boulevard and Inwood Road, and in an unknown area near the city of Carrollton, Texas. Another site owned by Henry Dorsey Jr. on Ferndale Road about a mile east of White Rock Lake hosted a three-day camp for African American Scouts in 1943.[14]

IN ALL AREAS THROUGHOUT THE COMMUNITY, THE COUNCIL'S MEMBERSHIP WAS GROWING. AND BY DECEMBER 1941, THE COUNTRY WOULD NEED EVERY ONE OF THEM.

chapter 10

A PRIME DECADE FOR PATRIOTISM (1941–1949)

"One Council, one program, one objective. Always good Scouting for the boy."

A SLOGAN OF CIRCLE TEN COUNCIL, BSA
CIRCLE TEN REPORTER, 1953

As the county entered the war years of the 1940s, downtown Dallas was still abuzz with nightlife action down Elm Street most evenings.

IN EARLY 1941, the initial rumblings of war made their way to American shores. After the successful invasion of Poland in 1939 by the Nazi war machine, German dictator Adolph Hitler declared the beginning of his "Thousand-year Reich," a pronouncement that shook world leaders to their cores. Predictably, the conquest of Europe followed with the Battle of Britain pitting London citizens against German air raids commencing in July 1940. Even though our European allies requested American military manpower, President Franklin D. Roosevelt needed a more direct reason to enter World War II, not only to help European forces end the reign of Hitler, but also to get the country out of its 10-year economic depression.

That day came on December 7, 1941, when the Japanese Empire attacked American warships stationed in Pearl Harbor, Hawaii. Led by Admiral Yamamoto and his Imperial Naval Fleet containing

ENSIGN EARL ROE DONNELL JR. *was a 1933 Eagle Scout from Troop 20 in Oak Cliff (far top right). The son of Earl R. Donnell Sr. and the former Lucretia Ayers of Oak Cliff, the family owned the Donnell's Ice Cream, soon to be purchased by the Borden Ice Cream Company in their national expansion program. As a young person, Earl Jr. had an appreciation for art, being both the progeny of an artist as well as the brother to another. He, himself, had the privilege of studying with legendary Texas "longhorn" artist Frank Reaugh during the summer of 1932.*

In 1935, Donnell graduated Sunset High School with the rank of lieutenant colonel in the ROTC and entered the University of Texas' School of Engineering to specialize in aeronautics. Graduating in 1939, he put his sketching skills to work and took employment at the Curtiss-Wright Aircraft Company in Saint Louis, Missouri, before accepting his commission into the Naval Reserve in Pensacola, Florida.

Ensign Donnell was assigned to Scouting Squadron Six on the USS Enterprise *stationed in Pearl Harbor, Hawaii (near top right and below middle left). During the Japanese surprise attack on December 7, 1941,* Enterprise *was still patrolling the Pacific. Donnell participated in the battle for the Marshall Islands, in which he lost his life on February 1, 1942. As noted, he battled "in the face of enemy fighter opposition and heavy anti-aircraft fire." Donnell was Circle Ten Council's first Eagle Scout to be missing or killed in action during World War II.*

In his brief yet distinguished career, Ensign Donnell received the Purple Heart and the Air Medal (both posthumous) for heroic and meritorious achievement while participating in an aerial fight.

The USS Donnell *(DE-56)—a Buckley-class naval destroyer escort (middle right)—was named in his honor and christened by his mother on March 13, 1943 (below right).*

After performing several years of service in both the Atlantic and Pacific theatres, the USS Donnell *was torpedoed by a German submarine off the coast of France. Crippled, it made its way to the port city of Cherbourg, where its generator was stripped off and used to light the city during the remainder of the war.[A]*

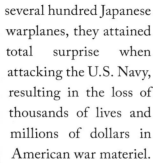

LEFT: After the Dallas Gas Company's adult Troop 80 dissolved, that number was re-assigned to a traditional troop of boys. Upon the outbreak of World War II, they performed service projects where needed, such as assisting at demolition sites and collecting much-needed scrap metal. BELOW LEFT: The ever-cheerful Tommy Tenderfoot appeared in a *Dallas Morning News* photo essay depicting the twelve points of the Scout Law.

several hundred Japanese warplanes, they attained total surprise when attacking the U.S. Navy, resulting in the loss of thousands of lives and millions of dollars in American war materiel.

Yet even in their hour of victory, a restrained Yamamoto, who understood the repercussions of his actions, supposedly uttered to one of his officers, "I fear that all we have done is to awake a sleeping giant and fill him with a terrible resolve."

Within mere hours, America was at war and, within days, nearly 2 million patriotic Boy Scouts were called into national service with Circle Ten Council Scouts leading the way in North Texas.

Foreseeing the potential for mass utilization of these boys, Region 9 Director James P. Fitch already had formed a "rigidly picked emergency corps" for a civilian defense service made-up of local Scout troops.

"We are not changing the program of the Boy Scouts," Fitch told critics of militarism. "[Scouting] is non-military in every sense of the word, but we do want them to be prepared for any emergency."[1]

Emergency service training for events like "attack during war, flood, fire, or earthquake" was held at Camp Wisdom.

Further pre-war preparations included hanging 8,000 posters that promoted the purchase of United States Defense Bonds and stamps from the Treasury Department. Other assignments involved the remainder of the 4,450 Scouts and 1,200 leaders that gathered in the Dallas Gas Company auditorium for instructions issued through Scout Executive Loys Hotchkiss.

By November 1941, Hotchkiss, now basing Council operations from Suite 100 of the Thomas Building at 1314 Wood Street next to the Cotton Exchange Building, directed several paper drives held not

New Office Building for Cotton Men

ABOVE: The Thomas Building was constructed on Wood Street in downtown Dallas in 1924 next to Cotton Exchange Building. Since the city served as the southern region's clearinghouse for raw textiles, the Thomas Building was meant to provide additional office space for cloth merchants. ABOVE RIGHT: Unfortunately, the demolition of its lower level began on October 24, 2012, which was completed the following month after all interior materials had been removed due to asbestos concerns. This photograph was taken by John K. Shipes on that day as the demolition permits were being served by the Dallas Fire Department. It was the Thomas Building's final grand protrait.

only "to cut down the high percentage of the wasted [resource] now being lost" but also to prepare for impending hostilities. Until then, monies raised from its collection and sale by Scouts were used to purchase defense stamps, make donations to the Red Cross or other agencies, and for the purchase of new troop equipment. But within two weeks, their sole objective would be to support the national war effort.

"There is a genuine need [for waste paper] and the call is urgent," said Hotchkiss. Some paper collections involved a door-to-door canvass for the "sorely needed wastepaper to feed mills in imperative war production."[2]

By mid-February 1942, one troop in Oak Cliff's Arcadia Park, led by U.S. postal carrier and Scoutmaster James E. Nicholl, collected 6,010 pounds of scrap newspaper and sold them to the American Paper Stock Company in Dallas (now defunct) for proceeds of $36.43. The Southwestern Life

BOBBY KEYES— A 10-YEAR-OLD CUB SCOUT HERO

ON APRIL 2, 1944, three-year-old Lapat Johnson, the daughter of Private and Mrs. Jack Johnson, was playing in a 7-foot deep pond near Love Field with her brother and neighbors from a nearby farm. Suddenly, she disappeared under the water. About five minutes later, her lifeless body surfaced due to the trapped air in her clothes.

Spotted by her screaming mother who waded out to pull the unconscious little girl to shore, 10-year-old Cub Scout Bobby Keyes of the Love Field Pack rushed to the scene and performed artificial respiration—miraculously reviving her. The child was taken to Parkland Hospital where she recovered fully from the trauma.[B]

Insurance Company offered a framed reproduction of the 1942 Boy Scout calendar by Brown & Bigelow to the two troops that collected the most paper in March.

Results showed 97,000 pounds were collected that month with Dallas' Troop 123 amassing a total of 16,000 pounds, an average of 821 pounds per youth member. Troop 90 brought in 14,300 pounds, a 753 pounds per boy average.

In support of this national conservation initiative, the customary "big dinner" associated with Circle Ten's annual fund-raising banquet was called off to "conserve foodstuffs." All attendees were requested to eat at home before arriving.[3]

Other types of war material drives were held. "Keep 'em Smiling" was the Cub Scout slogan for the Victory Book Campaign as the young lads went about town collecting reading material for the country's military forces, both domestically and overseas. Jointly sponsored by the American Library Association and the American Red Cross, 1,500 Cubs in 35 packs

TOP: The Cub Scouts of Pack 194 sponsored by the C.P. Russell Elementary School Dad's Club work on arts and crafts projects utilizing wood and tools. TOP LEFT and ABOVE: Sea Scouting was introduced to Scouting in 1912 and Circle Ten Council eventually formed several Ships that cruised on local lakes.

FOR SOME LUCKY *Circle Ten Council Scouts, 1942 marked the year of their first trek to the new Philturn Rocky Mountain Scout Camp near Cimarron, New Mexico. Donated to the Boy Scouts of America's national organization by Oklahoma oilman Waite Phillips in 1938; he wished to provide Scouting with a fully functioning high-adventure experience for older boys. To do so, he deeded 137,500 acres of land in the Sangre de Cristo mountain range in the Rockies and his large, multi-room ranch villa valued together at about $5 million ($76.5 mil today). During that first summer of hiking and camping in 1939, a total of 189 Scouts were "welcomed" in.*

A year earlier during Philturn's third camping season, three Circle Ten Scoutmasters (top and bottom)—Jim Clardy (bottom left), Dave Robb (bottom middle), and Clarence Gardner (bottom right)—had "tried it out." Loving the experience, the Council sent six car-loads of Scouters to Philturn in May 1942 for a long weekend of camping and hiking to assess its suitability for Council Scouts.

Approved, the first eight local Scouts arrived only weeks later in June (middle). They were A. W. Wortham of Athens, Bob Gammon of Waxahachie, Bobby Miller and Richard Baxter of Dallas, Alison Clayton of Greenville, Bobby Godden of Oak Cliff, James Watson of Hillsboro, and Kenneth Parker of Frisco.[C]

Seen by all campers since the beginning, the Tooth of Time (across right) remains the eternal symbol of Waite Phillips' landmark gift.

HERBERT L. CHAMBERS— DALLAS' FIRST AFRICAN AMERICAN EAGLE SCOUT

ON JULY 14, 1942, *at a ceremony at the St. John's Baptist Church on the corner of Allen and Guillot Streets north of downtown (now the Notre Dame School), 15-year-old Herbert Lowe Chambers (below on the left side) of Troop 164 made front page news—he was the first African American boy to earn the rank of Eagle Scout.*

Urged into Scouting by Council field executive Harvey L. Price (eventually to become BSA's Chief Scout Executive from 1976–1979), Chambers joined his troop in 1939 when there were no black executives yet employed by Circle Ten.

"[Mr. Price] helped us get started," recalled Chambers. "He brought other white Scouts to help us out."

Born in Dallas on July 4, 1927, to local tailor Miler W. Chambers and his wife, the former Durinde Amboree, Herbert was their third child behind 10-year-old brother Bonzo and 2-year-old sister Willie.

After graduating L. G. Pinkston High School at 2314 Dennison Street north of Singleton Boulevard in 1944, he continued his education at Prairie View A&M University in Houston. Chambers received his undergraduate degree in 1948 after having distinguished himself not only in the classroom but also on the athletic field. His track and field prowess gained him entrance to the Prairie View Hall of Fame in 1998.

Moving back to Dallas, he took a teaching position at the Dallas Vocational School and moved into a house at 2110 Boll Street in present day Uptown. He married his wife Danita on August 24, 1952, and eventually moved to Des Moines, Iowa, to further his education. Wishing to be in the medical field, he entered the Des Moines College of Osteopathic Medicine & Surgery, where he graduated with a doctorate in osteopathy in May 1959. After interning for a year in Warren, Ohio, at the Mahoning Valley Green Cross Hospital, the couple moved back to Dallas where he opened his own clinic in the summer of 1960 at 1831 Singleton Boulevard.

Dr. Herbert L. Chambers died in Dallas on March 2, 2002, at the age of 74.[D]

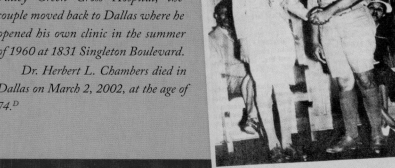

and eight Scout troops collected more than 10,000 volumes throughout Dallas. All booty was taken to Dallas' Carnegie Free Library at the southwest corner of S. Harwood and Commerce Streets (now torn down and having been replaced with the empty, six-story Old Dallas Central Library next to the Dallas Statler Hilton) for distribution to the various camps and USO clubs. Eventually local Girl Scouts and Camp Fire Girls joined in.[4]

Circle Ten Scouts were also trained as Defense Aids and local messengers under the civilian protection program. More than 600 boys 14-years-old and older joined as Scouts. Not to be left out, the Silver Palm District saw 150 new African American boys register as reported by J. J. Cross, the director for the training. Even 600 Senior Scouts, made-up of Explorers and Sea Scouts, were trained.

By May 1942, the call went out to collect scrap metal, as in scrap coat hangers and other bits of castoff metals that could be used to feed the nation's steel mills for plane, tanks, and gun fabrication. Proceeds were used to support the Dallas City-County Civilian Defense Council.[5]

By the end of June, local Scouts began working in earnest on the scrap rubber drive in Dallas as boys went into their neighborhoods asking that one's entire house "be ransacked for rubber scrap." Any material found could be taken to their local filling (gas) station or be picked up by the 4,000 Scouts and Cubs of the 122 participating troops and packs. Within three days, rubber collection spiked upward by 15 percent resulting in 100,000 pounds of new stock for national use.[6]

"When you get thousands of flyswatters, dish scrapers, sink stoppers and things like that," said Council Field Executive Harvey L. Price, "it shows that a whole lot of families are digging right down to the bottom to help out in the rubber campaign."

"I remember we worked really hard trying to make a difference," recalled Oak Cliff Scout Eddie Reitz. "We believed it to be our duty to help in the war effort."

Another large project performed by Scouts was the fats and kitchen grease collection drive that worked alongside Girl Scouts in distributing "salvage information cards" in Dallas neighborhoods. Collecting for the Dallas Community War Chest, Boy Scout troops received money at the rate of 4 cents a pound to be used in their programs. For those individual boys who collected a minimum of 25 pounds, certificates of accomplishment were awarded from Texas Governor Coke Stevenson through Les Harris, county chairman of the fats and grease collection campaign.

"They have been asked to help in a task where adults, to a large extent, so far have failed," reported the *Dallas Morning News*. As there was no quota, the collection was an ongoing enterprise throughout the war.[7]

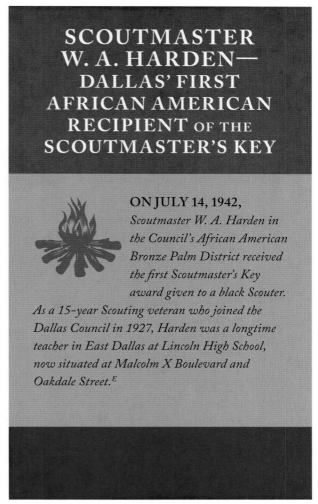

SCOUTMASTER W. A. HARDEN— DALLAS' FIRST AFRICAN AMERICAN RECIPIENT OF THE SCOUTMASTER'S KEY

ON JULY 14, 1942, *Scoutmaster W. A. Harden in the Council's African American Bronze Palm District received the first Scoutmaster's Key award given to a black Scouter.*

As a 15-year Scouting veteran who joined the Dallas Council in 1927, Harden was a longtime teacher in East Dallas at Lincoln High School, now situated at Malcolm X Boulevard and Oakdale Street.[E]

And in the midst of all this, in 1943, Council membership surpassed 10,000 registered Scouts for the first time in its history, with African American Scouts making up 10 percent of total registered

During World War II, Circle Ten troops performed a variety of local service projects. Those included taking traffic censuses (far left) and collecting thousands of pounds of newspaper (near left).

SAVE WASTE PAPER!
BOY SCOUTS WILL PICK UP WASTE PAPER
THE FIRST SATURDAY OF EACH MONTH
If you have paper prepared for collection, place this card in your front window the preceding Friday. If the weather is favorable for collecting, paper should be placed at the curb or on the front porch early Saturday morning. Tie mixed paper, including small cardboard cartons, into flat, compact bundles, or pack it in large cardboard cartons. Tie magazines and newspapers in separate bundles.
Paper is a War Material!

Star Scout Jerry McKinsey was one of nearly 400 who pacy was one of nearly 400 who participated in Wednesday's count. At one of the traffic hot tipated in Wednesday's traffic count. At one of the traffic hot spots, Ross and Akard, he he provided himself with a chair to make his six-and-a-half-hour shift easier.

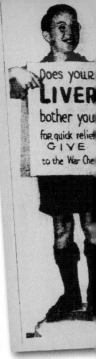

Scouts and 20 percent of the troops. To keep things in perspective, Council President Milton Brown reminded the Dallas citizenry, "Although 10,089 seems large enough," he advised, "I wish to emphasize that even this is just scratching the possibilities of the boy crop of our Council."[8]

By July 1944, the Council had participated in a drive to collect spent tin cans during the war salvage metal campaign as well as having performed a local service project to harvest a county fruit orchard in danger of suffering "severe losses" from a labor shortage. Similar to "Camp Service" in 1918 where Scout picked two trainloads of peaches in East Texas, Dallas Scouts were paid 30 cents an hour to pick 12,000 bushels of peaches and plums (500–800 baskets a day average) saving the La Reunion Fruit Farm near Grand Prairie from certain bankruptcy.

Afterward, they planted 25,000 sweet potato slips for the H. E. Cannon Nursery Company in Arlington and "worked the truck garden [or *trade* garden] of James Demases near the Santerre farm."[9] Another type of service project followed—taking a census of automobile traffic on local roads for the state.

As waste paper campaigns continued into 1945, BSA's partnership with the future president of the United States and current Supreme Allied Commander in Europe, General Dwight D. "Ike" Eisenhower, flourished as a result of the success of the General Eisenhower Waste Paper Medal. For any Scout who turned in 1,000 pounds of paper he collected during the March and April drive, he received the red and white ribbon bar with Ike's image on a round bronze medal suspended below.

Other war service projects included money drives for the local Community or "War" Chest (far left) and the gardening program (below) that was recognized with presentation of the McArthur Garden medal (near left) named after General Douglas McArthur. To earn it, a Scout had to tend to a garden of at least 400 square feet, make it a "good producer," harvest it properly, and have it inspected by Council representatives. Twenty thousand medals were issued nationally during the war. All Council service projects were itemized and reported to national BSA managers (far below).

One hundred Dallas Scouts earned it out of the 2,000 Scouts who collected paper locally. The campaign succeeded in collecting over 700,000 pounds of wastepaper materials in a "successful county-wide salvage paper drive."[10]

As World War II came to a close, Circle Ten Council had numerous things to boast about. The most obvious was its membership in excess of 12,422 persons, which included 2,206 Boy Scout leaders for 6,306 Scouts in 314 troops, and 695 adult Cub leaders for 3,215 Cub Scouts in 95 packs. Service wise, those Scouts had collected 5.5 million pounds of wastepaper, 8,000 pounds of scrap rubber, 1,500 pounds of tin metal, and 5,010 pounds of grease, along with three tons of old clothes during the length of the conflict.

Even sweeter was the fact that the Council was now completely free of debt with the Dallas County War Chest having paid off all outstanding bank loans as a "thank you" for the dedicated service performed by Scouts during the war effort. Circle Ten Council was now a positive force for good to be reckoned with in terms of both manpower and financial health.[11]

Expansion continued to be a goal of Scout Executive Hotchkiss with its most important attraction being the camping experience. As such, 1946 would be an exceedingly bountiful year for Circle Ten Scouts with the acquisition of two new camps—Constantin and Texoma.

Scout overnighters at Camp Constantin began on August 4, 1946, where as described by the *Dallas Morning News*, the "fish at Possum Kingdom Lake are going to have a hard time" when 175 "fish-hungry Senior Scouts descend that day." Circle Ten hosted a Council-wide two-week Wilderness Camp in Constantin's untamed brush and trees, that was flush with native animals.

Within a year, BSA's national engineering executive, William Hall, would survey the property and declare it "one of the best camp locations in the country."[12]

ACROSS: During World War II, Circle Ten troops performed a variety of local service projects that included the collection of newspapers that was recognized by the presentation of the Eisenhower Waste Paper medal (across top). Other projects in 1942 included scrap metal collection that were performed by units like Oak Cliff's Troop 2 (bottom).

BEGINNING IN MARCH 1945, *Circle Ten Council leaders opened discussions to form a quad-council partnership for a new Scout camp on the Texas/Oklahoma border on Lake Texoma to be named aptly, Camp Texoma. To manage it, a board of trustees from the local Region 9 councils would be formed to discuss a lease* for the 2,000 acres of shorefront from the U.S. Army Corps of Engineers, who had built the dam and lake and wanted it protected from squatters.

Circle Ten's representative, executive board member Ben R. Newberry, agreed to join economic forces with the three neighboring councils—the Red River Valley Council headquartered in Denison; the Lone Star Council based in Paris; and the Sherman Area Council. The partnership funded an endowment to develop the Texoma camping area with massive facilities proposed to house 8,000 Scouts during a multi-session summer camp season.

Lake Texoma itself had been authorized for construction by the federal government in 1938 with the passing of the Flood Control Act. The Corps of Engineers built Denison Dam and Lake Texoma to minimize local flooding and utilize the power of the water by constructing a hydroelectric power generation facility for the region. The dam, spillway, and generation facilities were begun in August 1939 and completed in February 1944. As noted by the Corps of Engineers, the dam was the 12th largest in water volume in the United States at the time.

Unfortunately for the Sherman Area Council, when the land was flooded to create the lake, their first Scout camp that dated to 1928, Camp Grayson, was submerged. However, Camp Texoma certainly would fill their requirements for a summer camp. (The Camp James Ray of today is the second location of Camp Grayson and sits some distance south of the original site lost to the waters.)

By June 1946, enough work had been done at Camp Texoma to permit the first regional meeting of Scout representatives from Texas, Oklahoma, and New Mexico, to be hosted on premises. The delegates earned the right to attend by winning local competitions in Scout skills like axemanship, sailing, and stalking. This session was a trial run for the upcoming six-week summer camp, of which the last week was reserved for African American troops. This was Circle Ten's second operating summer camp-site for minority Scouts. The first was at Richey Farm in the Bear Creek area west of the town of Irving.[F]

TOP and MIDDLE: The first patches for Camp Texoma in the 1950s and 1960s. LEFT: The Sherman Area Council's Camp Grayson, which sits about a mile to the northwest of Camp Texoma, is known today as Camp James Ray.

BELOW: Scouts look across Possum Kingdom Lake from atop Johnson's Peak. BOTTOM: One way to access Camp Constantin was by private single engine plane. This image was taken on June 5, 1948 before the Region 9 Camp School. The attendees ate under canvas as the dining hall had not yet been constructed.

BEING THE SON *of the founder of the Constantin Oil and Refining Company in Tulsa, Oklahoma, who had struck it big in the south Arkansas oil boom of 1921, Eugene Pierre Cyprian Constantin Jr. was a man of means. Constantin Oil's Hill Number 1 well released a huge stock of oil and gas reserves that enabled the family to live in extreme luxury. Eugene Jr. was the president of the company upon the retirement of his father.*

Born on February 22, 1896, in Lockport, Louisiana, as the eldest child of French immigrant Eugene Constantin Sr. and his wife, the former Alice Bouras, Eugene the younger learned that hard work often resulted in great things. As many fortunes were made in the twentieth century oil boom, he was determined to do good deeds with his family's vast wealth as an adult.

Marrying Miss Ruth Fitzpatrick by 1924, the couple lived in Wichita Falls, Texas, where their only child, Eugene Constantin III was born in 1925. Eugene Jr. moved his family to Dallas in 1931 as it had blossomed into a regional center for oil producers.

Eugene III was a good student who intended to make his own way in life, spurred on by his membership in the Scouting movement in the 1930s. However, his short life ended on April 16, 1945, during World War II as a second lieutenant in the U.S. Marine Corps at the bloodiest fight in the Pacific Theatre— the Battle of Okinawa during the invasion of Japan. He was killed-in-action as a member of the largest amphibious assault force in our nation's history.

His body was brought back to Dallas and buried at the Calvary Hill Cemetery at 3235 Lombardy Lane just north of the Murchison Scouting Center.

In May 1946 to honor their son's memory, the Constantins donated 772 acres of land on a peninsula at Johnson Bend stretching into Possum Kingdom Lake to the two organizations that best developed character in local youth: the YMCA of Metropolitan Dallas and the Circle Ten Council, BSA.

Divided down the middle, each had common ownership of the mountain overlooking the Lake called Johnson's Peak. It was named for local pioneer J. A. Johnson and his wife, Florence, who settled on the peninsula in 1888 and took "legal" ownership of it. Formerly, it had been under the control of the Comanche Indian Nation before their forced relocation to Oklahoma by the U.S. Government.[G]

RIGHT and BOTTOM LEFT: Eugene Constantin III as he appeared before being deployed in World War II. LOWER RIGHT: This deed for title transfer was issued for the Constantin lands at Johnson Bend on Possum Kingdom Lake to Circle Ten Council, which became Camp Constantin in 1946. ACROSS: A variety of Camp Constantin/Jack D. Furst Aquatics Base patches have been issued to campers since the 1950s.

LT. EUGENE CONSTANTIN III

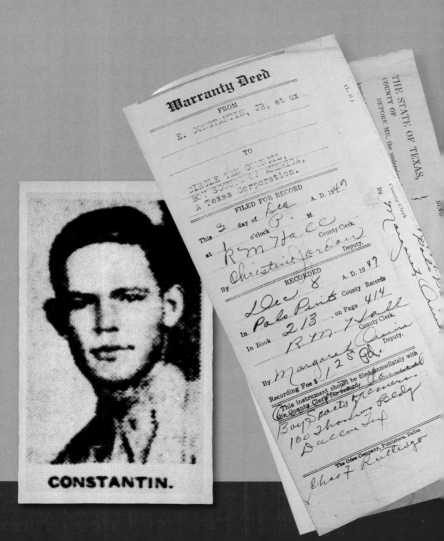

CONSTANTIN.

CIRCLE TEN EXPANDS NORTHWARD

IN 1947, *Circle Ten Council was debt free and able to flex its financial muscle in North Texas by aiding another regional council that was not as fortunate. The Red River Valley Council headquartered in Denison, Texas was in dire straits that made its independence untenable.*

During a presentation to Circle Ten's executive board at the Denison Hotel, Red River Valley's Treasurer Hal Watkins reported that his council had a $5,000 budget shortfall at the end of August 1947 and needed financial relief. Their solution was annexation by Circle Ten Council. Under the October 17, 1947, resolution, the deal included the Denison precinct in Grayson County, along with the whole of Cooke County, Texas, and Oklahoma's Bryan County. It read,

That in view of the request of Red River Valley Council that it is permitted to merge with Circle Ten Council and following the unanimous recommendations of the Committee appointed by President [Dechard A.] Hulcy (below) to meet with the Committee from Red River Valley Council, President Hulcy and Scout Executive Hotchkiss be authorized to proceed with the necessary details to complete the merger of the two Councils.[H]

The motion carried unanimously. Circle Ten was now in Oklahoma.

By March 1947, the waterfront was cleared and permanent latrine and shower facilities were installed in preparation for the 1947 summer camp season, its first "under canvass." But the true test would come merely two months later in May 1947 when BSA's assistant national director of camping, Ken Wells, would serve as the director for Region 9's camp school for executives attending the upcoming World Jamboree in France that August.

In mid-July 1947, Camp Constantin hosted its first 150 summer campers as Scouts from across North Texas made their way to the peninsula northwest of Mineral Wells, Texas, ripe with "adventure [in] every thicket."

Hikes up Johnson's Peak, canoe trips across the lake to the rocky walled formation known as Hell's Gate, and the marvelous fishing opportunities entranced the initial class of Constantin's campers. They lived in ten campsites with intriguing names like Hawk's Nest, Indian Mounds, Buffalo Pass, Crow Point, and Wolf Hollow, all under the watchful eye of Constantin's first camp director, the Council's Oak Cliff district executive, Robert C. Glew.[13]

In American Scouting's anniversary month of February 1949, BSA's national office began preparations to celebrate its 40th anniversary in 1950. That included a new annual slogan and plans for the next National Jamboree. Under the national theme of "Adventure—that's Scouting!" 2.2 million members rededicated themselves to the Scout Oath and Scout Law. For the kickoff celebrations in Dallas, guest speaker H. Roe Bartle, the patriarch of Kansas City Scouting proclaimed, "The call to Scouting is a call to brotherhood. If we strengthen the arm of liberty, we will have to take hate out of our hearts. Scouting must teach brotherhood for all men."[14]

In April 1949, the Council put on its annual Scout Exposition in the General Exhibits Building at Fair Park. It was replete with 129 booths set-up and manned by 10,000 Scouts. One impressed father of a 12-year-old Scout exclaimed to his wife standing next to him, "My dear, there's no question about it. If [son] Albert and I were stranded in the woods, I'd be completely dependent on Albert."[15]

Scouts demonstrated how to handle snakes, created useful items from old tin cans, offered tips on cooking and zoology, as well as taught the war dance of the Navaho Indian nation. When the dances were over, an African American troop sang campfire songs and "gave talks on good citizenship." One boy was heard declaring that he wouldn't mind if the event

ACROSS TOP: Scouts prepare to canoe at Camp Constantin during the 1949 season. ACROSS BOTTOM: Circle Ten Council President Dechard A. Hulcy in 1947.

A SCOUT HIKES 14 MILES—ON CRUTCHES

AFTER JOINING SCOUTING *in 1946, thirteen-year-old Perry Holestin Spencer of Oak Cliff wanted nothing more than to earn the rank of First Class (left). However, that included the completion of a 14 mile hike. It would not have been a problem had he not been a victim of infantile paralysis, but he was. Perry had little use of his legs and got around on crutches and a leg brace.*

Undeterred, he and three troopmates from Troop 2 at the Margaret B. Henderson Elementary School in Oak Cliff set-off from the home of Scoutmaster Charles W. Barton at 1710 South Edgefield and hiked to Mountain Creek Lake—seven miles away—and back in a time of six hours.

"We walked in pairs, and sometimes the two boys ahead of us would get far ahead," recalled Perry. "But their speedy pace tired them and they had to rest often. We kept overtaking them."

The long hike resulted in sore arms but a sense of accomplishment. When asked if it hurt to walk, Perry replied, "not a bit." But his mother had the last word adding, "The only time it hurts is when I ask him to go to the store for me."

In continuing his Scouting experience, Perry also spent a month at Camp Constantin and passed the requirement to swim 50 yards.

"We don't know just exactly how Perry gets around in the water without being able to use his legs," said his mother. "But he stays on his back and has figured out a style of his own."

Graduating Sunset High School in the Class of 1953, Perry married Judy P. Chitwood in Mangum, Oklahoma, in April 1966. They had one daughter, Perilyn, and eventually retired to Louisville, Kentucky, in 1995. Judy passed away in November 2011 after 45 years of marriage.[J]

Boy Scout Perry Spencer . . . even on crutches, a 14-mile hike is fun.

THE MINIMUM SCOUTING AGES DROP

ON JUNE 28, 1949, *after a three-year study on the suitability of Scouting for younger boys, BSA's national headquarters announced the lowering of its minimum age in several programs. First, Cubbing age requirements were lowered to 8-years-old from 9, Boy Scouts dropped to 11 from 12, and Senior Scouts (Explorers, Sea Scouts, and Air Scouts) fell from age 15 to 14. All changes were effective September 1.*

This was a boon to Circle Ten Scouting. Council executive and future national BSA Chief Scout Executive Harvey L. Price commented that Circle Ten could now recruit from the 7,200 local 8-year-olds—quickly expanding their membership numbers.[1]

lasted for a whole month. But in the end, the tired Scouts were prepared—to go home.

In January 1950, Circle Ten Council leaders began preparations for sending a contingent of Dallas Scouts to BSA's second National Jamboree at Valley Forge, Pennsylvania, scheduled for June 30 through July 6. The local Jamboree chairman was an old friend, former Council President George R. Angell, now living in Fort Worth. When Angell heard that "his boys" would be camping on the same field that General George Washington had spent the fateful winter of 1777–1778, he jumped at the chance to lead it. Side trips were planned for Washington, DC, New York City, and Philadelphia.[16]

BELOW: Entrance tickets to the Scout Exposition held at Fair Park's General Exhibits Building in April 1949. ACROSS: The members of Cub Scout Pack 3162 sponsored by the J. W. Ray Elementary School meet at the Park Theater in 1944.

CIRCLE TEN COUNCIL, BOY SCOUTS OF AMERICA
1949 SCOUT EXPOSITION
General Exhibits Building, Fair Park
DALLAS, TEXAS

Admission . 42c
Fed. Tax . . 8c
Total . . . 50c

Friday, April 29 . . . . 7:00 P.M. to 10:00 P.M.
Saturday, April 30 . . . . . . 1:30 P.M. to 9:30 P.M
THIS TICKET GOOD AT ANY TIME

SEE

200 Scouting Skills and Hobbies demonstrated by 10,000 Cubs and Scouts. Our country's future leaders demonstrating how they are preparing themselves to serve others. "Be Prepared" for the future, and how they are helping to "Strengthen the Arm of Liberty" in America.

GREATEST BOYS' SHOW IN THE SOUTHWEST

IN THE PRESENCE OF 40,000 OTHER SCOUTS AND LEADERS, THE
1950 NATIONAL JAMBOREE CONTINGENT FROM CIRCLE TEN COUNCIL
EXPERIENCED THIS MOMENTOUS EVENT MADE SOMEWHAT TENUOUS
AS ANOTHER WAR LOOMED ON THE HORIZON—SPECIFICALLY ON THE
KOREAN PENINSULA—JUST DAYS BEFORE PRESIDENT HARRY S. TRUMAN
WAS TO ARRIVE TO ADDRESS THE LARGEST MASS OF AMERICAN YOUTH
EVER ASSEMBLED IN ONE SPOT.

chapter 11

THE GOLDEN AGE (1950–1959)

"Put a boy in a Scout uniform and give him adventurous activity, tempered with patriotism and reverence and you will have a future to behold."

CIRCLE TEN REPORTER, 1953

President Harry S. Truman addresses the attendees at the 1950 National Jamboree at Valley Forge, Pennsylvania just after the outbreak of hostilities on the Korean Peninsula.

ON THE EVENING OF JUNE 30, 1950, the 47,000 national and international Scouts attending the second National Jamboree at Valley Forge, Pennsylvania were abuzz with excitement awaiting the arrival of President Harry S. Truman. It had been 13 years since the last jamboree due to the outbreak of World War II and Scouts hungered for the excitement of this national gathering.

Only four days earlier, Truman had ordered U.S. air and sea forces to the Korean Peninsula to aid South Korea in its defense against the invading Communist forces of North Korea.

A TWENTY-YEAR-OLD DALLAS SOLDIER RE-REGISTERS AS A BOY SCOUT DURING DEPLOYMENT

WHEN 20-YEAR-OLD
Dallas soldier Aubrey Wilford Pollard, a light weapons infantryman, approached the shores of the Korean Peninsula in August 1950, he wanted to serve his nation knowing he was a registered member of Circle Ten Council. Stationed in Pusan for training, he mailed a letter along with his Explorer Scout rechartering dues to University Park's Troop 70.

A graduate of Crozier Technical High School and having completed two years at Texas A&M University in College Station, Texas, he believed it his duty to enter the military. Should he be killed-in-action, Pollard wanted to die a member of Circle Ten Council.

On September 19, 1950, Private First Class Aubrey W. Pollard was killed in action as a member of Company I of the 5th Regimental Combat Team in South Korea. He is buried in Laurel Land Memorial Park south of downtown Dallas.[A]

In Washington, DC, the president's schedule filled-up quickly with strategy meetings. But in the midst of international chaos, President Truman left the White House at the end of the week and boarded a train at Washington's Union Station that took him to the Scout encampment.

Truman arrived at the site at 9 p.m. and took the stage five minutes later. Addressing the cheering masses, he recounted George Washington's saga at Valley Forge during the winter of 1777–78 and alluded to the aggression that was taking place overseas.

"If we are to succeed in our common struggle for peace," he said, "we must know and work with these freedom-loving people of other countries." He hoped this Jamboree would encourage "cooperative human action" among nations.

Present in the audience that evening were 3,000 Texas Scouts and leaders, of which 274 hailed from Circle Ten Council. Having arrived four days prior via the special "Big D" Texas & Pacific train on June 26 from their tour of New York City, all were looking forward to the landmark experience—eventually seeing and hearing speeches from two American presidents, the current one and his eventual successor, Dwight D. Eisenhower.[1]

The contingent, led by Executive Board Member Dr. Harvey J. Piercy, met at Dallas' Union Terminal downtown where the lads loaded their packs, colorful rolled blankets, and trading items into the train cars and took their seats for the ride east. Sitting in one boys' lap was a caged pigeon.

Approached by a civilian passenger walking through the aisle who had never been a Scout asked, "What's that for?"

Answered the lad, "It's a Swap, mister."[2]

Other boys brought the ever-popular horned frogs that reportedly "traded like hotcakes." Others brought Indian arrowheads to sell. When those ran out, they made new stock from Pennsylvania stone and sold more. As the event lasted through July 8, the majority of local Scouts who stayed behind in Dallas had the opportunity to dedicate a unique shrine in the city on Independence Day.

As part of the two-year national "Crusade to Strengthen the Arm of Liberty" program, only five months earlier, 200 Dallas Scouts assembled on the steps of city hall for a torch-lighting ceremony on February 12, 1950, with Ms. Anita Ardinger dressed as the Statue of Liberty from New York City's harbor.

ACROSS LEFT: The Quartermaster position patch issued in the 1950s. TOP: University Park's Troop 70 prepares to leave for the 2nd National Jamboree at Valley Forge led by Scoutmaster Lon Sailers (standing, far right). ABOVE RIGHT: A sample of Circle Ten Council's letterhead in 1950. ABOVE LEFT: The First Class rank patch presented in the 1950s.

LEFT: A different ribbon was presented to each troop that fulfilled the recruiting requirements for the "Forward on Liberty's Team" recruiting campaign from 1952–1955. BELOW LEFT: Miss Anita Ardinger represents Lady Liberty in February 1950. BELOW and FAR BELOW: These small metal pins and pocket pins were worn on the shirt pocket of a Scout or donor who participated in the annual recruiting, funding, or advancement campaigns of the 1950s. RIGHT: Scouts Bill Ewing (left) and Alfred Anderson Jr (right) in a photo published by the *Dallas Morning News.*

corner of the Hall of State Building at the intersection of Grand Avenue and Admiral Nimitz Circle. [3]

At the ceremony inside the Cotton Bowl, "Americans from all walks of life stood in silence" as the 8-foot "Little Sister" was dedicated in solemn reverence. Fourteen-year-old First Class Scout and Woodrow Wilson High School freshman Bill Ewing of Troop 2 chartered by the Greenland Hills Methodist Church at 5835 Penrose Avenue in University Park was chosen by Governor Allan Shivers to accept the statue on behalf of the Council "and for the people of Texas." Ewing's alternate was Alfred W. Anderson Jr., a 13-year-old Scout from Troop 66 at the Oran M. Roberts Elementary School on E. Grand Avenue. Scout George Shaftner of Troop 134 was the official flag bearer at the ceremony.

Now in July, 8-foot-tall copper replicas of the Statue of Liberty called "Little Sisters of Liberty" were being dedicated in cities and towns across the country. Texas State Fair chairman and future Circle Ten Council President Robert Lee Thornton approved the purchase of one statue to reside at Fair Park. It now sits at the northwest

Among the estimated attendance of 26,000 Texans were 5,000 Council

WITH THE FAITH AND COURAGE OF THEIR FORE-
FATHERS WHO MADE POSSIBLE THE FREEDOM OF THESE
UNITED STATES.... THE BOY SCOUTS OF AMERICA
DEDICATE THE REPLICA OF THE STATUE OF LIBERTY
AS A PLEDGE OF EVERLASTING FIDELITY AND LOYALTY.

40th ANNIVERSARY
CRUSADE TO STRENGTHEN THE ARM OF LIBERTY

1950

Flagbearer George Shaftner of Troop 134 (near left) at the dedication ceremony for the "Little Lady of Liberty" (far left) at Fair Park in July 1950.

Scout George Shaftner of Troop 134 holds a flag in Fourth of July ceremonies at the Cotton Bowl in which Boy Scouts of Texas received a replica of Miss Liberty.

Scouts who enjoyed the thrill of a lifetime and experienced an exciting fireworks show at its conclusion.

"The value of the symbol depends on the public understanding of the idea itself which stands behind the Statue of Liberty," explained guest speaker and President of Southern Methodist University Dr. Umphrey Lee. "Liberty is the foundation stone upon which the nation has been built. This symbol is given to the Boy Scouts in keeping with the Scout drive to strengthen the arm of liberty."[4]

"IT IS IMPOSSIBLE TO MEASURE THE VALUE TO SOCIETY CREATED BY THE LEGIONS OF SCOUTS DOING 'GOOD TURNS DAILY' DURING THE 100 YEAR HISTORY OF CIRCLE TEN COUNCIL. THIS COMMUNITY IS BLESSED TO HAVE CREATED THE ICONIC COUNCIL OF THE BEST CHARACTER-BUILDING AND LEADERSHIP INSTITUTE IN HISTORY— THE BOY SCOUTS OF AMERICA."

JOE CRAFTON, EXECUTIVE BOARD MEMBER, CIRCLE TEN COUNCIL, BSA

At the end of 1950, Circle Ten stood at 19 districts with 14,046 Scouts and 5,124 adult leaders. There were 168 packs, 325 troops, and 96 Explorer posts. Over 1,700 African American boys were Scouts in 106 of those units. Thirty-nine boys had earned the rank of Eagle Scout during the year, while 281 Cubs earned the Webelos rank. The sum of 4,301 merit badges were presented with Home Repairs coming as the most earned at 312, while Textiles, Skiing, Signaling, and Citrus Fruit Culture were avoided.

In Council-wide service projects, 285,000 pounds of waste paper were collected along with four tons of clothing in 46,350 Smile Day bags for Goodwill

BELOW: The Circle Ten Council annual banquet in 1950 during the "Strengthen the Arm of Liberty" national BSA campaign that ran in 1950 and 1951.

ACROSS TOP LEFT: Boy Scouts from Troop 161 sponsored by the Munger Avenue Baptist Church exhibit at the 1955 Scout Exposition.

ACROSS BOTTOM LEFT, ACROSS BOTTOM RIGHT, and ABOVE LEFT: Circle Ten Council Scouts participate in the annual clothes collection drive to benefit Goodwill Industries of Greater Dallas. Over the years, hundreds of thousands of bags were collected for the benefit of needy families in the area.

ABOVE RIGHT: Dallas Cub Scouts prepare for a television segment on WFAA-TV promoting the upcoming Scout Circus in 1958.

LEFT: A plaque of appreciation is presented by Circle Ten Council to KRLD radio for their support of Scouting in 1956.

THE GET OUT TO VOTE SERVICE PROJECT

IN SEPTEMBER 1951, *Circle Ten Council participated in the national "Get Out to Vote" drive co-sponsored by BSA and the Freedom Foundation. Scouts placed cardboard door hangers in the shape of the Liberty Bell at 46,000 houses across the territory. Scout Executive Loys Hotchkiss noted the hangers would be "on the doorknob of every home in America." As a popular national Scouting effort, it continued throughout the decade.*[B]

Industries, and 2,950 pounds of food for the poor. Scouts also distributed 4,035 public service posters. They planted 1,650 trees locally and performed 21 wildlife protection projects. These thousands of service hours assisted the American Red Cross, Fire Prevention Week committee, American Legion, Rotary International, Kiwanis and Elks Clubs, Veterans of Foreign Wars, the YMCA, the Chamber of Commerce and Junior Chamber of Commerce (Jaycees), the National Tuberculosis Association, the March of Dimes, the Community Chest, the local Parent Teacher Association, as well as the State Fair of Texas and Goodwill Industries.[5]

The New Year looked promising.

At a meeting of the Council's executive board on April 26, 1950, Health and Safety Chairman A. W. Breeland, the assistant director of personnel at the Lone Star Gas Company, read a letter from Dallas County Health Officer Dr. J. M. Pickard regarding the poor conditions that, once again, existed within Camp Wisdom's dining and food preparation facilities. As the structure had been constructed 27 years earlier in 1923 when Council membership was at 1,200 Scouts, it was not feasible to give the mess hall a facelift because, in his opinion, the building was "worn out."

Likewise for Camp Texoma, the usefulness of the temporary army buildings that had been moved-in five years prior had been "pretty well depleted." For Camp Constantin, the only permanent structure on site was the stone kitchen building that required meals to be served and eaten under canvas. The impact of 2,000 campers a year would soon overwhelm the Council's resources.[6]

LEFT: The Second Class rank badge as presented to Circle Ten Scouts in the 1950s. ABOVE: This patch was awarded to Scouts who attended Camp Wisdom during summer camp sessions in the 1950s. ACROSS, NEAR TOP RIGHT: Scouts take part in a flag ceremony during a summer camp session at Camp Wisdom. ACROSS, FAR TOP RIGHT: Camp Constantin staffers handle a skunk during a merit badge class. ACROSS MIDDLE: Circle Ten Explorers prepare for their high adventure hiking trek at Philmont Scout Ranch.

AS THE SUMMER camping season rolled in, 2,500 Circle Ten Scouts participated in activities held at all three Council camps. Camp Wisdom, now about 400 acres, hosted a number of first-year campers who arrived for basic Scout skills training. Experienced leaders attended training sessions as well. Camp Constantin attendees participated in sailing and fishing and Camp Texoma hosted the local African American Scouts in its final week.

Elsewhere, local Explorer Scouts trekked off to the Philmont Scout Ranch in New Mexico for burro packing and a wagon train trip, with some excursions lasting as long as 23 days.

The price for camp at Wisdom and Texoma ranged from $1.50 for troops that brought their own food to $11.50 for those that did not. Camp Constantin's rates ranged between $3 and $14. By the end of the following year, Constantin had a new dining hall.[C]

BELOW: This piece of Circle Ten Council promotional literature includes an equipment catalog for the upcoming summer camping season. BELOW RIGHT: A Scoutmaster teaches knots to his Scouts at Camp Constantin.

ANGUS G. WYNNE JR. *appreciated local Scouting so much that he became Circle Ten Council's president from 1954 to 1956—the first former Council Scout to do so. Born on January 9, 1914, in Kaufman County, Wynne joined his local troop in the mid-1920s and began his Scouting experience.*

Graduating from Highland Park High School in 1931, he received his bach-  *elor's degree from the University of Texas in Austin in 1938. After working in the Texas oil fields, Wynne joined the U.S. Navy as an ensign during World War II and received six service stars for action seen in the Asiatic and European theatres.*

He founded Wynnewood, a real estate company that developed one of the Southwest's largest suburban tracts in Oak Cliff, which led to other ventures. Following a trip to Anaheim, California's new Disneyland amusement park in 1959, Wynne decided that Texas needed its own large entertainment center.

As a result, he founded the Great Southwest Corporation with New York investors and began construction on their first "Six Flags" park in Arlington, Texas in August 1960. Originally to be named Texas Under Six Flags (referencing the national banners that had flown previously over the state) wife Joanne reminded him that "Texas ain't under nothing."

The Six Flags Over Texas concept developed into parks within Georgia and St. Louis. With success, he remained dedicated to philanthropy and dedicated large amounts of his time and resources to serving as an officer on the boards of 24 organizations and associations of which one of his favorites was Circle Ten Council.

Angus G. Wynne Jr. died in Dallas on March 12, 1979, not having lived long enough to see his latest park concept come to fruition—a water amusement park. That concept, however, lives on through the New Braunfels, Texas-based Schlitterbahn Waterparks company.[D]

After some discussion, the executive board appointed Camp and Activities Chairman Carl J. Rutland to contact a local contractor for advice and a proposal to update all three Council camps. The result was the most aggressive capital campaigns in Council history to date for facility, activity field, and sanitation construction.

Wisdom was to be the Council's main training center while Constantin and Texoma, with their waterfronts, would serve as the Council's summer camps as well as destinations for activities like archery, rifle shooting, boating, and aquatic sports. The preliminary goal was $368,000 but it was quickly bumped to $500,000.[7]

The bequest of 20-year Council Vice President Frank V. Faulker, who died on January 30, 1951, provided $350,000 to the Circle Ten Foundation. Faulkner, reputed to have produced "more crude oil than anyone in the Southwest," had been a 43-year executive with the Magnolia Petroleum Company.

Included with the gift was a stipulation that all proceeds were to be used solely for the benefit of Camp Wisdom until 1972. At which time, all monies would be freed for general Council funding. (By January 1971, proper fiscal management, along with other generous donations, enabled the Circle Ten Foundation's assets to rise to a value of about $2 million.)[8]

On November 14, 1951, the *Dallas Morning News* reported the Council's drive for $525,460 to build-up their three overnight camps, along with two other Council properties that were used for "day hikes." They were little-known Camp Murchison in the Wilmer-Hutchins area and Camp Shuler near Lake Whitney, about 15 miles west of Hillsboro.

1953 ANNUAL REPORT
Circle Ten Council
Boy Scouts of America

As each district had their own financial quota to collect, the Dallas County District was responsible for raising about $400,000 of the total sum beginning in late April 1952. Chairman and future Council President John E. Mitchell Jr. was in charge of the event. His assistants were J. D. Francis and Angus G. Wynne Jr., a real estate developer and future council president as well.[9]

The two week general campaign began with a luncheon in the Baker Hotel's posh Peacock Terrace on May 7. By the next day, a quarter of the goal had been met with receipts of over $144,000 coming in and aided by the *Dallas Morning News* publishing a Page 2 editorial declaring Council donations as a "safe investment that will pay off better than a flowing wildcat oil well."

TOP: The cover of Circle Ten Council's 1953 Annual Report handed out to banquet attendees.

CIRCLE TEN SCOUTS CHOSEN TO REPRESENT REGION 9

DURING BOY SCOUT WEEK 1952, *a six-foot tall, 16-year-old Eagle Scout named Frank E. McLain of University Park's Troop 70 (below) was chosen as one of a dozen Scouts to deliver BSA's Annual Report to the Nation to President Dwight D. Eisenhower in the White House (middle, and far below).*

"I haven't gotten over the excitement yet," McLain told Council President John E. Mitchell, who nominated him as Region 9's youth representative after witnessing his work at the most recent Junior Leader Conference held at Southern Methodist University. McLain had presided over a mass meeting of 4,000 Scouts from Texas, Oklahoma, and New Mexico, where he showed an impressive grasp of parliamentary procedure.

As a gift to his 11 colleagues from the other BSA regions, McLain presented each with a certificate from Texas Governor Allan Shivers citing them as "Honorary Texans."

Similarly in December 1954, 16-year-old Eagle Scout Jerry Phillips of Garland was nominated by Circle Ten Council to help deliver the Report to the State as well as represent Region 9 for BSA's Annual Report to the Nation in 1955.

Arriving in Austin on Saturday, February 19, 1955, the Council's representatives included Phillips, Charles M. Cooper III of McKinney, Joe Poitt of Cleburne, Howard Hardy of Malakoff in Henderson County, Wesley Howard of Ennis, and Albert Allison and Richard Beaupre, both of Dallas. About 2,500 other Texas Scouts joined in the ceremonies that "swarmed" the capital building after a parade was held along N. Congress Avenue.[E]

But by May 17 only about half the goal had been raised, so the original end date of May 20 was moved out. By June 4 about $394,000 had been committed to. When the official drive closed a short time later, Circle Ten Council had finished with a grand total of $478,300, but there was "every indication" that suggested it would "secure the complete goal."[10]

As allotted, $98,000 went towards new water and sanitation facilities and $165,000 for new dining facilities at all camps. Camp Texoma received a 250-person capacity mess hall with Camp Constantin's dining facility costing $45,248. Camp Wisdom got a 300-seat dining hall for nearly $65,000. A large portrait of Daddy Wisdom, now hanging in the Harbin Scout Museum, kept watch over the boys eating in the new facility. Camp Wisdom also received a large training lodge attached to its dining hall.

There was $9,000 allotted for health lodges at Camps Texoma and Constantin, along with $25,000 for camp office buildings and staff quarters, $87,780 for waterfront equipment and development, and $35,000 for general grounds improvements.

A stipend of $22,325 was made for the purchase of canvass tents, cots and portable wooden floors, with another $9,600 for program equipment, and $1,500 to construct trading posts. An additional $10,000 was given to develop Explorer bases within the Council, with $20,000 used for lodges and another $15,000 for cooking shelters, water supply, and sanitary facilities at Camps Murchison and Shuler.[11]

By the 1953 summer camping season, all three main camps had new dining halls with full kitchens that were reputed to be better furnished than some luxury hotels. There were over three miles of new water lines ranging from 4 inches in diameter down to ½ inch in size, and updated sanitation facilities.

While Camp Wisdom got its new training center, Camps Constantin and Texoma received new water storage tanks and over 80 new canoes and rowboats. The Camps Constantin and Wisdom dining facilities are the same ones used today; although, Camp Constantin's has been expanded in recent years and Camp Wisdom's new dining hall is under construction as of this writing.

When BSA's 44th anniversary came around in February 1954, Camp Constantin had its first health lodge donated by Southwestern Bell. The *Dallas Morning News* donated both the staff quarters and the George B. Dealey Office Building in honor of their former chairman and vocal Scouting

ACROSS TOP: The Circle Ten Council *Camping Guide* advertised the exciting times to be had at its three summer camps during the 1953 season. ACROSS FAR LEFT: A Scout prepares his meal over an open campfire at Camp Wisdom. ACROSS RIGHT: Scouts at Camp Constantin could participate in many different activities ranging from archery (across top right and lower left) to rifle and shotgun shooting (across lower and top left). Another popular activity was arm wrestling (left) during their down times or before meals that were announced with the ringing of the "dinner bell" outside the mess hall (lower left).

DOAK WALKER AND THE SCOUT EXPOSITION

ON APRIL 17 AND 18, 1953, *the Boy Scout Exposition, also known as "the greatest boy show in the Southwest," was held in the General Exhibits Building at Fair Park. More than 6,000 Scouts from 187 local troops attended. Like previous Expos, units built towers, bridges, canoes, and tended to honeybees. One lucky troop had the honor of wrapping first aid bandages around the body of SMU's famous Heisman Trophy winner and professional football star, Doak Walker.*

"The men and women who devote literally thousands of hours a week to Scouting deserve a lot of credit," declared Scout Executive Loys Hotchkiss. *"If even more of them could give of their* experience and time during the few short years that boys are boys, it would help keep America free."*[F]

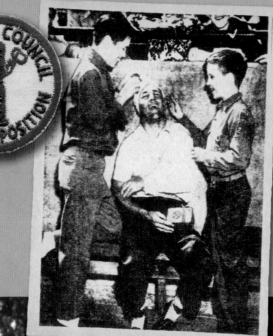

LEFT: Doak Walker, professional football hero and Heisman Trophy winner from SMU, gets bandaged by Circle Council Scouts. FAR LEFT: Several patches issued to attendees of the Circle Ten Council Scout Expositions during the 1950s. ACROSS TOP LEFT and ACROSS TOP RIGHT: Scouts perform for the crowds at the Scout Exposition. BELOW: Scouts performing in the Cotton Bowl at Fair Park.

TANDEM FATHER/SON EAGLE SCOUT CEREMONIES IN CIRCLE TEN COUNCIL

ON OCTOBER 7, 1952, *several pairs of father/son Eagle Scout ceremonies took place in Circle Ten Council. (In 1965, national BSA policy would change to permit only those holding a youth leadership position to be eligible for the award.)*

Receiving the medal on that October day were Troop 19 Scoutmaster Dr. Tom E. Smith and son McKamy. Assistant Scoutmaster Clayton Ayers and son Norman did so as well.

Other notable Circle Ten father and son recipients were Scoutmaster O. R. Hendricks and son Earl of Troop 17 at the Oak Cliff Christian Church at 300 E. 10th Street in August 1948. A. E. Harris Sr. and son A. E. Jr. of Troop 6 at the W. E. Greiner Junior High School at 501 S. Edgefield Avenue received it in September 1942. Orville Mitchell Sr. and son Orville Jr. earned the awards from Troop 55 at the East Dallas Christian Church at 629 N. Peak Street in March 1942, while D. H. McAnally Sr. of the Church of the Incarnation's Troop 34 at 3966 McKinney Avenue received the medal with his son D. H. McAnally Jr.[G]

supporter. Also added were a large warehouse, swim and boat dock, the Ray Foley memorial trading post, and the Lou Guthrie memorial Explorer Base. United Fidelity Life Insurance Company gave the chapel in memory of their former chairman, D. E. Waggoner.

Camp Wisdom had its new camp headquarters donated by the Haggar family; the administration building was donated by R. B. George & Company, along with the four Austin F. Allen memorial Troop Lodge buildings. The "Winter

BELOW LEFT: The Star rank patch as presented to Scouts in the 1950s. BELOW: Second Class Scout Bobby Webster of Troop 12 receives the Certificate for Heroism from BSA's National Court of Honor on May 19, 1955.

THE FIRST CIRCLE TEN COUNCIL WOOD BADGE REUNION

ON JANUARY 28, 1956, *the first "fellowship meeting and dinner" for "Wood Badge Men" was held at 4 p.m. at Camp Wisdom. Any graduate of the Council's first leadership course under Melvin Smith or any other person who had completed the advanced training course elsewhere could attend.[1]*

Camp site" was given by Mosher Steel in honor of their founder, W. S. Mosher. That gift included several Adirondack shelters, one of which still exists at Sailers Point campsite. In 1956, the Council began construction on a new house for Camp Wisdom's Camp Ranger.

ABOVE: The official gold training neckerchief earned by Boy Scout leaders prior to the adoption of the Wood Badge adult leadership course in 1955. The Owl head and totem base were earned with the "satisfactory completion of Basic Training for Leaders." The Raccoon head followed by qualifying for the adult leader Oak Leaf "Acorn Patch" along with completion of an additional training session. The Fox head was added when the Scouter completed the Outdoor portion of his training that included 24 hours in the field. The Eagle head completed the training program after completion of 7 hours of courses in troop operations. RIGHT: The felt patch once worn by the Camp Wisdom Ranger.

Camp Texoma's main expenditures were the $48,462 for its dining lodge along with $16,500 for the new water supply and sanitation system.[12]

By mid-May 1958, it was becoming apparent that change was coming to the position of Scout Executive as Loys Hotchkiss underwent surgery to remove a cancerous portion of his colon. The Council's executive board sent him "wishes for a speedy recovery" with individual members

BY 1955, *Circle Ten Council boasted membership of 19,001 Scouts—a new high. But Scouting in Dallas would reach another milestone within the year as a new adult training course was adopted by the Council. Known as Wood Badge and symbolized by two wooden beads suspended on a leather thong around the neck, it originated in England in 1919 with its first official course.*

Migrating to the United States by 1936, the first two-week trial courses were taught in May

and June at BSA's official training center located at the Schiff Scout Reservation in Mendham,

New Jersey. One of the graduates from both sessions was William "Green Bar Bill" Hillcourt, the author of the Patrol Leader's Handbook *and frequent* Boys' Life *magazine columnist.*

Hillcourt's expansive knowledge of Scouting and dedication to the program vaulted him into the position of course director (Scoutmaster) for the first two official events held in 1948 at Schiff and at the Philmont Scout Ranch. Attending the Philmont course from October 2–10 was Dallas' own Dr. Harvey J. Piercy.

By 1953, the Dan Beard Council in Cincinnati, Ohio, held the first council course in August 1953. Its success spawned eight more courses the following year held throughout the country. In June 1955, Circle Ten's leadership training committee chairman, P. M. Rutherford Jr., authorized the Council to hold its first Wood Badge course at Camp Constantin from November 5–13, 1955.

It was led by Scouters who had attended Wood Badge in other councils. Circle Ten staff member Melvin R. Smith served as its course director. Dr. Malcolm B. Bowers, a University Park dentist and the Scoutmaster of Troop 82, acted as senior patrol leader, while George C. Frickel, Circle Ten's director of training and eventual assistant national director of Cubbing, was quartermaster. O. R. Hendricks of Dallas' Troop 17 was his assistant.

The first specially selected training class of 30 men was invited to attend. Two more courses followed in 1956, another in 1957, and Wood Badge course No. 5 occurred in April 1958. As of this writing, there have been over 105 Circle Ten courses that have trained thousands of men and women in the methods and skills of Scouting.[H]

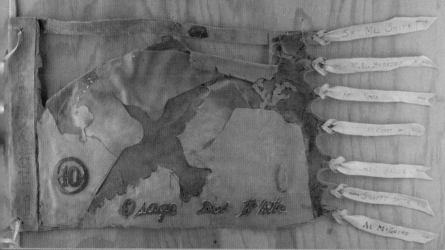

LEFT: A Dallas Scout holds a Liberty Bell symbolizing BSA's national theme of "Forward on Liberty's Team" as depicted on the cover of the 1955 Circle Ten Council Annual Report. BELOW: The Red and White community strips that originally designated a Scout's city developed into ones that stated the Scout's home council. Eventually, they became the Council Service Patches of today.

ACROSS LOWER LEFT: The Bobwhite Patrol's leather flag from Wood Badge #1 held at Camp Constantin in November 1955. ACROSS TOP LEFT: The Fox Patrol of Wood Badge #1 practices basic Scouting knots. ACROSS BOTTOM RIGHT: The Fox Patrol of Wood Badge #98 held at the Philmont Scout Ranch in the summer of 2011. ACROSS TOP RIGHT: The official Wood Badge course neckerchief worn by William "Green Bar Bill" Hillcourt when he was the Course Director of BSA's first two American Wood Badge courses in 1948. This thong of beads was once owned by Region 9 executive M. H. McMasters that includes an original Chief Dinizulu bead presented to him during the completion of his Wood Badge course held at Gilwell Park in England in the 1930s. TOP RIGHT: Members of Troop 156 sponsored by the Hamilton Park Elementary School prepare for a campout. ABOVE RIGHT: A Scout reads his new copy of the Boy Scout *Handbook* featuring the "walking Rockwell" cover – Norman Rockwell's iconic painting of a smiling Boy Scout in full stride.

adding their own personal correspondence. Although Hotchkiss returned to work, his tenure came to an abrupt end on March 11, 1960, when he died as a result of the cancer spreading to his lungs.[13]

Scout Executive Loys Leon Hotchkiss' tenure had lasted over 23 years—the longest to date. Five days later and with heavy hearts, the executive board appointed an executive search committee to find his successor.

At his passing, there were over 28,000 Council Scouts within 960 units led by 10,568 leaders and volunteers. Cub Scouts made up about 60 percent of the youth membership numbering 15,000 members and Explorer Scouts coming in just below 2,000. There were now three fully functioning camps with land and

equipment valued at $425,000 (about $3.1 million today). During his lifetime, Council service projects included get out to vote drives, clothes collections that gathered about 150,000 bags of items, many tons of scrap metal, rubber items, and wastepaper. Total Scout Circus attendance numbered in the hundreds of thousands of visitors, along with thousands more for the Scout Expositions, merit badge shows, and camporees.

The Council remained debt free with an annual budget that approached $500,000—a number that would keep growing as donations and programs expanded within Circle Ten's boundaries.

For sure, "Hotch" had left the Council better than he had found it—placing it on its present trajectory of sustainable growth within the community. The incoming Scout Executive would have huge shoes to fill. And by late April, that person was named—Charles F. Grable — the executive at Tulsa, Oklahoma's Indian Nations Council.[14]

A NEW ERA HAD BEGUN.

ACROSS LEFT: Den Mothers from Pack 105 in Garland in 1952. TOP LEFT: A promotional photograph for a 1950s Scout Circus featuring boys from Troops 82 and 70 based in the Park Cities. TOP RIGHT: Troop 70 Scouts pose for a photograph at a Court of Honor. ABOVE LOWER LEFT and ABOVE MIDDLE RIGHT: Each year, the youth representatives from many Texas Councils gathered in Austin, Texas to deliver Texas Scouting's Annual Report to Governor Price Daniel – an event hosted today by the Capital Area (Austin) Council. ABOVE MIDDLE LEFT: The Eagle Scout patch that was presented to Scouts in the 1950s. ABOVE LOWER RIGHT: The Life rank patch presented to Scouts in the 1950s.

Part III

SECURING THE FUTURE
(1960-2013)

THE MAN WHO IS TWELVE YEARS OLD

I know of a man who lives nearby
In a land called Everywhere,
You cannot tell from the hat that he dons
Or the clothes that he chooses to wear.

But 'neath his coat with many a patch
Lies a heart more precious than gold,
The heart of a man, 'neath the coat of a boy,
A man who is twelve years old.

We cannot tell what the future will bear
For the boys that we carelessly meet.
For there's many a Congressman doing his chores,
And President out in the street.

For the hands that lay grasp to the toys of today,
Will soon - reins of power they'll hold,
So, I raise a strong arm, and I proudly salute
That man who is twelve years old.

—UNKNOWN

chapter 12

THE COUNTER-COUNTER REVOLUTION (1960–1972)

"Camping is the base upon which Scouting grows. Group living, in summer camp and on short-term camping trips in the other seasons, provides a springboard for the development of character and citizenship."

JOHN D. MURCHISON
CHAIRMAN, "BUILDING FOR YOUTH" CAMPAIGN
DECEMBER 18, 1965

New Scout Executive Charles Grable upon his arrival in Dallas in 1960 and a 1st place ribbon awarded at the Scout Exposition held that year.

CHARLES F. GRABLE stepped into his new post of Scout Executive on June 1, 1960, intent to build upon the strong legacy left by his predecessor, Loys Hotchkiss. Standing about six-feet tall with well-groomed black hair, a strong jaw, and a pleasant smile, the affable Grable attended his first executive board meeting on October 4.

Introduced by Council President Gus Bowman, the new executive paid tribute to Hotchkiss noting, "It is a real pleasure to follow a man who was as dedicated as he was." Next, he revealed his initial goals such as funding the Council's first headquarters building, making Camp Wisdom "the camping and training showplace of America," and ridding the budget of any wasteful spending. Grable closed his presentation with a poignant reminder to the board, "the only limits are the ones we draw are around ourselves."[1]

BOY SCOUTS OF AMERICA
1910
1960
50TH YEAR
EXPOSITION
1
AWARD

BY OCTOBER 1960, *420 Council Scouts returned from their summer trip to the fifth National Jamboree held in Colorado Springs, Colorado celebrating Scouting's Golden Anniversary. As such, the event garnered the attendance of 55,000 Scouts from across the nation as well as a visit from President Dwight D. Eisenhower. He arrived on July 28 and was driven in an open-air car between several miles of Scouts who lined both sides of the road, cheering and waving, all trying to get his attention.*

Twenty-five percent of the Council's contingent came from two units —Troop 57 in Garland and Troop 70 in University Park. Troop 57, Gray Owl District's oldest unit chartered by the First United Methodist Church, brought 37 Scouts. Troop 70, known as the "Jamboree Troop" as it was their fourth consecutive jamboree under Scoutmaster Lon Sailers, brought a symbolic 70 boys with them. Their unit was the single largest troop to attend the event overall.

Enterprising Circle Ten Scouts brought with them unique local items to swap, such as rattlesnake rattles, legendary horned toads, and the "Most Valuable Swap of All"—cellophane bags filled with Texas soil.

"For us, the big things to trade with were armadillo tailbone neckerchief slides," recalled Brad Smith, a Tenderfoot Scout in Troop 70 at the time. *"When trading with other Scouts, the older guys looked out for us little guys, so that we wouldn't get the short end of a swap, since we were new."*

Another Scout, Harold Smith (no relation to Brad), was working as a Philmont ranger and drove north with friends on their day off to visit the Jamboree.

"We were sitting in the Philmont headquarters building with nothing to do at the time," he reflected, *"so four of us piled into my 1948 Dodge and we headed north."*

ABOVE and TOP RIGHT: The 28-foot tall Old Man Texas served as the official jamboree gateway for Troop 70 between 1957 and 2010. It was designed by *Dallas Morning News* artist John Knott and made with 2x4 lumber sheeted on both sides with painted plywood. RIGHT: The official neckerchief, backpatch, and two special event pocket patches issued for the 1960 National Jamboree in Colorado Springs, Colorado.

Laden with 25 Golden Anniversary Philmont patches that he had purchased at the trading post for 50 cents apiece, each was sold at a tidy profit.

Another popular activity was eating—made possible by a "staggering stockpile" of 123,360 cans of condensed soup provided by the Campbell's Soup Company to be used as an ingredient in all meals. For example, at breakfast, the soup was drunk straight out of the can. At lunch, it worked as the base for the cheese sauce served over toast as Welsh rarebit (also known as Welsh rabbit).

At dinner, it was a key ingredient in a fanciful meat dish known as "Chuckwagon Burgoo." The Burgoo featured "1 can of condensed cream of celery soup" and "2 cans of condensed tomato soup" along with several pounds of meat, a pound of elbow macaroni, and a pound of onions.

"It was a great experience and I wouldn't trade those memories for anything," affirmed Harold.[A]

CAMP CONSTANTIN-1961

STRENGTHEN AMERICA

CHARACTER COUNTS

46th ANNUAL MEETING-ANNUAL REPORT
Circle Ten Council – Boy Scouts of America
Dallas Memorial Auditorium • January 24, 1961

RECRUITER '61

Following the two decade long Hotchkiss era, Grable's tenure would last but a mere four years.

In 1961, Circle Ten Council representatives presented the Eagle medal to three brothers in one ceremony—Texas' first. Held at the Pleasant Grove Shopping Center, twins Ronnie and Donnie Parrish along with brother Leon gathered with family and friends from Explorer Post 91 for the event. But this would be a temporary record. Three years later, the four Blackburn brothers of Explorer Post 38—Thurman, Joe, Walter, and Roger—received the rank at ceremonies held at the Lakewood Methodist Church at Lakeshore Drive and Abrams Road. The *Dallas Morning News* believed this event to be the first of its kind in the nation.

TOP LEFT: The members of Troop 8 in Oak Cliff at Camp Constantin in 1961. TOP RIGHT: The Circle Ten Council Annual Meeting program from 1961. ABOVE MIDDLE: A scene from the 1961 Annual Meeting and banquet. ABOVE: The Recruiter patch given to any Scout who registered a new member during the 1961 membership campaign. LEFT: Texas Governor Price Daniel signing autographs for Circle Ten Scouts.

But boys were not the only ones showing tenacity towards a goal. In 1962, 26-year-old George A. Stuart, a polio-stricken worker at Goodwill Industries and a seven year tenured Assistant Scoutmaster at Troop 555, set a tireless example of how to *never* give up. George "exercised with withered muscles day and night and swam with his Scouts regularly."

In recognizing another example of Scouting excellence, the Council awarded the Silver Beaver medal to 36-year-old Gene Brown of Corsicana, Texas—a blind

ABOVE: Scouts perform a flag ceremony at Camp Constantin around 1963. RIGHT: A disabled Cub Scout on a field trip with his den in 1962. FAR RIGHT: The felt patch awarded to Scouts who participated in the annual clothes collection drive for Goodwill Industries in 1963.

CIRCLE TEN COUNCIL'S FIRST HISPANIC EAGLE SCOUTS

ON TUESDAY, JANUARY 22, *1963, Circle Ten Council presented the Eagle medal to its first two Hispanic recipients. Making this an extra special event, they were father and son. Raymundo "Tata" Rubio Sr. was a 37-year-old handyman born in Aquila, Texas, south of Hillsboro. Raymundo Jr. was a 13-year-old Scout who excelled in an active program put on by Oak Cliff's Troop 75 sponsored by St. Cecilia's Catholic Church at 1809 West Davis Street.*[B]

A NEW UNIFORM!

THE GROWING AFRICAN AMERICAN SCOUTING PROGRAM

IN 1962, *Scouting in the local African American community was growing. Due to the success lodged by the first minority district (Silver Palm), the Bronze Star district was formed in October 1962 under the Council's new African American District Executive Noble Gilstrap*

(right) *from nearby Greenville, Texas. District Chairman T. Z. Davis, the principal of the K. B. Polk Elementary School east of Love Field in Dallas, challenged his district committee to oversee the immediate recruitment of 350 boys and the necessary adult leadership.*

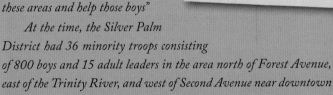

NOBLE GILSTRAP
Mustang District Executive

"When our men learn more about Scouting," said Assistant District Executive Abraham Eatmon, *"they will become more interested in it. Let's go back into these areas and help those boys"*

At the time, the Silver Palm District had 36 minority troops consisting of 800 boys and 15 adult leaders in the area north of Forest Avenue, east of the Trinity River, and west of Second Avenue near downtown Dallas.

Already organized were Troop 905 at Hamilton Park Methodist Church, Troop 941 at the Roseland Home, Troop 167 at the Good Street Baptist Church, Troop 160 at the J. P. Stark School, Troop 171 at the K. B. Polk School, Troop 158 at the Bethany Baptist Church, Troop 163 at the Munger Avenue Baptist Church, Troop 909 at the John Henry Brown School, Troop 920 at the St. James African Methodist Episcopal Temple, Troop 916 at the Christopher Attucks School, Troop 162 at the B. F. Darrell School, and Troop 903 at the Arlington Park School.[C]

ABOVE: A page from the Council's 1963 Annual Report that featured an advertisement for local Scout uniform distributors. RIGHT: A troop of African American Scouts that attended a week-long summer session at Camp Texoma in 1963.

man who served as the Navarro District's training chairman.

In White Rock District, Troop 862 was formed to serve disabled students at Angels Inc., a day school located at 2860 Peavy Road for boys in the special education classes in the Dallas public schools.

Children Inc., a similar organization, organized a troop for mentally challenged Scouts at their 110 Oregon Avenue facility in Oak Cliff.[2]

RICHARD W. JUNG—CIRCLE TEN COUNCIL'S FIRST ASIAN EAGLE SCOUT

ON MAY 26, *1964, 16-year-old Richard W. Jung of Troop 45 was the first Scout of Asian descent to earn the rank of Eagle Scout in Circle Ten Council.*

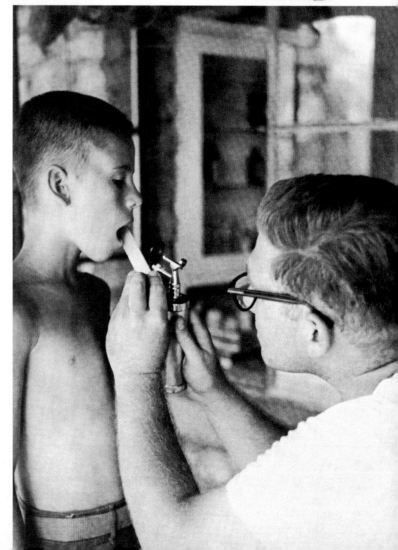

TOP: Texas Governor John Connally receiving a delegation of Circle Ten Scouts during the Annual Report to the State in February 1964. The Governor, shown with his am in a sling, was recuperating from the gunshot wound suffered in Dallas during the assassination of President John F. Kennedy on November 22, 1963. TOP RIGHT: The patch and segments awarded to a Scout who completed and eventually staffed the Council's Oak Leaf Training course. RIGHT: The camp doctor examining a Scout during a summer session at Camp Constantin in 1964.

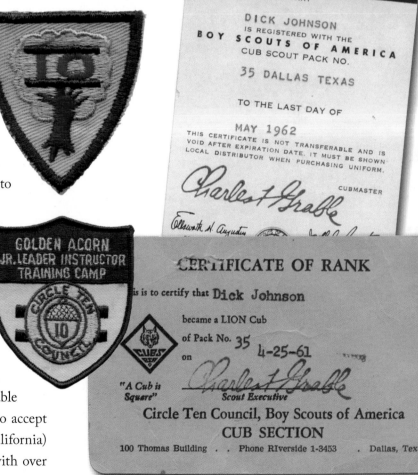

S cout Executive Grable, dedicated to improving the quality of boy leaders within the Council, initiated plans to begin training older youth in a new leadership course known as "White Stag" during the summer of 1963. The following year, the course was renamed "Golden Acorn" and became the follow-up course to the Oak Leaf training sessions initiated over a decade earlier. Held as three, 1-week gatherings at Camp Wisdom in June 1964, Golden Acorn's success ushered in a new syllabus and name change in 2003—National Youth Leadership Training or NYLT.

After nearly four years of program growth in Circle Ten Council, Scout Executive Grable resigned his position effective June 1964 to accept the same post in the Los Angeles (California) Council, the third largest in the nation with over 70,000 members.

Under Grable's leadership, Circle Ten membership expanded from over 38,500 members (28,000 boys and 10,500 leaders) in 960 units when he arrived in 1960 to about 45,000 total members in 1,109 units when he left.[3]

TOP: The first graduates of the 1964 Golden Acorn Junior Leader Training course. MIDDLE LEFT: The Oak Tree Training patch awarded to Scoutmasters and their assistants who completed the course after April 1964. ABOVE LEFT: The Golden Acorn patch presented to Scouts who completed advanced junior leader training and put their training into action. Attendance was by invitation only. MIDDLE RIGHT and ABOVE RIGHT: The registration and rank certificate of Cub Scout Dick Johnson in 1961. Johnson was the son of Eagle Scout Lemuel Johnson III who attended the 1937 National Jamboree with the Circle Ten Council contingent.

ROUND-UP
10 '61 AWARD

To be expected, Charlie Grable's successor was a magnificent leader as well—just what the Council needed during the turbulent social climate of the Vietnam War era. Arriving in Dallas in August 1964, Scout Executive James L. Tarr came from the 23,000-member Covered Wagon Council based in Omaha, Nebraska, where he had been their chief executive for the previous seven years.

Tarr had begun his career some years earlier as a district executive in Austin's Capital Area (Texas)

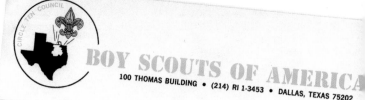

Council and received a promotion to the Scout Executive's post in Galveston's Bay Area (Texas) Council in 1952.

As a youth, he had been a Cub Scout who eventually joined the Boy Scout program and attained the rank of Eagle Scout. Tarr attended the 1937 National Jamboree in Washington, DC—the place where he decided to make Scouting his life's vocation.

"Scouting builds self-reliance and encourages concern for others," he proclaimed years later. "For God and Country' is not only what the Boy Scouts stands for, but what it accomplishes."

Upon taking the reins of Circle Ten Council, Tarr had several objectives: increase membership, draft its first non-discrimination policy statement, fund a new Council camp, and build a permanent headquarters/service center. By the end of 1964, one item was checked off that list—the membership drive.[4]

ACROSS TOP LEFT: Circle Ten Cub Scout Billy Brummitt plays with his pet iguana during a den meeting in 1965. The small reptile also served as his Pack's official mascot. ACROSS TOP RIGHT: The patch presented to Scouts who participated in the Circle Ten membership Round-up in 1961. ACROSS BOTTOM LEFT: Scouts collect bags of clothing during the 1963 Scout Good Turn Day. TOP LEFT: A Scout receives swimming instruction in Possum Kingdom Lake at Camp Constantin in 1964. TOP RIGHT: The Circle Ten Council letterhead in 1963. MIDDLE LEFT: Circle Ten Council Scout Executive James L. Tarr in 1964. LOWER LEFT: A troop of African American Scouts around 1966.

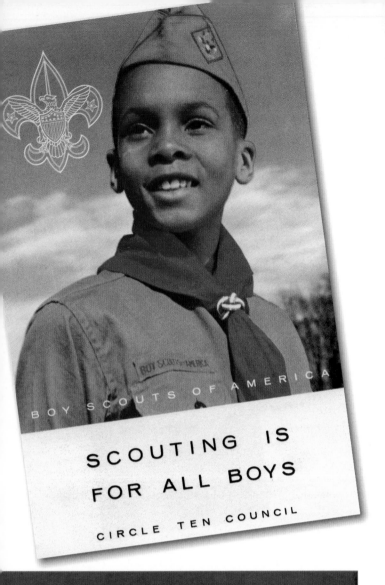

SCOUTING IS
FOR ALL BOYS

CIRCLE TEN COUNCIL

THE MITCHELL-HEAD SERVICE CENTER

IN JUNE 1965, *Circle Ten Council's executive board was prepared to fund and build its first Scouting service center building. Board member and former Council President Austin F. Allen reported that the building's cost came in at a "reasonable" $259,000 with an additional $10,000 allotted for furniture. To pay for it, Council leaders voted to take a $200,000 loan from the Circle Ten Foundation at an interest rate of 4 percent per annum for 40 years. To ease these funding pains, an additional $115,000 in donations was raised but not yet allotted to the building's costs.*

On August 12, 1965, the Mitchell-Head Service Center at 1922 Anson Road was dedicated. Named in honor of SMU law professor Homer R. Mitchell and Texas Power and Light Company Chairman W. B. Head, it contained 5,304 luxurious square feet and a whopping 65 parking spaces for staff and visitors. The 44,728 Scouts and leaders in the 25 districts now had a place to call their own.

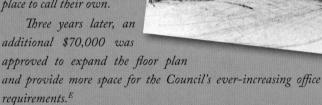

Three years later, an additional $70,000 was approved to expand the floor plan and provide more space for the Council's ever-increasing office requirements.[E]

CIRCLE TEN COUNCIL'S FIRST NON-DISCRIMINATION POLICY

ON FEBRUARY 23, 1965, *under the leadership of Scout Executive James L. Tarr, the executive board approved Circle Ten Council's first Non-Discrimination Policy Statement. It read,*

Services of the Circle Ten Council, Boy Scouts of America are rendered without discrimination or segregation because of race, creed, color or national origin.

It is the policy and practice of the Circle Ten Council, Boy Scouts of America that its Executive Board and its Committees are open to representation from all segments of the public.

It is further the policy and practice that there be no discrimination with regard to hiring, assignment, promotion or other condition of staff employment.[D]

ACROSS FAR LEFT: The cover of the Circle Ten Council's 1966 Annual Report that first expresses its official policy of non-discrimination among members and employees. BELOW: A map of Camp Wisdom that shows the proposed path of the new Spur 408 (to the west) and Interstate Highway 20 through camp. The dotted line with the "x" runs directly through the present Jim Sowell Administration Building. Through intense negotiation, the highway was moved slightly southward to its current location (and now through the original campsite where Daddy Wisdom witnessed Troop 1's prayer service in 1920). BOTTOM RIGHT: A dump truck removes dirt during the construction of Interstate Highway 20 in 1974.

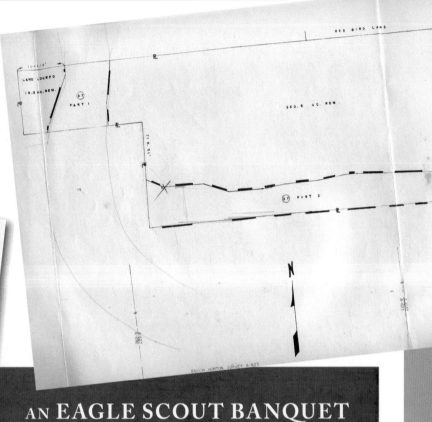

INTERSTATE HIGHWAY 20 AND CAMP WISDOM

IN MAY 1965, *the Texas Highway Department sent Circle Ten Council preliminary plans that condemned about 140 acres of Camp Wisdom land to make way for the proposed Interstate Highway 20. Meeting with county planners, Scout Executive James L. Tarr was shown aerial photographs depicting the probable route (through the current Sowell Center Headquarters Building and Harbin Scout Museum) and what it would leave for the Council—about 260 acres. Tarr left the meeting intent upon "continuing to make effective use of the property for training and overnight camping." Refusing to allow a coup by the county, Council leaders appointed a committee to negotiate with the highway department for both a fair price and a more southern route through camp property.*

To blunt the effects of the annexation, the Council purchased as much land bordering Camp Wisdom as was available. In July 1965, a 20-acre parcel in the southwest corner of the camp was targeted. Council Camping Chairman William P. Clements Jr. purchased the land for $5,000 and donated it to the Council "in the interest of Scouting."

By April 1969, the highway department was ready to begin construction and submitted their requisition to purchase a sum of 109 acres of Camp Wisdom for $220,000—amounting to $1,800 per acre. Believing the land value to be significantly higher, Council representatives led by Clements and attorney Robert Richie rejected the offer and countered with a revised $3,000-per-acre price based on comparable sales in the area.

On April 28, 1970, the southern and western portions of Camp Wisdom were sold for $314,500 for the right-of-way construction of Interstate 20 to the south and Spur 408 to the west.

Unfortunately, the Council would not receive payment for that land for nearly 40 years. In November 2009, Dallas County's check finally arrived in the Council's office for the full amount due—lacking any accrued interest for the overdue payment.[G]

AN EAGLE SCOUT BANQUET AND SPEAKER

ON THURSDAY, *February 24, 1966, 234 Eagle Scouts assembled at the downtown Sheraton-Dallas Hotel for one of the first Eagle Scout banquets held by the Circle Ten Council. Featuring Southwestern Bell Telephone Company President R. A. Goodson as the evening's guest speaker, each boy was accompanied by a member of the business community "from the vocational field the boy is interested in." The master of ceremonies was the alumni director of Southern Methodist University and fellow Eagle Scout Pierce Allman.*

Each Scout received a memorable dinner along with a certificate of commendation signed by Texas Governor John Connally.[F]

THE FORMATION OF THE CLEMENTS SCOUT RESERVATION

IN MARCH 1966, *the $1,310,000 "Building for Youth"* *fundraising campaign formally kicked off with Dallas businessman John D. Murchison as its general chairman. Phillip T. Bee and William P. Clements Jr. served as its vice chairmen. Although monies raised would be used for multiple purposes, the most important expenditure was for the purchase of the Council's new camp that totaled 3,000 wooded acres in Athens, Texas, about 60 miles southeast of Dallas in Henderson County. Other sites previously under consideration were at Lake Whitney near Cleburne and a "large area in Oklahoma near [the town of] Antlers."*

Included in the Athens land were six lakes and ponds, beaver dams, forest-covered hills, and wildlife ranging from rabbits to deer to bobcats and coyotes. In sum, the property was a consolidation of seven land parcels belonging to prominent families like the Howells, the Bells, the Carrigans, the Kirklands, the Halls, the Downses, and brothers John and Clint Murchison Jr. The Circle Ten Foundation made the mass purchase over twelve months, all orchestrated by Clements.

"The fact that the future Governor was able to put together such a large parcel of land was absolutely incredible," recalled former Council

President John Stuart III. "His ability and purpose were quite laudable."

A 250-acre lake located in the northernmost section of the property was named in honor of John D. Murchison, who donated back 2/3s of the $200,000 sales price to the Foundation.

Another large lake at the property's southern end was dubbed "Jonsson Lake" in honor of Dallas Mayor Erik Jonsson, whose $300,000 campaign donation was put toward the purchase of the rest of the Henderson County camping paradise.

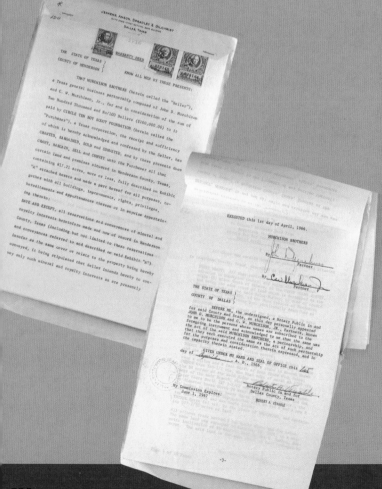

ABOVE: Dallas Mayor J. Erik Jonsson receiving a neckerchief in 1964. LEFT: The land title issued by brothers Clint and John D. Murchison to Circle Ten Council for the property that would become the Clements Scout Reservation. ACROSS RIGHT BOTTOM: The main entrance to the Clements Scout Reservation in the 1970s. ACROSS TOP RIGHT: The official Clements Scout Reservation patch with "charter year" rocker issued at summer camp.

By the end of March, over $900,000 had been raised in the span of two weeks. Ending on April 22, the final tally surpassed $1.4 million that enabled the purchase of an additional 500 acres adjoining the property. Proudly, Clements declared the Circle Ten Scout Reservation would serve the Council's needs well into the year 2000.

By summer, the first honorific was announced—the shooting area dubbed the Thomas A. Hord Rifle Range in honor of the 50-year tenured Scoutmaster of Troop 1.

Three years later, in October 1969, Clements committed funds from his personal foundation to "fully develop at least three additional camps at the Circle Ten Scout Reservation." In the proposal titled "Commitment to Scouting," the Clements Foundation reserved naming rights for the whole of the Reservation as well as the two camps currently inside.

On April 28, 1970, a motion was made by Council Camping Chairman and future Council President Omar Harvey to rename the Circle Ten Scout Reservation as the Clements Scout Reservation. Humbled, Clements gave tribute to his parents and placed a memorial plaque at the main entrance to honor them, Mr. and Mrs. W. P. Clements Sr.

The Reservation was divided into two properties: Camp Cherokee on the west side and Camp Comanche to the east. The former received a health lodge and a chapel, with one of the first buildings to be constructed being a natural history museum to house the "specimens of animals, birds, reptiles, and fish indigenous to East Texas." An extensive collection of American Indian artifacts followed.

The latter had a few permanent structures (latrines) and was to be used as a primitive camping area. The collective property eventually was renamed the Clements Scout Ranch in 1983.[H]

"Operation One Hundred" kicked off in September 1964 intended to charter 100 new units. Led by Chairman Joe Dealey, president of the *Dallas Morning News*, the program sought "to introduce the benefits of Scouting to boys in the area who had not yet joined organized groups." Local Scout officials met with many potential chartering organizations including schools, churches, and citizen groups. When the results were tabulated, 44 troops, 31 packs, and 25 Explorer Posts had been organized in the effort.[5]

Tarr's work was becoming increasingly important as the 1960s ushered in dramatic social change. Accentuated by the country's involvement in an unpopular war, the rise of the women's liberation movement and the prevalence of loose morals, the nation's young people rebelled against authority, effectively pitting young Americans against the traditional values of its older citizens.

Through riots in the streets, the prolific use of mind-altering substances, and sometimes-peaceful sit-ins, the country's youth sought attention and societal change based on social "fairness" with regard to wealth re-distribution and commune-style living. To BSA, these were radical ideas and something the organization fought hard to defeat.

"Hippie [is] the something-for-nothing attitude of many young people, [as is] the 'God is dead' illusion, [the] moral decline in some areas, [and] the shadow of international communism," declared BSA's 1968 Annual Report. "It becomes readily apparent that a positive force to capture the attention and interest of youth is essential."

TOP: the logo for Circle Ten Council's newsletter, *The Circler*. MIDDLE: The national patch issued during the BoyPower '76 membership campaign. RIGHT: Boy Scouts on the lakefront of Camp Texoma around 1963.
ACROSS LEFT: Circle Ten Council Scouts during the 1969 National Jamboree. ACROSS BELOW: A postcard of the Arena area at the Idaho Jamboree. ACROSS FAR RIGHT: The Circle Ten Council contingent neckerchief, leather back patch, and pocket patch issued to local participants.

The result was an eight-year membership-building program known as BoyPower '76 that led up to the nation's Bicentennial celebration in 1976. Through it, BSA intended to reestablish traditional American values of behavior and morality throughout the country by holding every council "accountable" to reaffirming the objectives of the program.

It was to be a three-pronged attack. First, baseline membership numbers were established at the end

THE 1969 NATIONAL JAMBOREE

THE SEVENTH NATIONAL JAMBOREE *was held at Farragut State Park in Idaho in July 1969. Traveling aboard a chartered Braniff Airways flight from Love Field to the cry of "Farragut or bust," 305 Scouts and 33 leaders formed the enthusiastic Circle Ten Council contingent. They arrived on July 13 for the 10-day event and joined 40,000 Scouts from across the nation in the heavily wooden park on the shores of "crazy cold" Lake Pend Orille.*

"You'd dip your whole body up to your shoulders in the 40-degree water until you started shivering and then you'd come out," recalled Life Scout Burton L. Scott. "But it felt glorious after running around all day or when coming back from hiking up Bernhard Peak overlooking the Jamboree."

But attacking the Peak was no easy task. It took eight Circle Ten Scouts about three hours to hike the seven miles up to the 2,881-foot summit. Led by Patrol Leader Steve Crocker, his unit included brother Paul Crocker, Ty Brown, Doug McGregor, Mike Ballew, Buzzy Joplin, Tommy Crook, and Warren Wright.

When they did return some time later, an amazed Chief Scout Executive Alden Barber exclaimed, "You made it!" To which a delighted Steve Crocker panted, "Sure did."

But for most boys, the highlight of the Jamboree was the moment when they assembled in the grassy amphitheater where two huge television screens had been set up behind the performance stage.

"It was the most amazing thing," recalled Eagle Scout Jim Lankford." We all sat there and watched Neil Armstrong walk on the moon! He also gave a big 'hello' to us back at the Jamboree."[1]

THE SUPPORT OF H. ROSS PEROT

IN SEPTEMBER 1969, *Dallas entrepreneur H. Ross Perot made a $1 million donation to Circle Ten Council to help launch its BoyPower '76 fund-raising campaign. As the largest gift ever made to the Council at the time, Perot restricted the donation to solely fund Scouting expansion in the area. Focus was to be placed on low-income and rural areas as well as an "extension of the Explorer program with young men in high school." The gift also provided $50,000 to hire additional staff to grow the program in targeted areas.*

Two years later, Perot committed an additional $5.4 million (80,000 shares of Electronic Data Systems stock) to 19 charitable organizations. About 1,220 shares ($83,000) went to Circle Ten Council.

"These will be substantial cash awards," commented Perot to the Dallas Morning News. *"They will be given to people who have gone beyond the usual realm of their activities and performed with excellence."*

A separate large gift endowed a fund to provide all rank patches for Circle Ten Council Scouts in all programs. The most coveted of these is the Eagle Scout Award kit that still includes a small card with a congratulatory greeting from Mr. Perot.[J]

of 1968 and from them each council set its goal to increase membership "to one boy out of three."[6]

"We must assume responsibility for the success or failure of Scouting in our nation, region, or district," BSA proclaimed in their 1968 Annual Report. "BoyPower '76 challenges each of us to do precisely that."[7]

Next, BSA sought to improve Scouting's positive influence within its inner city and urban areas.

Those areas were designated as "vital targets." For the first time, BSA's National Council offered financial assistance to those potential members in order to defray costs. However, membership fees for everyone else doubled to $1 per year for Scouts and $2 for leaders.

BSA also sought to train *all* registered leaders but set a more realistic goal of 65 percent of them by 1976. At the time, few councils had more than 48 percent of their unit leaders trained. Circle Ten's percentage, however, stood at a strong 56.[8]

Last, a push was made to increase the pay of Scouting professionals in order to attract the best possible candidates to carry out the organization's new message into the nation's communities.

As the decade neared its end and the advent of the OPEC oil cartel and energy shortages loomed, the country became more concerned with conserving its limited natural resources. Scouting tried to keep step with the changing national attitude and developed Project SOAR—Save

Our American Resources. Inaugurated in summer 1969, it was praised by President Richard M. Nixon.

"Our young people have an enormous interest in the environment and Scouts have had that from the time of their foundation," he said. "They know of the natural beauty of this country and they want to preserve it—preserve it for their children and for all the generations to come."[9]

By the end of 1970, Circle Ten Council troops were fully engaged in cleaning up locally trashed areas in its 12 districts and

ACROSS TOP LEFT: Circle Ten Council President William P. Clements Jr. (left) presenting a small R. Tate McKenzie statue to H. Ross Perot (right) in thanks for his substantial financial gift to the Council in 1969. ACROSS BELOW: John D. Murchison speaking at the celebratory banquet for Mr. Perot. ABOVE: The national patch awarded to Scouts who participated in Project SOAR ("Save Our American Resources") in 1969.

THE FIRST FEMALE EXPLORERS

ON APRIL 1, 1971, *BSA allowed female Explorer Scouts to officially join their male counterparts. Although girls had been unofficial members of the program for several years prior, BSA's national policy was changed and they became dues-paying members of the organization. Circle Ten Council followed suit and "extended a formal welcome to all present and prospective girl Explorers" on that date.*

"It's an extension of what already has been happening here [in Girl Scouts]" commented Mrs. Claude O. Boothman, the president of Tejas Council of the Girl Scouts of the USA regarding BSA's progressive decision. "[It's] part of our way of life within our council."[K]

MARY JANE STEVENS ECKSTEIN— 1971 SILVER FAWN RECIPIENT AND FEMALE CIRCLE TEN PIONEER

AS WOMEN'S CONTRIBUTIONS *became more prevalent in Scouting, BSA's national office created the Silver Fawn award to recognize those achievements. On par with the Silver Beaver that previously had been awarded only to men, the Silver Fawn was given to ladies from 1971 through 1974, when it was incorporated into the Silver Beaver.*

One of the seven earliest Circle Ten recipients of the Silver Fawn was Jane Eckstein, a devoted volunteer Den mother and Cub leader for many years. Born in 1918, she married Arnold Carter Eckstein in Dallas in the 1940s and had two sons, Steven and Gary. When they joined Cub Scouting, her dedicated work with the Council began.

Over her Scouting career, she created a Cub Scout craft book that incorporated "drawings, skits, and ideas of interest" for young people. She illustrated the book, wrote the text, and even spiral bound it—eventually witnessing its translation into 14 languages—for which she received no compensation. When asked why not, she replied, "It doesn't matter. I did it for the children."

Passing away on December 2, 2010, at the age a 92, Jane Eckstein's life was filled with volunteerism that included work with the USO during World War II, the American Red Cross in Dallas, Kiwanis International, and the Southeast Dallas Chamber of Commerce.[L]

recycling used materials like paper and aluminum under the "Yes We Can" program sponsored by aluminum giant Alcoa.

In early 1971, First Lady Pat Nixon presented Grand Prairie's Mayor Joe Colwell with the Ernest T. Trigg Trophy for being the "nation's cleanest city" in its population bracket. Scouting played a large part in the earning of that award. As reported in the *Dallas Morning News*, Grand Prairie Scouts picked up 1 million beer cans in 18 months of work, earning over $10,000 in funds for their local troops.

In another campaign, Dallas Mayor Wes Wise led a cleanup called "Keep America Beautiful Day," where 15,000 of the city's Scouts and leaders participated in a massive litter collection project. The National Guard provided "trucks and drivers for the trash pickup."

THE **FIRST CUB** WORLD DAY CAMP

IN THE SUMMER OF 1971, *after some time of non-use, overnighters resumed at Camp Wisdom beginning with the inaugural "Cub World" day program to be held over eight Saturdays. On June 19, 250 boys from 36 Scouting units joined together at camp for the inspired outdoor program. At the end of the season, over 1,200 Cubs had attended. Two years later, the sessions would host 2,676 youth.*[N]

THE **ACQUISITION** OF **CAMP TRINITY TRAILS**

IN JANUARY 1971, *Circle Ten Council's executive board announced a gift of land and supporting funds to be used for a new camp that potentially could relieve the overuse of nearby Camp Wisdom. Mr. P. W. Gifford, the co-founder of the Gifford-Hill Construction Company, donated 554 acres of land in Henderson County along with $22,500 to purchase additional adjoining property. It was dubbed Camp Trinity Trails in May 1972 and plans were made to develop a minimalistic building infrastructure.*

Council monies authorized for its construction amounted to $35,000—equaling the interest to date booked from the sale of the Camp Wisdom's property to the state of Texas for the new Interstate Highway 20 and Spur 408 that would begin to break ground in August 1973.[M]

It is the purpose of the Boy Scouts of America to provide for boys an effective program designed to build desirable qualities of character, to train in the responsibilities of participating citizenship, and to develop in them personal fitness, thus to help in the development of American citizens who:

■ Are physically, mentally, and emotionally fit.

■ Have a high degree of self-reliance as evidenced in such qualities as initiative, courage, and resourcefulness.

■ Have personal and stable values firmly based on religious concepts.

■ Have the desire and the skills to help others.

■ Understand the principles of the American social, economic, and governmental systems.

■ Are knowledgeable about and take pride in their American heritage and understand America's role in the world.

■ Have a keen respect for the basic rights of all people.

■ Are prepared to fulfill the varied responsibilities of participating in and giving leadership to American society and in the forums of the world.

The Boy Scouts of America accomplishes this purpose by making its program available in partnership with existing groups having compatible goals, including religious, educational, civic, fraternal, business, labor, and governmental bodies.

CIRCLE TEN COUNCIL
ANNUAL BUSINESS MEETING
RECOGNITION DINNER
December 19, 1972
S.M.U. STUDENT CENTER

Local Explorer Scouts aged 15 to 20-years-old went so far as to hold their own SOAR litter pickup project on a 100-acre tract on the Elm Fork of the Trinity River near downtown. Over 1,000 Scouts showed-up and spent the day serving their community.

In April, the Councils hosted an Explorer SOAR Exposition to promote Scouting's dedication to conserving community resources at Market Hall downtown.[10] Over 385 units signed-up to have demonstration booths and Council members sold over 20,000 tickets.

As Scouting rolled into 1972, things were changing dramatically on both national and local levels. The BoyPower '76 recruitment program seemed to be performing well throughout the nation and the organization's membership ranks grew steadily. From 4.6 million Scouts at the beginning of 1969 when the campaign began to 4.9 million Scouts at the end of 1972, BSA was expanding.[11]

Circle Ten, however, was not seeing that same positive growth. In fact, youth membership had actually dropped from 36,000 traditional Scouts (Boy Scouts, Cubs, and Explorers) to about 34,000. Membership problems had first appeared in early 1968 as Cubbing's rank of Lion was dropped for the new Webelos (standing for "We'll Be Loyal Scouts") program. Council executive board minutes note there was a "substantial decrease" in advancements marked by the adoption of Webelos.[12]

To help counteract the decreasing membership, Council executives sought help from those who had the ability to act quickly—Wood Badge graduates. They were expected to fill open troop leadership positions, lend units their expertise, improve their

ERIC E. HILLARY— AN EAGLE AT THE WHITE HOUSE

IN FEBRUARY 1972, *19-year-old Eagle Scout Eric Eugene Hillary, a freshman at East Texas State University, was selected as one of BSA's presenters of the National Annual Report to President Richard M. Nixon.*

Recognized as a natural leader while attending J. N. Ervin High School at 3722 Black Oak Drive in South Dallas (now the J. N. Ervin Elementary School near Paul Quinn College), Hillary set a strong example for his classmates to follow as the editor of both the school newspaper, the Ervin Monitor, *and the school yearbook, the* Prowler. *He was a member of the Highland Hills United Methodist Church and president of the youth fellowship and youth usher board. He was a person driven to succeed.*

"Competition is probably one of the things that kept me going," he recalled. "Seeing all those guys with their awards made me say, 'If they can do it, I can do it.'"

Aging out of the ranks of Scouting's youth membership, Hillary continued as an Assistant Scoutmaster for Troop 998 at St. Luke's Methodist Church in East Dallas south of Interstate 30 between East Grand Avenue and Dolphin Road.

"Every time I start to slow down in Scouting," he said, "They come up with something else that gets me involved."

Sadly, within a few years, it all would come to an end. Eric Hillary passed away in 1975 at the tender age of 24 having lived a life filled with achievement.○

ACROSS LEFT: The program for Circle Ten Council's Annual Dinner held at the SMU Student Center in 1972.

programs, and, thereby, stem the loss of members. It worked to some extent as membership quickly rebounded to about 40,000 traditional Scouts and leaders by the end of 1972.

ABOVE LEFT: A promotional photograph advertising one of the final Scout Expositions held at Dallas' Market Hall near downtown. ABOVE: Champion Olympic swimmer and Dallas native Jerry Heidenreich displaying his 2 gold, 1 silver, and 1 bronze medals in a promotional photograph for Circle Ten Council's Good Turn Day in 1972.

HOWEVER, BY 1976, COUNCIL EXECUTIVES EXPECTED THE LOCAL ORGANIZATION TO REALIZE A TOTAL OF 57,000 TRADITIONAL SCOUTS—A LOFTY NUMBER THAT, SADLY, IT WAS UNLIKELY TO HIT DUE TO THE DEVASTATING DECISION BY NATIONAL BSA OFFICIALS TO RELEASE THE NEW EIGHTH EDITION OF THE BOY SCOUT *HANDBOOK* IN SEPTEMBER 1972. THIS BOOK WOULD SINGLE-HANDEDLY CRATER NATIONAL MEMBERSHIP WITHIN A YEAR AND SEND CIRCLE TEN GROWTH INTO A TAILSPIN.[13]

chapter 13

STEMMING THE LOSS (1973–1978)

"Camp is where it is all at."

John F. Stephens
President, Circle Ten Council
June 27, 1978

A view of downtown Dallas looking northward in 1978 after the completion of Reunion Tower.

AT THE END OF 1972, national BSA membership was diving.

From 4.9 million registered Scouts in 1972, there were only 3.15 million Scouts at the close of 1979. In the same time period, total BSA membership (which included its leaders) fell from 7 million members to 4.6 million—a staggering loss of over a third.[1] A revolt was in progress against Scouting's new direction and its members were voting with their feet.

As a part of the BoyPower '76 campaign, the new Boy Scout *Handbook* was released in September 1972 with updated rank requirements. The most dramatic of these changes involved the Eagle award. Now, a boy could earn Scouting's "ultimate" rank without ever having camped, hiked, or cooked

TOP: The 1972 Boy Scout *Handbook* with updated requirements for the rank of Eagle Scout did not entail the completion of Cooking, Camping, and Hiking merit badges. ABOVE: The red and white Council Service Patch.

in the outdoors, as those merit badges were no longer required for the recognition. Additionally, the total number of merit badges required for Eagle was increased to 24 from the traditional 21.

For the ranks of Tenderfoot through First Class, a series of "skill awards" was introduced to supplement the loss of the formerly Eagle required merit badges of Camping, Hiking, and Cooking.[2]

Other "facelift" changes included modified uniforms for both Scouts and leaders. Den mothers could choose newly designed "hot pants" and Scouts could don red berets.

The final straw to many was the removal of the word "Boy" on the "Boy Scouts of America" uniform strip above the right pocket and replacing it with "Scouting U.S.A." A perturbed columnist for the *Dallas Morning News* awarded BSA a "de-merit badge" for "de-boying the Boy Scouts."

"The lengths people will nowadays go to disclaim their heritage!" wrote the editorialist. "We could love [Scouting] even more, but it's terribly hard to love clumsy, silly, misguided attempts at—you'll excuse the expression—relevance."[3]

Beginning in February 1979, national BSA began evolving back to its outdoor roots with the help of newly named Chief Scout Executive James L. Tarr. But before gaining BSA's highest national professional management office, Tarr skillfully led the Council away from certain membership devastation beginning in 1973 by utilizing new ideas like sponsored membership drives and garnering positive news coverage as times were changing rapidly.

For those with long Council memories, the deaths of 50-year tenured Troop 1 Scoutmaster Thomas Alan Hord, and both Mr. and Mrs. Eugene Constantin symbolically ended the golden era of local Scouting, as they were the last tangible links to the expansionary age of Scout Executive Loys Hotchkiss. In spite of these events, Council leaders had to press on and continue to promote and grow the program.

Ever-decreasing membership numbers revealed future problems. Circle Ten had experienced an increase of 600 boys and 22 units over 1973 putting membership at an all-time high of 42,079 traditional Scouts serving in 1,417 units. But they still lagged behind their stated BoyPower '76 goal of 47,000. Realizing they could not grow at an 11 percent rate, the executive board voted to modify the goal downward to 45,000 traditional Scouts by the end of 1974—a more realistic growth rate of 7 percent over the year.

THE EIGHTH NATIONAL JAMBOREE *held in 1973 was a "split" event—Jamboree West took place at Idaho's Farragut State Park and Jamboree East was at Pennsylvania's Moraine State Park. Promoted under the national theme, "Growing Together," nearly 74,000 Scouts gathered at the two locations to symbolically renew national fellowship through technology. One part of the Jamboree included a video link between both sites.*

"We all gathered in the arena and sat in front of those huge screens," recalled University Park Eagle Scout William P. "Bill" Hemenway II, the great-grandnephew of former BSA National Scout Commissioner Daniel Carter Beard. *"Then we heard a cheer from the other Scouts across the country, cheered back, and waved our hands around. That was the best part of the Jamboree."*

Prevalent at Jamboree West were international contingents from Canada, Taiwan, Guam, Korea, and Puerto Rico. Jamboree East claimed honors for the "largest steel reclamation project in the nation's history" as some 25 tons of the material—500,000 soft drink cans—were collected and recycled by attending Scouts on a huge "Save Our American Resources" conservation project.[A]

LEFT: The neckerchief, pocket patch, and leather back patch that were issued to Scouts attending the 1973 National Jamboree. BELOW: 1973 National Jamboree attendee and Eagle Scout William Hemenway in 1979. Hemenway would attend several more national and world jamborees during his celebrated Scouting career that included his appointment to the National Volunteer Training Team at BSA's National Training Center in Westlake, Texas and the presentation of the Silver Beaver medal in 2012.

As small consolation to the dejected board, Scout Executive Tarr read a note written to him by Lt. Col. Elmo Baker, a prisoner once held in the infamous "Hanoi Hilton" during the Vietnam War.

"Of all the [500] prisoners-of-war who tried to escape," explained Baker, "Each had been a Boy Scout. Scouting helped prepare them to face and overcome all obstacles."[4]

Meeting adjourned.

By the end of April 1974, attrition further lowered membership levels to 33,000 boys in 1,342 units, which prompted the board to modify its previous goal downward again to 35,000 in 1,327 units by year's end. May's tally was even worse—3,000 more boys had dropped out and nine more units had folded. Subsequently, goals were lowered to 34,400 traditional Scouts in 1,354 units. Trying anything to stop the mass exodus, Dallas Cowboys Head Football Coach Tom Landry was asked to lead the Council's annual recruitment roundup. From his endorsement, membership immediately jumped by 6,000 boys to 36,000 traditional Scouts serving in 1,460 units.[5]

Sadly, the numbers did not hold and soon membership waned to below 29,000 traditional Scouts within a year. But number tracking was not the only problem plaguing the Council.

TOP: The patch awarded to Scouts who participated in the 1973 membership recruitment campaign. ABOVE: The patch presented to Scouts who participated in the membership drive during America's Bicentennial year of 1976. NEAR RIGHT: The program for Circle Ten Council's Annual Dinner in 1975. FAR RIGHT: A promotional photograph for the recruitment of Scouts in 1975.

ON FEBRUARY 8, 1975, *Circle Ten Scouts swarmed the Capitol Building in Austin as part of Texas Scouting's Annual Report to the State and Governor Dolph Briscoe (right, middle and below, center).*

Selected to make the presentation was Troop 167 sponsored by the Good Street Baptist Church in Oak Cliff's Mustang District (formerly the Bronze Star District). Scoutmaster Warren G. Moore recalled that his boys were "very happy to have been selected to represent some 14,000 adult volunteers, 1600 Cub Packs, Scout Troops, Explorer Posts in Circle Ten Council's dynamite Scout program."[B]

CIRCLE TEN COUNCIL'S SCOUT SHOW, *started in 1973 under the theme "New World of Scouting," was the direct descendant of the amazing Scout Circuses and Expositions put on by local Scouts during the previous four decades. Wishing to recapture the feel of earlier Scout Expos held at Fair Park, Council leaders created the "Scout Show" and held the first few events in Loos Field House in North Dallas. The second Show scheduled for May 4, 1974 was scheduled for an estimated 42,000 participants.*

Featuring cooking and pioneering proj-ect, many local troops dazzled the community with their skills. Troop 831 of Carrollton cre-ated shish kabob and cherry cobbler in dutch ovens cooked over hot coals. Attendees tasted Scout-made doughnuts, pancakes, and turkey roasted on a spit.

Other projects included a maze created by Troop 887 of Garland consisting of 1,400 pounds of cardboard and five gallons of glue, and a sponge throwing event featured by Cub Pack 1031, also of Garland.

Using the traditional Scout sales-manship model, ticket sellers received a commission on each sale they made, which resulted in 60,000 tickets being sold throughout the Dallas area at $1 each. Any Scout who sold at least 100 tickets was entered in a drawing to win one of three trips to Disney World in Florida. Other prizes based on sales levels also were awarded.

The Council's top seller was eight-year-old Cub Scout Darry Dabbs from Pack 995 (below left). He sold 500 tickets and won a 10-speed Huffy bicycle, five entrance tickets to Lion Country Safari near Lewisville, and a trip to Disney World

The Show featured Scout units demonstrating skills in crafts, aquat-ics, cooking, and camping. It became an annual event until 2010 when the last one was held at the Texas Rangers' Ballpark in Arlington.[C]

ACROSS TOP RIGHT: The patches and ribbons from the Scout Shows from 1973–1977 given to participating Scouts and troops. ACROSS BOTTOM RIGHT: Patches from 60 years of Scout Shows, Expositions, and Circuses. RIGHT: The program for Circle Ten Council's Annual Dinner held in 1976. ACROSS BOTTOM LEFT: Circle Ten Council's top Scout Show ticket seller in 1974, Darry Dabbs of Pack 995.

1976 ANNUAL RECOGNITION DINNER
CIRCLE TEN COUNCIL
BOY SCOUTS OF AMERICA

In April 1974, eight-year-old girl Carrie Crosman joined Pack 842 as a Wolf Cub in Coppell, Texas—she wanted to be a Scout like the boys. But Circle Ten officials declared her ineligible because "the national charter says a Cub Scout must be a boy." With that, the "gender shot" had been fired across the bow of Scouting—something that the national office had to address with Carrie quickly becoming its symbol. Over the following weeks, little more was made of it. [6]

"STRONG CHARACTER TRAITS ARE DEVELOPED IN YOUNG MEN AT AN EARLY AGE THAT REQUIRE THE GUIDANCE AND SUPPORT OF ADULTS, WHO TAKE THE TIME TO MENTOR AND ENCOURAGE THEM. THERE IS NO OTHER ORGANIZATION QUITE LIKE THE BOY SCOUTS THAT SERVES OUR YOUTH IN JUST THIS WAY—PROVIDING POSITIVE ROLE MODELS THROUGH DEDICATED VOLUNTEERS AND STAFF, AND ENCOURAGING YOUNG MEN TO WORK HARD, RESPECT OTHERS, ENJOY THE GROWTH AND FELLOWSHIP THAT COMES WITH OUTDOOR EXPERIENCES, AND DEVELOP THE MORAL CHARACTER AND SKILLS THAT WILL BRING THEM SUCCESS AS OUR NEXT GENERATION OF LEADERS."

—TREVOR REES-JONES, FOUNDER AND CHAIRMAN, CHIEF OIL AND GAS

THE COUNCIL CAMP GAS LEASES

IN 1975 *as membership continued to wane, Circle Ten had to make up lost revenues in an ever-constricting budget. To its good fortune, several Council camps now had operational gas wells either on them or being proposed.*

Camp Constantin was slated for up to five wells that would produce about $500 per month in royalties, maxing out at an estimated $287,000 in total revenues by 1988.

At the Clements Scout Reservation, the Delhi Gas Pipeline received the right-of-way lease for their gas wells. Also there, a 5-year gas lease contract was awarded to the Texas Oil and Gas Corporation that would pay a base rental price per acre in addition to a one-eighth royalty. A cool $18,910 was placed into the Circle Ten Foundation after the first year of royalties from the Reservation's gas lease in 1979.[E]

BREAKING THE GENDER BARRIER

IN JANUARY 1976, *women broke into Scouting's top leadership positions by being allowed to register as Cubmasters with the understanding that "the program have predominately male leadership," according to national BSA official, Arch Monson Jr.*[D]

In mid-June, the executive board voted to renew the lease for Camp Texoma at the rate of $1 per annum to the U.S. Corps of Engineers. But there were reservations as an oil well was scheduled to be drilled on property within a year. Also, the camp's expenses were not being divided equally among the remaining member councils because its operation had become mainly a Circle Ten responsibility. In April 1978, the executive board voted

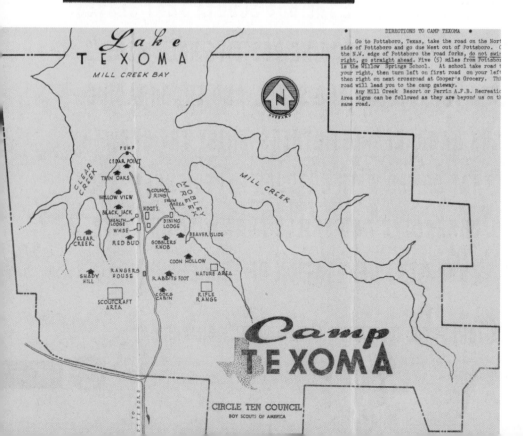

DIRECTIONS TO CAMP TEXOMA

Go to Pottsboro, Texas, take the road on the North side of Pottsboro and go due West out of Pottsboro. the N.W. edge of Pottsboro the road forks, do not swing right, go straight ahead. Five (5) miles from Pottsboro is the Willow Springs School. At school take road your right, then turn left on first road on your left, then right on next crossroad at Cooper's Grocery. This road will lead you to the camp gateway.

Any Mill Creek Resort or Perrin A.F.B. Recreation Area signs can be followed as they are beyond us on the same road.

ACROSS LEFT: The official map of Camp Texoma given out to Council members in the 1970s. ABOVE: Summer activities at Circle Ten camps included carving totem poles at Camp Wisdom (above top right), cooking on an open fire at Camp Constantin (above top left), and constructing monkey bridges (above) at Camp Texoma.

against holding a Council summer camp at Texoma in 1979—a critical first step to eventually divesting itself of the property lease.[7]

In a statement from Scout Executive Tarr dated June 21, 1978, he outlined the Council's desire to sell its share in the lease and recoup sunken costs for the buildings it had constructed. He also noted that four Council camps were unnecessary with ever-decreasing membership. He believed Camps Wisdom, Constantin, and the Clements Scout Reservation would adequately serve Circle Ten's summer camping needs.

"It is estimated that maintenance, repairs, and improvement expenses of Camp Texoma will be $60,000 to $90,000 in the next twelve months," wrote Tarr. "The Council needs to economize in all areas of operation." He ended, "It is my further recommendation that we take steps to void our lease."

In April 1979, Circle Ten's interest in Camp Texoma was sold for $140,000 to the Texas Outdoor Ministry of the Lutheran Church, being

monies received as reimbursement for building improvements made on the property—thereby ending Circle Ten's 33-year relationship with the camp. But this would not be the only property that Circle Ten had divested itself of.

Two years prior, Beckett Place, received by bequest in 1961, had become a burden to maintain as well, even though it was one of the two Council camps that allowed co-ed overnight Explorer camping. (The other was Camp Texoma until 1979.)

In March 1976, the Council conferred with the Thomas G. Beckett family and received their permission to sell the property. On July 22, the Beckett Place property was sold for $175,000 and the receipts were placed in the Circle Ten Foundation in the name of its donor, Thomas G. Beckett Sr.[8]

Camp Wisdom, on the other hand, was getting more attention as it was vital to the inner-city camping program that Tarr had promoted since his Council tenure began. In an analysis by the Camp Wisdom Committee led by Dallas psychologist Dr. Prior Shelton, the report concluded that Camp Wisdom was the centerpiece camping experience for Dallas' urban Scouts due to its close geographic proximity to downtown.[9]

TOP LEFT and LEFT: A Scout at Camp Texoma constructs an arrow for his Archery merit badge (top), while a Scout attending Camp Constantin aims at his target (below).
ACROSS BOTTOM RIGHT: Thomas G. Beckett Jr. as the vice president of First Southwest Company in 1954. ACROSS RIGHT: Circle Ten Eagle Scout Beckett in 1927 after earning the Council's first Silver palm ever presented.

By the end of the BoyPower '76 campaign, BSA was down 775,000 members nationally—a loss of 13 percent of its membership in eight years.[10] Circle Ten had devastating results to report as well—a loss of almost 26 percent to 25,000 traditional Scouts from 34,000 youth only eight years earlier in 1968.

With diligent attention to promoting the program, Council membership rebounded to 29,500 at the end of 1977—a massive 25 percent increase in one year.[11] Tarr's turnaround efforts were taking hold.

THE GIFT OF CAMP BECKETT

IN LATE 1961, *the Council gained its fourth camp as the result of the passing of Scouting supporter Thomas Gervas Beckett Sr.*

"I hereby give, devise, and bequeath . . . my said home estate, in its entirety to Circle Ten Council, Boy Scout Foundation . . . in fond memory of my deceased son, Thomas Beckett, Junior," instructed Beckett Sr. in the first codicil of his Last Will and Testament.

The elder Beckett's bequest included a lump sum of $25,000 and 60 acres of lakefront land just north of Dallas on Grapevine Lake. Within three years, the interest gained on the assets allowed "Beckett Place" to open for Council Scouts. Its small size was well suited for weekend camping for Explorer Scouts.

Thomas Jr. had grown-up in the Council and credited the program with developing his tenacity to duty and solid work ethic as an adult. Earning the Eagle award at University Park's Troop 32 in 1926, Beckett kept earning merit badges and leading his troop.

In May 1927, when the "Eagle palm" was introduced by the National office to recognize achievement while an Eagle Scout, 15-year-old Thomas Beckett Jr. was the first Circle Ten Council Scout to receive the silver palm, which represented a minimum of 36 merit badges earned.

The Dallas Morning News *declared, "Thomas Beckett has more medals than most people including admirals and athletes." He responded humbly, "Scouting brings out talent in any particular field. It brings out the best in anyone."*

The young Junior Assistant Scoutmaster had a productive future ahead. Graduating from both Harvard College and Southern Methodist University, Beckett joined the United States Navy in 1942 after the outbreak of World War II. In 1946, he founded the investment banking firm of First Southwest Company taking the position of vice president, a title he held until his death in 1956.[F]

NATIONAL ORATORY CHAMPION—ERNEST TUTT JR.

IN 1976, *Dallas Eagle Scout Ernest Tutt Jr. won the* Reader's Digest National Public Speaking Award, *which was presented to him by Scout Executive James L. Tarr (below, right). Tutt was a member of the Mustang District's Troop 169, formerly known as the Bronze Star District. But his was not a case of "beginner's luck." Tutt was a talented speaker. Only two years earlier, he had been invited to speak at his district's Annual Appreciation Dinner for the Wilmer-Hutchins and South Dallas areas, where he dazzled the crowd with inspirational oratory held in Bishop College's Union Building on February 4, 1974.*

Recalling anecdotes gained from his experiences at the 1973 National Jamboree, local media picked up the story, netting him an appearance at the Region 9 Board Meeting later that year—that eventually lead to his Reader's Digest championship.

Born in Houston, Texas, in 1959, Tutt was adopted by Mr. and Mrs. Ernest Tutt Sr. at age three. Moving to Dallas in 1971, he showed early promise at public speaking, eventually entering and winning several youth oratory contests. Graduating Skyline High School in 1978, Tutt had become an acclaimed orator now having won several regional and national competitions, including a contest sponsored by the National Podium Association.

After earning an associate's degree in business from Grayson Community College in 1980, he left for the University of Texas at Austin where he majored in philosophy and political science. Selected as a Diversity Enhancement Fellow, he took a master's degree in education from Texas A&M University in College Station, Texas, before earning his doctorate from Texas A&M in Commerce, Texas.

He worked as the Director of Special Projects to the President of A&M at Commerce before moving in 2003 to Skagit Valley College in Mount Vernon, Washington, where he presently teaches ethnic studies and speech communication.[G]

In September 1977, Scout Executive Tarr received two reports commissioned from Texas Field Research analyzing "How Boys View Scouts" and "Scouting: A Parental Perspective" that helped him determine the Council's best youth recruiting path.

The first one noted that team sports were most popular among boys who had never joined Scouting or were Scouting "dropouts." Current Scouts,

LEFT: Scout Ernest Tutt speaking at Bishop College in February 1974. BELOW: Circle Ten Council Scout Executive Jim Tarr presenting Tutt with the *Reader's Digest* National Public Speaking Award in 1976.

ERNEST TUTT RECEIVES READER'S DIGEST NATIONAL PUBLIC SPEAKING AWARD 1976

DALLAS' TROOP 20 CELEBRATES 50 YEARS IN SCOUTING

IN FEBRUARY 1977, *Scout Executive James L. Tarr announced to the executive board that Troop 20 at the Tyler Street Methodist Church at 927 W. 10th Street in Oak Cliff was celebrating their 50th Anniversary during Scout Week that month. Originally chartered at the Kessler Park Methodist Church in Oak Cliff in 1927, Troop 20 had presented a total of 130 Eagle Scout awards to its most achieving Scouts over the years. Among them was sitting Dallas Mayor Robert "Bob" Folsom.*[H]

however, preferred its outdoor activities to team sports and, also, were more likely to have a paper route or similar job. This suggested a Scout had a "willingness and ability to accept responsibility." To boys who had never joined Scouting, "making the team" was more important.

Scouting dropouts believed the program to be "much like school" and they disliked the uniform. Current Scouts enjoyed learning leadership skills and "earning achievement badges" more than their counterparts who believed those opportunities to be "boring" after a while.

With regard to the parents of non-Scouting boys, they believed that developing sports skills was superior to self-development. However, Scouting parents saw the experience as providing "more opportunities" to their sons than other programs, including sports.

Parents of Scouting dropouts preferred the summer camp opportunities to weekly meeting programs. Scouting parents appreciated all meetings, as well as the belief that Scouting's tenets helped their sons internalize their family's own value system. To them, Scouting's best asset was its method of "showing" a boy what he could do rater than doing it for him.

The resulting recommendations were used to "promote Scouting heavily before school starts" and "hook them" before [boys] joined organized sports, as well as to promote the summer camping experience.

National managers saw the problem as well and began incorporating organized sports (like basketball) into meetings as games, along with providing more outdoor experiences like canoeing, camping, and hiking. In other words, BSA began to put the outdoor program back into Scouting—the part they had removed with the release of the 1972 *Handbook*.[12]

Beginning in 1978, a special push was made to attract boys classified as "handicapped." As a previously underserved market segment, national BSA executives created special requirements for those Scouts with disabilities, so they could get the same character training experience as other Scouts. Now, medically certified

THE CAMP TRINITY TRAILS' GRASS LEASE

ACROSS RIGHT: Circle Ten Council Scouts enroute to the 1977 National Jamboree stop in Washington, DC to visit Dallas Congressman James M. "Jim" Collins at the Capitol Building.

BY 1979, *Camp Trinity Trails in Henderson County had only the most primitive of camping facilities built on it, which included "four troop sites, roads, and a parking lot." But only the central water system awaited completion.*

To help fund its upkeep, local farmer Hollis Gassett entered into an agreement with the Council to fertilize and harvest the hay meadows—splitting the profits with Circle Ten from their sale. In the "bottom land," Gassett would seed, plant, and harvest oats, wheat or milo, with the Council receiving one-third of the gain. Although minimal, the land was used as a new profit center for the Council.[1]

CAMP BROOKLAWN

WITH THE GIFT OF 170 ACRES *in Oak Cliff's Kiest and Hampton Roads area, the Brooklawn Farms camp was born. Eventually to be known as Camp Brooklawn, the land was gifted by Dallas oilman Wirt Davis II and his sisters, Mrs. Patricia Davis and Mrs. Camilla Davis Blaffer. The acreage, valued at $1.6 million, was accepted by the Circle Ten Foundation Committee in June 1978. Wishing to develop the property for nearby urban troops that could not travel easily to other Council camps, bathroom facilities quickly were rented and located on the property at an annual cost of $1,000 per pair. But over the next few years, little else was invested into the property.*

In 1981, the City of Dallas requested that it be deeded one-quarter acre of Brooklawn property for use as the new hospital road entrance planned for the adjoining property. Council board members agreed to the sale, as they believed it would enhance the marketability of the property.

The camp's noted lack of use encouraged a "would you take" sale offer from land developers in 1985, which was rejected but prompted the Council to pursue its release at a better price. After years of trying, Camp Brooklawn in Oak Cliff was sold in 2000 for $1.2 million to the Southwest Dallas Housing Company, the builders of senior assisted living facilities.[J]

disabled Scouts could earn the rank of Eagle without age limitation on completing the requirements.

Simultaneously, Scout Executive Tarr initiated Circle Ten's dedication to serving disabled Scouts as well. By the end of 1980, the enrollment of these boys jumped 250 percent to several hundred over the year before. The Council set a goal to serve at least 1,000 special needs Scouts by the end of 1981.[13]

By the end of 1978, enormous change had come to Scouting both nationally and locally, and not just in programs. Within Circle Ten, the Denison (Texas), and Bryan County (Oklahoma), districts "requested transfers to the Texoma Valley Council" based in Sherman. With the release of Camp Texoma, it did not make financial sense for their Scouts to have to travel so far south into the Council's established camps on the weekends, when they could make a short trip to nearby Camp Grayson. Circle Ten's executive board unanimously approved their request to transfer.

Nationally, BSA's leaders announced its intention to move its New Jersey headquarters to a 10-acre site in Las Colinas, Texas, and construct a three-story, 150,000-square foot office building the following summer.[14]

ITS NEW CHIEF SCOUT EXECUTIVE WOULD BE JAMES L. TARR, MEANING CIRCLE TEN NOW HAD TO FIND A NEW LEADER. THE MAN CHOSEN FOR THE JOB WOULD TAKE THE COUNCIL INTO ITS NEXT 20-YEAR MEMBERSHIP EXPANSION.

chapter 14

TURNING TIDES (1979–1992)

"The Council is at a crossroads."

Thomas A. O'Dwyer
President, Circle Ten Council
February 27, 1979

AN ENTHUSIASTIC William C. "Billy" Gamble became Circle Ten's new Scout Executive in March 1979 having served at the same post in Birmingham, Alabama. Present at the March executive board meeting was outgoing Scout Executive James L. Tarr, who had accepted national BSA's top role as its Chief Scout Executive/CEO.

After Circle Ten Council President Thomas A. O'Dwyer made introductions, he screened a film depicting the recent Golden Acorn Training session held at the Clements Scout Reservation, followed by Tarr's *Check Out Report* that ended with his traditional salutation of, "Thanks, you are appreciated."

Gamble recalled years later, "I felt honored and privileged that the selection committee chose me to follow Jim Tarr. I had tremendous respect and admiration for Jim, and over the years, he became one of my dearest friends and fishing buddy."[1]

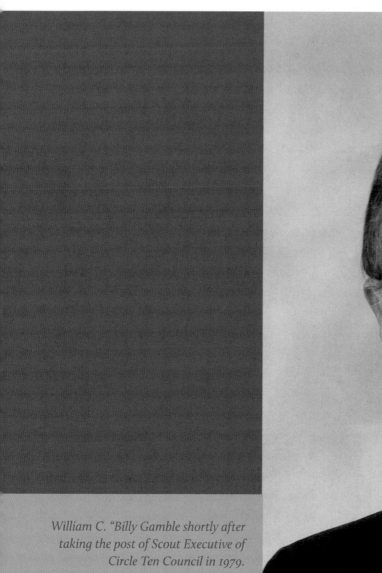

William C. "Billy Gamble shortly after taking the post of Scout Executive of Circle Ten Council in 1979.

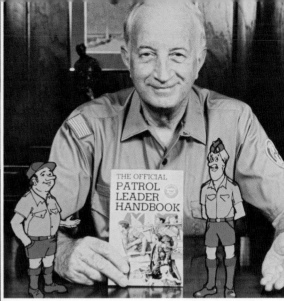

LEFT: Mementos from the Scouting career of James L. Tarr that include his official position patch, business and registration cards, Covered Wagon Council thank you plaque, and Chief Scout Executive key chain and watch fob. ABOVE: This photograph was used to promote the release of the new Boy Scout *Handbook* authored by William "Green Bar Bill" Hillcourt that replaced the 1972 edition.

According to President O'Dwyer, Circle Ten Council was "at a crossroads," suggesting that changes needed to be made in order to survive the new decade. Their choice of a "no nonsense" leader like Gamble paid off as he threw himself into the job—working under his personal mantra of "On my honor, I will do my best."

First up was the creation of a complete long-range strategic plan that emphasized better recruiting, improved facilities, excellent programs at all council camps, and a realignment of the districts.

Second, he sought to develop a high-quality professional staff that would be able to support the most important people in the Council—the ones who made it all work—the unit leaders. Third, Gamble

called for the recruitment of top local business and civic leaders who had the ability to finance the program and mobilize the community's resources. Finally, a surge was made to recruit new members into the budding inner-city youth program.[2]

The "Gamble Law" of having no dropped units during the year was instituted and included every current troop, pack, and post. After his first year, the membership loss had been reduced from 12 percent down to 1 percent. From that point on, Gamble expected his executives to deliver consistent membership growth.[3]

As the new decade of the 1980s dawned, Gamble found success in all areas of management and delivering the program to the Scouts. First, the Council remained fiscally

262

CIRCLE TEN'S FIRST COMPUTER SYSTEM

IN THE LATE 1970s, BSA's national office provided computing services to councils through their use of commercial and military-designed software packages.

"For word processing we used IBM Wordstar, which was a nightmare to learn," recalled Council Director of Support Services Scott Ferguson. "That's why we had so many excellent administrative assistants. They could handle it."

In October 1982, the executive board voted to buy their first system to perform general ledger and accounting calculations, word processing, registration, and maintain records of sustaining membership contributions.

The system consisted of a TI 990 CPU that came with a 256K processor and "basic memory." Included was a 96 MB disk drive, a backup pack, a 150 CPS dot matrix printer, a 45 CPS letter-quality printer, a letterhead stacker, and seven CRT workstations—all for the princely sum of $50,000, which included $2,500 for the "one-time startup charge."

The single CPU alone accounted for $14,125. But such was the price for state-of-the-art technology in 1982. The Council's field staff would not receive their own laptops for another decade.

After some early apprehension, the computer system proved successful but had one flaw—no one on staff was truly proficient at repairing it.

"For years, [fellow executive] Bart Green and I were the oldest employees in the office," recalled Ferguson, "and we were the de-facto heads of the Circle Ten IT Department. Our motto was, 'If you give us enough time, we'll either fix it or break it trying.'"[B]

These days Greg Taylor keeps Circle Ten Council's servers humming along.

THE 1979 SWEDEN JAMBOREE

THE 15TH WORLD JAMBOREE was scheduled to be held in Nishapur, Iran, in the summer of 1979. However, due to the increasing tensions in the Middle East that capitulated with the storming of the American embassy by Iranian students that November, the Jamboree was moved to Sweden. Council executive board member Ray Marr led the South Central Region contingent as its Scoutmaster.

The Scouts traveled to London, England, and Vienna, Austria, for tours before embarking for the Jamboree site. Although the 10-day experience of international fellowship was exciting, the trip home was welcomed as well. With many gifts to pack, some Scouts chose to lighten their loads.

"Ray was just a wonderful man and an outstanding leader, yet a strict Scoutmaster in Sweden," recalled Eagle Scout Bobby Higginbotham, "but you knew that if you lived by his rules, you would have a great time."

"We cooked on 'fire tables,' which were a series of side-by-side logs atop two parallel cross members on four log "legs," said Higginbotham. "A layer of dirt was put on top to make a safe burning area. But on that last day, we decided to use it to burn our grungy clothes."

Piece by piece garments were disposed of with "whoops" and "cheers" as new ones were added.

"When Scoutmaster Marr caught us, it was not a pretty sight," Higginbotham lamented. "I don't really remember what he said but I'm sure it was pretty to the point."

Higginbotham received the Silver Beaver award in North Trail District in April 2012 and serves as the Scoutmaster of University Park's Troop 82. Reports suggest that he has held many memorable flag retirement ceremonies since taking over the unit in 1999.[A]

strong as the Circle Ten Foundation's trustees took advantage of the nation's extraordinarily high interest rates. With 30-day corporate paper earning a staggering 16.5 percent annually, the trustees expanded the Council's highly profitable portfolio.

Also in 1980, Gamble initiated the Cub Leader Pow Wow training program for active Scouting parents, as well as a Commissioner College at Camp Wisdom to train Boy Scout leaders who mentored multiple troops within their districts.

ABOVE: A typical scene from the rotunda inside SMU's Dallas Hall during the University of Scouting. RIGHT: Circle Ten Council President W. Herbert Hunt in 1984. ACROSS LOWER RIGHT: An adventurous Scout participates in the horse program at the Clements Scout Ranch around 1985. ACROSS UPPER RIGHT: The patch awarded to Scouts who completed the hiking of the Governor's Trail.

Around 1984, at the urging of Council President W. Herbert Hunt, the College program, now known by its current moniker of the University of Scouting, was moved to Southern Methodist University for its first sessions.

Another improvement was the effectiveness of making quality long-term hires like the new Director of Camping Richmond "Ric" Wilkins. Over his 20-year tenure, he oversaw the latest building and improvement plans for all Council camps, and he was the professional advisor to the Mikanakawa Lodge, Order of the Arrow.

A third goal was to re-build the underused Clements Scout Reservation as it contained uncomfortably hot and humid campsites sitting atop a hard-to-access hill in the south central area of camp.

THE **THURBER RANCH FACILITY**

IN MAY 1981, *Circle Ten Council was given a training facility in Thurber, Texas, by the Texas Pacific Oil Company known as the Thurber Ranch. Arranged for by Council President Louis Beecherl Jr. and valued at about $450,000, the 120 acres of land was located 60 miles west of Fort Worth off Interstate Highway 20. Unfortunately, the Ranch had operating costs of about $5,000 for the first two years. The Council sought a corporate sponsor to act as benefactor and pay those expenses, else it would be sold. As none was found, the parcel was disposed of in May 1984 with the $350,000 in proceeds going into the Circle Ten Foundation.*[c]

THE 5-MILE CREEK CAMP

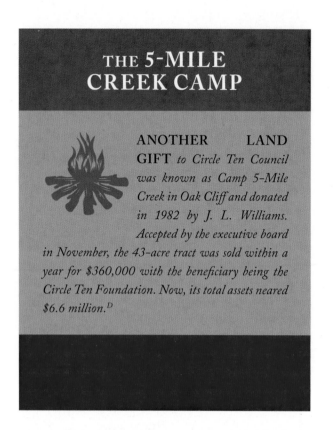

ANOTHER LAND GIFT *to Circle Ten Council was known as Camp 5-Mile Creek in Oak Cliff and donated in 1982 by J. L. Williams. Accepted by the executive board in November, the 43-acre tract was sold within a year for $360,000 with the beneficiary being the Circle Ten Foundation. Now, its total assets neared $6.6 million.*[D]

To do so, Scout Executive Gamble first appealed to Governor Clements for assistance in revitalizing his namesake camp. Clements responded by making a $1 million gift that initiated construction of new campsites down around Perryman Lake near the headquarters building. Also, a new swimming and boating area was built on nearby McElvaney Lake, a new dining hall was constructed on property, and the "Governor's Trail" was cut in – the large hiking loop around Lake Murchison named in Clements' honor. It was dedicated in May 1981. Today, the Trail is a staple of weekend activities for hundreds of visiting troops.[4]

Last, the Council presented its first Whitney M. Young Jr. Service Award that honored an adult individual or organization that had performed dedicated work in assisting rural or low-income youth.

Named in honor of the MIT-trained civil rights leader who died in 1971, the Council's first recipient of this national BSA award in 1979 was Mr. Alma Hawthorne, a 1975 Silver Beaver awardee. The second honoree was Mr. Michael Alexander of Troop 169 in the Council's Mustang District in 1980.[5]

In May 1982, the Tiger Cubs BSA program was introduced nationally, allowing first grade boys and their parent or guardian to enter Scouting as part of the new "Foundations of Growth" program begun in 1983, that was designed to increase local membership. Circle Ten took the lead as it was gaining a reputation for being a model Scouting council through its expanding facilities and programs.[6]

In May 1983, Fort Worth's Longhorn Council agreed to transfer portions of Carrollton and Farmers Branch residing within Denton County, along with parts of the Lewisville Independent School District, into Circle Ten. Approved in June, an agreement was drawn up and completed that October.

Future Council President Jim Sowell took his seat as the newest executive board member and former Scout Executive Charles Grable rejoined the Council as its new development director in charge of cultivating donors. A year later, he would receive his 50-year service pin denoting his many continuous years of service to the Scouting movement.

ACROSS LEFT: A den of enthusiastic Tiger Cub Scouts around 1985.

SERVING DISABLED SCOUTS

BY JUNE 1982, *Circle Ten Council had 1,500 special needs Cubs and Boy Scouts registered. Six months later, that number had increased to 2,000, which caught the attention of the Special Olympics organization, who asked the Council to help sponsor the games coming to the Southern Methodist University campus in 1985. With considerable credit given to the publicity surrounding Scouting and the Special Olympics, the special needs Scout membership within the Council skyrocketed to several thousand registered boys.*

The main draw for these young men was Scouting's outdoor experience. With Council facilities now being built with handicapped access, more Scouts than ever were able to enjoy weekend camping.

"Since the early 1980s, all of our new facilities have complied with the requirements set forth in the ADA—the Americans with Disabilities Act," noted Council Camping Director Scott Arrington. *"But moreover, we want to remove every obstacle to Scouts who wish to participate in the program—both physical and financial. We must enable every young person to have the opportunity to enter the program and love it."*

To help facilitate their ability to camp, a $24,000 requisition was authorized to equip a handicapped troop site at Camp Wisdom.

Disabled Scouts also would be consolidated within the Golden Eagle District—soon to include 4,500 Scouts in 96 units by 1991.

One Golden Eagle success story was that of Plano Troop 45's David Brady. As a youth born with Down syndrome, Brady rose through the ranks with the goal of being an Eagle Scout. He earned it after three years of work, "an accomplishment that takes longer for most Scouts," commented District Executive Ron Frederich.

"I really like the Boy Scouts because it gets me in busy stuff," recalled David. *"The thing I like about being an Eagle Scout is you can never quit being it. Once you're an Eagle, there's no quitting [it]."*[E]

THE FIRST DANNY WHITE GOLF CLASSIC

AS THE COUNCIL EXPANDED, *new sources of income needed to be generated. One idea was a golf tournament with Dallas Cowboy quarterback Danny White as its chairman. Featuring individual corporate hole sponsors, the event was designed to attract local executives who supported Scouting.*

White's celebrity allowed him to bring in nationally known entertainers and sports figures to attend the post-tournament dinner party usually held at a local hotel. Movie stars and musicians like Danny Thomas, Ray Price, and Louise Mandrell put on highly memorable shows for the Council. Other special guests included the likes of western actor Dale Robertson and New York Yankees baseball legend Mickey Mantle. Soon, Golf Digest *declared the Danny White Golf Tournament as the best celebrity golf event in the country.*

Over the years, profits from the tournament rose from $3,000 in 1979 to over $115,000 in 1985. Some proceeds even were used to pay off the Council's $10,000 loan to the Circle Ten Foundation for the computer system purchased in 1982.[F]

It continues today as the popular Circle Ten Council Golf Classic held at various professional courses around the Metroplex.

The Council's World Jamboree contingent to Alberta, Canada, consisting of several troops was led by executive board member Ray Marr. Featuring a bus trip from Dallas through Yellowstone National Park, Mount Rushmore in the Black Hills of South Dakota, and other sites of interest, the 2-week excursion proved a hit.

THE HISPANIC TOGETHER PLAN

AS THE HISPANIC COMMUNITY *in Dallas continued to expand, Circle Ten Council created the "Hispanic Together Plan" led by Council Membership Chairman Ray Robbins. Within a year, community leaders like Troy Marceleno and Sam Moreno promoted the program throughout Dallas. Similar to the urban recruitment emphasis of the 1970s, these two programs (along with the disabled Scout program) took center stage within the Council in the early 1980s. Dallas-based actor, singer, and guitarist Trini Lopez even served as its chairman one year.*

At the time, the Hispanic youth market was estimated at 14,000 Scouting aged boys with an additional 10,000 potential recruits in the Dallas Independent School District.

In 1986, Executive Board Member Al Gonzalez accepted the chairmanship of the effort and from his leadership the Council's initiative boasted 8,700 Hispanic Scouts by the end of its first year.[G]

ABOVE: A Circle Ten Council Contingent to the 15th World Jamboree to Calgary, Alberta, Canada during a bus stop at Mount Rushmore in South Dakota. LEFT: Circle Ten Council World Jamboree contingent Scoutmaster Ray Marr.

THE CLEMENTS NAME CHANGE

IN OCTOBER 1983, *the Clements Scout Reservation's name was changed to its present moniker of the Clements Scout Ranch.*[H]

THE FIRST SCOUTFITTER

BY JULY 1986, *the Council decided to provide uniforming assistance to underserved market segments in town. To do so, they raised a 20 x 40 foot metal building at the back lot of the Mitchell-Head Service Center. Named the "Scoutfitter," they received donations of used or "experienced" uniforms from donors and had them cleaned, pressed, and put on hangers for presentation to needy Scouts.*[I]

The size of Camp Wisdom again increased by 52 acres due to a generous gift from Industrial Properties owned by Dallas businessman John M. Stemmons. The Council hoped that with positive publicity other companies would make similar land donations. In response, the Clements Scout Ranch received a parcel of an additional 71 acres from the Governor himself, again showing his support for his namesake camp.[7]

As 1985 came to a close, the Council celebrated a new high with 192 young men having earned the rank of Eagle Scout during the year. Additionally, over 18,000 merit badges were awarded, prompting Council Advancement Chairman Bud Porter to declare, "This committee is functioning better than ever."[8] Further progress was expected on all fronts.

BSA'S VARSITY PROGRAM ADOPTED

BSA CREATED *the Varsity program for Boy Scouts aged 14 and older with a sports-based theme. It was adopted by Circle Ten Council as short time later.*[J]

Financially, Council board members set several goals that included growth of the Foundation's assets to $20 million, making a solid support system in potential down years of fund-raising. By the end of 1987, Circle Ten

TRAMMEL CROW'S ANNIVERSARY DONATION

LEADING UP TO BSA'S *75th Anniversary year in 1985, Dallas real estate mogul and former Circle Ten Scout Trammell Crow donated $10,000 to pay for all rank advancement patches earned during that year.*[K]

THE **MEXICAN** SCOUT EXCHANGE

IN AN ATTEMPT *to reach out a hand of brotherhood across Texas' southern border, Circle Ten Council engaged in an international Scout exchange program with Mexico. Ten of Circle Ten's Scouts swapped countries with ten Mexican Scouts and lived in the homes of local sponsor families for the duration of July and August 1985. Its success resulted in an expansion of the program the following month where some Circle Ten families hosted a total of 52 Mexican Scouts.*[L]

Foundation assets had risen above $10 million. Other facilities gifts followed.

Camp Constantin received a gift of $100,000 from the Sturgis Foundation to be used to build a new staff center on premises, and be dubbed the Sturgis Center.

Circle Ten received a $1.3 million gift as the result of terminating the trust established by the will of Ruby Trim Meisenbach, the widow of long-time Council executive board member, Kurt K. Meisenbach. The trust's last income beneficiary, Troop 70 Scoutmaster Lon Sailers, had passed away only months earlier.

In honor of the gift, Camp Comanche at the Clements Scout Ranch was re-named Camp Meisenbach. Funds received were used to make much-needed improvements and create its current endowment.[9]

Other improvements were closer to home. Answering the call was former Council President John D. Murchison's widow, Lupe, and their daughter, Ginger, who committed $1 million toward building a new Council headquarters to be named in his honor. Murchison had passed away in June 1979 while serving as BSA's national president.[10]

In May 1987, the Council's Scout Show again was planned for Texas Stadium (it's seventh to date) at a rental fee of $2,000 for the day. At it, hundreds of Scouting units put on "improved displays" of skills to a record number of attendees estimated at 30,000 people. Also, over 162,000 tickets

A LAWYER BY PROFESSION, *Lon Clayton Sailers Jr. (right and below) was a highly regimented leader as the tenured 38-year Scoutmaster of University Park's Troop 70. Regarded by his many former Scouts as a "tough but compassionate drill sergeant," Sailers mentored 238 boys through to the rank of Eagle Scout, possibly the most by a single troop in the area.*

Born on September 28, 1917, Sailers earned his Eagle rank in 1932 as a member of Dallas' Troop 34 led by another legendary local Scoutmaster, Rufus A. McClung. Attending the University of Texas in Austin, Sailers earned a bachelor's degree in business administration in 1940 and a law degree in 1941.

As a patriotic American during World War II, he joined the U.S. Navy on July 4, 1942, as an ensign, where he served on the USS Minneapolis. Honorably discharged in April 1946, Sailers returned to Dallas and began his practice of law at the firm of Turner Rogers Winn and Scurlock on McKinney Avenue. Knowing Sailers to be an Eagle Scout, one of the law partners asked him to take over the leadership of Troop 70.

Agreeing to do so, he asked fellow lawyer, Jerry Jordan, to help.

"He convinced me to be his assistant in the late 1940s and I just couldn't say no. I saw what those boys meant to him," recalled Jordan. "Lon was very organized when it came to things needing structure and Scouting fit that bill."

Former Troop 70 Scout and one of its future Scoutmasters, Charles Holmes added, "The Boy Scout troop was his family and Lon dedicated his life to it."

With an eye toward discipline and excellence, Sailers led his boys with a characteristic wide smile when pleased and stern look when not. His unit was run with timed precision and attention to detail. He insisted every Eagle Scout in his troop earn the Cooking merit badge, which was usually completed at the same time as the Camping merit badge. Also, each Eagle candidate had to construct a table, using spars and lashings, which was thrown off the University Park Elementary School's fire escape—twice. If it survived the fall, maintained secure joints, and supported the weight of Sailers standing atop it, the candidate was "officially" declared an Eagle Scout.

By the summer of 1985, Sailers' health began to fail and he passed away from heart disease on December 8.

"He didn't build a stadium or a highway, but he influenced the lives of 1,000 to 2,000 boys," recalled former Troop 70 Scout and Addison City Manager C. J. Webster. "For at least a hundred boys, he is equal to their father. I would call him my second father."M

TOP: Troop 70 Scoutmaster Lon Sailers at a Circle Ten Council banquet in the 1950s. BOTTOM: Scoutmaster Sailers (left) poses with Troop 70 Eagle Scouts in May 1963.

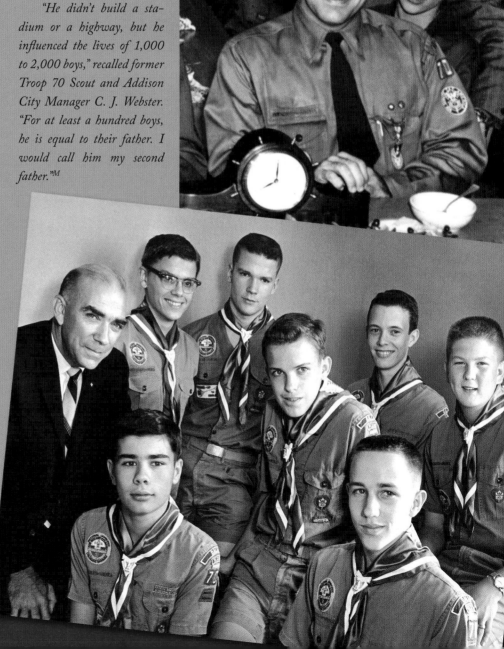

TECHNOLOGY EXPLORING POSTS

IN JANUARY 1986 *as Circle Ten Council continued to embrace technology, Council executives encouraged their Scouts to do the same. The Exploring program, which boasted a 6 percent increase in membership over the previous year, made the first definitive move. Responding to the increasing numbers of boys interested in electronics and science, a "Video Production Post" and a "Robotics Post" were established to serve the growing population of tech savvy youth.*[P]

were sold by Scouts and Cubs canvassing their neighborhoods.

Scout Executive Gamble instituted his plan to prevent child abuse through an "all-out" effort to support better training for all leaders, both junior and adult. In tandem, there would be a new Drug Awareness Program complete with "special unit level presentations"—the precursor to the Youth Protection Training program of today. The classic Scouting video detailing this program called "A Time to Tell" was released by October 1989.

With new national BSA policy changes, women were allowed to hold the position of Scoutmaster, as more youth were coming from one-parent households and many men simply could not dedicate enough time to the program as in previous years.

Clearly, Scouting was expanding across the nation and leadership positions needed to be filled.[11]

Women volunteers were becoming prevalent on the national scene and populous at national events like the 12th National Jamboree at Fort A. P. Hill held in August 1989 with the 360 Scout council contingents. That year, Circle Ten hosted 900 non-Texan Scouts on its pre-jamboree tour of Philadelphia, New York City, and Washington, DC.

As the decade came to a close, Scout Executive Gamble commented, "the 80s were very productive times for Circle Ten Council." But better times were in store as new ideas for expansion surfaced.

One of those new ideas was the publication of a new book by local well-known motivational speaker, Randy G. Pennington, called *On My Honor, I Will*,

THE FIRST SCOUTING FOR FOOD DRIVE

THE FIRST *"Scouting for Food"* drive was announced by Executive Board Member Steve Winn at the Council's annual dinner in January 1987. Believing Circle Ten to lack a significant community-wide service project like the Smile Day Good Turn clothing drives of past decades, Scout Executive Billy Gamble pressed for its approval.

With support of Chairman Tom McCartin, the 51-year-old publisher of the Dallas Times Herald newspaper and former Hall of Fame quarterback of the Dallas Cowboys Roger Staubach, the project was launched later that year.

Sponsored by Tom Thumb food stores, Scouts annually walk door-to-door on a canned food canvass for the food banks of North Texas.[N]

IN 1988, *Circle Ten was looking for new ways to raise revenue. One idea was to sell cans of Fix-A-Flat used to re-inflate automobile tires. It was adopted by the Council's fund-raising committee that included Scoutmaster Gene Smith of Troop 3 at the Oak Cliff Presbyterian Church. But before receiving authorization to proceed, Smith was called into the office of Scout Executive Billy Gamble to explain it.*

"He asked what I thought about it and I let him know that I would help promote it in any way that I could," recalled Smith. "It seemed like a good option, so we began selling the kits the following year."

But this short-lived fund-raiser was dropped when Council executives discovered that the product voided the warranty of tire manufacturers. So, the Council adopted the sale of popcorn instead after Ray Marr proposed it at the January 1990 executive board meeting. Proposed for the fall, a trial sales effort was scheduled for the spring. But the Council had little to worry about as Boy Scouts had been selling popcorn for the past decade across the nation.

Originating at the Buffalo Trace Council in Evanston, Illinois, after their funding had been cut in 1978, their executive board had two sales ideas to make up the financial shortfall—sell either gym socks or popcorn. Fortunately, one Buffalo Trace board member was an officer at the Pop Weaver Company, a local popcorn manufacturer, so the deal was struck. In the first sales season of 1980, Pop Weaver produced a simple white tub with black letters denoting "Scouting Popcorn," and filled them with kernel corn.

Word spread the following year, in which three councils made it their official fund-raiser. By 1982, seven councils had adopted it. But in 1984, national BSA's lawyers sent a letter to Pop Weaver declaring their use of the word "Scouting" as prohibited per act of Congress in 1916 as it infringed on BSA's rightful trademark. To accommodate, the company formed their philanthropic division named "Trail's End."

Circle Ten Council held a kickoff meeting in October 1990 that was attended by 323 local units. By the sales' end in November, total proceeds had "exceeded expectations," earning the Council a profit of $130,000—more than two times the funds budgeted. Over 70,000 units of popcorn were sold by Cub and Boy Scout salesmen, who received $136,000 in commissions. The first co-chairmen were executive board members Al Cloud and former Dallas Cowboys quarterback Danny White.[o]

From this modest start, a local Scouting classic was born.

BELOW LEFT: The original containers for Boy Scout popcorn from the 1970s. BELOW: A sampling of prizes awarded to the best Scout popcorn salesmen in Circle Ten Council over the years. ACROSS: The annual patches awarded by the Pop Weaver Company to their Scout salesmen across the country.

Chris Neukranz (left) and Jordan Christian (right) lead Plano's Troop 221 in performing the closing flag ceremony at summer camp.

which was brought out mid-year. From his royalties, Pennington donated 10 percent to the Council in support of Circle Ten Scouting.

The founding of Explorer Post 111 sponsored by the East Dallas Police Storefront was an important development in serving the local minority community—all members were Asian immigrants seeking U.S. citizenship. The Council had the opportunity to impress itself and its values onto these new Americans seeking a new life.

Council board members knew Circle Ten had to continue to promote its brand. To update its image, it commissioned the current logo that reflected its fresh goals and community objectives in service. The position of finance director was created as well and the new site for the Murchison Scouting Center was chosen.

The four-year search had netted three possible locations by mid-year 1991 that included: LBJ Freeway near Josey Lane, Dallas Technology Center on Stemmons Freeway, and the corner of Regal Row and Harry Hines Blvd. It was decided that the 36,000-square-foot Regal Row site was the best location. Offered at a cost of $527,500 plus the additional cost of the 17,000-square-foot building on the corner, several funding grants brought the cost down by $200,000. The sale of the old Mitchell-Head Service Center brought the net outlay of the new land to *zero* dollars.[12]

Other building projects were being planned as well. Camp Cherokee's headquarters had burned in January 1991 and a new headquarters building was being planned. It was completed by June.

Also, a ham radio system was approved for installation in a new building constructed at Camp

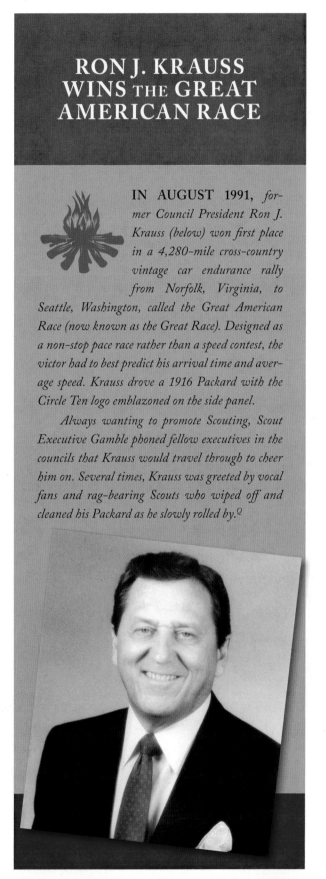

RON J. KRAUSS WINS THE GREAT AMERICAN RACE

IN AUGUST 1991, *former Council President Ron J. Krauss (below) won first place in a 4,280-mile cross-country vintage car endurance rally from Norfolk, Virginia, to Seattle, Washington, called the Great American Race (now known as the Great Race). Designed as a non-stop pace race rather than a speed contest, the victor had to best predict his arrival time and average speed. Krauss drove a 1916 Packard with the Circle Ten logo emblazoned on the side panel.*

Always wanting to promote Scouting, Scout Executive Gamble phoned fellow executives in the councils that Krauss would travel through to cheer him on. Several times, Krauss was greeted by vocal fans and rag-bearing Scouts who wiped off and cleaned his Packard as he slowly rolled by.[Q]

Wisdom—the Metrocell Building—eventually to be under the direction of new camp ranger, Phil Augsburger, who had assumed the oversight of Camp Wisdom after the retirement of longtime Camp Ranger Bill O'Pry and a temporary successor. Southwestern Bell Mobile Systems eventually leased 3,000 square feet of space at the camp to place a much-needed cell phone tower.[13]

There were 16,000 inner city Scouts meeting within the Council weekly and a new national program was launched—Learning for Life. Designed as an in-school classroom program to develop self-esteem, ethical behavior, and decision-making processes in students from kindergarten through high school, Circle Ten chose to adopt it for career awareness.

In mid-1992, plans were developed to build a "Cub World" at Camp Wisdom to provide a fun place with activities to serve the youngest patrons of Scouting. To necessitate these and other building projects, Council treasurer and future Council President Douglas D. Hawthorne proposed a $7 to $9 million capital fund-raising campaign.

Scout Executive Gamble reminded the executive board that it had been over 25 years since Circle Ten had embarked on such a campaign, and this would be the last one needed for the foreseeable future.[14]

LEFT: Former Council President Douglas Hawthorne at his presentation ceremony for the Distinguished Eagle Scout Award in 1995. ACROSS RIGHT: A happy Circle Ten Council Scout enjoying a meal at summer camp around 1984.

AND THE COUNCIL WOULD NEED THOSE FUNDS TO CONTINUE
DEVELOPING A ROBUST PROGRAM—ESPECIALLY SINCE IT WAS ABOUT
TO ACQUIRE MUCH MORE SCOUTING TERRITORY.

chapter 15

EXPANSION (1993–1999)

"Work hard, think big, stay alert, and success will follow."

JOHN P. "JACK" HARBIN
PRESIDENT, CIRCLE TEN FOUNDATION [1]

In the executive board meeting of November 1992, the proposed merger between the Circle Ten and Texoma Valley Councils was announced as the Sherman-based council sought financial and managerial relief as their expenses were increasing faster than new funding. With half of their $290,000 budget coming from the United Way and their annual Friends of Scouting campaign (both decreasing), the Texoma Valley Council soon would be forced to take on debt to support operations without some relief.

For Circle Ten, the addition of 2,700 youth members, 800 adult volunteers, 60 chartering organizations, and a new summer camp (Camp Grayson) would be welcomed additions within the Council's goals of expanding its regional Scouting program. By March 1993, Scout Executive Billy Gamble reported that a joint meeting between the two councils had taken place and that a merger agreement was eminent. The goal for completion was July 1.[2]

On June 10, Circle Ten Council President Jim Oesterreicher put the proposal up for a vote to the Special Committee with the comment, "No negatives are seen in the planned merger."

Unanimously passed, the announcement was made to the executive board a week later and Texoma Valley's three districts became Circle Ten's one.

RIGHT: Circle Ten Council President Jim Oesterreicher in 1993.
ABOVE: The first summer camp patch for Camp Grayson under the new ownership of Circle Ten Council in 1994.

"There were about 700 councils across the nation in the 1950s," recalled Circle Ten Council Operations Manager Dick Corcoran. "So, it was natural that these mergers take place to better deliver the program to our kids. Now, Grayson and Bryan County Scouts would have access to three additional camps as members of Circle Ten."

Another issue involved the reconciliation of the two Order of the Arrow lodges—they had to be combined into one entity. Up for negotiation were each lodge's totem: Mikanakawa's owl and Okiciapi's thunderbird. The stalemate was broken in April 1994 with the adoption of both totems on all future lodge patches, flaps, newsletter banners, and artwork. However, all Circle Ten Order of the Arrow members would be part of Mikanakawa Lodge 101.[3]

"DAILY, WE WITNESS THE NEAR-TERM IMPACT OF SCOUTING ON THE LIVES OF YOUNG PEOPLE IN OUR COMMUNITY. HOWEVER, THE LONG-TERM BENEFIT WILL BE FELT FOR GENERATIONS TO COME AS THESE YOUNG PEOPLE TAKE ON LEADERSHIP ROLES AS ADULTS IN DALLAS AND CITIES AROUND THE WORLD. THE VALUES THEY ARE LEARNING IN SCOUTING TODAY WILL LEAD TO TRANSFORMATIONAL CHANGE IN OUR COMMUNITIES TOMORROW."

—BOBBY B. LYLE, FOUNDER & CHAIRMAN, LYCO HOLDINGS INCORPORATED

The year 1993 featured another landmark event—the Council's partnership with the Dallas Youth Crime Commission. Beginning in 1994, the Police Department chartered 30 new units "to target Cub Scout age youth in high-risk areas." Dubbed "Partners in Youth Crime Prevention," police officers were tapped as unit leaders.

The program proved a success as national BSA publications *Boys' Life* and *Scouting* magazines featured articles on the Council's initiative in 1996. Even sitting U.S. Supreme Court Associate Justice Clarence Thomas came to Dallas and visited a Dallas Police Cub Scout pack on September 9, 1999. Regaling the lads with stories from his childhood regarding his growing up under the

ACROSS LEFT: The Mikanakawa Lodge and Okiciyapi Lodge merger flap produced in celebration of the landmark event in 1994. ABOVE: Members of the Cub Scout Pack sponsored by the Dallas Youth Crime Commission of the Dallas Police Department around 1995.

wing of his grandparents and being forced to "do his homework," he stressed the importance of staying in both school and Scouting.[4]

Another major initiative was the kickoff of a new $7 million capital campaign led by former Council President William C. "Bill" McCord. As the first major fund-raising effort in 25 years, Scout Executive Gamble called it "one of the most important things we have undertaken."

With the new funds, $5 million was allotted for various camp improvements and $2 million was set aside to increase the endowment of the Circle Ten Foundation. After six months, the initiative had raised $5.8 million that included two large gifts of $500,000 each. One was from Lupe Murchison, while the other was received from future Council President Jim Sowell. Sowell's gift endowed Camp Wisdom and created the Billy Sowell Boy Scout Camp on the west side in honor of his father. By the end of 1994, a total of nearly $7.3 million had been raised by the Council and camp improvement plans were finalized.[5]

LUCILLE G. "LUPE" MURCHISON – COUNCIL PATRON

BORN IN DALLAS *on November 4, 1925, Lucille Hughes "Lupe" Gannon always intended to make a positive difference in her community. The daughter of First National Bank of Dallas Vice President Edward James "Ward" Gannon Jr. and wife Ethyl, Lupe graduated Highland Park High School at age 16 in 1942.*

Marrying well-to-do real estate developer John D. Murchison on March 9, 1947, in her mother's home near the Brookhollow Golf Club, they set upon a course of giving back to the community that had given them so much. John, the son of oil and gas developer Clint W. Murchison Sr., made shrewd business deals that provided the monetary largesse for a lifetime of philanthropic gifts with Lupe.

Over the years, Lupe Murchison was a devoted patron of the arts and known for her "enormous generosity of spirit and immense size of her heart" when it came to supporting her favored organizations. Those included the Dallas Museum of Art, Southern Methodist University's Meadows School for the Arts, the Ford Museum in Michigan, the Georgia O'Keefe Museum in Santa Fe, the Vatican Museums, the Royal Academy Trusts, and the Boy Scouts of America, just to name a few.

As a valued member of Circle Ten Council's executive board in the 1990s, she helped expand the local movement with her leadership on various projects that included the John D. Murchison Scouting Center dedicated in 1996 to her husband's memory.

Lupe G. Murchison passed away on July 3, 2001, and is buried next to her husband and their daughter, Virginia "Ginger" Murchison, in the Athens (Texas) Cemetery in Henderson County near the Clements Scout Ranch.[A]

285

LEFT: Circle Ten Council President Jim Sowell in 1997. ABOVE: A portrait of Eagle Scout Billy Sowell as a youth, the namesake of the Billy Sowell Boy Scout Camp at Camp Wisdom. ACROSS BOTTOM LEFT: A Scout sits on a bridge at Camp Cherokee at the Clements Scout Ranch.

Construction began in early 1995 at Camps Constantin and Grayson with the former receiving a new swim dock and the latter getting an enlarged dining hall. The plan for Camp Wisdom/Billy Sowell Boy Scout Camp was to build a large amphitheater to be completed as a gift to the Council from the Mikanakawa Lodge. Named the Jim W. Ince Amphitheater in honor of the long-time Order of the Arrow lodge advisor (1976 – 1987), it was dedicated in August 1995.

Sadly, James William "Jim" Ince would pass away at his home in Richardson on May 29, 2012, after decades of devoted service and mentorship to the leaders of the Mikanakawa Lodge and Circle Ten Council Scouting.

"Jim Ince believed in his youth leaders and had faith in us," recalled former Lodge Chief Brian

DISTINGUISHED EAGLE SCOUT BILLY GAMBLE

AT THE EXECUTIVE BOARD *meeting on April 22, 1997, Scout Executive Billy Gamble was presented with the Distinguished Eagle Scout Award for to his years of dedicated service to the Scouting movement, which included 22 years as the head of Circle Ten Council.*

"It came as a complete surprise to me," Gamble recalled, "but I was truly humbled to be thought of in that way."[B]

Bennett. "That had a very powerful effect on a bunch of teenagers trying to find their way. He truly made a difference in our lives"[6]

In August 1997, construction at Camp Wisdom/ Billy Sowell Boy Scout Camp included a new combination headquarters, health lodge, and museum building. Dubbed the Jim Sowell Administration headquarters in honor of his generosity and service as the sitting Council president, half of the building was dedicated for use as the Council's museum and named in honor of John P. "Jack" Harbin, the longtime president of the Circle Ten Foundation. Only recently, Harbin had retired from its board of trustees having serving 28 years and having donated $1 million to fund the museum.

With the building completed in February 1998 and formally dedicated in June 1999, new Council

JOHN P. "JACK" HARBIN
By Bob Reitz, Curator, Harbin Scout Museum

JACK HARBIN *(below) was born in Waxahachie, Texas and became a Boy Scout when his father, Elijah P. Harbin, was Scoutmaster. He received his Eagle Scout award in 1931 and was a member of the White Sharks of Tahkodah, an early Scouting honor society in Circle Ten Council.*

After receiving a degree from the University of Texas in Austin in 1939, he served as a lieutenant in the U.S. Naval Reserve from 1942 until 1945, when he started his business career as an accountant with oilfield support company Halliburton. Rising through the ranks as a duty-driven leader, Harbin retired in 1983 as its chairman and CEO.

He was selected as a Distinguished Alumnus from the University of Texas in 1981 and elected into the Texas Business Hall of Fame in 1994.

Harbin served as the trustee of the Circle Ten Foundation board for 28 years, retiring as its president. He received his Silver Beaver award in 1971 and was awarded the Distinguished Eagle Scout Award, a national recognition, in 1972.

For his long-term service to local Scouting, the Harbin Scout Museum at Camp Wisdom/Billy Sowell Boy Scout Camp was named in his honor.[D]

THE JACK D. FURST AQUATICS BASE AT CAMP CONSTANTIN

IN 1997, *Executive Board Member Jack D. Furst and wife Debra made their first major commitment to Circle Ten Council that combined his fond memories of being an aquatics staffer in the 1970s with his desire to positively impact the lives of today's Scouts. The result was a $1 million gift to renew the waterfront at Camp Constantin and make it the best-equipped camp in the Council. The Jack D. Furst Aquatics Base was dedicated in June 1998, just in time for its first summer camp session.*

"It was the right thing to do," recalled Furst some years later. "I wanted to honor the Camp Constantin waterfront staff for having a positive influence on my life as a 15-year-old Eagle Scout from Paoli Troop #1 in Paoli, Pennsylvania."[C]

ACROSS TOP and ACROSS FAR MIDDLE: Executive Board Member Jack D. Furst and wife Debra at the June 1998 dedication ceremony of the Jack D. Furst Aquatics Base at Camp Constantin. At the waterfront, Scouts can participate in jumping on the blob (right), canoeing, water skiing, and sailing among other exciting water activities on beautiful Possum Kingdom Lake.

President Bobby Lyle commended Harbin for his "outstanding contributions of energy and financial resources."[7]

Further plans called for the creation of a playground for the Council's Cub Scouts. Dubbed "Cub World," construction commenced in March 1998 with a large wooden castle, a fort, and two land ships sitting on concrete bases with steel infrastructure. With much of the costs donated by Hill & Wilkinson Commercial Construction Company and stonemasons Dee Brown Inc., the Council incurred no added expense.

By November, Fort Farrington, given by Executive Board Member Jerry S. Farrington, was completed. Construction of the Cub World Space Station began in March 1999, which was paid for with a $75,000 donation made by Southwest Airlines. General Electric donated funds for the Nature

THE FIRST CELEBRITY SHOOT

THE FIRST CIRCLE TEN *Council Celebrity Shoot took place in September 1997 when kicked-off at the Eddie Dean's Ranch banquet hall in downtown Dallas. Named the Golden Chick/Jay Novacek Celebrity Shoot, it teamed the well-known restaurant sponsor with the former Dallas Cowboy All-Pro tight end in a shotgun marksman, fund-raising event. As designed, the four-man teams included one person of local notoriety that moved from station to station on the clay pigeon target range.*

This was the first major Council event chaired by Jack D. Furst, who had joined the Circle Ten executive board in January 1997. His 30-man committee arranged for corporate sponsorships in the vein of past Danny White golf tournaments.

The first year, the Shoot raised over $400,000 for the Council prompting sports cable channel ESPN to take notice and film its second annual contest for broadcast.

"This event has grown beyond our wildest dreams," said Golden Chick Chairman Mark Parmerlee. "When we started with the idea, we hoped it would become an annual event, but we had no idea how truly successful it would be."[E]

CIRCLE TEN COUNCIL'S R. TATE McKENZIE STATUE

IN HONOR OF *the thousands of dedicated Circle Ten volunteers over the years, Council President Jim Sowell donated a coveted R. Tate McKenzie statue of a Boy Scout* to be placed at the entrance of the new John D. Murchison Scouting Center in August 1998.

As specified by the McKenzie trustees, every potential statue recipient had to be "approved to be sold to" by passing a rigorous vetting and qualification process. The six-foot-tall bronze depicts an iconic Boy Scout in picturesque Scout uniform holding his campaign hat in one hand and holding his hatchet with the other.[F]

THE SALE OF THE ANSON ROAD SERVICE CENTER

WITH THE ACQUISITION *of the John D. Murchison Scouting Center, the old Mitchell-Head building was put up for sale in February 1996 with an asking price of* $495,000. It was purchased three months later for $450,000.[G]

ACROSS LEFT: Circle Ten Council President Bobby Lyle in 1999. BELOW: The commemorative patch issued at the time of the opening of Cub World at Camp Wisdom/Billy Sowell Boy Scout Camp in 1999.

Center, along with the large yellow and blue painted Cub World Activity Center. Work on the cave/mountain facility had not started but the Mikanakawa Lodge had begun construction on the Indian Village.

In September 1999, the Cub World facility was "built out and open to the public at Camp Wisdom/Billy Sowell Boy Scout Camp.[8]

Construction on the John D. Murchison Scouting Center began in mid-1995 at the corner of Harry Hines Boulevard and Regal Row. By January 1996, it was "65% complete and within

FAR BELOW: The John D. Murchison Scouting Center while under construction in 1996. ACROSS LEFT: The Murchison Scouting Center as it appears today. BELOW CENTER: The program from the Dedication of the Murchison Scouting Center. BELOW: Gov. William P. Clements Jr. (middle) with two Eagle Scouts at the dedication of the Eagle Plaza in October 1998. ACROSS BOTTOM RIGHT: Gov. Clements posing with two attendees at the Eagle Plaza dedication. ACROSS BOTTOM LEFT: A current image of the bronze eagle statue at Circle Ten Council's Eagle Plaza.

DEDICATION
JOHN D. MURCHISON
SCOUTING CENTER

CIRCLE TEN COUNCIL
BOY SCOUTS OF AMERICA

293

THE MURCHISON SCOUTING CENTER'S DONOR WALL

WISHING TO BETTER *publicize those who had given financially to the Council, Endowments/Development Committee Chairman Jack D. Furst proposed the creation of two new eight-foot tall "Donor Walls" to be placed in the main lobby of the Murchison Scouting Center.*

Dedicated on December 13, 2005, the walls listed grantors of deferred life insurance gifts (both individuals and corporations) as well as those who contributed funds at all levels for membership within national BSA's 1910 Society as well as some smaller gift acknowledgments.[H]

budget." Proposed for the site but not originally budgeted was a celebratory Eagle Scout Plaza that listed every boy or man who ever had accomplished that feat within the Council's current territory.

The names were to be engraved into many Texas granite tablet slabs laid in the ground that surrounded a ring of granite benches. Within the ring was to be a defined centerpiece. Eventually, that would become a large boulder topped with a dramatic bronze eagle with outstretched wings designed by Fort Worth–based sculptor Deran Wright.

His work was dedicated to the parents and Scoutmasters of those enshrined Eagle Scouts, and donated by Council member Pryor Blackwell and

family in honor of his father, longtime Circle Ten Scoutmaster Rebel Blackwell.

With a total cost of the Plaza being estimated at $150,000, Scout Executive Gamble was asked by the executive board to "discuss the plan with selected key Eagle Scouts and report back to the Committee."[9]

Its approval came a short time later but the hardest part was yet to come—fact checking the thousands of boys and men who had earned the rank over the previous 85 years. To the rescue came a group of senior volunteers within the Council, many of whom were also former Scouting professionals known as the Silver Scouters. Led by Circle Ten

EXPANDING THE CAMP WISDOM/ BILLY SOWELL BOY SCOUT CAMP

IN 1998, *Council President Jim Sowell negotiated the purchase of an additional 28 acres of adjoining land at Camp Wisdom/Billy Sowell Boy Scout Camp's northwest corner from the Grady Niblo family. Afterward, he dug a 6.8-acre lake and dubbed it Lake Shirley in honor of his mother. President Sowell also provided for a COPE (Challenging Outdoor Personal Experience) ropes course for older Scouts and Venturers to be installed in late 2000.[I]*

BILLY GAMBLE'S MEMBERSHIP EXPANSION

THE BILLY GAMBLE *years were a blessing for membership growth. By the end of 1999, the Council had over 35,000 traditional Scouts. Upon his retirement in 2001, Gamble had presided over 21 consecutive years of increasing membership and the naming of Circle Ten Council as the nation's fourth largest.*[J]

monument, replete with 13,000 names, was dedicated a year later on October 27, 1998.[11]

More camp improvements came in 1998. Camp Cherokee got its iconic 60-foot-high climbing-and-rappelling tower in June while Camp Grayson expanded its land holdings by an additional 230 acres to the southwest, which formerly had been owned and used by Perrin Air Force Base as its recreation area. The Council intended to utilize the land for outpost camping, as well as become the new home of an aquatics base and a Cub World.

employee Gene Smith, these gentlemen poured over the annual listings of Eagle award recipients culled from sketchy early national BSA records and affirmed their rightful place on the large, engraved granite tablets.

The Murchison Scouting Center was dedicated on October 6, 1996, with the completion of the Eagle Plaza to follow.[10]

In October 1997, Executive Board Member Jack D. Furst, a founding partner of the Dallas venture capital firm of Hicks, Muse, Tate & Furst, made a generous donation of $75,000 to jumpstart the Plaza project. Other donors included Past Council President Dick Brooks, Immediate Past President of the Circle Ten Foundation Jack Harbin, Gov. William P. Clements Jr., the Pryor Blackwell Family, and the John Loper Family. The impressive

LEARNING FOR LIFE

AT A TIME WHERE *students were performing unthinkable acts of violence against their fellow classmates in other parts of the country, Circle Ten Council sought a way to get Scouting's peaceful message into the local school systems. By November 1999, executive board member and former Richardson ISD Superintendent Linus Wright assisted in getting the Dallas Independent School District to adopt Scouting's Learning for Life program for its high school students.*

Recounted Scout Executive Billy Gamble, "Scouting and its values are needed more than ever as a partner to help save the lives of our youth in a real hands-on way."[K]

Building began on the Sanford Aquatic Center on the main campground property beginning in January 1999 from a sizeable gift made by Executive Board Member Robert F. Sanford and his wife, Lola. Dedicated on July 1, it included a new 280,000-gallon swimming pool and slide.

In September 1999, Circle Ten Council received a generous $2 million gift to make further improvements to Camp Grayson from Mrs. Ruth Ray Hunt, the widow of Dallas oilman H. L. Hunt Jr. Her desire was to assist the Council in "helping deserving rural needy Scouts or adults to attend summer camp, day camp, Wood Badge, and other events."

In honor of her donation, the Circle Ten leaders renamed the camp in honor of her brother (at her request), a 25-year Scoutmaster in Idabel, Oklahoma—James Ray, known to everyone simply as "Uncle Jimmy."

Under the direction of the James Ray Grant Committee, immediate projects included a new gateway, entrance road, and expanded parking lot.[12]

AS 1999 CAME TO A CLOSE, COUNCIL LEADERS LOOKED FORWARD TO TAKING THE MESSAGE OF SCOUTING FURTHER INTO THE COMMUNITY, EVEN AS THE NEW MILLENNIUM APPROACHED AND THE UNKNOWN CHAOS OF THE DREADED Y2K PROGRAMMING BUG LOOMED ON THE HORIZON.

The official Council portrait of the Hunt and Ray Families taken at Circle Ten headquarters before the dedication of Camp James Ray in 2000. "Uncle Jimmy" Ray appears in the back row next to Mr. Ray L. Hunt, who stands behind Uncle Jimmy's wife, Mrs. Mavis Ray. Mr. Hunt's wife, Mrs. Nancy Ann Hunt, is to the right of Mrs. Ray. The group is flanked by Council President Bobby Lyle next to Mrs. Hunt and Scout Executive Billy Gamble next to Mr. Hunt. Three special Circle Ten Scouts are in front.

chapter 16

NEW MILLENNIUM, FRESH START
(2000–2009)

"Scouts, when I started my professional career, I was told by my boss that working a half day was fine with him. I just had to tell him whether it would be the first twelve hours of the day or the second. Gentlemen, any form of success takes hard work and dedication to purpose."

GLENN E. "GENE" STONE
SCOUT EXECUTIVE, CIRCLE TEN COUNCIL
ADDRESS TO TROOP 750 IN GARLAND, TEXAS
DECEMBER 10, 2001

The Hon. Pete Sessions of Texas displays his Lone Star State cummerbund and bowtie with Scout Executive Billy Gamble at BSAs 90th Anniversary celebration in 2000 in Washington, DC.

A S MANUFACTURING and financial centers across the nation emerged from their self-made bunkers after the dreaded Y2K programming bug failed to shut down any vital national computer systems and send the world into economic Armageddon, Circle Ten employees returned to business as usual on January 3, 2000 when Council offices opened.

Also to the positive, Council camps were getting a lot of attention. A 153-foot waterslide and new cabin on Lake Murchison had been added to Camp Cherokee at the Clements Scout Ranch. A large waterfront pavilion and remodeled bath house now were built at the Camp Constantin/Jack D. Furst Aquatics Base. New latrines and camp pavilions had been installed at Camp James Ray, and Camp Wisdom/Billy Sowell Boy Scout Camp got a new assembly area in Cub World along with a remodeled warehouse. In addition, the latter camp's land had expanded by a half acre after the Council completed additional negotiations with the Niblo family to purchase more adjoining land that included the property containing the old log cabin of Dr. Grady Niblo Jr.

After giving 22-years of dedicated service to the Council, Scout Executive Billy Gamble announced his retirement effective November 2001 with his replacement to be named shortly. That man would be

the Chickasaw Council's Scout Executive Glenn E. "Gene" Stone. Travelling from Memphis, Tennessee, and introduced to the Circle Ten executive board in late November, Stone expressed his "excitement" at the opportunity being given him in Dallas. He declared his intention to bring Scouting into the lives of boys "who have never had a Scouting opportunity" and he invited all board members to "join him in this objective."[1]

And he meant it.

Stone, an Eagle Scout who had graduated Colorado State University in Pueblo with a degree in forestry, changed occupations to enter the management ranks of professional Scouting—a decision that brought him assignments at the Monterey Bay Area Council in Salinas, California, and the Cub Scout division at BSA's National Office in Irving, Texas before moving to Memphis and then back to the Dallas area, where he again put his work ethic to the test.

Within the upper leadership ranks of Circle Ten, the members of the executive board were pleased at his hiring as well. Council President John Stuart III, a Circle Ten Distinguished Eagle Scout and alumnus from Troop 32 (now Troop 68) at the Highland Park United Methodist Church, recalled

SCOUT EXECUTIVE GENE STONE IS OFFERED AN ASSISTANT SCOUTMASTERSHIP AT GARLAND'S TROOP 750

WHEN GENE STONE *arrived in Circle Ten Council, he made a point of visiting as many troops and districts as possible in his first months. Traveling to Garland in December 2001, he gave the keynote address at the annual Christmas Court of Honor of Troop 750 at the Monica Park Christian Church on Broadway Boulevard. After delivering a highly inspirational talk, Scoutmaster David D. Durrett approached the Scout Executive to thank him for attending the event.*

"You sure are nice to have come to see us," said Durrett. "Maybe we should promote you to Assistant Scoutmaster!"

A delighted Stone replied, "Check back with me again in a few months. I may take you up on it!"

"That was just the way he was," noted Council Director of Finance Don Burke. "Gene was a genuine and cheerful person, who tried very hard to take Scouting's values into the field. He was a great Scout leader as well as being my best friend."

Tragically, Gene Stone passed away at the age of 58 after battling a long illness on October 8, 2009, in Skillman, New Jersey.[B]

Stone as being "very open, a people person, and always transparent."

"He was a wonderful guy," Stuart added, "and we were glad to have him with us when he was here."[2]

In promoting the program, Stone wanted every boy to have a quality Scouting experience. One of those lads was Eagle Scout Paul Hedgecock of Troop 852 chartered by the Our Savior Lutheran Church in Mesquite. Paul had cerebral palsy and was confined to a wheelchair but that did not prevent him from earning Scouting's highest rank. Stone was so impressed by the boy's undefeatable spirit that he presented both Paul and his mother Gina to the executive board in April 2002.[3]

ACROSS LEFT: Circle Ten Scout Executive Gene Stone in 2002. BELOW: Scouts of Troop 714 sponsored by the Bent Tree Bible Fellowship in Carrollton serve freshly made kettle popcorn.

THE NEW LEADERS' TRAINING CONTINUUM

BEGINNING ON JANUARY 1, 2002, *Circle Ten Council converted to the "seamless" training continuum program that allowed graduation from preliminary courses to later ones with little duplication of material. The expectation was that Scouting units could better attain a level of 100 percent trained leaders.*

"The switch to the new system was important because before, we had the program but no true flow," recalled Council Training Chairman Daniel Zaccara. "The new training continuum tied all of the courses together, added some new ones, and made the experience more complete and effective."

New leaders began with Fast Start training and learned the basics of the Scouting program. Next came New Leader Essentials with a module on leader-specific training for those who held any adult leadership role. The Wood Badge training experience capped the training triumvirate with all graduates being able to provide their units with the most skilled and best-prepared leaders that Scouting could offer.[C]

302

SCOUTING AND SOCCER

SCOUT EXECUTIVE GENE STONE *recognized that Circle Ten Council was under-serving the ever-expanding Hispanic market segment in town. At the time, that portion made up about 30 percent of the entire Dallas population, and it was growing rapidly.*

Similar observations were being made across the country, causing national Scouting managers to take notice. Begun in Florida by Hispanic advocate Jose Niño, with the advice of advocate Michael R. Bradle, the Scouting and Soccer program combined sports and character building into something that was embraced by many Hispanic families. But in order to adopt the new program, the Council had to change the perception of Scouting within this market segment.

"Much of our Hispanic population had grown up in different countries with the Scouting program being only for children from well-to-do families," noted Council President John Stuart III. "We wanted them to know that Scouting is for everybody."

Stone and the executive board designed a "soccer-Scouting-soccer" style meeting, where the values of Scouting were taught at halftime by the Scoutmaster/Coach, when sandwiched within a healthy athletic game. The uniforms consisted merely of the team's jersey.[D]

ACROSS TOP and ACROSS BOTTOM: A Cub Scout from Pack 160 works on a construction project, while a Tiger Cub participates in the Raingutter Regatta at the 2008 Scout Show. TOP RIGHT and MIDDLE RIGHT: Scouts assemble for and perform a flag ceremony in June during summer camp. LOWER RIGHT: A Scout works at the forge in Camp Cherokee's Mountain Man area in 2004.

THE NEW DOCK AT THE CAMP CONSTANTIN/JACK D. FURST AQUATICS BASE

IN SEPTEMBER 2002, *the Camp Constantin/Jack D. Furst Aquatics Base was given permission by the Brazos River Authority to construct its new swimming dock. The dock included three specific areas reserved for the three classifications of Scout aquanauts—non-swimmer, beginner, and swimmer. It had three closed-in sections for each designation with non-swimmers being closest to shore and always able to touch the bottom of the lake.* [E]

Other success stories in Stone's first months were the awarding of the Medal of Merit in lifesaving from BSA's national office to Cub Scout Joshua Jordan and Boy Scout Matt Mullaney. Also, the Certificate of Merit was presented to Scout Adam Webb, whose heroic story was featured on an episode of the TV talk program, *The John Walsh Show* that ran from 2002 to 2004. Walsh's notoriety stemmed from his *other* show that featured the criminal end of the spectrum, *America's Most Wanted*.

At the terminus of Scout Executive Stone's first compete year in 2002, traditional membership had rebounded back to above 35,000—a 4.4 percent increase from the year before.[4]

TOP and ABOVE: Summer scenes from the Jack D. Furst Aquatics Base at Camp Constantin. LEFT: The patch issued to each Scout that attended summer camp during Camp Constantin's 60th Anniversary year in 2006.

LEFT and BELOW: A Scout descends down the climbing tower at Camp Cherokee as his fellow Scouts encourage him on.

In the case of Council management, Scout Executive Stone wanted to maintain its high level of integrity. One of his innovations was to form the "Audit & Ethics Committee" to review internal policies and reinforce the Council's image of incorruptibility within the community.

Another was recommended by Audit & Ethics Committee Chairman Michael F. O'Donnell as a requirement of employment—Council workers had to sign a Code of Conduct document. Later the Audit & Ethics Committee created a hotline for "reporting any alleged inappropriate behavior in the

THE CIRCLE TEN FOUNDATION

AS 2003 CAME TO A CLOSE, *Circle Ten was one of the best-funded councils in the country, coming in second to the Greater St. Louis Council in Missouri. Reaping the benefits of having excellent trustees for many years as well as strong donors who had given of their resources freely, the Council amassed nearly $26 million in assets by that time.*

President of the Trustees Bob Wooldrige reported that the Foundation had garnered a staggering 23.7 percent return on investments during the previous year being "a definite improvement over the past two years."

The addition of another $1 million donation from the founder of Fort Worth's Mesa Petroleum, T. Boone Pickens, put the Council closer to its goal of seeing the Foundation's assets increase to $100 million by 2012.[G]

THE FIRST WEBELOS-TO-SCOUT TRANSITION COMMITTEE

AN IMPORTANT ASPECT *of the Webelos Scout program is its ability to transition lads from Cub Scouting into Boy Scouting. To improve the conversion rate, the first Council Webelos-to-Scout transition committee was formed under the direction of Chairman David Klaudt, the troop committee chairman of Troop 838 at St. Rita's School in North Dallas.*

"We put that program in place as a 'best practices' system for inserting existing Cub Scouts over into Boy Scouts," recalled Klaudt. "We already had the customers. They just needed to be properly introduced to Boy Scouting, to keep them involved in the program."

Beginning in the spring of 2004, over time this effort has led to increasing numbers of Council Webelos Scouts remaining in the program each successive year.[F]

BELOW: A Scout leads the Pledge of Allegiance at the Friends of Scouting banquet on March 7, 2006 with Dallas Cowboys radio commentator Brad Sham behind him. ACROSS TOP RIGHT and ACROSS BOTTOM RIGHT: North Trail District Cub Scouts participate in Twilight Camp activities at Richardson's Breckenridge Park in June 2007.

Council" with a third party monitoring any activity. According to the Director of Support Service Scott Ferguson, "We haven't had a hit in years."[5]

Likewise in 2004, the Health and Safety Committee headed by Bassett Kilgore reported that BSA's new *Guide to Safe Scouting* books had been distributed to all units. This publication outlined in detail all

BECOMING A NATIONAL SCOUT SHOP

ALTHOUGH THE NATIONAL *economy was in a period of rapid expansion in 2004, Circle Ten Council's sources of income lagged while its expenses increased. One of the problems involved the Council-run Scoutfitter store. For several years, the Scoutfitter saw its income drop while its inventory had risen. Now facing competition from strategically placed national BSA Scout Shops around the territory, members no longer had to trek to the Murchison Scouting Center to buy their gear.*

Executive Board Member Jack D. Furst performed an analysis of the advantages of either keeping the Scoutfitter as an in-house operation or transferring the concession to BSA's National Supply Division as their newest store location.

Effective January 1, 2005, the Circle Ten Scoutfitter became the latest BSA Scout Shop. Current store employees could interview for new job positions, which two did. In the end, the Council began participating in the profits without bearing the expense of the operation.[H]

DISTINGUISHED EAGLE SCOUTS JACK D. FURST AND REX TILLERSON ARE APPOINTED TO BSA'S NATIONAL EXECUTIVE BOARD

BY MAY 2003, *as Jack D. Furst (below, on the right with Council Board Member Dan Zaccara) continued to serve Circle Ten Council, his contributions were recognized by national BSA officials with an appointment to the National Executive Board. Furst began by serving as the organization's vice president of the National Supply Division, as well as in other capacities like assisting on several Chief Scout Executive search committees and leading the committee that identified the location of BSA's future national high adventure base—the Summit Bechtel Reserve near Beckley, West Virginia.*

ExxonMobil chairman and former Circle Ten Council

Executive Board Member Rex Tillerson (right) became BSA's 33rd National President in May 2010, ushering in a new attitude of building the national membership base through the development of quality programs on a local level. His mantra of "Keep the Main Thing the Main Thing," that referred to delivering the best Scouting experience to the youth of America, was adopted as a rallying cry throughout the "Scouting Nation" during his tenure as president that ended in May 2012.

Both men were honored with the presentation of the Distinguished Eagle Scout Award for their service to Scouting.[1]

BELOW: A new Scout participates in Troop 81's marksmanship campout at Camp Wisdom in April 2006. FAR BELOW: Two Scouts prepare to rappel at Camp Cherokee during Winter Camp in December 2004.

official BSA policies pertaining to the protection of both Scouts and their leaders. Circle Ten's website linked to it electronically for downloading.

The Council's traditional membership numbers continued trending upward and ended 2004 with 36,304 members and 1,165 total units with the expectation of further growth.

CHARACTER CAMP

CHARACTER CAMP *is a program held annually in May at Camp Wisdom/Billy Sowell Boy Scout Camp for local public school students. They attend on one of three days: a middle school day, one for high school students, and one for special education students.*

Created to give an out-of-doors experience to non-Scouting, inner-city students within the Dallas Metroplex, the children participate in a "fun-filled day of activities" that includes archery, team-building games, nature study, crafts, and "lots of play" on the Cub World facilities. A total of 3,149 local kids "experienced" the camp in 2005.

By 2012, the program had developed into a five-day event staffed by Council executives and employees from supportive local organizations like AT&T and GEICO Insurance. Now designed for pre-kindergarten through sixth grade (with one day dedicated

One area of expansion was in the Learning for Life program with its membership being counted in addition to those registered in traditional Scouting. It now boasted 35,500 students in 150 public institutions in the Dallas, Grand Prairie, and Lancaster school districts. Portions of the city of Irving, Grayson County, the city of Carrollton, and a few private schools joined as well. The program was administered by five Council staff members with its minimum joining age requirement having been extended downward to the elementary school level from those just in high school.[6]

Stone's local success resulted in his promotion to Director of the Northeast Region based in Jamesburg, New Jersey. He resigned his position as Scout Executive effective August 23, 2005 and headed to the eastern seaboard.[7] Unfortunately, Stone would miss one of the landmark assemblies of business professionals the Council had ever hosted—the Gathering of Eagles—which initiated a reconnection with 2,500 local Eagle Scouts, many of whom were willing to get involved throughout the Council's ranks as new leaders or advisors.

In October 2005, new Council Scout Executive Ponce Duran Jr., formerly of the Alamo Area Council in San Antonio, Texas, took the reins of leadership from Circle Ten's Interim

to special needs children mainly in the Dallas Independent School District and several private institutions) some 1,700 young kids attend annually.[1]

309

CIRCLE TEN COUNCIL'S HURRICANE KATRINA SERVICE PROJECTS

WHEN HURRICANE KATRINA *hit New Orleans and the Gulf Coast states on August 29, 2005, millions of people were forced to flee northward, many with only the clothes on their backs. The Dallas area was one of the places into which they came.*

On September 4, Garland's Troop 57, founded in 1946, sent 15 Scouts and leaders to spend the day doing general cleanup and unloading of semi-trucks filled with pallets of supplies at the Salvation Army's warehouse at 9216 Harry Hines Boulevard. With additional acts of service that included pulling weeds in the lawn and sweeping the floors in between loads, the Scouts learned a lot about giving back to those in need.

"We were there to work and it did not matter who it was for. We had a job to do and we were going to do it," recalled Scoutmaster Robert Garrett. "We may have had some downtime at the beginning when we just cleaned up the warehouse property, but when the trucks started rolling in, we got very busy, very fast. We arrived when the sun came up and left when it went down. I was extremely proud of my young men."

Troop 605 in the Texoma Valley District performed a similar relief service.

"We helped the Red Cross (below) set up some shelters and take food inventories. Then we got clothing ready for distribution," said Assistant Scoutmaster and former Mikanakawa Lodge Advisor Wade Graves. "Since only one of four shelters was opened, we helped dismantle the others and took the perishable food to the Salvation Army."

Junior Assistant Scoutmaster Kevin Lovett Jr. of Troop 306 in Allen, Texas, worked with about a dozen members of the Sunnock Chapter of the Order of the Arrow at Texas Stadium. Called into service by Lodge Advisor Graves, Lovett led his group in offloading pallets and boxes of clothing for the hurricane victims.

"We wanted to reinforce our image within the community that the Order of the Arrow was here to help everyone," recalled Lovett. "But I got much more out of it than that. This was the first time that I truly realized that there were people much worse off than anything I had ever seen before. They came to us with no personal possessions, looking for any help that we could give them. And we helped them as best we could."

Lovett, elected Mikanakawa's Lodge Chief in 2009, was changed forever. "I don't take my blessings for granted anymore," he said. "I was put here to give back to my community."[L]

RIGHT: The program for the Gathering of Eagles event hosted by honorary chairman Mr. Ross Perot on July 16, 2005 at Camp Wisdom. BELOW: Circle Ten Scouts aiding Red Cross Disaster Services.

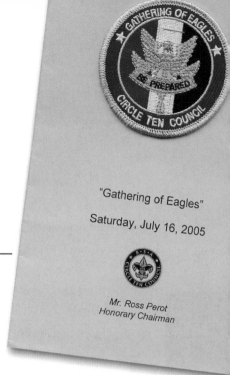

"Gathering of Eagles"
Saturday, July 16, 2005

Mr. Ross Perot
Honorary Chairman

Scout Executive (and the Council's sitting Finance Director) Don Burke on November 1. Burke had been serving in the temporary position at the request of Council President John Stuart III, who believed too many things were happening within the Council to leave the post empty during the selection process.

"I felt I needed to appoint someone to fill the last three months of Gene's contract and we were fortunate to have a lot of capable people to choose from," recalled Stuart. "I trusted Don."

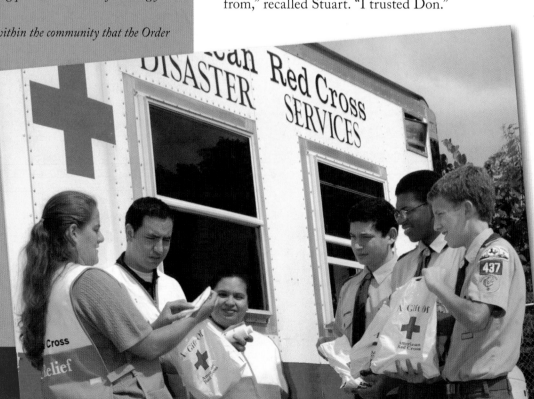

EAGLE SCOUT MICHAEL ROSS *is not your typical volunteer leader. In 2000, he approached Circle Ten Council executives about starting a new unit, but not in his comfortable North Dallas neighborhood.*

He wanted to be in an Urban Scouting location without functioning troops.

Sponsored by the J. Erik Jonsson Community School at the Salesmanship Club near 10th Street and N. Beckley Avenue, he began operations at Troop 2012 a short time later.

Situated in the "economically hard-hit" and heavily Hispanic part of North Oak Cliff, Ross began his tenure as Scoutmaster. Using his years of program experience as his knowledge base, Ross successfully recruited Scouts and assistant leaders.

"I didn't want to just provide Scouting where it was well established," Ross recalled. "I wanted to grow it where it was needed most in Dallas."

Scout Executive Ponce Duran Jr. concurred saying, "It's a demographic group that we haven't had as good a job in reaching as we should have."

In March 2007, high school senior Jose Contreras became Troop 2012's first Eagle Scout, earning the rank after several years of turmoil—nearly dropping out of both school and Scouting to help support his family. At the time, Ross intervened and convinced Contreras to finish his quest for Eagle Scout— ultimately proving his ability to succeed in life and becoming a role model in his community.

For his Eagle project, Contreras organized a community blood drive for the Carter Blood Center. But his volunteerism did not stop there—he also worked on Hurricane Katrina relief aid assignments through World Vision as well as several other projects during his Scouting career.

"Here, he is going to learn things we can't teach him because we don't know how," noted his mother, Adriana. "I know this is very important for him,"

Added his father Juan, "He's seen much more than I did at that age and experienced more things than I did."

In late 2007, both Ross and Contreras received the President's Volunteer Service award presented by Anne MacDonald, Associate Director of USA Freedom Corps, catching the attention of a proud Chief Scout Executive Robert J. Mazzuca.

"The BSA is proud of our many leaders and members who continue to give of themselves," Mazzuca said. "A Scout is taught to provide a good turn daily, which are often small, thoughtful acts, and are usually provided without any recognition."[K]

Jose Contreras and his mother during his March 2007 Eagle Scout award ceremony.

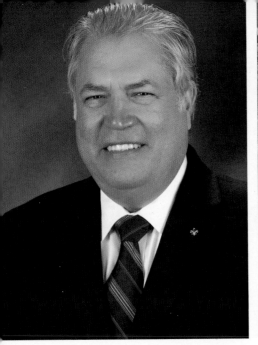

His hunch was right.

Burke entered the office and presided over the Council's response to the Hurricane Katrina disaster that hit New Orleans on August 25. Circle Ten Scouts and leaders rallied under the direction of volunteer Rob Kyker at Texas Stadium while serving a flood of incoming survivors. Many in the community regarded Kyker's work as "heroic."

Other acts of heroism included Eagle Scout James M. Griffin of Troop 543 in Dallas, whose "quick thinking saved a fellow Scout from drowning while on an outing to Austin." For it, he received the Heroism Medal. Another Heroism Medal recipient, Scout Philip Whitaker III, "saved his father from drowning while boating on Lake Lewisville."

Upon taking office, Scout Executive Duran made a list of several prime objectives to tackle immediately that included membership growth, launching a new $90-million fund-raising campaign, establishing a measurable strategic plan, and increasing the ethnic diversity of both membership and Council staff through targeted recruitment.[8]

The $90 million "Continue the Legacy Campaign" commenced in January 2007 with the goal of increasing the Council's Foundation by $90 million for various purposes. Proposed

THE WILLIAM C. GAMBLE ENDOWMENT FUND

IN DECEMBER 2005, *former Council President Bobby Lyle made a $1 million gift to establish the William C. Gamble Endowment Fund in honor of former Scout Executive Gamble's 42 years of service to Scouting. In a letter to Council President Jack D. Furst, Lyle expressed his great admiration for Gamble and that the unrestricted funds were to be used at the "discretion of the organization's executive board to enhance the programs of Circle Ten Council."*

"Billy has been a role model for both youth and adults throughout his distinguished career," Lyle said. "It is my pleasure to make this gift in honor of Billy Gamble."[M]

TOP LEFT: Circle Ten Scout Executive Ponce Duran. TOP RIGHT: Three Scouts express their unity during summer camp in 2007.

MIKANAKAWA LODGE'S NATIONAL SERVICE AWARD

IN MAY 2006 *at BSA's National Annual Meeting in Washington, DC, the Mikanakawa Lodge received the National Service Award at the Southern Region's luncheon. As cited, Lodge members performed a total of 62,245 man-hours of service to others during the previous year, which averaged out to 22 hours and 15 minutes per registered member. The Lodge was only one of the eight recipients of the award from over 300 lodges across the nation.*[N]

BOTTOM LEFT: Heroism Medal recipient Philip Whitacre III as he appeared in the Council's Annual Report in 2006. BELOW: BSA's National President Rick Cronk served as the guest speaker at Circle Ten Council's Annual Dinner in February 2007, where he posed with Julian, a Tiger Cub Scout. ABOVE LEFT: Tiger Cubs enjoy the 2005 Scout Show and a snack.

by Council President Jack D. Furst, the campaign included 248 camp projects and a new service center at an estimated cost of $28.5 million, and an endowment campaign of $61.5 million, putting the Circle Ten Foundation over $100 million. According to Furst, this would "endow Circle Ten Council for the next 100 years." Beginning quietly, the plan would not be announced publicly until $50 million had been raised.[9]

By March 2007, BSA's national office announced that Scout Executive Duran was a finalist for the position of Chief Scout Executive (the first Hispanic or minority candidate ever to have done so) along with former Circle Ten Scout Executive Gene Stone. Although both made it to the final six candidates (with Duran getting to the final four) Assistant Chief Scout Executive Robert J. Mazzuca got the nod.

Concurrently, international Scouting was ramping-up to its Centennial Jamboree being held in Chelmsford, England in late August 2007. BSA

BELOW LEFT: Circle Ten Council President Jack D. Furst in 2006. BELOW: Scouts participate in the 2007 Scout Show. ACROSS TOP: Mrs. Margaret Tarr posing with the portrait of her late husband, Chief Scout Executive James L. Tarr, at the June 24, 2008 dedication ceremony for the dining hall named in his honor. ACROSS BELOW: The Circle Ten Council staff poses in front of the new Jim Tarr Dining Hall at the Clements Scout Ranch on January 7, 2009.

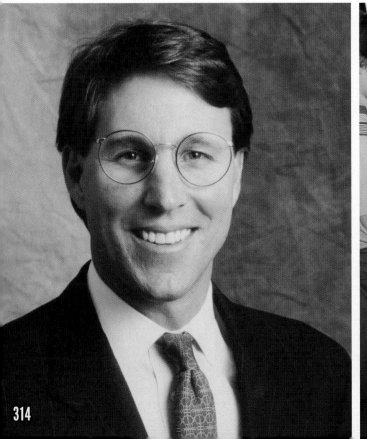

THE 2007 WORLD JAMBOREE

JOINING 45,000 SCOUTS *from across the globe, the 2007 Circle Ten Council contingent of World Jamboree participants traveled to England and eventually to Gilwell Park for festivities. Entertaining games and events tested the skills of the visiting Scouts and helped the to forge friendships during the Jamboree.*

"I ran one of the Scouting demonstration programs that involved a compass game," recalled Peter Culver of Plano's Troop 714. "The Scouts received orienteering instructions to step on a series of tiles on the ground bearing a single letter that constructed a phrase. Many 'foreign' Scouts just loved it and wanted to do more."

"It was the fellowship between Scouts of all nations that stood out for me," recalled Circle Ten contingent Assistant Scoutmaster John Stone of Troop 1776 in Plano. "Now, I tell my Scouts that the purple World Crest is the smallest patch on your uniform, but it is the one truly brought to life at the World Jamboree."

Since former council president Jack D. Furst led BSA's national contingent, he had the privilege of being present at the famed Sunrise Ceremony held on Brownsea Island—the location of the world's first Scout camp held in August 1907—on its 100th anniversary.

Visiting the island with two representative Scouts from each participating country, Furst admitted to the gravity of the ceremony. As the sun broke over the horizon, the sound of the kudu horn was blown to initiate the historic gathering, just like it had been done by Scouting founder, Robert Baden-Powell, a century before.

"It was spectacular," recalled Furst. "It was one of those magic moments that we have in Scouting; one hundred years and hundreds of millions of Scouts later. For me, it re-emphasized that one person really can make a difference."[P]

sent a contingent of 80 Scouts along with Circle Ten's own Distinguished Eagle Scout Jack D. Furst leading BSA's national assembly.

By 2008, the Council's membership was increasing steadily. Now boasting 36,585 traditional Scouts (a 3.4 percent increase over the previous year), Circle Ten was growing.

The Centennial Campaign had topped $27 million by early 2009 with several important projects being completed. Much of that work had been done at the Clements Scout Ranch with the construction of the Jim Tarr Dining Hall—named in honor of BSA's former Chief Scout Executive and Circle Ten Council's top leader. Tarr, who had died just months before its completion, was said to have been truly humbled by the Council's recognition of his service to Scouting. With assembled dignitaries that included his widow, Margaret, the ceremony recalled Tarr's laudable character and quality of leadership.

"Jim and I were good friends," said Executive Board Member Craig

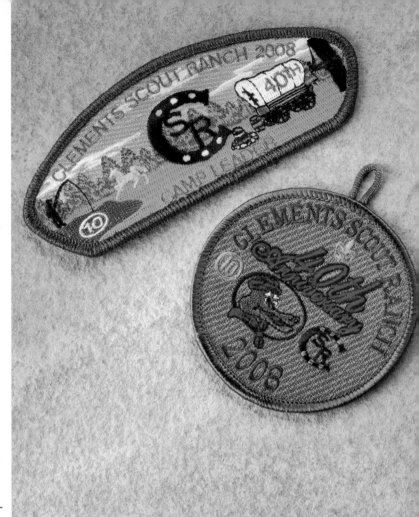

RIGHT: The 40th Anniversary patches of the Clements Scout Ranch presented to Scouts attending summer camp at Camp Cherokee in 2008. ACROSS LOWER LEFT: A Circle Ten Scout enjoys the thrill of the zip line. ACROSS LOWER RIGHT and ACROSS UPPER RIGHT: Several local Circle Ten Council Fire Explorer Posts participate in a skills competition held at the Dallas Fire Department Training Center.

Hutton. "He was another one of our great leaders that this Council has been so blessed to have over the years."

Scout Executive Duran recalled, "Jim Tarr was one of most honorable professionals I have ever met and he mentored me many years before coming to Circle Ten. He was a man of faith and inspired others to follow his example."

Camp James Ray in Grayson County received improvements of its own. According to a Letter of Commitment presented to Scout Executive Duran by benefactors Ray and Nancy Ann Hunt, they intended to donate $1.5 million toward the construction of a new dining hall in memory of their "Uncle Jimmy," the camp's namesake. The building, which included the latest, state-of-the-art equipment in food preparation, also contained a Founder's Hall presentation stage that showcased

THE 2009 SCOUT SHOW

BASED ON PREVIOUS *Scout Show ticket sales, the annual Circle Ten extravaganza scheduled for May 2009 anticipated 23,000 attendees during the daylong event. And for the third year in a row, instead of the Scouts selling tickets with just a couple of store discount coupons included, the Council arranged for a "Ticket/ Discount card" that was honored at a dozen businesses throughout the Circle Ten area.*

Unfortunately, with the outbreak of the dreaded H1N1 "swine flu" virus, the Show was canceled at the last minute. The last Circle Ten Scout Show was held in May 2010—national Scouting's Centennial year. By 2011, the "Camp Card" sales program replaced the Scout Show as the Council's official spring fund-raiser.[8]

CHRIS ROGERS AND JOSHUA RAINES—SCOUT HEROES

IN 2008, *Troop 444 chartered by the Arapaho United Methodist Church in Richardson, Texas, was in Bromide, Oklahoma, on their annual rocketry campout. Suddenly tragedy struck when an errant rocket ripped into the upper body of 16-year-old Scout Connor McNeil, breaking two* ribs, "*tearing his lung,*" *and lodging* "*an inch from his heart.*"

"*I felt the rocket moving in my body,*" *recalled the Richardson High School sophomore,* "*I just said, 'Please God, if you want to take me, take me, but I want to stay here for a while.'*"

Witnessing the horrifying sight, 14-year-old First Class Scout Joshua Raines and 15-year-old Life Scout Chris Rogers flew into action. Together they calmed young Connor and stopped the bleeding with cloth bandages—buying enough time for the emergency helicopter and paramedics to arrive and take the injured boy to the hospital.

For their rapid lifesaving actions, both Joshua and Chris were awarded with BSA's Heroism Award presented in January 2010 at the North Trail District Dinner. Boys' Life magazine recounted the inspiring story of the fast-thinking Scouts in their February 2010 issue.[9]

ten men who inspired Scouting's ultimate success both locally and nationally. The building's dedication ceremony was held on October 25, 2011.[10]

The Camp Constantin/Jack D. Furst Aquatics Base received a new shower house and restroom facility that became the prototype bathroom house to be placed at all camps. Constructed on

MIKANAKAWA LODGE AT ARROWCORPS 5

ARROWCORPS 5 *was a massive cleanup service project performed by Order of the Arrow lodges from across the nation and held at five U.S. National Forests. Members of the Mikanakawa Lodge participated. Assigned to the Mark Twain National Forest in Rolla, Missouri, the Lodge sent the nation's largest contingent of 86 arrowmen, who performed 12 days of work alongside 500 fellow Order of the Arrow members from other parts of the country.*

"The U.S. Forest Service asked us to remove the Eastern Red Cedar they consider as an invasive species of tree because it takes over all vegetation," recalled Lodge Advisor and future Council Commissioner Matt M. Walker. "We cleared 134 acres that the Forest Service estimated to be 284,000 trees and $1.6 million worth of work to them."

Not surprisingly, the Order of the Arrow was awarded Employer of the Year honors by the U.S. Forest Service.[R]

ABOVE: A wonderful example of "A Scout is Cheerful".
BELOW: Campers work on their canoeing skills at the Clements Scout Ranch in June 2008. ACROSS: The Texoma Valley District's Troop 1709 at the 2005 National Jamboree at Fort A.P. Hill in Caroline County, Virginia.

a large 20-foot-by-40-foot concrete slab, separate compartments included either flushing toilets or shower stalls. Readied for the summer 2009 camping season, these five facilities complied fully with the Americans with Disabilities Act (ADA) requirements as they contained built-in wheelchair access along with other accommodations.

As 2009 came to a close, more management changes were taking place as Scout Executive Duran accepted his new position as the Director of the Southern Region that November. An executive search committee was formed to find his replacement that would oversee Circle Ten during Scouting's centennial celebration year of 2010, as well as the Council's own centennial year events of 2013.[11]

THE MAN CHOSEN FOR THE JOB WAS A LONGTIME SCOUTING PROFESSIONAL WORKING IN THE SOUTHERN REGION OFFICES IN ATLANTA, GEORGIA NAMED PAT CURRIE. HE WOULD BE TASKED WITH TAKING CIRCLE TEN COUNCIL TO ITS NEXT LEVEL OF SUCCESS.

chapter 17

THE CENTENNIAL (2010–2013)

"I love Scouting. I think it's one of the great mentor programs in the country."

GEORGE W. BUSH
43RD PRESIDENT OF THE UNITED STATES
CIRCLE TEN COUNCIL FRIENDS OF SCOUTING BANQUET
MARCH 3, 2011

Dallas' newest landmark dedicated in 2012, the Margaret Hunt Hill Bridge over the Trinity River, serves as the connection between the Woodall Rodgers Freeway and Singleton Boulevard in West Dallas. This image was taken on Patriot's Day, September 11, 2012.

THE ARRIVAL OF THE YEAR 2010 brought with it an exuberant Boy Scouts of America organization that would commence its yearlong centennial celebration on New Year's Day with its first float entered in the Tournament of Roses parade in Pasadena, California since 1950. After that, other upcoming dramatic national events would include a summer parade through downtown Washington, DC, and the grand 2010 Centennial National Jamboree at nearby Fort A.P. Hill in Caroline County, Virginia.

More excitement was reserved for Dale Coyne Racing's sponsorship of BSA's first IndyCar driven by Englishman Alex Lloyd that was intended to promote Scouting on NASCAR's

Circle Ten Scout Executive Pat Currie poses with a special Cub Scout during a Council banquet.

platform and its new STEM/NOVA initiative. STEM, standing for Science-Technology-Engineering-Math, was designed to keep Scouting's program on the cutting edge of the digital age for the forseeable future. The showcase event would be car #19's inaugural entry into the legendary Indianapolis 500 auto race that May. On a grassroots level, a semi-truck known as Adventure Base 100 traveled to each council in the lower 48 states laden with interactive exhibits and activities for members of the community to visit and play on.

The "Words to Live By" national campaign, BSA's newest recruitment slogan, was being piloted within eight councils that included Circle Ten. For two years, those words would adorn the Council's letterhead and business cards in a national rebranding effort by top BSA professionals.[1]

Arriving at the John D. Murchison Scouting Center in January 2010, newly hired Scout Executive Pat Currie quickly got to work, fully intending to remain faithful to his personal mottos of "Continuous Improvement" and "Question Everything and Change What's Appropriate."

Introduced to the executive board at their meeting on January 26, Currie began a unique cross-Council introduction tour that got him out among the membership-at-large.[2]

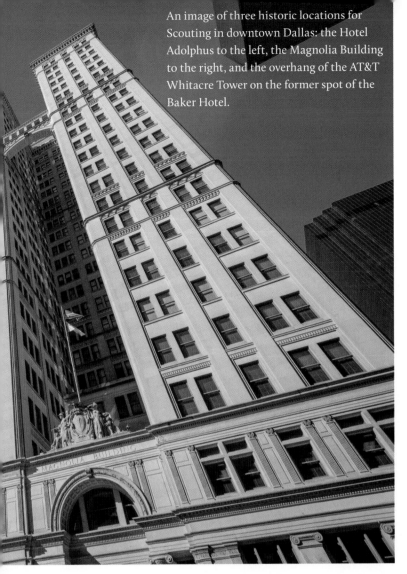

An image of three historic locations for Scouting in downtown Dallas: the Hotel Adolphus to the left, the Magnolia Building to the right, and the overhang of the AT&T Whitacre Tower on the former spot of the Baker Hotel.

"We wanted to listen to those in the field as to what we did well and what we needed to improve on," recalled Scout Executive Currie. "It was a great experience and extremely beneficial to me to get things going after I arrived."

Additional travels took Currie to all three Council summer camp sessions each week–a tradition that he continues to this day.

"From these interactions," he recalled, "I presented a report to the executive board that formed the basis for our new strategic plan, the one that we are executing today."

In short order, Scout Executive Currie assembled the *Circle Ten Council Strategic Plan 2011–2015* that set basic performance goals, such as increasing membership through recruiting and retention, and increasing Cub and Boy Scout advancement in excess of the national average. Other objectives included the training of 100 percent of the adult leadership and tracking each district's progress towards doing so. Also, he expected Council leaders to focus on helping each district formulate and execute activities that would involve every segment of their local Scouting population in tandem with increasing local participation at Council run summer camps.[3]

As the host of a series of "Fireside Chats" held in the far corners of the Council's vast territory, Currie had Council President Sherwood Blount Jr. and Council Commissioner Matt M. Walker appear with him on stage for the question-and-answer sessions.

"WE ARE IN THE BUSINESS OF CREATING THE NEXT GENERATION OF LEADERSHIP FOR THIS COUNTRY–THERE IS NO HIGHER CALLING."

–ERNEST J. CAREY, PRESIDENT, CIRCLE TEN COUNCIL (2012 – 2014)

AS LOCAL SCOUTING continued to grow north into the Collin and Grayson County regions, the concept of a new Scout Center north of Dallas in Fairview, Texas, was added to the Council's Strategic Plan. Designed to increase public awareness of Scouting and provide better service to its "customers," the project fell under the direction of Council Operations Manager Dick Corcoran.

From a bounty of 60 possible locations, the final site selected was on Highway 75 North that sees 175,000 vehicles a day pass by.

"It came down to making Scouting more accessible to the community," said Corcoran. "Now, the Scout office is easily available to 10,000 Scouts and leaders in our northern areas."

Added former Director of Field Services Russell Etzenhouser, "Circle Ten needed to make sure that we provided the best services to the most important people in our business—the Scouts and leaders."

As envisioned, the new building was to be a testament to the growth of Scouting in the region as well as celebrating the close and formidable partnership of the two men who helped make that happen—former Council President Bobby Lyle and 42-year Scout Executive Billy Gamble.

"Billy Gamble is an extraordinary Boy Scout," recalled President Lyle. "I really enjoyed working with him over those years."

Gamble had similar feelings for Lyle.

"Bobby is one of the finest, most respected, and generous business and civic leaders in Dallas, who lives his life by the principles found in the Boy Scout Oath and Law," said Gamble. "He is a trusted and loyal friend and brother."

With 1.3 acres of land donated to the north of Stacy Road by the MG Herring Group, a 13,000-square-foot building was conceived. Another positive indicator for the location was the success of the Allen, Texas, satellite Scout Shop, which had amassed over 24,000 individual customer transactions annually. In partnership with the Council, BSA's National Supply Division sought permission to build its prototype "Scout Shop of the future" within the facility.

"We wanted to have a new marketing concept for our store," said Scout Shop Manager Toni

Atwell. "Now products are featured with an out-of-doors theme that help our customers better imagine how they will use them, like tents and gear. The younger Scout climbing wall is also a hit because they can see what they can do when they get older."

In March 2010, former Council President Jack D. Furst donated $2.5 million toward the construction costs. With plans to open the office by the end of 2010, an additional $1 million was needed for furniture, fixtures, and a maintenance endowment.

Construction was completed on February 22, 2011—international Scouting founder Robert Baden-Powell's birthday anniversary—with the Bobby Lyle ♦ Billy Gamble Scouting Center being dedicated on April 26.[A]

Mid-year, BSA's national office announced the opening of its National Hall of Leadership to recognize the finest leaders in today's Scouting movement. With each council nominating its best candidates, a national panel would select the initial induction class. From Circle Ten, Eagle Scout Jared Lyons of Troop 876 at the Valley View Christian Church in Carrollton was chosen for inclusion.

"There aren't many 16- or 17-year-old Boy Scouts who know how to make an 11-year-old Tenderfoot Scout feel like he's the most important member in the troop," the nomination testimonial began. "Jared Lyons has that gift."

As Senior Patrol Leader, Jared set a strong example for quality Scouting in his troop and used "positive reinforcement to promote fun and friends."

I always knew Jared would wind up working with youth," declared one troop father. "He was devoted to his faith and often led the Sunday devotion service on weekend campouts. Today he is the Student Pastor of the MET Church in Fort Worth."[4]

The 2010 Centennial National Jamboree, the last to be held at Fort A.P. Hill in Caroline County, Virginia, featured an extravaganza not seen before—a live streaming Internet broadcast of the "Shining Light Across America" stadium show.

ACROSS TOP: Former Circle Ten Scout Executive Billy Gamble (left) and former Council President Bobby Lyle (right) in the lobby of the Murchison Scouting Center. TOP RIGHT: Circle Ten Council Scouts engage in patch trading at the 2010 National Jamboree at Fort A.P. Hill in Virginia. RIGHT: Circle Ten Council Scouts at the Statue of Liberty during their tour of New York City en route to the 2010 National Jamboree. ACROSS BOTTOM: The new Scouting Center in Fairview, Texas.

ACROSS FAR TOP LEFT: Executive Board Member Ray Marr. ACROSS TOP RIGHT: Troop 82 Scout Hollis Meacham salutes at one of the Jamboree Arena show. ACROSS MIDDLE RIGHT: Jamboree attendees from Troop 125. ACROSS BOTTOM RIGHT: Scout Benjamin Hamner in front of the Lincoln Memorial in Washington, DC. ACROSS FAR BOTTOM LEFT: Several Circle Ten Council contingent patches alongside a 2010 BSA Centennial belt buckle. BOTTOM LEFT: The Hon. Pete Session of Texas. BOTTOM RIGHT: BSA National President Rex W. Tillerson (right) riding in the 2010 Centennial Parade in Washington, DC. BELOW: Cable tv personality Mike Rowe speaks to the Scouts at the closing arena show. LEFT: The Arena Show patch presented to Jamboree participants and the most common piece of technology today—a cell phone.

LOUIS BENNO—CIRCLE TEN COUNCIL'S 80-YEAR VETERAN

By Robert Reitz, Curator, Harbin Scout Museum

BORN IN DALLAS on December 24, 1920, Louis Benno grew-up poor in South Dallas. He and his family attended Temple Emanu-el, where he joined Troop 29 and excelled under the direction of Scoutmaster Morris I. Jaffe, who became like a second father to him.

Attending BSA's first National Jamboree in 1937 in Washington, DC, Louis was one of two Scouts to receive a medal from President Franklin D. Roosevelt for high achievement in the program.

A year later on October 15, 1938, Benno earned his Eagle Scout award along with friend, Mashie Smith. Graduating Forest Avenue High School in June 1939, he already had earned five Eagle palms and would receive four more by October 1940.

By the end of his Scouting career, Benno racked up a staggering total of thirteen Eagle palms and 86 merit badges—tops in the Council at the time—earning him honor guard duty at the funeral services of former Council President Leslie B. Denning.

Benno left Scouting for the U.S. Naval Reserve and flew in World War II, the Korean War, and for ten months during the Vietnam conflict. Marrying his beloved wife Claire, he eventually retired as a lieutenant commander and returned to Dallas to help re-activate his old Troop 29 at his temple.

Currently, Louis Benno serves as a docent with the Frontiers of Flight Museum at Love Field and attends some Scouting functions donning the Scout uniform of his youth.[B]

TOP RIGHT and RIGHT: A Scout visits an exhibit at the 2010 National Jamboree featuring the 1937 National Jamboree uniform of Circle Ten Eagle Scout Louis Benno. Commander Benno (bottom picture in the middle) still is able to wear that uniform on special occasions. ACROSS FAR RIGHT: Circle Ten Council President John Stuart III in 2004.

Among the 43,400 Scouts in attendance, 496 Circle Ten Council Scouts and 100 adult staff members witnessed Chief Scout Executive Robert J. Mazzuca rappel down a 60-foot high tower onto the stage as his grand entrance. Included in the festivities was National Executive Board Member Jack D. Furst, who informed the assembled masses about the progress being made at the Summit Bechtel Reserve, the location of the 2013 National Jamboree and 2019 World Jamboree. Also speaking that evening was popular cable TV personality and Distinguished Eagle Scout Mike Rowe, the host of the Discovery Channel's hit program *Dirty Jobs*. In a show where he works in the least-desirable occupations across the country, the self-proclaimed "Ambassador of Dirt" delivered a memorable speech with the message, "A Scout is clean but not afraid to get dirty."

"People ask me all the time, 'What did you learn, what's the point [of Scouts]?'" Rowe postulated. "The truth is that everything that I needed to know to live my life, I learned in [my] first troop meeting . . . Scouting forces you to confront your discomforts. It trains you to like it [and] you're going to do well in whatever you try."

Eagle Scout Thomas Long of Carrollton's Troop 574 at the Holy Covenant United Methodist Church found Rowe's talk to be "one of the best parts of the stadium show." He added, "His speech was definitely inspirational and he got a lot of respect from me and from all the Scouts who were there."[5]

But Assistant Scoutmaster Joey Castleberry of Irving's Troop 175 got something else out of it. Although he labeled Rowe's speech "amazing" and "very inspiring," he said, "watching our Scouts interact and bond with other Scouts from around the country and seeing the joy on their faces as they told us about their day's adventures" was more impressive.

The entire Texas contingent—numbering 2,000 Scouts and leaders—was led by the Southern Region's Area 2 Area Director Rob Hoffman (a former Circle Ten Council executive) and former Council President and Distinguished Eagle Scout John Stuart III. To bring a little part of the Lone Star state to Virginia, they requested and received a Texas flag that had been flown over the State's Capitol building in Austin in honor of Scouting's 100th Anniversary. It included a citation from Governor Rick Perry, a Distinguished Eagle Scout himself.

"We flew it in our Area campsite for the entire event," recalled Stuart, "and we look forward to it eventually residing in the Harbin Scout Museum at Camp Wisdom/Billy Sowell Boy Scout Camp."[6]

THE LAST CIRCLE TEN COUNCIL SCOUT SHOW

THE CENTENNIAL SCOUT SHOW held in May 2010 at the Ballpark in Arlington, home of the Texas Rangers, would be the Circle Ten Council's last. With Cub Scout booths mostly in the stadium and Boy Scout activities held in the parking lot, it proved to be extremely fun for the thousands of attendees.

One of the exhibitors was Pack 630 of Allen, Texas, who sponsored a rubber band target shooting gallery.

"I wanted to give Cubs the opportunity to work at something and learn from it," recalled Den Leader James Alexander. "But I also wanted them to know that they can have fun while doing that and also be active members of their Council."[C]

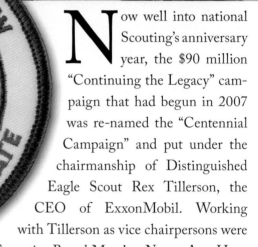

Now well into national Scouting's anniversary year, the $90 million "Continuing the Legacy" campaign that had begun in 2007 was re-named the "Centennial Campaign" and put under the chairmanship of Distinguished Eagle Scout Rex Tillerson, the CEO of ExxonMobil. Working with Tillerson as vice chairpersons were Executive Board Member Nancy Ann Hunt and former Council President Bobby Lyle. Lyle was placed in charge of the Steering Committee tasked with raising funds.

Moving forward with the campaign in March 2010, Chairman Tillerson and Scout Executive Currie approached the Rees-Jones Foundation in pursuit of a substantial gift to improve the aging camp facilities as well as to endow the Council's critical ScoutReach program. The initial response from Texas oilman and Distinguished Eagle Scout Trevor Rees-Jones and wife Jan was positive. Having made his wealth in the Barnett Shale oil

TOP: For nearly a decade after the commencement of the Iraq War in 2003, Circle Ten Council Scouts greeted returning veterans passing through DFW Airport each week of the "Welcome Home a Hero" program.
MIDDLE: The final Circle Ten Council Scout Show patch issued in 2010.
LEFT: A giveaway gift at the 2010 Scout Show held at the Ballpark in Arlington, the home of the Texas Rangers Baseball Club.

The Lone Star Gas Building at 301 South Harwood in downtown Dallas and the home of Circle Ten Council from 1935 to 1937.

Looking upwards at the Wilson Building on Main Street – the Dallas Council 's first home in 1913.

CIRCLE TEN COUNCIL'S CENTENNIAL CAMPOREE

ON SEPTEMBER 15, 2010, *the City of Dallas proclaimed October 29 to 31 as "Scouting Weekend." The Centennial Camporee, celebrating 100 years of Scouting in America, was held at the Dallas Executive Airport in Duncanville. Resembling a mini-Jamboree,* some 6,500 Scouts, leaders, and families were registered. Featuring a stage show, military flyovers, and a fireworks demonstration, the event was hailed as "incredible" and "excellent" by many attendees.

Council Vice President John Harkey summed it up, "The partnership between the City of Dallas and the Council proved to be a big success for this signature 100th Anniversary event. It was a tremendous celebration of Scouting."

"Camporee Chairman Charles Mohrle deserves a large amount of credit for making this event happen," recalled Scout Executive Currie. "He did a fantastic job."

"They had some really cool things in the Midway," according to Pack 516 Webelos Den Leader Don Birdsong. "They had signaling and Morse code with flashlights, pioneering and bridge building, and games sponsored by Boy Scout troops. But the rocket launching with 2-liter soda bottles off of a pressurized tank was intense!"

There were two air shows: one civilian and one military. Especially impactful was the Navy F-5 fighter jet flyover after the Marine Corps, in dress blues, concluded the Saturday morning flag ceremony.

"It was important for the boys to see the presence of the military," recalled Troop 759 Scoutmaster and air show organizer Kip Lankenau. "Their presence put a face on what our kids saw on television. Periodically, Scouts need to be reminded of what patriotic pride in duty and service looks like."

"My Cubs were amazed at the air show," said Pack 826 Cubmaster Ange Elliott. "They couldn't believe what those planes did!"

Another, Cubmaster Bianca Goolsby of Pack 939 in Rockwall, thought that it was memorable for a multitude of reasons, not just because of one single thing—"it was the entire experience."

"We drank homemade root beer, played Chinese checkers, rode on a hover seat, made rope, learned astronomy, and played the numerous games offered by the different packs, troops, and crews," she said. "We ate box cookies, dutch oven masterpieces, and learned how to stamp leather. Out of all of these, the best thing our Cubs took away from the event was that we are all one. No matter what numbers are sewn onto the sleeves of these boys, we are all there for the same purpose—our love of all things Scouting."D

Scenes from Circle Ten Council's 2010 Centennial Camporee held at the Dallas Executive Airport in Duncanville for 6,500 attendees.

BELOW: University Park Scout Benjamin Smith was one of the first boys to earn to new Robotics merit badge in Circle Ten Council. A member of Troop 70, he was one of six Scouts to earn it in April 2011.

IN AUGUST 2000, *Council Vice President of Operations and eventual Council President David Biegler proposed three "Program Managers" to be hired at $1,000 per month to run a Scouting program within urban zones. Utilized from October through December, the program's success prompted continued funding.*

In 2002, petition was made to Mr. H. Ross Perot and the Texas Instruments Foundation for additional monies to create permanent jobs for eight Program Managers "who are serving as Scoutmasters and Cubmasters in the urban area." As designed, they would run up to 10 Scouting units within their assigned areas. With both answering the funding call, by October, nine managers were in place and serving 63 units containing 1,000 members.

Renamed "ScoutReach" in January 2004, it received a massive injection of funding in August 2010 from the enormous generosity of the Rees-Jones Foundation established by Distinguished Eagle Scout and former member of University Park's Troop 70 Trevor Rees-Jones and wife Jan.

Through their transformational gift to the Council in the amount of $25 million—the highest single gift to any Council in the history of BSA—$5 million was to be used immediately to upgrade facilities at the Clements Scout Ranch and the remaining $20 million to endow the Rees-Jones ScoutReach program. From that endowment, over $1 million a year in interest will be generated to fund the Scouting experience of thousands of inner-city children who otherwise will not have the opportunity to partake in the Council's character-building program.

To honor their generosity and devotion to Circle Ten Scouting, Camp Cherokee was renamed Trevor Rees-Jones Scout Camp, and dedicated for use on March 24, 2012.[E]

fields of East Texas, the couple had set aside a significant portion of the profits for such a philanthropic purpose.

In August, Jan and Trevor Rees-Jones awarded Circle Ten Council with the staggeringly large gift of $25 million—a transformational gift—that ranked as the largest single donation ever made to one council in the history of the Boy Scouts of America.

As stipulated, $20 million of the sum was used to endow the Trevor Rees-Jones ScoutReach program to improve Scouting opportunities for inner-city youth. The remaining $5 million was to be used for upgrading

THE COURT OF HONOR FOR 11 EAGLE SCOUTS

IN NOVEMBER 2010, *St. Luke Community United Methodist Church's Troop 914 in Dallas made local history— they hosted a massive Court of Honor for 11 new African American Eagle Scouts (below).*

"It doesn't matter whether they're black, white, purple or orange—that's an amazing accomplishment," said Scout Executive Pat Currie to the Dallas Morning News. *"As far as we can determine, there's only been one other time in the history of the Boy Scouts where there were more African Americans at one time, from one troop, receiving the Eagle award."*

Under the direction of Scoutmaster Keith Kennedy, the 14-year-old troop had been founded in 1996 to serve inner-city youth. With just "six boys, two tents, and one piece of outdoor cooking equipment" in that first year, it had grown to 60 Scouts with nearly 40 of them having earned the Eagle rank.

"I finally made it," said new Eagle Donald Erick Thomas. "All the hard work comes to this moment right here."[F]

camp facilities at the Clements Scout Ranch. In honor of the Rees-Joneses magnanimous gift, the Council Executive Board voted to rename Camp Cherokee as the Trevor Rees-Jones Scout Camp.

Construction on about 15 projects began at the Trevor Rees-Jones Scout Camp by mid-October 2010 with an estimated completion date set for June 1, 2011. Included in the projects were eight miles of repaved roads, a new pool house, a new water delivery system, 16 new campsites with tent platforms, 25 campsite pavilions, new bath houses, an improved staff area with 10 new cabins, a rebuilt chapel, and general vegetation clean up. The dedication of the magnificent Trevor Rees-Jones Scout Camp was held on March 24, 2012.

"This is one of the greatest Scout camps in the entire nation," exclaimed Council Camping Director Scott Arrington. "With this unbelievable gift, the Clements Scout Ranch was rebuilt from the ground up and with incredible facilities like these, it would be exceedingly difficult to run a subpar summer camp. The takeaway for our Scouts is that they have been given a huge 'attaboy' to keep doing what they're doing from the sizeable generosity of Jan and Trevor Rees-Jones."[7]

As the year 2011 opened, plans were finalized for the most impressive Friends of Scouting campaign to be held to date. Not since baseball slugger Babe Ruth's address in 1929 had the Council invited a speaker of this magnitude. On March 3, former President George W. Bush stood at the podium and made a short speech to introduce the evening's keynote speaker, Distinguished Eagle Scout and former Secretary of Defense Robert Gates.

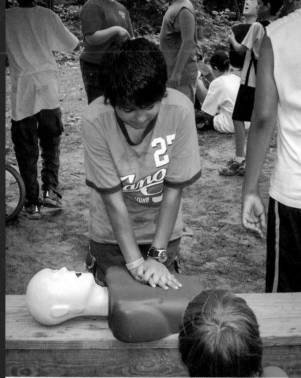

Scouting benefactors Jan and Trevor Rees-Jones alongside scenes from the Circle Ten camp that their generosity re-built.

Beginning with the statement, "I love Scouting. I think it's one of the great mentor programs in the country," President Bush touted the positive effects of the program, as well as the qualities of his former employee. And ending with the comment, "It's my honor to bring to this podium one of the finest secretaries of defense this country has ever produced," the President yielded the stage to enthusiastic applause.

As the ovation died down, Secretary Gates took the stage, looked the crowd over, and firmly thanked President Bush for allowing him to serve in his Administration. Easing into his address, Gates made reference to his short stature and tied it to an observation of hope made to Scouts in the audience of similar build.

"Stature is about character, not about height," he advised.

Continuing, Gates acknowledged how Scouting made a difference in this world.

"At a time when many American young people are turning into couch potatoes and, too often, much worse," Gates told the 1,500 donors in the audience, "Scouting continues to challenge boys and young men, preparing them for leadership."

"We in Scouting believe that personal virtues— self-reliance, self-control, honor, integrity and morality—are absolute and timeless," Gates added. "There are in too many places too few people with Scouting values—people who say, 'On my honor, I will do my best to do my duty,' and mean it."

In closing, he challenged all Scouts to "learn skills, to master challenges, to strive to live up to high principles and moral values, to find the greater

TOP: Two members of the Circle Ten color guard assigned to present the colors at the 2012 Friends of Scouting banquet. At the event, guest presenter, former First Lady Laura Bush (left), introduced former Secretary of State Dr. Condoleezza Rice to the crowd. ABOVE: Circle Ten Council President Ernest J. Carey at Fair Park in 2012. ACROSS: Two patches celebrating the Mikanakawa Lodge's 75th Anniversary celebrations held during the 2012 Fall Fellowship weekend at Camp Wisdom/Billy Sowell Boy Scout Camp.

beauty in a life of cheerful service, to build strong character" because Scouting will make them "strong leaders for tomorrow."

The event raised approximately $2 million that night prompting Vice President of Finance Stanley Allred to declare that Friends of Scouting Chairman and future Council President Ernest J. Carey had "knocked it out of the park."

When asked about it some months later, a humble Carey responded, "I had a lot of help."[8]

In an attempt to build on the prior year's success, the 2012 Friends of Scouting committee brought in former First Lady Laura Bush to introduce the evening's guest speaker, former Secretary of State

Condoleezza Rice. In her introduction, a congenial Mrs. Bush quickly put the crowd at ease.

"President Bush and I both participated in Scouting [as young people] and we were both fortunate to have our mothers serve as our troop leaders when we were growing up in Midland," she began. "My mother-in-law, Barbara Bush, was George's Cub Scout leader and, actually, that's when her hair turned white."

After the laughter settled down, she continued, "I wanted to make a difference [in the world] and Scouting gave me the confidence to be a leader, and I want to thank you for the opportunities that you are giving the boys."

As the former First Lady left the podium, a well-rested Secretary Rice took the stage and opened with an observation regarding her newfound pleasure of being able to read the morning newspaper and not see her name in it.

"The thing that's most different now is that I get up every day, I get my cup of coffee, and I open the newspaper (on the Internet) and say to myself, 'Isn't that interesting,'" she quipped. "And then I go on to do whatever else I want to do because I am no

RIGHT: The Statler Hilton on Commerce Street sits on the site of the former Dallas YMCA Building – the place where Scouting first was introduced to the city in November 1910 by Claude M. Richmond.

longer responsible for what is *in* that newspaper. It's a wonderful station in life."

Her speech included how the American spirit drives its own special kind of democracy and hypothesized as to why foreign peoples continue to flock to our native shores.

"They know it doesn't matter where you come from, it matters where you are going," she advised. "You can come from humble circumstance and you can do great things here . . . That is the strength of our democracy. That is the strength of America."

In closing, Secretary Rice offered her analysis as to why Scouting has lasted over 100 years.

"You are helping to strengthen the communitarian spirit—that civil society in one very specific and important way . . . Boy Scouting teaches young men responsibility and to honor accountability and integrity," Rice said. "It teaches them not to feel entitled to anything because there is no greater enemy to a strong democracy than a sense of entitlement."

THE JOURNEY TO EXCELLENCE DASHBOARD

IN ORDER TO *become Scouting's Iconic Council, Circle Ten leaders had to improve in all prescribed measurable areas of performance as required by national BSA's Journey to Excellence program. Financially, the objective was to have 90 days worth of cash on hand for any potential lean times. Membership goals included improvement on market share of Total Available Youth (TAY), youth retention, and increasing total membership and units.*

Program goals included having more Scouts advance and attend Council-run summer camps. districts needed to recruit new unit commissioners in service areas, while the Leadership and Governance objective was to increase the percentage of trained leaders across all units.

Should the Council meet national standards, they would be awarded either the Bronze, Silver or Gold Recognition for the year. For the year 2011, Circle Ten Council earned the exemplary rating of Gold.[H]

Clearly a hit in Dallas, Circle Ten Council set a new one day fund-raising record by raising nearly $2.59 million that evening, which also set a national BSA fund-raising record for a single Council event. This came as both good and bad news to Finance Director Don Burke—the good being that the Council had an extremely successful night, and the bad, because now he was expected to better it next time.

"I don't know how we're going to do it in 2013 but the committee will meet soon to figure it out," Burke commented. "Friends of Scouting Chairman Curt Farmer and lead sponsor Comerica Bank really made it happen this year and they deserve a tremendous amount of credit. It just keeps getting better each time and that makes me very proud to be a part of this organization."[9]

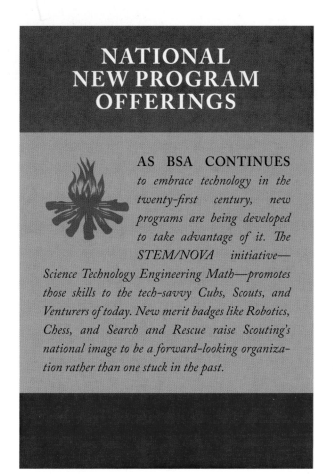

NATIONAL NEW PROGRAM OFFERINGS

AS BSA CONTINUES *to embrace technology in the twenty-first century, new programs are being developed to take advantage of it. The STEM/NOVA initiative— Science Technology Engineering Math—promotes those skills to the tech-savvy Cubs, Scouts, and Venturers of today. New merit badges like Robotics, Chess, and Search and Rescue raise Scouting's national image to be a forward-looking organization rather than one stuck in the past.*

Other national Scouting developments kept Circle Ten leaders on their toes. The Journey to Excellence program was introduced at BSA's National Annual Meeting in San Diego, California in May 2011. Covering the critical areas of finance, membership, program, unit service, and leadership and governance, the Journey to Excellence "dashboard" goals focused on a council's resources to meet certain levels of expected performance. Circle Ten executives decided to exceed those minimum requirements en route to their long-range goal of becoming Scouting's "iconic council"—meaning that the Council's performance in all areas of operation will become the exemplar of excellence for all other councils to emulate.

"This image of becoming Scouting's 'iconic council' is something we discussed when hiring Scout Executive Pat Currie," recalled Council President Ernest J. Carey. "He had the same vision as we did and wanted to be a part of that process. There is no question that his foresight and leadership will help make that happen."

To help Scout Executive Currie better focus on that goal, the executive board believed that a new position was in order. The result was the office of Chief Operating Officer/Deputy Scout Executive who would oversee the day-to-day office operations. David M. Williams, an executive from the Middle Tennessee Council in Nashville, Tennessee, assumed the role on December 1, 2011.

"The opportunity to work in this Council was an opportunity that I simply could not pass up," said Williams. "Circle Ten is one of the finest councils in the country and I wanted to play a part in increasing its reach into the community."[10]

To better deliver the program to its youth, Scout Executive Currie saw a problem—many of the districts were too large and needed to be split up for better management. For example, the North Trail District stretched from the Park Cities through Far North Dallas and into Richardson making it as large as some entire councils elsewhere in the country.

To tackle the realignment process, Currie recruited a committee of 41 dedicated volunteers in May 2011 to discuss all options for its full implementation on January 1, 2012.

"It had been 30 years since the last major district realignment," said Currie. "It was time."

"With the way the Dallas area had grown in size in the last 30 or 40 years," explained Circle Ten Council Commissioner Matt M. Walker, "we had some areas that were way out of the norm of what they should have been in size."

After six months of negotiations, the largest districts were split into two and three new districts to be under the direction of one district executive each. As their new boundaries materialized, Scouts were encouraged to submit new district names, and from them the new identities would emerge, as well as a new way of doing business.

Commissioner Walker believed every district should change its name because it was "a great way to start fresh and not be encumbered by the 'way we have always done it' attitude."

He expected the best practices from each district to survive and flourish under new nomenclature.[11]

In the end, the vast majority of districts changed names with only a handful maintaining their old titles. The Council now had 23 separate areas plus the ScoutReach district—a far cry from the original four districts assigned in 1913.

"It was a hard sell to some leaders," recalled Executive Board Member John Copley, "but it was best for all in the end."

For certain, local Scouting was continuing to evolve and grow, just as it had done for the past century. Circle Ten Council was now the home of 54,000 total youth across all programs in 12 counties—a far cry from the four boys in one city a century prior.[12]

EAGLE SCOUT NICHOLAS COBB SPEAKS TO THE IMPORTANCE OF SCOUTING

Presented at the Friends of Scouting Banquet—March 6, 2012

MY NAME IS NICHOLAS COBB (below) and I am a 15-year-old sophomore at Allen High School. I am not too different from most boys my age. I like to hang out with my friends, I like to play video games, and I like to eat.

Outside of that I guess you could say I am involved in a few things. I am a straight "A" student, I sing in 2 choirs, I am in the National Honor Society, the Student Council, and the Scholarship Ministry at my church. The biggest thing that I am involved in outside of school is Boy Scouting, which I have been a member of since I was 6.

As a Cub, I was a Bobcat, a Wolf, a Bear and, of course, a Webelos Scout who earned the Arrow of Light award.

My mom likes to tell the story of when I saw my first Crossover ceremony. She says I ran out to the bridge because I wanted to crossover too. She explained to me that I couldn't just walk across it because I had to earn the right to do it. Since then, I have tried to show myself worthy of every rank I earned.

In the end, I did get to crossover into a great unit, Troop 306. I know there are other troops represented within the Council but I have to say that I think my Scoutmaster, Mr. Bahnman, is the best Scoutmaster, of the best troop, in the best district, in the best council in the world.

Everyone in my great troop worked with me in everything I did and helped me learn everything that I wanted to learn. That is what Scouting is all about. It gave me confidence to feel like I could do anything I set my mind to, and it built my leadership abilities as well!

For me, I always worry about homeless people, especially in a country as wealthy as America. To help me cope with it, I performed little projects for years. When I was 12-years-old, I started thinking about doing something bigger that could be ongoing. Therefore, I started my own non-profit organization called Comfort and Joy with the goal of providing warm clothing to less fortunate individuals and families—especially around the holidays.

Its inaugural project was my Eagle Scout project. I set a goal of raising $3,400 to purchase 129 coats for families at the Samaritan Inn Shelter in McKinney. Some people thought that was a big deal, but that is the thing about Scouting—if you can conceive it, you can achieve it. Everyone in the community helped me and we did raise the money, we did buy the coats, and I did become an Eagle Scout at age 13.

The feeling of helping others is just so strong that you can't stop. Last year I set of a goal of raising $4,500 and we raised that too. This year we gave coats to City House shelter in Plano and to the Allen Community Outreach Center (right), along with starting a healthy eating garden at City House as well. I plan to continue to give back to the community for years to come.

In sum, Comfort and Joy has raised $25,425.48 and the best part of the whole deal is that every boy in Circle 10 Council is just like me.

We can do anything we want to do and be anything we want to be because we have been taught leadership qualities in Scouting.

But my story is just one story. I have friends who have installed conservation programs in conservatories, or rebuilt parts of churches or sent supplies abroad to victims of natural disasters. And they are all just as passionate about their projects as I am about mine.

That is why Scouting is so important. Every Scout needs the same opportunity to develop leadership characteristics as me. Scouting opens up doors that would never have been opened before.

I have big plans for my future and plan to attend the SMU Bobby Lyle School of Engineering. I am going to be a computer analyst and give back to my community right here in North Texas. I want to be a Scout Leader someday. Who knows maybe someday I can fund the Circle Ten Nicholas Cobb Boy Scout Center. Scouting really makes you feel like anything is possible.

God bless each of you. God bless the Boy Scouts and God bless the United States of America.

The arrival of Circle Ten Council's centennial year of 2013 is a grand time for North Texas Scouting as its members and supporters look to the future of the organization after having re-visited its glorious past.

Few institutions—much less *franchises*—can boast a record of success like Scouting can in Texas and Oklahoma, but Circle Ten Council's achievement was not attained overnight, nor did it occur in a vacuum. It occurred as the result of decades of hard work performed by hundreds of thousands of volunteers who believed that communities are made better one person at a time. And with a vehicle like Scouting, no other result could be expected.

Surely the Dallas Council's first apostle, Scoutmaster, and Scout Commissioner Claude M. Richmond would be duly impressed with how that vision has thrived. But like other success stories, it quickly transcended his initial groundwork and flourished under like-minded individuals who followed his example and gave liberally of their minimum "one hour a week."

The result continues to be legions of well-trained young people who are versed in the skills of life and filled with a resolve for clean living and ethical behavior.

TROOP 44 OF VAN ALSTYNE, TEXAS—100 YEARS OF SCOUTING IN 2013

IN 1939, *District Scout Commissioner Rae A. Nunnallee of Van Alstyne had a lot to say about the start of Scouting in North Texas—he was there.*

In late 1912, three local boys named Rowland Barnett, Otis White, and Nunnallee himself received their first Boy Scout storybooks and took interest in this relatively new movement. Barnett, as the story goes, made a Christmas wish for a Boy Scout troop to be formed in the town—a wish realized on April 2, 1913, with the founding of Van Alstyne's Troop 1.

The unit's first Scoutmaster was Prof. W. F. Barnett, Rowland's father, who also served as the principal of the Van Alstyne Agricultural School. He served as Scoutmaster until April 19 when he moved his family to Corsicana to take the position of Superintendent of the State Orphans' Home. The first meeting place was the old school building as the trustees had granted the troop use of a third floor room for meetings.

In 1917, the First United Methodist Church in town became the troop's chartering organization—certainly to be one of the longest continuous associations with a single Scout troop in the country.

Operating without national documentation for a dozen years, on July 8, 1925, troop leaders announced receipt of their official BSA charter listed under the direction of Scoutmaster W. J. White and his assistants, 21-year-old Edgar Sledge and 30-year-old Rae Nunnallee.

Three years later in August 1928, Troop 44's first Eagle Scout award was presented to 15-year-old Surce John Taylor, the son of a local farmer. Taylor would eventually move to Garland and become a ballistics expert.

Nunnallee became the troop's second Eagle Scout in 1930 and earned a total of 84 merit badges. He would serve his unit and Scouting for the next 53 years (logging over 70 continuous years total) and have the chapel at Camp Grayson, now Camp James Ray, named in his honor.

Troop 44's, Scoutmaster Brian Hendricks continues to mentor the youth of Van Alstyne in the lessons and values of Scouting.[1]

Former secretary of education William J. Bennett said at a recent national gathering of Scouting professionals in Orlando, Florida, "In society today, we must teach boys what a man must be."[13] And Circle Ten Council is doing exactly that.

As we all reflect upon what Circle Ten Council means to each of us individually, remember that it can only continue to expand with the aid and support of the same. Its unparalleled success is in direct correlation with its responsiveness to the needs of the community and its ability to develop young people with character.

So, here's to the next 100 years of Scouting in Circle Ten Council and to the building of its youth into the citizen-leaders of tomorrow. And as we are fully aware, no cross-generational gift is greater than that.

THREE CHEERS FOR CIRCLE TEN COUNCIL!

HIP HIP HOORAY!

OH, BY THE WAY, CIRCLE TEN COUNCIL WILL PRESENT ITS 30,000TH EAGLE MEDAL TO A LUCKY SCOUT IN DECEMBER 2013.

THE LEGACY CONTINUES.

ACROSS: Without question, Circle Ten Council is one of the finest Scouting organizations in the country today, as it is made up of many duty-driven youth, adults, supporters, and professionals, who singularly care for their community and those living in it. This image re-envisions the classic "Scout Salute" photo in front of the Camp Wisdom gate in 1932 as seen on page 134. As we close the year on our first century, may the Scouts of Circle Ten Council continue to lead the way towards a better America. They are the future leaders of this great country.

THE SECOND CENTURY

BY AMIT BANERJEE
PUBLISHER, *PHILANTHROPY KIDS*
EAGLE SCOUT, 2012

For my earliest days, I saw that Boy Scouting's slogan, "Do a good turn daily," was all around me and better yet, Scouts were living it. I saw them create flowerbeds for their schools, craft handmade cards for the elderly at retirement homes, and raise money for others by selling lemonade at corner stands. These simple acts of kindness made a big difference to me in my life because I saw how they helped other people.

As I moved through the ranks of the Scouting program, I better understood the close relationship between philanthropy and Scouting and wanted to make it a bigger part of my life. For my Eagle project, I chose to work in the area of youth and giving but on a grand scale. So, I founded a publication dedicated to telling the stories of good kids and how they helped people in need. That became *Philanthropy Kids* magazine.

However, creating a magazine and actively Scouting on a weekly basis was not an easy path. At times, schoolwork and extra-curricular activities zapped away my time and energy. But I was surrounded by very passionate Scouts and leaders who became my friends. I was blessed. But the one BIG thing that tied us together was the unwavering support given us by the dedicated people at Circle Ten Council.

I AM AMIT BANERJEE, an Eagle Scout from Troop 51 in Frisco, Texas. When I joined Cub Scouting as a six-year-old in the first grade, I knew very little about it. I was just happy to spend that extra hour a week with my friends. But what an amazing experience it turned out to be! We earned belt loops, designed and built pinewood derby cars, and waited anxiously for the Blue and Gold Banquet where we formally advanced to the next rank. I remember it being five years of non-stop learning and having fun with my friends.

That was when the Cub Scout motto, "Do your Best," became a part of me. But that was not the end of the trail—Boy Scouting awaited.

When I "crossed over" into Boy Scouts, I exchanged monthly pack meetings for weekly troop meetings. Belt loop advancements became merit badges and seasonal campouts became frequent events. It was a journey from adventure to adventure.

COVERING 12 COUNTIES in North Texas and Oklahoma, Circle Ten Council is the umbrella organization under which all our local troops operate—hundreds of them. When new Scouts or Venturers join, they have the opportunity to make new friends through their Scouting adventures. With time, shared experiences forge strong bonds among them. From that, something much bigger happens—they become part of the Scouting family. For me, having valued friends on my Trail to Adventure was very motivating and enabled me to focus on helping others and eventually earn that red, white, and blue Eagle Scout patch.

THE PROFESSIONALS AT Circle Ten Council desire to give the Scouting experience to everyone within its borders because it impacts society for the better. As Scouts grow through the ranks and become experienced in their unit, they are obliged to mentor the less experienced Scouts—something that we need more of in this world. I have seen this philosophy applied in so many ways over my eight years in the program.

I credit the success I have had in Scouting to the adult leaders who have served as my mentors. But those leaders couldn't have done it without the troop. And the troop wouldn't be there without the district. Finally, the district wouldn't be there without the support and organization of the magnificent Circle Ten Council.

This Council, standing tall since its formation in 1913, always has supported the community in a symbiotic partnership of service and citizen-building. Within its territory, the Council promotes the doing of good turns to all in need. For Scouts and leaders, Circle Ten advocates living the tenets contained within the Scout Oath and Scout Law in one's everyday life.

Scouting is not limited to any particular section of society and embraces diversity because its members come from many different cultural and religious faith backgrounds—making it a great integration tool. And for youths with troubled pasts, Scouting is a "safe haven" where they can share their life's experiences with others in their age group, build friendships, and self-confidence. In sum, I believe that Scouting should be a part of every kids's life for the mere fact that it builds undeniable character in a person.

Thank you Circle Ten Council for all you have done for us and I wish your continued success as you build more citizen-leaders of quality well into your second century!

AWARD RECIPIENTS

SILVER ANTELOPE RECIPIENTS

H. Ross Perot 1974
John D. Murchison 1974
Omar Harvey 1978

Paul Thayer 1978
T. Louis Austin Jr 1972
John Cooper 1986

Ray H. Marr 1987
Merle Borchelt 1995
Jack D. Furst 2007

Charles Holmes 2007
John Stuart III 2010

SILVER BEAVER RECIPIENTS

1931 George R. Angell | George H. Bird | Thomas E. Cox | Frank V. Faulkner | Col. Albert E. Humphries | Rev. W. H. Meyers Jr. | John S. Wisdom | Archie Wood | Frank W. Wozencraft

1933 T. A. Hord

1934 W. A. Goodwin | R. S. Reading

1937 W.C. Stainman | N. H. Talley

1938 R. A. McClung

1940 Milton Brown | B. R. Newberry

1941 R. A. Kilpatrick

1942 George T. Hemmingson | Orville Mitchell

1943 Glen Cloeman | E. P. Harbin | Graham Pierce

1944 E. L. Craig | Clifford Dinsmore | Joe F. Etters | J. V. Folsom | Arthur C. Hopkins Sr. | Eric B. Nelson | W. R. Richardson | Otto F. Vehle

1945 B. J. Jackson Jr. | J. Tip Newell | Rea Nunnallee | J. C. Tyler | Cyril E. Wyche

1946 R. M. Allman | Oscar Bilger | Wesley T. Hook | Roy Kyle

1947 John R. Santerre | Chris W. Scheurer | Clyde Tomlinson

1948 Rev. F. L. Becker | J. C. Cantrell | J. V. Conatser | O. Jack Hammock | Lionel C. Hardie | Dr. Harvey J. Piercy | Fred A. Ryle

1949 J. W. Crozier | J. Cook Evans | Dechard A. Hulcy | John E. Mitchell Jr. | C. Hansford Ray

1950 E. E. Collins | W. E. Cox | G. B. Gaston | Paul K. Purcell | P. M. Rutherford Jr. | Joe B. Stuart

1951 John Daffron | M. E. Dobbins | Earl C. Entrekin | O. R. Hendricks

1952 Austin F. Allen | E. C. Anderson | Dr. Malcolm B. Bowers | Hubert C. Davis | John B. Mills | Stuart Leslie Reed | William B. Thompson

1953 Dr. S. L. Brown | John F. Buckner | Joe P. Cox Jr. | Sam M. Davis | Frederick Dickson | W. R. Lovejoy | David W. McCord | Boone Powell Sr. | J. D. Clifford Smith | G. H. Wilcos

1954 A. W. Breeland | Richard F. Chapman | Clarence S. Cone Jr. | Pierre A. Fontaine | Richard R. Lipscomb | James H. Penny | Dr. Charles P. Pitts | F. M. Rawlins | Carl J. Rutland | William Ray Saunders | Rev. Abraham L. Schley | Maynard Shearer | Paul Kincaid Wilson

1955 Lester E. Allen | Morris S. Battle Sr. | Gus Bowman | Jack Hannah | Guy Henry | Leslie E. Hoover | R. H Jennings | Charles S. Johnson Sr. | Lon Clayton Sailers Jr. | E. G. "Pat" Simpson | August H. Tiemann

1956 William H. Boyd | Robert L. Clark | James M. Cumby | Nathan Kopel | Dr. D. A. McCall | Laurence R. Melton | Alton B. St. Clair | C. D. Taylor

1957 E. J. "Jimmy" Bowles | Vernon H. Brown | Paul Carrington Sr. | Theodor R. Clancy | Frank Clark | Ray Foley | Arnold Latschar | E. Robert Riddle Jr.

1958 Dr. Gough Hall Alexander | Carey L. Anderson | Edward F. Bilger | Joe G. Buch | Clifford R. Byrd | David Daniels | R. Shelton Goode | Alfred L. Myers | Rev. William J. Stack | J. W. Bob Vinson | Homer L. Walker | Henry A. Warren Jr. | Jack Allen 1959

1959 R. L. Redellium Atnip | Estabrook Glosser | Samuel D. Gratke | L. T. Gunter | Arthur G. Hopkins Jr. | Samuel W. Hudson | Kellum Johnson | John Harwell Jones | John R. Kilgore | Neth Leachman | Nick Miller | Miro Arthur Pavelka Sr. | Brookin N. Wadley Jr. | Augus Gilchrist Wynne Jr.

1960 John Biggerstaff | C. Loyd Brown | Paul Wesley Calvin | Carl L. Collins | Eugene P. C. Constantin Jr. | W. A. Denton | G. Brice Gaston | W. Z. Hayes | Rev. Harry C. Hoy | Wilson Otto Kaden | Alfred G. McGuire | Joseph McMillan | John Joseph Patterson | Ryal L. Skaggs | Dr. John Joe Stowe Jr. | Edward Williams

1961 H. C. Barnes | Thomas H. Barnett Jr. | Alfred H. Benjamin | Dr. Elmer P. Cheatum | Jack W. Foote | Howard A. Hestand | Samual Weldon Jackson | Rev. T. Herbert Minga | Chester I. Motes | Raymond E. Neal | B. T. Nurre Jr. | Robert A. Polson | Lester T. Potter | Dr. Ronald M. Shifflett | G. Raymond Stephens | O. V. Stewart

1962 Robert M. Allen | John C. Clary | Ottis J. Cottrell | Dan M. Dennis | Samuel E. Garrett | John M. Grover | James H. Harris | James E. Huffstutler | Robert E. Jones Jr. | James W. Lee Jr. | Asa L. Leger | Eugene McElvaney | Kenneth H. McMullen | Joseph C. Moore | Ben W. Munson II | C. A. Tatum Jr. | Edwin E. Wright

1963 Walter A. Alderfer | Duward C. Bean | Curtis Calhoun | William Perry Clements Jr. | Dr. Jonathan Halsey | Darrell F. Manley | Abe Marks | Ford Molen | Rebel Mosby | Ben W. Munson III | Fred Roberts | David F. Robertson | Earl Spooner | Robert L. Thornton Jr.

1964 H. F. Aubel | Charles M. Cooper | Toice Z. Davis | Louis H. Groves | Evans T. Hardeman | Rufus A. Hauerwas | Paul T. Mathews | William V. Mowlam | Edward E. Murphree | George A. Scott Jr. | Bloomer Sullivan | J. Wilbur Thompson | John W. Vaughan | Dee Brown Walker

1965 Charles E. Beard | Maurice Beck | William P. Bowling | Percy Brooks | John M. Brown | Willis Currens | Milton Dr. Curry Jr. | Rev. William Fry | Robert W. Gillespie Jr. | Erik Jonsson | Truman David Matthews | Warren A. McCreight | Robert L. Richards | W. P. Robertson | Thomas C. Schneider | Dr. William P. Shelton | James E. Tisdale | Arthur D. Wilson | Clayon Wright

1966 J. Linwood Barton | Eugene H. Brooks | Paul H. Carter Sr. | W. F. Fitzsimmons | William H. Frazier | Kay Allen Griffin | Duane C. Holford | Melvin H. Hunter | O. B. Lawrence | Lum Lewis | Bob Lockhart | Henry F. Lote | Avery Mays | John H. McLearen | Robert W. Miller | James E. Rider | Carl J. Schoberle Jr. | Thomas J. Speed | Bernard Whitten

1967 Louis E. Adin Jr. | M. T. Buhl | Roy D'Avignon | Howard L. Day | Donald Fielding | Issac E. Harder | Felix L. Jones | Jones McConnell Sr. | Lloyd McKinney | Drewey D. McKnight Jr. | Alfred Metz | Rev. William Moran | Joe M. Nall | Carl H. Neal | Trent C. Root Jr. | Gene R. Rutherford | Hoyt M. Sessions | T. Webster Six | Anson VanSlyke | Jack T. Williams | Robert M. Wilson

1968 William G. Alsabrook | Turner Baxter | John Bradenburg | Walter A. Carter | Jack W. Chumley Sr. | Paul M. Cork | Arnold C. Eckstein | C. Bennett Harrington | Conrad D. Hendrix | Keith W. Hubbard | Victor B. Isbell | Carl Johnson | Charles D. Mohrle | George E. Moore | Wesley Moss | William C. Perryman | Jack E. Pratt | Allie Slider | R. C. Vaughan

1969 Jack C. Allen | Jack K. Bradley Jr. | Charles W. DeVoll | Joe D. Dusek | Francis X. Fallwell | Homer L. Gilkeyson | John B. Hickman | Dr. James M. Johnson | Dr. Frank H. Kidd Jr. | Clinton B. McNabb | Cottrell M. Mosby | Saturnino Perez | Erwin K. Shellenberger | Roscoe C. Smith | Haskell P. Taylor | Thomas W. Tully | Norbert E. Weiler

1970 Thomas Anderson | Olan Atherton | Don R. Chaney | George E. Choate | Patrick Darnell | Byron Davis | Fred A. Ludwig | Robin D. Moffat | Olan Monk | Charles E. Mull | Aaron E. Plaxco | Robert F. Richie | Raymond L. Smith | Russell Smith | Buddy Tommer | Arthur H. Waddell | Fred A. Zimmerman

1971 Richard A. Arnett | Jack A. Barnes | Charles W. Baxter | T. J. Collette | Thomas F. Cook | Edward L. Cowens | Mary Crawford | C. Milton Daniels | Juanita Darnell | Jane Eckstein | Frank B. Egan | Mary Virginia Egan | Robert E. B. Fielder | Dr. Clyde Hall | John P. Harbin | Everett King | Joseph L. Klein | Rev. Thurman Levacy | Altha Pond | Edward G. Rayson | Fred H. Rolke | Jennings Rucker | Carolyn Sutton | Guy Weathers | Ruth Wilson

1972 George Alford | Emily L. Bird | Hubert G. Brown | W. Ted Colglazier | Mrs. Ralph Courteney | Estella Doty | W. Jack Frazier | Marge Griffin | Cletus J. Hakert | H. Cecil Hicks | Jake Hopkins | James W. Ince | Sara Johnston | Harry A. King Jr. | George A. Landrum | W. David Lewis | William E. McCommons | Mary E. McDermott | Dr. B. Willie Mooring | James M. Murphy | Ruth Potter | Harold K. Sohner | O. Mike Strohl | Robert E. Verinder | David E. Wilson

1973 Madrom J. Bankston | Howard Barrar | Robert L. Bird | Elaine Blair | Warren E. Brashier | George M. Brewer | Jean Brown | Leonard Burris | Sybil Euraine Cooley | Donald Coppedge | William Alfred Craven | Bertha Fore | Richard Garcia | George Glaspie | Martin G. Hall | Dr. Larry J. Hines | Janet E. Knapp | Norma Kronenberg | William C. McCord | Larry Roark | James F. Stuart | Dr. Truman Wester | George O. Wills

1974 Billy F. Adair | John E. Bement Sr. | Edmund D. Bloom | Clark W. Breeding | Ray J. Butler | Harvey E. Elkins | Terrence W. Freeman | Johnny D. Gimarc | James H. Harris | William D. Harris | Omar Harvey | Charles Y. Hendricks | R. D. Hughes | Donald L. Lindsey | Lloyd B. Miller | Marion Mohrle | Lloyd Perkins | Richard Riggins | Ben S. Skinner Jr. | Clarence J. Spangler | Cecil Ray Tarver | Anthony J. Thomas | Vincent W. Thompson

1975 Edwin I. Aduddel | Donald W. Anderson | Ann Callahan | John W. Collins Jr. | Mrs. Ralph E. Cummings | Joe D. Denison | Robert E. Dickerson | Lewis M. Duca | Alma Hawthorne | Richard A. Hester | John Hinkel | Lyle Hunt | Richard A. Johns | Frank T. King | T. R. Lee Jr. | James T. Lineback | Robert E. Little | William D. Manahan | Norman W. Meador | Alfred L. Pierce | Charles W. Potter | Hill P. Read Jr. | Mrs. Ralph F. Sanders | Jerry L. Talley | Lewis F. Tidwell | Evelyn Womble | James F. Young

1976 Rosa L. Bookman | Billy Joe Brown | Paul Bruns | Randolph R. Carlisle | Alvis R. Coffman | Hugh H. Cotton | Ann M. Cox | Brady Cox | John Dannel II | Rev. James F. Dean | J. S. Fore | Roland E. Goss | Dr. Gilbert Hatcher | Ralph E. Jenkins | Walter Johnson | Paul K. Landtiser | James N. Livezey | James C. Lovelace | William Mowlam Jr. | B. W. Northrup | Richard R. Rubottom | Manning B. Trewitt | Cortis R. VanCleve | Marshall H. Warder | Dr. Otto L. Willbanks | Alice E. Williams

1977 Charles I. Acker | Charles W. Calhoun | Thomas A. Caverly | Betty Christenson | Douglas Coffin | Horace R. Crawford | Roy E. Hill Sr. | Harrison Holloway Sr. | Fred Kersting | Charles H. King III | Ray H. Marr | Ronald E. Martin | Ray F. Mathis | Louie McQuirter | Lloyd C. Riddles | Luther B. Terry | Andrew Triche Jr. | William B. Welch | Roy T. White | Norman E. Williams | Reba Wright

1978 Tom Beauchamp | Lloyd W. Birdwell | Billy Blinn | William Bonds | Dr. Hugh Brown | Horace Claire | Ken Clardy | Duane Collier | Harlin Dauphin | Jerry Dollison | George Dykes | Edward Farris | Harry Furst | Roger L. Hanson | John Hochgraf | William Holtz | Peter Lutken Jr. | Francis McDermott | Thomas A. O'Dwyer | H. Ross Perot | Ray C. Robbins | John Shelton | Gene Stewart | Frank Thixton

1979 Willie Alton | N. Alex Bickley | Lillie Brown | Dr. Jefferson Bruton | O. V. Cartwright | Edward R. Cave | Ted D. Cox | Ann Dunfield | Bennie Finn | Gene Foster | David H. Hitt | Marcus Hubbard | William R. Mahaffey | Rufus McKnight | Calvin Myers | Shirley Oktay | Roger D. Osterhout | Russell Pierce Jr. | Raymond A. Reed | John F. Stephens | Fred R. Watson | Charles A. Wood

1980 Daniel D. Adams | Ronald D. Bauer | Mac Book | Bernard M. Coffey | Thomas H. Covington Jr. | David Jackson | Alan H. Lee Jr. | Charles Marcus | James F. McHugh | C. K. Pool | Altus Bing Scherzer | Rev. C. B. T. Smith | George N. Soderstrom | Craig L. Stephens | Charles Strong | John D. Stuart | Paul S. Thomas | Bob O. Weeks | Lewis J. Wertheimer | Peter J. Weyrens

1981 Louis A. Beecherl Jr. | Rebel E. Blackwell Jr. | M. Browning Combs | Jess Covey | Robert Etzell | Billy Langley | Kay Manley | Joseph A. Mehan | Cecil C. Mills | John Munson | Jimmy Sutton | Richard B. Williams

1982 Paul K. Baker | Cleeta Burton | Robert K. Campbell | Mildred C. Coffey | Dr. Billy E. Dade | Wayne R. Fisher | Kenneth S. Goldstein | Marshall L. Hall | L. Drew Humbert | Stan Keese | William H. Mathewes | Walter W. McCabe | Robert McCollum | Joyce Meeker | Jack E. Morman | Fred M. Ramsey Jr. | Janet Schulz | Bobby Joe Simmons | Edward Valentine | Charles L. L. Vogel | Theodore Wallace Sr. | Larry F. Walls | Gerald H. Weghorst

1983 Herbert T. Boyd | Charles E. Bunnell Jr. | Robert K. Campbell | Larry Clark | Chancey Corse | Elmer Diggs | Warren S. Ekis | W. Herbert Hunt | Robert L. Johnson | Dr. Jesse W. Jones | Sharon J. Lee | Barbara S. Myers | Joy Ondrusek | Dr. Percy M. Pentecost Jr. | John D. Phillips | J. C. Riza | Donald Schuhmann | Jack Daffron | Richard B. Sperry | J. Wesley Thorn | Claude Watson | Timothy A. Whisler | Jim Bob Wilson

1984 Jerry Farrington | Joe L. Gary | Richard M. Hart | Randy Hopkins | Raymond Morra

1985 Billy Arnold | Al Carson | James A. Cavalleri | Daniel Cheatham | Albert H. Cloud | Forest Dodson | Mack Estes | Frank B. Hacker | Dan Herndon | Dan Jackson | Tom Lear | Ken Long | Roy Luckett | Dana Mackison | Hobart Marple | Frank Marrero | John McCaulie | Vera McGruder | Raymond Morrow | Bruce O'Neal | Paula Price | Faye Purnell | Richard M. Raitt | Michael Shaw | James Sinclair | Doug Stiegler | Allene Tollison | Jeanne A. Tolzmann | Bishop Thomas Tschoepe | Rev. James Tucek | Charles Wickersham | Claude Wiseman

1986 Harry Bubek | Rosi Criswell | Glenn Dickerson | Cleve Hundley | Kenneth V. Jenkins | Jimmy King | Spencer Lengyel | C. H. Poole | Bob Prowse | Danny White | Dr. Jim M. Williams | Linus Wright

1987 Dennis R. Arnold | Lynda L. Bailey | Robert L. Beck | Lloyd A. Behm | Donald J. Carter | Dr. Norman E. Dyer | Robert D. Hawthorne | Donald L. Hook | David MacDonald | Raymond Mehan | Mike Moore | Trinidad Munoz Sr. | Roy O'Neal | Doyle D. Rogers | Kay Sanders | Val Schrumpf | Jerry Stiles | Waggoner L. Tipps | Allene Tollinn | Newton Wade | H. Eugene Wenzel | Nat Williams | W. C. Youngblood

1988 Nancy Adamson | Taylor August | Eddie Baker | Hank Caruso | Durwood Chalker | Emmert Dill | Maurice Edwards | Richard Griffith | Mary Hall | Richard Hogue | Paul Johnston | Fred Kibat | Rowland Lewis | Thomas Lipscomb | Dr. Milton Lowrey | Larry Marcy | George Miller | Willard Moon | Lucille Murchison | Terrence Peake | Donor Penn | George R. Schrader | Terry Snook | Lewis Sweeney | Robert Sypult | Marshall Tyre | James Vornberg

1989 Mike Alexander | Edwin Barker | Joe Bicik | Gordon Christian | Edward Crumley | Ruben Esquivel | Michael Flagg | David Gish | Mart Hamilton | Bill Hawkins | Joe Hilbun | Mary Hogan | Gerhardt Krawitz | Cindra Morgan | Bobby Rutherford | Jerry Tucker

1990 Harold R. Ashby | Dr. Joe Barner | Jerome L. Bell | Merle L. Borchelt | John Bradley | Patricia M. Cummings | Jimmy Dale Sr. | Mary H. Gonzales | David Hall | Eileen Henry | Darell J. Herbst | Charles D. Holmes | Steve E. Howie | William Innes | Steve Jung | Sandra Malone | Ray McClary | Judith K. Raitt | Russell Rose | Gary Schulz | Betty Tucker | Bill Tucker | Sam Tucker | George VanDerven | Charles Vickers | Merrell W. Williams

1991 Denise Backers | Alva H. Bandy | Brian Barnette | Kent M. Black | John Burrows Jr. | Tommy L. Cruce | William L. Dorsey | Judy Eastburn | George Etier | Alan B. Gage | Douglas D. Hawthorne | Kenneth G. Kahler | Dr. Larry Melton | Staley W. Mims Jr. | Karen L. Mindrup | Dr. Yondell E. Moore | Fred Petry | Mark W. Richmond | William O. Scherzer III | Paul Schieffer | Clair Schultis | Ronald G. Steinhart | Marie VanArsdale | Cynthia Whisennand

1992 Marilyn Bechtol | Sherwood Blount Jr. | Gary Brewer | Mack Broiles | John Burke | Homer Canada | Dr. Larry Carter | David Dees | Dr. Marvin Edwards | Kevin Fagan | Ben Ford | Robin Goss | Chuck Haseman | Jack Helmbrecht | Mike Henrichsen | Sylvia Herrington | Curtis Kitchens | Dr. Paul Lonquist | Pam Peveto | James W. Porter | James Scott | Dale Smith | Robert Turner | Claudine Williams

1993 James Bell | Dr. James Brooks | Mark Carpenter | Cliff Clark | Jim Corvey | Jeffrey English | Jack Evans | Jack Ferguson | John Gary | Benjamin Hartsell | Glenn Haynes | Jay Holmes | Jimmy Hooks | Galen Johnson | Jeff Kerr | Richard Logue | Odis Luper | Donald MacLellan | Roy Miller | Agnes Monzingo | Ray Pinson | Homer Rodriguez | Danny Sherrer | Frances Walker | Bob Wooldridge | Ronald York

1994 Mike Blew | Jim Bourn | Don Cameron | Glenda Curts | Scott Dillard | Eric Graham | Alan Gray | Rochester Harper | Shane Herrington | Terry Krawitz | Larry Kuhlken | Brad Manson | Darryl Odom | James E. Oesterreicher | Tom Pierson | Hal Todd | Terry Winborn

1995 Gerald R. Albert | Sylvia Augsburger | Gary E. Bechtol | Mark A. Brown | Sunni Craig | Rodger Cramer | Margaret Duncan | Mike Gibbs | Jeffery Hendricks | Tom Holder | Clarence Hollie | Barbara Murry | Robert Pierce | Roger Sanderson | Steve Schmidt | Jim R. Smith | Jim Sowell | George Westmoreland | Julius Zsohar

1996 Jonas Berk | E. R. "Dick" Brooks | Michael Busby | Ed Dayton | Lisa Earl | David Edwards | Richard Franco | Al Gonzales | Danny Hagel | Gerry Hooks | Martin Korn | Stephen Leake | Bill Lee | Rex Lewis | Tom Malorzo | John McClerran | John Miller | Gerald Palmeri | Jethro Pugh | John Richardson | Ray Rogers | Larry Seidemann | Donovan Sisson Jr. | John St. Denis | Sim Stokes | Don Wallace | Patricia Wilkerson | Melvin Ziegenbein

1997 Bill Benson | David Blair Jr. | Marshall Garcia | Paul Hargrave | Gary Hill | John Fox Holt III | Guy Knoll | Bobby Lyle | Ernest Muegge | Mike O'Quinn | Sheryl Pierson | Ervin Richards | Gail Richards | Barbara Rookstool | Carl Schieffer | Jim Whaley | Lometa Williams | Carol Witt | Paul Witthoeft

1998 Patrick Adams | Bob Brand | Joni Chatwin | Terri Cody | Ronald Coker | Chuck Currie | Mike Fry | Bob Gates | Lorne Grasse | William Hammon | Frank Horak | David James | Rick King | Cindy Liddy | Georgia Mason | Frank Mills | C. H. Moore | David Nunn | Tom Shane | Jack Singley | David Watkins | Joseph Williams

1999 Kresha Alvarado | Brian Bender | Dennis Garcia | Randall Graham | Wade Graves | Milburn Gravley | Robert Harris | John Judah | Roger Knapp | Frank Krizan | Dr. Howard Linn | Gayther Shane McBride | Michael F. O'Donnell | Donald Rabon | Steve Ramsey | James Sweat | Liz Vinton | Lloyd Yost

2000 Raul Aguilar | Clark Allen | Michael Bigbee | Kathy Bratcher | Reynolds Chapman | Cody Crider | Odis Dossett | Jack D. Furst | Daniel Gessley | Carter Hallmark | Cody Crider | Donald Lindsey | Ronald Malouf | Kent Metzger | Marc Migliazzo | Douglas Molepske | Conrad Renner | Sherrie Sanders | William Webb | Dietrech Whisennand

2001 Benjamin Barber | William Bliss | William Clif Chamberlain | Ralph Evans | Tony Gobar | Raymond Harris | Steve Healy | John McCollum | Markie Nathan | Bernard Nguyen | Edwin Reitz | William Richardson | Robert F. Sanford | Danny Shaw | John Stuart | Scott Thompson | Jeanne Tunks | David Wakefield | Gerald Williams | Margaret Wunsch

2002 Bob Beard | David Biegler | Dr. Rev. C. A. Clark | Clifford Harmon | Jim Marshall | Keith Nathan | Dr. Marvin Noble | Robert Packard | Roy Lynn Rea | Sheri Robson | Pete Sessions | Ralph Smith | Ed Thatcher | Duwaine Thomas | Todd Washburn | Don Wendell | Royce West | Calvin Winchester

2003 Hugh David Arant | Bill Bexley | Sylvia Cass-Freyling | George DeLacerda | James A. Fry | Steve Goff | Pat Goold | Gina G. Hedgecock | Wilmer Griffin Jones Jr. | Dr. Bassett Kilgore | Richard Knight | Jerry Lewis | Bennie McBride | William S. Robson IV | Dr. George B. Theilen | Robert Burdette Tomes | Dennis Weigel | Paul White

2004 Tom Baker | John Bristow | Ragan Broyles | Tony Dayton | Leslie G. Harris | Robert W. Higgins | Chris Jackson | David E. Lindsey | Phil Lipoma | Mathis Perkins | Jim T. Phillips | Tom Poindexter | Robert W. Pospick | Robert Reitz | Leonard Robertson | Mike Snyder | Dennis Wayne Teel | Greg Wilkinson

2005 Brian Bennett | Gloria G. Blum | Al J. Boudreaux | James H. Cash | Billy R. Chambers Jr. | Perry G. Fisher | Teresa L. Harner | John Michael Hayes | Nancy Ann Hunt | Robert Paxton Kyker | Hudson Coleman Lockett III | Jack Martin | Ronald Netherland | David Nutt | Mark Parmerlee | Gary Pierce | James C. Shepherd | Joe Walker | Kent Wilson

2006 Johnny R. Almanza | Pryor Blackwell | Debbie Chesley | Tim Conard | Drew Dickens | Noble Hetherington Jr. | J. Roland Jeter | Dianne K. Jones | G. Alan Joyce | Karen M. Lipoma | Janet McGrath | Vernon Mullen | Larry Nixon | William O'Neal | Laura Petrash | Dr. John R. Richmond | Dr. Jerry L. Sims | Richard W. Thiot | Tucker Thompson | Henry J. Voegtle

2007 Gordon Wright | Jerry Wayne Tolbert | Paul Andrew Nolte | Randy Bradshaw | Wallace T. Ford Jr. | Cathy Netherland | Jeri Marold | Robert Lyons | Richard Dawson | Tom Manley | Dayne Scott Woodall | Roger B. Foltz | Bobby G. Littlefield | Duncan L. Clore | Charles Mohrle | Dr. Michael J. McGuire | Jim Conrad | Mary Lorraine Almanza | Stanley E. Allred | David P. Poole

2008 L. David Johnson Jr. | Bob Fries | Harold L. Sickler | Jeanine Robinson Stevens | Mark Baland | Jan Baland | Monika Kriechbaum | Victor Kriechbaum | Lester Hunter | David K. Marold | Robert McCullough | Lloyd Harold Duty Jr. | Lynne Downs | Tony Reynolds | Annette James | Connie Deckard | Edward Yost | Mary R. Buenrostro | Randy Svajda | Joseph V. Alexander | Dr. John Price | Kimberly Colonnetta | Lance Pool

2009 Hilda K Griffin | Kevin Harrison | David S Matthewson | David Joseph Fornadel | Kathryn Chesley | Randy Konkel | William Moser | Reno Morris | Dennis O'Hara | Glenn Moore | Charles W Doolin | Susan Lovett | Susan L Bishop | Ernest Joseph Janecka | James Wintle | Peter McNabb | Rosa Gordon | Ken Gordon | Edwin Darrell | James Wesley Russell Sr. | John Harkey | Liz Minyard

2010 Judy K. Johnson | Alvin Creighton Gary | Barbara Rust Powers | Thomas E. Cooper | Bart Brion | Judge Cheryl Williams | Stephen Shore | Elaine Miller | Dale Grantham | Stephen Carpenter | Scott Rohrman | Bill Thompson | Ralph Courtney Jr. | Grace Davidson | John E. Thompson Jr. | Mary Kate Akkola | Harry O. Sivess | George H. Tarpley | Stephen Andre Houser | Mark E. Wood | Leldon Echols

2011 Ronald Davis | Barry Dana-Bashian | John Dougherty | John Stone | Ramsay Ellis | Robert Phillips | John Copley | John Wilhite | Cecelia Stevens | Robert Higginbotham | John Slaughter | Harry Yankuner | David Ragsdale | Ken Fulk | Howard James | Samuel Tates | Joe Griffis | Diana Griffis | Jose Garcia | Christopher Wilt | David Ketchum | Rex Tillerson

2012 Rita Anderson | Allen Avery | Michael K. Black | Naomi Ann Boudreaux | Earl Keith Brown Jr. | Max Carrier | Debra Copley | Jay Dalehite | James Greenwood Jr. | William P. Hemenway II | Chuck Holden | Dr. Michael Holub | James M. Johnston | Ernie E. Koestner | Alan R. Larsen | Douglas Keith Latimer | Kevin Lovett Sr. | Leigh Anne LeBlanc | Homer Phelps | R. Gray Powers | David C. Scott | David Wade Stevens

SILVER BUFFALO RECIPIENTS

George W. Truett 1940
Frank W. Wozencraft 1943
John D. Murchison 1978

William P. Clements Jr. 1980
R. Dan Matkin 1993
R. Richard Rubottom 1993

Herbert T. Olson Jr. 1998
Daniel Zaccara 2008
Jack D. Furst 2010

Rex Tillerson 2010
Matt M. Walker 2012
Randall Stephenson 2012

SILVER FAWN RECIPIENTS

Mary Crawford 1971
Juanita Darnell 1971
Jane Eckstein 1971
Mary Virginia Egan 1971

Altha Pond 1971
Carolyn Sutton 1971
Ruth Wilson 1971
Emily L. Bird 1972

Mrs. Ralph Courteney 1972
Estella Doty 1972
Marge Griffin 1972
Mary E. McDermott 1972

Ruth Potter 1972

DISTINGUISHED EAGLE SCOUT AWARD RECIPIENTS

William P. Clements Jr. 1969
H. Ross Perot 1970
Darrell F. Manley 1971
John P. "Jack" Harbin 1972
Boone Powell Sr. 1974

Robert F. Richie 1975
N. Alex Bickley 1984
Thomas A. O'Dwyer 1985
Douglas D. Hawthorne 1995
William C. "Billy" Gamble 1997

James E. Sowell 1998
Ray H. Marr 1998
John Stuart III 2002
Tom Hicks 2009
Jack D. Furst 2009

Rex Tillerson 2010
Trevor Rees-Jones 2012

HEROISM AWARD RECIPIENTS

John M. "Don" Clardy Jr. *Gold* 1926
Paul J. Mertens *Heroism Award Certificate* 1929
J. W. Lindblom Jr. *Heroism Award Certificate* 1931
Leo McDaniel *Heroism Award Certificate* 1931
Nathan White Sr. *Letter of Commendation fron Dan Beard* 1931
Charles Clark *Letter* 1934
Bernard Wentworth *Gold* 1934
Peter Leadholm *Heroism Award Certificate* 1955
Bobby Webster *Heroism Award Certificate* 1955
Jimmy Marshall *Certificate of Merit* 1957
Bill Owen Jr. *Certificate of Merit* 1960
Randel Sergi *Certificate of Merit* 1960
Peter Carpou *Heroism Award Certificate* 1962
James Estil Wood *Certificate of Merit* 1963
Robert Wayne Williams *Certificate of Merit* 1964
Cedric Britt *Certificate of Merit* 1965
Robert M. Spence Jr. *Honor Medal* 1969
Dan D. Parker *Medal of Merit* 1971
Bernard Roth Jr. *Heroism Award Certificate* 1971
Rodney Van Stewart *Heroism Award Certificate* 1976
William A. Bonds *Medal of Merit* 1977
Courtenay Mathey II *Medal of Merit* 1977
Wilie N. Ross *Medal of Merit* 1977
Heath Alan Williams *Heroism Award Certificate* 1977
William Allen Grasse *Heroism Award Certificate* 1979
Preston R. Knight *Medal of Merit* 1980
Justin Boone *Medal of Merit* 1983
Jack Brixey *Medal of Merit* 1983
Justin Beights *Heroism Award Certificate* 1984
John Russell Holloway *Heroism Award Certificate* 1984
Neal Shea *Heroism Award Certificate* 1984
Phillip Haberman *Heroism Award Certificate* 1985
Bill Alsup *Medal of Merit* 1987
David Pat Ebner Jr. *Honor Medal* 1987
Seth Alan Heidman *Honor Medal* 1987
Phillip Anderson *Heroism Award* 1992
Corey Howard *Marr Honor Medal* w/Crossed Palms 1993
David Aaron *Goode Heroism Award* 1994
Richard W. Hamill *Honor Medal* w/Crossed Palms 1994
Brandon Brake *Heroism Award* 1995

Randall Lee Crane Jr. *Heroism Award* 1995
Israel Freeland *Certificate of Merit* 1995
Gregory or Clifford Hammond *Honor Medal* w/Crossed Palms 1995
Jacob Todd Hight *Certificate of Merit* 1995
Monica Kriechbaum *Certificate of Merit* 1995
James Logue *Medal of Merit* 1995
Justin Penney *Certificate of Merit* 1995
Curtis W. Brancheau *Heroism Award* 1996
Victor McConnell *Heroism Award* 1996
Steven Sparks Jr. *Heroism Award* 1996
Clark Allen *Medal of Merit* 1997
Joshua C. Allen *Medal of Merit* 1997
Ben McCaleb *Medal of Merit* 1997
Bradley Michael Burt *Heroism Award* 1998
Derek Lee B. Homolka *Heroism Award* 1998
Joshua S. Smith *Honor Medal* w/Crossed Palms 1998
Tommy Stallings *Heroism Award* 1998
Todd Wagner Bentley *Medal of Merit* 1999
Mark Munoz DeLaCruz *Medal of Merit* 1999
Tim A. Billingham *Heroism Award* 2000
Scott Moore *Honor Medal* 2000
William Moore *Heroism Award* 2000
Jeffrey Robinson *Medal of Merit* 2000
Michael Heatley *Medal of Merit* 2001
Jonathan S. Kelley *Heroism Award* 2001
Michael Schmidt *Heroism Award* 2001
Jordan Stubbs *Certificate of Merit* 2001
Melvin Hall III *Honor Medal* w/Crossed Palms 2002
Joshua Jordan *Medal of Merit* 2002
Matthew James Mullaney *Medal of Merit* 2002
Michael Soler *Heroism Award* 2002
Adam Webb *Certificate of Merit* 2002
Alex Mears *Medal of Merit* 2003
C. L. Tanner Mendel *Medal of Merit* 2003
Stephen Staebell *Heroism Award* 2003
Matthew Standley *Certificate of Merit* 2003
Nick Copeland *Heroism Award* 2004
Joseph Matthew Croll *Medal of Merit* 2004
Sam Roberts *Certificate of Merit* 2004
Kris Carroll *Medal of Merit* 2005

Westn L. Childs *Heroism Award* 2005
Sean Gresham *Certificate of Merit* 2005
Brian P. McWilliams *Medal of Merit* 2005
Emanuel Meloul *Heroism Award* 2005
James Griffin *Heroism Award* 2005
Cameron R. Broussard *Heroism Award* 2006
Tate Chanler *Heroism Award* 2006
Aaron D. Chapman *Certificate of Merit* 2006
John Douglas Harrell *Honor Medal* w/Crossed Palms 2006
Phillip R. Whitaker III *Heroism Award* 2006
Brendin Hart *Medal of Merit* 2007
Greig Latham *Certificate of Merit* 2008
Joshua Longley *Heroism Award* 2008
Jessica Carson *Certificate of Merit* 2008
Justin Carson *Certificate of Merit* 2008
Blake Fisher *Certificate of Merit* 2008
Kenneth Hughes *Certificate of Merit* 2008
Logan Latham *Certificate of Merit* 2008
Jeffrey Bell *Certificate of Merit* 2009
Chris Rogers *Certificate of Merit* 2009

Joshua Raynes *Certificate of Merit* 2009
Grayson James *Heroism Award* 2010
Dillon Kennedy *Certificate of Merit* 2010
Jimmy Wolfson *Certificate of Merit* 2010
David Lambeth *Certificate of Merit* 2010
Hunter Lambeth *Certificate of Merit* 2010
Jacob Wizeman *Heroism Award* 2010
Forest Hallstrom *Medal of Merit* 2011
Drake Robinson *Heroism Award* 2011
Christopher Morgan *Certificate of Merit* 2010
Dennis Denson Jr. *Heroism Award* 2011
Carter Fiffick *Heroism Award* 2011
Baylor Fain *Heroism Award* 2011
Noah Satele *Heroism Award* 2011
Tristan Vowell *Heroism Award* 2011
Rafe Sinclair *Certificate of Merit* 2011
Seth Riddle *Certificate of Merit* 2012
Grieg Riddle *Certificate of Merit* 2012
Steve Bohn *Medal of Merit* 2012

WHITNEY M. YOUNG AWARD RECIPIENTS

Alma Hawthorne 1979
Michael Alexander 1980
Hazel Partee 1983
U. S. Hammond 1984
Marguerite Foster 1985
Dr. Frank H. Jordan 1986
Louis Smith 1986
Dr. Roscoe C. Smith 1987
Patricia Pickles 1987
Dr. Yondell E. Moore 1987
Ted McIntosh 1987
Dietrich Whisennand 1987
Mildred Daniels 1990
Rochester Hooper 1990
Dorothy Hooper 1990
Rev. John L. McCaulie 1990
Roy Adams 1991
Marilyn Calhoun 1991
Toice Davis 1991
Clarence Hollie 1991
John F. Lubbin III 1991
Paul S. Thomas 1991
Dr. Caesar A. W. Clark 1992
Albert Lipscomb 1992
Rev. Zan Holmes 1993

Annie Smith 1993
Claude Watson 1993
Edward Joe Bagsby 1994
Dr. Norman E. Dyer 1994
Donald W. Hills Sr. 1994
Dr. Mannie McKnight 1995
Judge Charles Rose 1995
Taylor D. August 1995
Clarence W. "Tom" Bohanan 1996
Ben R. Click 1996
Jimmy King 1996
Mayor Ron Kirk 1996
Dr. Raymond Reed 1996
Don Serna 1997
Robert Ward 1997
Hattan W. Sumner Foundation 1997
Victor Burke 1998
Richard Knight Jr. 1998
Steve Polansky 1998
William Blair 2000
Terrell Bolton 2000
Dr. Franklin Jennifer 2000
Levi Davis 2001
Dr. Theodore Lee 2001

State Sen. Royce West 2001
Reginald Gates 2002
Willis Johnson 2002
Dr. Delores Seamster 2002
Dr. Frederick Todd 2002
John Stuart III 2003
Texas Instruments Foundation 2003
Vernon Mulin 2003
Comer Cottrell 2003
Ruben Esquivel 2003
Dr. David Barbosa 2004
Thomas B. Lipscomb 2004
Ron Martin 2004
Jethro Pugh 2004
Wells Fargo Bank 2005
Dr. Craig Thomas 2005
Trinidad Munoz 2005
James Fry 2005
David W. Biegler 2005
DART 2006
Judge Dianne K. Jones 2006
James Sweat 2006
Officer Eric Conde 2006
Don Lindsey 2006
TXU 2007

Bobby B. Lyle 2007
Richard Franco 2007
Johnny F. Stevens 2007
Theodore "Ted" Wallace 2007
Martin Burrell 2008
Barbara and Johnny Ives 2008
James "Jim" Sanders 2008
Bruce Khanhkham 2008
Gene and Jerry Jones Family Charities 2009
Frank Beverly 2009
Santiago Jimenez 2009
Michael Ross 2009
Edna Pemberton 2009
ExxonMobil Foundation 2010
Jerome Garza 2010
Odis V. Luper III 2010
Dr. John Ellis Price 2010
Cecelia Stevens 2010
H. Ross Perot Sr. 2011
Ron Davis 2011
Connie Deckard 2011
Mauricio Mazurra 2011

appendix b
CIRCLE TEN LEADERSHIP

COUNCIL CHIEF EXECUTIVES

SCOUT COMMISSIONERS

Claude Marion Richmond	January 14, 1913–February 3, 1915
James Arthur Glidewell	February 20, 1915–October 6, 1915
George Wesley Keeley (Interim)	October 6, 1915–August 13, 1916

SCOUT EXECUTIVE

Robert Chester McDowell	August 14, 1916–April 2, 1918
Walter Sanders Lee	April 4, 1918–December 7, 1918
Harrison Holman McGill (Interim)	December 7, 1918–January 7, 1919
Walter Scott Barcus	January 8, 1919–bet Sep 20 - Oct 28, 1921
Hubert E. Ratliff	bet Sep 20 - Oct 29, 1921–November 1, 1922
Jack R. Berry (Interim)	November 2, 1922–February 26, 1923
Clinton B. Harris (Interim)	February 27, 1923–March 25, 1923
Jack R. Berry (Interim)	March 25, 1923–May 16, 1923
Howard Winfrey Wester	May 17, 1923–bet Sep 19 -Sep 23, 1925
Oscar "Otto" Avery Kitterman	bet 9/20 - 9/24/1925–May 3, 1930
Orton Lorraine Duggan	July 9, 1930–September 1, 1936
Loys Leon Hotchkiss	October 22, 1936–March 11, 1960
Charles F. Grable	April 27, 1960–August 3, 1964
James L. Tarr	August 4, 1964–March 27, 1979
William C. "Billy" Gamble	March 27, 1979–September 30, 2001
Glenn E. "Gene" Stone	October 1, 2001–August 23, 2005
Don Burke (Interim)	August 24, 2005–October 31, 2005
Ponce Duran Jr.	November 1, 2005–December 31, 2009
Pat Currie	January 1, 2010–current

CIRCLE TEN COUNCIL PRESIDENTS

Joseph Eastman Farnsworth	January 14, 1913–November 22, 1914	Robert Lee Thornton Jr.	January 1, 1966–December 31, 1967
Judge Quentin D. Corley	November 22, 1914–October 6, 1915	William Perry Clements Jr.	January 1, 1968–December 31, 1969
Otto Henry Lang	October 6, 1915–December 31, 1917	Darrell F. Manley	January 1, 1970–December 31, 1971
Elias Louis "Eli" Sanger	January 1, 1918–December 31, 1919	William McCord	January 1, 1972–December 31, 1973
Major Leigh Hill French	January 1, 1920–August 16, 1920	Omar Harvey	January 1, 1974–December 31, 1975
Charles Louis Sanger	August 18, 1920–December 31, 1921	John J. Casey	January 1, 1976–December 31, 1977
Walter Elliott Kingsbury	January 1, 1922–December 31, 1922	John F. Stephens	January 1, 1978–December 31, 1978
Frank Wilson Wozencraft	January 1, 1923–December 31, 1926	Thomas A. O'Dwyer	January 1, 1979–December 31, 1980
Harry Elmer Hobson	January 1, 1927–December 31, 1927	Louis A. Beecherl Jr.	January 1, 1981–December 31, 1981
George Robinson Angell Sr.	January 1, 1928–December 31, 1928	Jerry S. Ferrington	January 1, 1982–December 31, 1983
Franklin Pierce Holland Jr.	January 1, 1929–December 31, 1930	W. Herbert Hunt	January 1, 1984–December 31, 1986
Fred Farel Florence	January 1, 1931–December 31, 1932	Richard M. Hart	January 1, 1987–December 31, 1988
Leslie Burke Denning Sr.	January 1, 1933–December 31, 1939	Ron J. Krause	January 1, 1989–December 31, 1990
Milton Brown	January 1, 1940–December 31, 1945	Douglas D. Hawthorne	January 1, 1991–December 31, 1992
Dechard Anderson Hulcy	January 1, 1946–December 31, 1948	James E. Osterreicher	January 1, 1993–December 31, 1994
Felix R. McKnight	January 1, 1949–December 31, 1949	E. R. Brooks	January 1, 1995–December 31, 1996
Austin F. Allen	January 1, 1950–December 31, 1952	James E. "Jim" Sowell	January 1, 1997–December 31, 1998
John E. Mitchell Jr.	January 1, 1953–December 31, 1953	Bobby B. Lyle	January 1, 1999–December 31, 2001
Angus Gilchrist Wynne Jr.	January 1, 1954–December 31, 1955	David W. Biegler	January 1, 2002–December 31, 2003
Carl J. Rutland	January 1, 1956–December 31, 1958	John Stuart III	January 1, 2004–December 31, 2005
Gus Bowman	January 1, 1959–December 31, 1960	Jack D. Furst	January 1, 2006–December 31, 2007
Charles E. Beard	January 1, 1961–December 31, 1961	Thomas L. Baker	January 1, 2008–December 31, 2009
C. A. Tatum Jr.	January 1, 1962–December 31, 1963	Sherwood Blount Jr.	January 1, 2010–December 31, 2011
Lester T. Potter	January 1, 1964–December 31, 1965	Ernest J. "Ernie" Carey	January 1, 2012–current

CIRCLE TEN HEADQUARTERS

(John B.) Wilson Building 818 1623 Main Street at S. Ervay Street January 14, 1913–bef. July 16, 1914
624 by July 16, 1914–January 3, 1915

Dallas Terminal Railway & Union Depot (Greyhound Bus Terminal) 7 808 Commerce Street at S. Lamar Street January 4, 1915–bef January 15, 1916

Chamber of Commerce Building 1101 Commerce Street at N. Griffin Street by January 15, 1916–August 22, 1916 torn down

Single Office Address (former Beeman Shoe Co. offices) 1214 Main Street between N. Griffin and N. Field Streets August 23, 1916–December 21, 1916 torn down

Rock Island Railway Freight Office 1312 1/2 Commerce Street at Field Street December 22, 1916–April 2, 1918 torn down

Busch (Kirby) Building 1213 1501 Main Street at N. Akard Street April 4, 1918–December 7, 1918

Multi-Suite Office Building 108 1/2 Field Street at Main Street by January 15, 1919–bef. January 15, 1921 torn down

Multi-Suite Office Building 1931 1/2 Main Street at N. Harwood Street by January 15, 1921–bef October 31, 1921 torn down

Dallas County State Bank Building 522 1700 Main Street at Lamar Street (SW corner) by October 31, 1921–aft. Sept 5, 1922 torn down

Chamber of Commerce Building 1101 Commerce Street at N. Griffin Street bet. Sept 6, 1922 and Dec. 31, 1922–bef. January 15, 1923 torn down

Board of Education Administration Building S. Akard Street at Royal Street in NW corner by January 15, 1923–bef. July 31, 1925 torn down

Dallas City Hall 107 106 S. Harwood Street between Main and Commerce Streets by July 31, 1925–bef Aug 8, 1925
406 aft. Aug 8, 1925–bef. July 31, 1926

Linz (Brothers) Building 224 1608 Main Street at Lane Street by July 31, 1926–bef. July 31, 1927 torn down
603 by July 31, 1927–bef. July 31, 1928
403 by July 31, 1928–bef. May 14, 1930

Santa Fe (Railway) Building 721 1122 Jackson Street at N. Griffin Street aft May 13, 1930–bef. July 31, 1935

Dallas Gas Company Building 617 1915 Wood Street at S. Harwood Street by July 31, 1935–bef. July 31, 1937
706 by July 31, 1937–bef. Jul 31, 1941

(Mike H.) Thomas Building 100 1314 Wood Street next to Cotton Exchange Bldg. by July 31, 1941–August 11, 1965 torn down

Mitchell-Head Service Center 1922 Anson Road at Harry Hines Bouvelard August 12, 1965–October 5, 1996

John D. Murchison Scouting Center 8605 Harry Hines Boulevard at Regal Row October 6, 1996–current

notes

AM   Arlene Mason (Johnsey) Family Archive (Lewisville, Texas)

APT   Austin Presbyterian Theological Seminary Archive (Austin, Texas)

BEC   Thomas G. Becket Family Archive (Sunnyvale, Texas)

BG   William C. "Billy" Gamble Archive (Plano, Texas)

BSA   National Archive, Boy Scouts of America (Irving, Texas)

BSC   Brad Shine Collection (Garland, Texas)

CG   Calvin Grubbs Collection (Garland, Texas)

CMR   Claude M. Richmond Family Archive (San Antonio, Texas)

CTC   Letter and Document Files, Circle Ten Council Archive (Dallas, Texas)

DCS   David C. Scott Collection (Dallas, Texas)

DHS   Photographic Files, Dallas Historical Society Archive (Dallas, Texas)

DMN   Dallas Morning News Archive (Dallas, Texas)

DPL   Photographic Files, Dallas Public Library Archive (Dallas, Texas)

EBM   Executive Board Meeting Minutes, Circle Ten Council Archive (Dallas, Texas)

ETS   Ernest Thompson Seton Fonds, Canadian National Archive (Ottawa, Canada)

GRI   Joe Griffis Collection (Dallas, Texas)

GS   Gene Smith Collection (Duncanville, Texas)

HIG   Robert "Bobby" Higginbotham Sr. Collection (Dallas, Texas)

HIL   William "Green Bar Bill" Hillcourt Trust (Houston Texas)

HSM   Harbin Scout Museum Archive, Camp Wisdom/Billy Sowell Scout Camp (Duncanville, Texas)

HOL   Charles Holmes Archive (Garland, Texas)

JQT   Jon Q. Thompson Family Archive (Lubbock, Texas)

LC   Photographic Files, Library of Congress (Washington, DC)

MR   Mitch Reis Collection (Windsor, Connecticut)

RM   Ray Marr Archive (Dallas, Texas)

RR   Rick Rembisz Archive (Garland, Texas)

SM   Seton Museum Archive, Philmont Scout Ranch (Cimarron, New Mexico)

SMS   Stephen M. Shore Archive (Annandale-on-Hudson, New York)

SMU   DeGolyer Library, Southern Methodist University Archive (Dallas, Texas)

T70   Troop 70 Archive, University Park Elementary (Dallas, Texas)

TBC   Clarence W. "Tom" Bohanan Jr. Archive (Dallas, Texas)

TPL   Harry S. Truman Presidential Library (Independence, Missouri)

UNT   Portal to Texas History, University of North Texas (Denton, Texas)

INTRODUCTION: THE STORY OF THE CENTURY

1. Dallas Morning News, Mar. 16,1913, p. 11; Frank White Johnson, A History of Texas and Texans (American Historical Society: New York, 1916) vol. 5, p. 2176; Hopkins, C. Howard, History of the YMCA in North America (Association Press: New York, 1951) p. 203. Hopkins notes that although "rescue missions were available for the neglected boy," the YMCA publication The Watchdog argued that it was "more strategic to attempt to reach the lower class of boys by means of the upper class than to try the opposite." This reasoned shift away from troubled urban youth to those of the middle class "was to trouble the YMCA conscience from then on." Hopkins continues: "Many Associations did maintain work for boys from distressed areas and classes, but this received relatively minor emphasis."; Ibid., p. 469

2. According to Leonard Clark, the first "Seton Indian" camp took place for one night during their Easter vacation. Since Easter was on April 14, 1902, the camp probably began on Thursday April 11 or Friday April 12; Ernest Thompson Seton, "The Boy Scouts in America," Outlook Magazine, Aug. 1910, pp. 630–5; Farida A. Wiley, ed., Ernest Thompson Seton's America (New York: Devin-Adair, 1954) pp. 344–54; H. Allen Hugh Anderson, The Chief: Ernest Thompson Seton (College Station: Texas A&M Press, 1986) pp. 106–8; Francis W. Halsey, ed., American Authors and Their Homes (New York: James Potts & Company, 1901) pp. 281–92. Cos Cob was a well-known artists' colony that gave birth to the Cos Cob School. Seton advised Lincoln Steffens that he should not buy in nearby Greenwich because only the very rich lived there and land cost $1,000 per acre. But Cos Cob land was going for no more than $25 per acre. Lincoln Steffens, The Autobiography of Lincoln Steffens (New York: Harcourt, Brace & World, 1958) pp. 436–7, 440.

3. "Indians at Wyndygoul," Greenwich News, Oct. 23, 1903; "Are You a Seton Indian? Whoop!" New York Herald, Oct. 11, 1903; W.W. Storms, "The Woodcraft Indians," Holiday Magazine, Oct. 1904; John Henry Wadland, Ernest Thompson Seton: Man in Nature and the Progressive Era, 1880–1915 (New York: Arno Press, 1978) p. 344; Seton, "The Twelve Secrets of the Woods," Craftsman, Jun. 1916, cited by Wadland, Man in Nature, p. 354

4. Richard Allan Whitmore, Beard, Boys, and Buckskins: Daniel Carter Beard and the Preservation of the American Pioneer Tradition (Northwestern University Press, 1970) pp. 165–166; Ibid., pp. 177–178; Draft of the Constitution of the Sons of Daniel Boone, undated, Beard Papers, LC.

5. Whitmore, Buckskins, pp. 180–181; Arthur Mead to Beard, Feb. 9, 1906. Beard Papers, LC.

6. William Hillcourt, Baden-Powell: The Two Lives of a Hero (New York: Putnam, 1964) p. 244; Piers Brendon, Eminent Edwardians (New York: Houghton Mifflin, 1980) p. 239; Baden-Powell to Seton, Jun. 17, 1907. SM; Draft of contract with C. Arthur Pearson, Ltd., Jul. 30, 1907. BSA; Pearson to Baden-Powell, Oct. 22, 1907. BSA; Hillcourt, Two Lives, pp. 264–265; Dan Lipton, "Where Scouting Began," Scouting, May–June 1983. According to Hillcourt, a Dane by birth, the term "Brownsea Island" is redundant because the final "ea" is old Danish that means island. The name Brownsea is a contraction of either "Brown's Ea" or "Bronk's Ea," possibly referring to an ancient island inhabitant during the reign of Edward the Confessor named Bruno, who was the Lord of the Manor of Studland and the owner of the island at the time.

7. Baden-Powell Diary, Dec. 26, 1908. BSA; Baden-Powell to Peter Keary, Dec. 27, 1907. Richards, Paul, ed., The Founding of the Boy Scouts as Seen through the Letters of Lord Baden-Powell, October 1907–October 1908. (East Bridgewater, MA: The Standish Museums and Unitarian Church, 1973); Baden-Powell to Keary, Mar. 1 and Sept. 9, 1908; Richards, Founding of the Boy Scouts; Baden-Powell to Seton, Jul. 9, 1908, SM; Baden-Powell to Frank N. Doubleday, Jul. 31, 1910. SM; Baden-Powell Diary, Sept. 24, 1910. BSA; Baden-Powell to Seton, Sept. 24, 1910. ETS.

8. In his noteworthy legal career, the Honorable Towne Young would end up as the Judge of the 44th District Court and the firm would have in its offices one of Dallas' first and most distinguished 1914 Eagle Scouts, future U.S. Supreme Court Associate Justice Tom C. Clark.

9. DMN, Aug. 27, 1910, p. 7; John L. Alexander to Towne Young, Sept. 8, 1910, CG. The new YMCA Building (formerly at 416 – 418 Jackson Street running north-south alongside the Trinity River before it was moved), whose address was changed to 1910 Commerce Street in 1911, stood just a few steps down from Dallas' Carnegie Library built in 1896, currently a historic city block that holds the now-abandoned structures of the Dallas' Old Central Library and the 800-room Statler-Hilton. The Statler-Hilton Hotel is also remembered as being the place from which entertainer Tina Turner left her abusive husband, Ike, in 1976 before their concert. After Ike had gone to bed, Tina snuck down the back staircase with only "a Mobil credit card and thirty-six cents" to her name. "Ike and Tina in Dallas," DMN, Dec. 13, 2007.

PART I: FOUNDING THE VISION

1. "A Word to Parents" Dallas Council, BSA, DMN, Apr. 27, 1913, pt. 1, p. 13.

CHAPTER 1: BUILDING BRIDGES (1910–1913)

1. DMN, Oct. 5, 1910, p. 5; Darwin Payne, Dallas: An Illustrated History (Woodland Hills, CA: Windson Pubs, 1982) pp. 12–31.

2. Ruth Miller Fitzgibbons, "Dallas' First Families: Old Money Still Survives," D Magazine, Aug. 1982.

3. Doc Holliday had been in partnership with fellow dentist J. A. Seegar, but that relationship dissolved in 1874. Seegar worked out of his office on Elm Street above Cochrane's Drug Store, while Holliday's office was on the second floor of the Dallas County Bank at the corner of Main and Lamar Streets. Dallas Daily Commercial, Mar. 2, 1874. Holliday would eventually make his way to Tombstone, Arizona, join forces with Wyatt Earp and his brothers, and gain fame at the legendary Shootout at the OK Corral against Ike Clanton and his gang of lawbreaking hooligans. Karen Holliday Tanner, Doc Holliday: A Family Portrait (Norman, Oklahoma: University of Oklahoma Press, 2001) p. 91.

4. DMN, Oct. 5, 1910, p. 5; DMN, Nov. 2, 1910, p. 4; Elizabeth York Enstam, When Dallas Became a City (Dallas: Dallas Historical Society, 1982); DMN, Nov. 9, 1910, p. 6; DMN, Sept. 3, 1911, p. 28; DMN, May 11, 1913, p. 8; DMN, Jul. 6, 1913, p. 7.

5. Ibid.

6. DMN, Nov. 5, 1910, p.16; DMN, Nov. 10, 1910, p. 7; DMN, Nov. 25, 1910, p. 16; DMN, Nov. 11, 1913, p. 2.

7. DMN, Nov. 11, 1910, p. 16; DMN, Nov. 25, 1910, p. 16; DMN, Dec. 7, 1910, p. 15.

8. DMN, Jan. 18, 1911, p. 14; DMN, Jan. 21, 1911, p. 3; DMN, Jan. 22, 1911, p. 8; DMN, Feb. 11, 1913, p. 11.

9. DMN, Feb. 3, 1911, p. 4; DMN, Feb. 19, 1911, p. 22; DMN, Apr. 15, 1911, p. 5.

10. DMN, Nov. 10, 1911, p. 4; DMN, Nov. 15, 1911, p. 5; DMN, Nov. 16, 1911, p. 5; DMN, Aug. 15, 1912, p. 6; DMN, Jan. 11, 1913, p. 8.

11. DMN, Jan. 11, 1913, p. 8; DMN, Jan. 15, 1913, p. 4; DMN, Feb. 15, 1913, p. 15; DMN, Feb. 20, 1913, p. 4; DMN, Feb. 22, 1913, p. 4.

12. DMN, Dec. 19, 1912, p. 4; DMN, Dec. 22, 1912, p. 3; DMN, Feb. 23, 1913, p. 9; DMN, Feb. 25, 1913, p. 4; DMN, Mar. 2, 1913, p. 10; DMN, Mar. 20, 1913, p. 4.

13. This is the current location of Two AT&T Plaza.

14. This is the present location of the Bank of America Plaza; DMN, May 17, 1914, p. 4.

15. DMN, Mar. 2, 1913, p. 10; DMN, Mar. 5, 1913, p. 4; DMN, Mar. 19, 1913, p. 4; DMN, Mar. 30 1913, p. 3; DMN, Feb. 25, 1922, pt. 1, p 4.

16. www.HellaShriners.org; DMN, Mar. 15, 1913, p. 18; www. GilchristCompany.com.

17. DMN, Mar. 19, 1913, p. 4; DMN, Mar. 29, 1913, p. 4; DMN, Apr. 9, 1913, p. 4; DMN, May 9, 1913, p. 3; DMN, May 10, 1913, p. 6; DMN, May 16, 1913, p. 4; Boys' Life, Aug. 1913, p. 25.

18. DMN, Apr. 17, 1913, p. 4; DMN, May 13, 1913, p. 6; DMN, May 14, 1913, p. 8; DMN, Mar. 22, 1914, p. 10; DMN, Jun. 21, 1913, p. 5; DMN, Jul. 6, 1913, p. 1; Boys' Life, May 1914, p. 29 .

19. DMN, Jul. 8 1913, p. 18; DMN, Aug. 1, 1913, p. 4; DMN, Sep. 25, 1913, p. 3.

20. DMN, Jun. 22, 1913, p. 5; DMN, Aug. 20, 1913, p. 4; DMN, Aug. 22, 1913, p. 4; DMN, Sept. 9, 1913, p. 16; DMN, Oct. 8, 1913, p. 16; DMN, Oct. 26, 1913, pt. 4, p. 4.

21. DMN, Sept. 12, 1913, p. 4; DMN, Sept. 24, 1913, p. 16; DMN, Oct. 10, 1913, p. 16; DMN, Oct. 12, 1913, p. 5; 1914 Charter Renewal, CTC.

22. DMN, Nov. 8, 1913, p. 12; DMN, Jan. 11, 1914, pt. 4, p. 6; Boy Scouts of America, Scoutmaster's Handbook (New York: Boy Scouts of America, 1913-1914) pp. 59–60; DMN, Mar. 6, 1914, p. 18.

A. Payne, Dallas, pp. 12–31; Boys' Life, Jan. 1915, p. 21.

B. DMN, Nov. 9, 1910, p. 6.

C. Jim Guildart, Interview, Jun. 27, 2012; Texas Certificate of Death #13387; Texas Death Certificate #16162.

D. DMN, Jan 18, 1911; DMN, Jan 21, 1911; DMN, Jan 22, 1911, p. 8; DMN, Feb 11, 1913, p. 11; DMN, Feb 19, 1911, p. 22.

E. DMN, Aug. 26, 1911, p. 14; DMN, Aug. 27, 1911, p. 40.

F. George M. Haas, Daddy Wisdom: Scouting Benefactor (Dallas, Texas: Cockrell & Son, 1937) p. 26; DMN, Apr. 25, 1913; DMN, May 10, 1913; DMN, Nov. 10, 1913; DMN, May 31, 1916, p. 5; "History of Troop One," Troop One Signal Newsletter, Nov. 2, 1928, vol. 1, No. 3, p. 1, HSM; DMN, May 19, 1923, pt. 2, p. 18.

G. DMN, Apr. 12, 1913, p.

H. Ted Dealey, Diaper Days of Dallas (Nashville, TN: Abingdon Press, 1966); DMN, Mar. 20, 1913, p. 4; DMN, Apr. 4, 1913, p. 4; DMN, Apr. 13, 1913, p. 8; DMN, Apr. 16, 1913, p. 4; DMN, Apr. 23, 1913, p. 4; DMN, Apr. 29, 1913, p. 16; DMN, May 18, 1913, p. 7; DMN, May 20, 1913, p. 4; DMN, May 29, 1913, p. 4; DMN, Jun. 1, 1913, pp. 8, 10; DMN, Jun. 9, 1913, p. 18; DMN, Jun. 11, 1913, p. 4; DMN, Jun. 14, 1913, p. 4; DMN, Jun. 21, 1913, p. 4; DMN, Jun. 29, 1913, pp. 10, 14.

I. DMN, Jul. 14, 1913, p. 16; DMN, Jul. 26, 1913, p. 5.

J. DMN, Jul. 14, 1913, p. 16; DMN, Jul. 20, 1913, p. 7; DMN, Aug. 11, 1913, p. 14; DMN, Dec. 9, 1925, p. 8; DMN, Jun. 1, 1939, p. 8; DMN, Feb. 11, 1940, p. 13; DMN, Feb. 11, 1945, p. 10; Cody Stevenson, email, May 27, 2012.

K. DMN, Apr. 6, 1913, pt. 4, p. 16; DMN, Apr. 7, 1913, p. 14; DMN, Jun. 22, 1913, p. 5; DMN, Aug. 22, 1913, p. 4; DMN, Sept. 11, 1913, p. 4; DMN, Oct. 12, 1913, p. 9; DMN, Oct. 26, 1913, pt. 4, p. 4.

CHAPTER 2: COMMISSIONER RICHMOND STAKES THE CLAIM (1914)

1. Membership Numbers, BSA; DMN, Jan. 12, 1914, p. 3.

2. DMN, Mar. 10, 1914, p. 6; DMN, Mar. 18, 1914, p. 6; DMN, Mar. 20, 1914, p. 8; DMN, Mar. 31, 1914, p. 8; Boy Scouts of America, Handbook for Boys (New York: Boy Scouts of America, 1914) pp. 30–31.

3. DMN, Jan. 12, 1914, p. 3; DMN, Feb. 20, 1914, p. 18; DMN, Apr. 1, 1914, p. 20; DMN, Apr. 28, 1914, p. 4; DMN, May 8, 1914,

p. 4; DMN, May 20, 1914, p. 9; DMN, May 24, 1914, pt. 1, p. 4; Boys' Life, Jul. 1914, p. 19, 22; Boys' Life, Nov. 1914, p. 22.

4. DMN, Jan. 21, 1914, p. 4; DMN, Mar. 9, 1914, p. 5; DMN, Mar. 14, 1914, p. 6; DMN, Mar. 15, 1914, pt. 1, p. 8; DMN, Mar. 18, 1914, p. 6; DMN, Apr. 9, 2011, p.

1914 Charter Renewal, CTC; John Neal Phillips, Running with Bonnie and Clyde (Norman, Oklahoma; University of Oklahoma Press, 1996) p. 44.

5. DMN, Mar. 21, 1914, pt. 3, p. 5.

6. DMN, Sept. 21, 1914, p. 14; DMN, Sept. 22, 1914, p. 16; DMN, Sept. 24, 1914, p.14; DMN, Nov. 22, 1914, pt. 1, p. 4.

7. DMN, Sept. 27, 1914, pt. 4, p. 4; DMN, Dec. 9, 1914, p. 9; DMN, Dec. 11, 1914, p. 15; DMN, Dec. 12, 1914, p. 9.

8. DMN, Jan. 3, 1915, pt. 2, p. 12; DMN, Jan. 20, 1915, p. 4; DMN, Jan. 24, 1915, pt. 4, p. 6; DMN, Feb. 13, 1915, p. 4; DMN, Feb. 21, 1915, pt. 1, p. 4.

A. DMN, Sep. 14, 1913, p. 6; DMN, Sep. 25, 1913, p. 13; DMN, May 24, 1914, pt. 1, p. 4.

B. DMN, Mar. 27, 1913, p. 4; DMN, May 18, 1913, p. 7; DMN, May 28, 1913, p. 13; DMN, Jul. 16, 1913, p. 4; DMN, Aug. 3, 1913, p. 1.

C. DMN, May 30, 1915, pt. 4, p. 7.

D. DMN, Jul. 23, 1914, p. 9; DMN, Jul. 28, 1914, p. 4; DMN, Aug. 15, 1914, p. 16; DMN, Aug. 18, 1914, p. 4; DMN, Aug. 20, 1914, p. 16; DMN, Aug. 27, 1914, p. 16; DMN, Oct. 21, 1914, p. 6; DMN, May 10, 1916, p. 11; DMN, Jan. 21, 1917, pt. 5, p. 10; DMN, Jan. 24, 1917, p. 5.

CHAPTER 3: SCOUTS TO THE RESCUE (1915–1918)

1. Feb. 21, 1915 pt. 1, p. 4; Jun. 26, 1915, p. 4; DMN, May 19, 1916, p. 6; Jim Wheat's Dallas County Texas Archives, http://freepages. history.rootsweb.ancestry.com/~jwheat/#anchor2033590.

2. DMN, Feb. 21, 1915, pt. 1, p. 4; DMN, Mar. 28, 1915, pt. 1, p. 8; DMN, Apr. 9, 1915, p. 15; DMN, May 26, 1915, p. 6; DMN, May 27, 1915, p. 7; DMN, Jun. 9, 1915, p. 6; DMN, Jun. 20, 1915, pt. 4, p. 7.

3. DMN, Jul. 10, 1915, p. 11; DMN, Jul. 31, 1915, p. 16; DMN, Apr. 18, 1916, p. 8; DMN, May 11, 1916, p. 7; DMN, May 19, 1916, p. 4.

4. DMN, Jul. 23, 1915, p. 6; DMN, Jul. 31, 1915, p. 16; DMN, Apr. 15, 1916, p. 6.

5. DMN, Apr. 15, 1915, p. 6; DMN, Oct. 5, 1915, p. 7; DMN, Oct. 7, 1915, p. 4; DMN, Oct. 27 1916, p. 16.

6. DMN, Apr. 15, 1916, p. 6; DMN, May 4, 1916, p. 6; DMN, Apr. 18, 1917, p. 8.

7. DMN, May 14, 1916, pt. 3, p. 3; DMN, May 16, 1916, p. 8; DMN, May 17, 1916, p. 18; DMN, May 20, 1916, p. 9; DMN, Jun. 17, 1916, p. 13.

8. DMN, Nov. 19, 1915, p. 4; DMN, May 31, 1916, p. 5; DMN, Jul. 2, 1916, pt. 4, p. 2; DMN, Jul. 14, 1916, p. 5, 9; DMN, Jul. 16, 1916, pt. 4, p.14; DMN, Aug. 19, 1916, p. 4.

9. DMN, Jul. 22, 1916, p. 6; DMN, Jul. 25, 1916, p. 6; DMN, Jul. 30, 1916, pt. 1, p. 7; DMN, Aug. 25, 1916, p. 13.

10. In early April 1918, Frank P. Margolin was promoted by his employer, the Selig (auditing) Company, to the position of assistant to the president in Atlanta, Georgia. Upon moving, Troop 1's Drum and Bugle Corps was disbanded. It was re-started again on July 29, 1920, consisting of 40 pieces under the direction of Gaddis Taylor, a former drum major in the Texas Infantry Band on Texas-Mexico border service from 1916–1917, DMN, Apr. 14, 1918, p. 2; DMN, Jul. 30, 1920, p. 6.

11. DMN, Aug. 15, 1916, p.11; DMN, Aug. 16, 1916, p. 4; DMN, Aug. 19, 1916, p. 4; DMN, Aug. 21, 1916, p. 10; DMN, Aug. 24, 1916, p. 3;DMN, Sept. 10, 1916, p. 4.

12. DMN, Sept. 20, 1916, p. 16; DMN, Oct. 1, 1916, pt. 1, p. 10.

13. DMN, Dec. 24, 1916, pt. 1, p. 7; DMN, Dec. 31, 1916, pt. 1, p. 8; DMN, Jan. 2, 1917, p. 15.

14. DMN, Mar. 5, 1917, p. 6; DMN, May 13, 1917, pt. 4, p. 7; DMN, Jul. 13, 1917, p. 13.

15. DMN, May 27, 1917, pt. 4, p. 3; DMN, May 27, 1917, pt. 3, p. 3; DMN, Jun. 3, 1917, pt. 7, p. 12.

16. DMN, Jun. 5, 1917, p. 6; DMN, Jun. 6, 1917, p. 14; DMN, Jun. 11, 1917, p. 12; DMN, Jun. 12, 1917, p. 7.

17. DMN, Jun. 15, 1917, p. 15; DMN, Jun. 16, 1917, p. 13; DMN, Jun. 17, 1917, pt. 3, p. 2; DMN, Jun. 20, 1917, p. 10; DMN, Aug. 26, 1917, pt. 4, p. 12.

18. DMN, Oct. 2, 1917, p. 6; DMN, Oct. 26, 1917, p. 6.

19. DMN, Oct. 26, 1917, p. 6; DMN, Oct. 27, 1917, p. 8; DMN, Oct. 28, 1917, pt. 1, p. 7; DMN, Dec. 29, 1917, p. 7.

20. DMN, Feb. 10, 1918, pt. 4, p. 4; DMN, Feb. 13, 1918, p. 4; DMN, Feb. 21, 1918, p. 7; DMN, Feb. 27, 1918, p. 16.

21. DMN, Mar. 12, 1918, p. 7; DMN, Mar. 13, 1918, p. 9; DMN, Mar. 19, 1918, p. 6; DMN, Mar. 25, 1918, p. 12.

22. DMN, Apr. 3, 1918, p. 13; DMN, Apr. 5, 1918, p. 7.

A. Margery Ruth Glidewell, "Research Notes on James Arthur Glidewell," unpublished ms; DMN, Jun. 30, 1914, p. 7; DMN, Oct. 6, 1914, p. 9; DMN, Dec. 15, 1920, p. 15; Margery Ruth Glidewell, email, Nov. 6, 2011.

B. DMN, Sept. 20, 1916, p. 16; DMN, Oct. 1, 1916, pt. 1, p. 10.

C. DMN, Feb. 9, 1917, p. 5; DMN, Feb. 13, 1917, p. 8.

D. DMN, Jan. 31, 1917, p. 4.

E. DMN, Mar. 21, 1917, p. 19.

CHAPTER 4: EXPANDING MEMBERSHIP AFTER ADVERSITY (1918–1920)

1. DMN, Dec. 8, 1918, pt. 2, p. 12.

2. DMN, Apr. 13, 1918, p. 15; DMN, Apr. 17, 1918, p. 14.

3. DMN, May 5, 1918, pt. 1, p. 10; DMN, May 16, 1918, p. 9; DMN, Jul. 1, 1918, p. 3; DMN, Jul. 10, 1918, p. 4.

4. DMN, Jul. 1, 1918, p. 3; DMN, Jul. 10, 1918, p. 4; DMN, Jul. 16, 1918, p. 7; DMN, Jul. 28, 1918, pt. 4, p. 7.

5. DMN, Aug. 1, 1918, p. 9; DMN, Aug. 21, 1918, p. 5; DMN, Sept. 3, 1918, p. 4; DMN, Sept. 15, 1918, pt. 4, p. 12; DMN, Sept. 27, 1918, p. 13; DMN, Oct. 4, 1918, p. 3.

6. It was built in 1906 by architects C. W. Bulger and Sons. The historic building later housed Dallas' Hard Rock Café and was torn down on January 20, 2008.

7. Walter Sanders Lee, Death Certificate, Dec. 7, 1918; DMN, Dec. 8, 1918, pt. 2, p. 12.

8. Thomas Alan Hord, "History of the Scouting Movement in Dallas" (unpublished ms) pp. 14–15, HSM; DMN, Jan. 9, 1919, p. 6; DMN, Jan. 11, 1919, p. 13.

9. DMN, Jun. 15, 1919, p. 3; DMN, Jun. 21, 1919, p. 13.

10. DMN, Jun. 22, 1919, pt. 3, p. 14; DMN, Jun. 30, 1919, p. 12; DMN, Jul. 3, 1919, p. 15.

11. DMN, Jul. 21, 1919, p. 10.

12. DMN, Nov. 2, 1919, pt. 1, p. 4; DMN, Oct. 21, 1919, p. 12.

13. Minor Huffman, History of Region Nine, Boy Scouts of America, 1920–1967 (private printing, 1967) pp. 70–72; DMN, Nov. 8, 1919, p. 11; DMN, Dec. 26, 1928, p. 14.

14. DMN, Oct. 21, 1919, p. 12; DMN, Oct. 23, 1919, p. 11; DMN, Oct. 27, 1919, p. 11; DMN, Dec. 7, 1920, p. 7.

15. DMN, Oct. 3, 1919, p. 15; DMN, Oct. 29, 1919, p. 6; ; DMN, Nov. 2, 1919, pt. 1, p. 4; DMN, Nov. 23, 1919, pt. 1, p. 9.

16. The Dallas Scout, vol. 2, no. 1, p. 1, HSM; DMN, Jan. 1, 1920, p. 10.

17. DMN, Mar. 21, 1920, pt. 5, p. 7; DMN, Aug. 17, 1920, p. 8; DMN, Aug. 19, 1920, p. 8.

18. DMN, Feb. 4, 1920, p. 7; DMN, Jul. 16, 1920, p. 7; DMN, Jul. 20, 1920, p. 5; George M. Haas, Daddy Wisdom: Boy Scout Benefactor (Dallas, Texas: Cockrell & Son, 1937) p. 26.

A. DMN, Aug. 8, 1918, p. 6; DMN, Aug. 16, 1918, p. 5; DMN, Dec. 18, 1918, p. 19; DMN, Dec. 24, 1918, p. 7; The Dallas Scout, Apr. 1919, vol. 1 no. 8, p. 1, HSM.

B. DMN, Jun. 3, 1915, p. 6; DMN, Sept. 26, 1917, p. 6; DMN, Dec. 29, 1917, p. 7; DMN, Jun. 27, 1924, p. 6; DMN, Nov. 17, 1938, p. 10; DMN, Dec. 16, 1943, p. 14; Missouri Dept. of Health—Standard Death Certificate #13439.

C. DMN, Feb. 28, 1924, p. 7.

CHAPTER 5: THE BENEFACTOR AND CAMP WISDOM (1920–1923)

1. Haas, Daddy Wisdom, p. 26; Ferdinand Eugene Daniel, ed., Medical Insurance: Devoted to the Insurance Examiner and Clinical Diagnostician, Vol. 36, p. 434; DMN, Mar. 25, 1923, p. 6.

2. DMN, Jul. 7, 1922, p. 1; Haas, Daddy Wisdom, p. 27, 9.

3. DMN, Sept. 5, 1920, pt. 2, p. 5; DMN, Dec. 3, 1920, p. 6; DMN, Dec. 7, 1920, p. 7; DMN, Dec. 10, 1920, p. 11.

4. DMN, Dec. 12, 1920, pt. 2, p. 2; DMN, Apr. 14, 1921, p. 7; DMN, May 22, 1921, pt. 1, p. 12.

5. DMN, May 16, 1921, p. 6; DMN, Oct 30, 1921, pt. 3, p. 7; DMN, Oct 5, 1922, p. 13.

6. Although it filled to capacity within the year after construction ended, increasing usage demanded that additional water be brought in. The damming of White Rock Creek to produce White Rock Lake would follow in 1911 as city growth required more potable water, Preservation Dallas and Dallas Heritage Village, Dallas Landmarks (San Francisco, CA: Arcadia Pub., 2008) p. 59; Eventually, to maintain the water level of the newly constructed dam to hold water in Bachman Lake, a 36-million-gallon water pump was installed to move water into the dam from the Elm Fork of the Trinity River; Engineering and Contracting, Vol. 37, May 1, 1912, p. 67.

7. DMN, Nov. 10, 1921, p. 6; DMN, Jan. 22, 1922, pt. 3, p. 7; DMN, Mar. 28, 1922, pt. 1, p. 5.

8. DMN, Apr. 11, 1922, p. 22; DMN, Apr. 12, 1922, p. 2; DMN, Apr. 13, 1922, p. 10; DMN, May 14, 1922, pt. 1, p. 2.

9. Wisdom Deed, May 28, 1923, p.1, CTC; DMN, Jul. 7, 1922, p. 1; DMN, Jul. 9, 1922, p. 10.

10. DMN, Aug. 6, 1922, p.14; DMN, Aug. 14, 1922, pp. 5, 7; DMN, Aug. 29, 1922, p. 20; DMN, Aug. 30, 1922, p. 9.

11. DMN, Aug. 20, 1922, p. 16; DMN, Aug 27, 1922, p. 4; DMN, Aug. 31, 1922, p. 9; DMN, Sept. 11, 1922, p. 6.

12. 1923 Charter Renewal, CTC.

13. DMN, Jan. 1, 1920, p. 10; DMN, Sept. 17, 1922, p. 9; DMN, Sept. 18, 1922, p. 14; DMN, Nov. 3, 1923, p. 12; DMN, Jan. 6, 1924, p. 13.

14. Now known as Grove Hill Memorial Park.

15. DMN, Mar. 27, 1923, p. 13; DMN, Feb. 25, 1923, p. 8; Huffman, History of Region Nine, pp. 70–72.

16. DMN, Mar. 10, 1923, p. 11; DMN, Mar. 16, 1923, p. 13; DMN, Mar. 18, 1923, p. 3; DMN, Mar 28, 1923, p. 6.

17. DMN, Mar. 28, 1923, p. 6; DMN, Mar. 29, 1923, p. 15; DMN, Mar. 30, 1923, p. 4; DMN, Mar. 31, 1923, p. 4.

18. DMN, May 18, 1923, pt. 2, p. 24; DMN, May 19, 1923, pt. 2, p. 18; DMN, Nov. 3, 1923, p. 12; DMN, Sept. 1, 1922, p. 13; DMN, Oct 3, 1923, p. 13.

19. DMN, Oct. 11, 1923, p. 15.

20. 1924 Charter Renewal, CTC.

A. Hass, Daddy Wisdom, pp. 5–11; Wisdom Deed, Mar. 26, 1923, Stewart Abstract Co., CTC.

B. DMN, Dec. 12, 1920, pt. 2, p. 2.

C. DMN, Feb. 13, 1922, p. 11; DMN, May 14, 1922, pt. 1, p. 2; DMN, May 31, 1922, p. 22; DMN, Mar. 19, 1923, p. 4.

D. DMN, Apr. 6, 1913, p. 8; DMN, May 9, 1913, p. 3; DMN, May 13, 1913, p. 7; DMN, Jul. 14, 1916, p. 9; DMN, Oct. 1, 1916, p. 10; DMN, Dec. 8, 1918, p. 12; DMN, May 14, 1922, p. 2; DMN, Nov. 23, 1923, p. 13; Thomas A. Davis, ed, Annual Circular Letters of the Active Chapters of the Phi Delta Theta (Collegiate Press, Menasha, Wisconsin, 1912) Vol. 26, p. 127.

E. DMN, Nov. 30, 1922, p. 20; DMN, May 12, 1940, p. 12.

F. DMN, Sep. 9, 1922, p. 9; DMN, Jun. 13, 1935, p. 9; DMN, May 19, 1936, p. 8; DMN, Oct. 3, 1935, p. 6.

CHAPTER 6: GROWING INTO CIRCLE TEN COUNCIL (1924–1927)

1. DMN, Apr. 6, 1924, p. 12.

2. DMN, Jan. 2, 1924, p. 13; DMN, Feb. 3, 1924 p. 1.

3. DMN, Jan. 22, 1924, p. 22.

4. Ibid.

5. Cliff Temple Baptist Church, "Cliff Temple Baptist Church: A Century of Serving," http://www.clifftemple.org/church-history.php.

6. DMN, Feb. 3, 1924, p.1; DMN, Feb 18, 1924, p. 7.

7. DMN, Apr 22, 1924, p. 1; DMN, May 18, 1924, p.1; DMN, May 25, 1924, p. 1; DMN, Sept. 11, 1924, p. 12.

8. DMN, Jun. 10, 1924 p. 13.

9. DMN, Jun. 15, 1924, p. 6.

10. DMN, Jun. 8, 1924, p. 1; DMN, Jun. 10, 1924, p.13; DMN, Jun. 15, 1924, p. 6; Boyce House, Oil Boom: The Story of Spindletop, Burkburnett, Mexia, Smackover, Desdemona, and Ranger (Caldwell, ID: The Caxton Printers, Ltd., 1941) pp. 132–133.

11. DMN, Sept. 1, 1924, p. 16; DMN, Sept. 21, 1924, p. 13; DMN, Sept. 23, 1924, p. 8.

12. DMN, Jul. 13, 1925, p. 3; DMN, Jul. 14, 1925, p. 13.

13. DMN, Feb. 5, 1925, p. 9; DMN, Dec. 4, 1929, p. 13.

14. DMN, Apr. 17, 1924, p. 11; DMN, Jan. 6, 1926, p. 18; DMN, Feb. 25, 1926, p. 11; DMN Feb. 26, 1926, p. 4; DMN, Mar. 2, 1926, p. 4; DMN, Mar. 4, 1926, p. 3; DMN, May 6, 1926, p. 5.

15. DMN, May 8, 1926, p. 17; DMN, May 18, 1926, p. 10; DMN, Jun. 29, 1926, p. 6.

16. DMN, Jun. 4, 1927, p. 13; DMN, Sept. 1, 1927, p. 13; DMN, Sept. 16, 1927, p. 7.

A. Dallas County Deeds, Nov. 1915; DMN, Nov. 27, 1920, p. 13; Dallas County Deeds, Mar. 1922, Mar. 1924, May 1924; DMN, Jun. 10, 1924, p. 13; Dallas County Deeds, May 1924 (CTC); Bowles to Wozencraft, May 20, 1924 (CTC); Humphreys to BSA Deed, Jun. 9, 1924 (CTC).

B. DMN, Feb. 26, 1913, p. 7; DMN, Jul. 6, 1913, p. 1; DMN, Mar. 20, 1924, p. 15; DMN, Apr. 1, 1924, p. 19; DMN, Apr. 4, 1924, p. 15; DMN, Mar. 6, 1927, p. 10.

C. DMN, Sept. 1, 1924, p. 16; DMN, Feb. 15, 1933, p. 6; DMN Nov. 9, 1963, p. 4; State of Texas Death Certificate #68733.

D. DMN, Jun. 8, 1924, p. 1.

E. Haas, Daddy Wisdom, pp. 44–47; DMN, May 3, 1925, p. 5.

F. DMN, Nov. 27, 1926, p. 15; DMN, Aug. 30, 1927, p. 15.

G. DMN, Nov. 13, 1926, p. 18; Dan Beard, Boy Heroes of Today, (New York: Boy Scouts of America, 1930) pp. 34–35, 51.

PART II: GROWTH AND DEVELOPMENT

1. DMN, Oct. 6, 1930, p. 9.

CHAPTER 7: CREATING THE BASE (1927–1931)

1. Circle 10 Reporter, 1953, CTC

2. DMN, Sept. 25, 1927, p. 2; DMN, Oct. 5, 1927, p. 13.

3. DMN, Sept. 25, 1927, p. 2; DMN, Jan. 1, 1929 p. 22.

4. DMN, Jun. 20 1928, p. 15.

5. DMN, Jul. 11, 1928 p. 13.

6. DMN, Jul. 24, 1928, p. 15.

7. DMN, May 4, 1930, p. 3; 1926 Charter Renewal, CTC; 1930 Charter Renewal, CTC.

8. Oscar A. Kitterman, "Final Report," Jun. 1, 1930, CTC.

9. Report of the Regional Executive, Aug. 1, 1930, CTC.

10. DMN, Jul. 10, 1930, p. 17.

11. DMN, Sept. 7, 1930, p. 12; DMN, Sept. 10, 1930, p. 10; William P. Clements Jr. to DeWitt Thompson, Jun. 3, 1985, JQT; Pat Bywaters Interview, November 30, 2012.

12. Haas, Daddy Wisdom, p. 89.

13. DMN, Mar. 9, 1931, p. 9.

14. DMN, Mar. 10, 1931, p. 13.

15. DMN, Mar. 11, 1931, p. 17; DMN, Mar. 15, 1931, p. 9; DMN, Jun. 8, 1932, p. 1; DMN, Jul. 4, 1932, p. 4.

A. DMN, Sept. 20, 1927, p. 13; DMN, Sept. 28, 1927, p. 13; DMN, Oct. 4, 1927, p. 17.

B. DMN, Jan. 27, 1928, p. 13; Boys' Life, Apr. 1928, p. 61.

C. DMN, Apr. 4, 1929, pp. 17, 23; DMN, Apr. 6, 1929, p. 13; DMN, Apr. 18, 1929, p. 11; Babe Ruth and Robert Johnsey, Image, AM.

D. DMN, Oct. 13, 1928, p. 6; DMN, Oct. 15, 1928, p. 3.

E. DMN, Jul. 21, 1929, p. 1.

F. DMN, Jan. 14, 1931, p. 4; William D. Murray, The History of the Boy Scouts of America (New York, Boy Scouts of America, 1937) pp. 386–389; Annual Charter Renewal 1930, CTC; Annual Charter Renewal 1932, CTC; DMN, Apr. 27, 1932, p. 12.

CHAPTER 8: SURVIVING THE DEPRESSION (1931–1936)

1. DMN, Jun. 28, 1931, p. 3; DMN, Jun. 29, 1931, p. 1; DMN, Jun. 10, 1936, p. 2.

2. DMN, Jul. 5, 1931, p. 14; Dec. 19, 1931, p. 10.

3. Charleston Gazette, May 28, 1927; Tom Noel, "Where the Ghost of A.E. Still Roams," Denver Post, Oct. 25, 2009; EBM, Jan. 23, 1932.

4. DMN, May 6, 1932, p. 2; 1932 Charter Renewal, CTC.

5. National Cub Scout Committee, History of Cub Scouting (New York: Boy Scouts of America, 1897) p. 55.

6. Murray, History of the Boy Scouts, p. 196; History of Cub Scouting, p. 13; 1932 Charter Renewal, CTC; 1933 Charter Renewal, CTC; DMN, May 6, 1932, p. 2; DMN, May 9, 1932, p. 1.

7. DMN, Jan. 11, 1936, p. 11; DMN, Feb. 3, 1936, p. 1; DMN, Mar. 27, 1936, p. 1; DMN, May 23, 1926, p. 3.

8. DMN, May 30, 1936, p. 4; DMN, Jul. 17, 1936, p. 1.

9. DMN, Jul. 20, 1936, p. 4; DMN, Jul. 22, 1936, p. 1.

10. Ibid.

11. DMN, Aug. 3, 1936, p. 11; DMN, Aug. 8, 1936, p. 1.

12. Duggan to Members of the Executive Committee, Aug. 14, 1936, CTC; DMN, Aug. 15, 1936, p. 10; DMN, Sept. 2, 1936, p. 12.

13. Scout Executive Report, Aug. 14, 1936, CTC; DMN, Aug. 15, 1936, p. 10; 1937 Charter Renewal, CTC; DMN, Oct. 22, 1936, p. 10.

A. DMN, Jan. 12, 1933, p. 4; DMN, Mar. 7, 1933, p. 4; DMN, Mar. 8, 1933, p. 5.

B. DMN, May 17, 1932, p. 1.

C. DMN, Jun. 30 1935, p. 5; DMN, Dec. 19, 1938, p. 10; "History of Troop 42, Whitewright," provided by Enoch Heise and Don Rhodes of Troop 42, Nov. 9, 2011.

D. Thomas Alexander Lee, The Development of the American Public Accountancy Profession (New York: Routledge, 2006) p. 77; EBM, Nominating Committee Report, Jan. 24, 1961; EBM, Scout Executive's Report, Sept. 19, 1961, p. 3.

E. DMN, Jan. 25, 1933, p. 1; DMN, Jan. 3, 1935, p. 4.

F. DMN, Mar. 31, 1934, p. 1; DMN, Mar. 17, 2006, obituary.

G. DMN, May 6, 1932, p. 2; DMN, May 9, 1932, p. 1.

H. DMN, Jan. 9, 1926, p. 13; DMN, Jan. 27, 1928, p. 13; DMN, Apr. 7, 1929, p. 8; DMN, Aug. 24, 1929, p. 3; DMN, Feb. 26, 1933, p. 8; DMN, Apr. 6, 1933, p. 16; DMN, Jun. 29, 1933, p. 1; DMN, Dec. 1, 1934, p. 6.

I. DMN, Apr. 5, 1933, p. 10.

J. DMN, Nov. 5, 1933, p. 1.

K. DMN, Nov. 1, 1931, p. 4; DMN, Dec. 16, 1931, p. 2.

L. DMN, Jan. 21, 1934, p. 6.

CHAPTER 9: SCOUTING FOR ALL BOYS (1937–1940)

1. DMN, Sept. 15, 1936, p. 9.

2. DMN, Oct. 22, 1936, p. 10.

3. DMN, Dec. 6, 1936, p. 8; DMN, Dec. 18, 1936m p. 3; DMN, Dec. 21, 1936, p. 4.

4. DMN, Nov. 2, 1936, p. 5; DMN, Dec. 6, 1936, p. 8; DMN, Dec. 18, 1936, p. 3; DMN, Dec. 21, 1936, p. 4;
DMN, Dec. 9, 1936, p. 9; DMN, Jan. 2, 1937, p. 1.

5. DMN, Feb. 25, 1937, p. 11; DMN, Apr. 4, 1937, p. 4; DMN, Jun. 20, 1937, p. 4; DMN, Jul. 10, 1937, p. 1; Richard Johnson, Interview, Dec. 8, 2011.

6. George Lankford, Interview, Dec. 13, 2011 and Jan. 2, 2012.

7. 1937 Charter Renewal, CTC.

8. 1938 Charter Renewal, CTC.

9. DMN, Feb. 19, 1938, p. 10; DMN, Feb. 25 1938, p. 38; DMN, Feb. 27, 1938, p. 7.

10. DMN, Feb. 25, 1938, p. 5; DMN, Feb. 26, 1938, p. 9.

11. DMN, Nov. 13, 1938, p. 14; DMN, Dec. 10, 1938, p. 1.

12. DMN, Feb. 8, 1940, p. 7; 1941 Charter Renewal, CTC.

13. DMN, Mar. 30, 1940, p. 6; DMN, Apr. 11, 1940, p. 2; EBM, Scout Exec Report, Sept. 12, 1940, p. 1.

14. DMN, May 5, 1940, p. 6; EBM, Scout Exec Report, Sept. 12, 1940, p. 2; DMN, Nov 22, 1943, p. 1.

A. DMN, May 20, 1937, p. 6; DMN, May 24, 1937, p. 12; DMN, Jun. 23, 1937, p. 1; DMN, Jun. 30, 1937, p. 5; DMN, Jul. 1, 1937,

p. 14; DMN, Jul. 2, 1937, p. 11; DMN, Jul. 7, 1937, p. 1; DMN, Jul. 8, 1937, p. 5; DMN, Jul. 9, 1937, p. 11; DMN, Jul. 11, 1937, p. 3; http://www.loc.gov/pictures/item/hec2009009566/.

B. EBM, Finance Report, Nov. 1, 1937; DMN, Dec. 29, 1938, p. 10; Peter McNabb, I Go to Prepare a Trail for You: Mikanakawa Lodge 1937–1987 (Wolfe City, Texas: Hennington, 1987) p. 11, 7, 8; DMN, Jun. 11, 1939, p. 9; DMN, Nov. 19, 1939, p. 13.

C. Nelson R. Block, A Thing of the Spirit (New York: Boy Scouts of America, 2000) p. 46; DMN, Sept. 26, 1917, p. 6.

D. DMN, Jan. 16, 1938, p. 5; DMN, Mar. 18, 1938, p. 6; DMN, Aug. 5, 1938, p. 6; DMN, Aug. 19, 1938, p. 9.

E. DMN, Dec. 21, 1937, p. 14; DMN, Dec. 28, 1937, p. 3.

F. DMN, Sept. 8, 1938, p. 1; DMN, Oct. 18, 1938, p. 5.

G. DMN, Jul. 10, 1940, p. 1.

H. DMN, Apr. 24, 1938, p. 12; DMN, May 8, 1938, p. 12; EBM, Aug. 22, 1935; DMN, Nov. 2, 1938, p. 8; DMN, Nov. 13, 1938, p. 14; DMN, Dec. 8, 1938, p. 6; DMN, Dec. 10, 1938, p. 1; DMN, Dec. 11, 1938, p. 10.

I. DMN, Jan. 9, 1940, p. 1.

CHAPTER 10: A PRIME DECADE FOR PATRIOTISM (1941–1949)

1. DMN, Mar. 11, 1941, p. 1.

2. DMN, May 31, 1941, pt. 11, p. 3; DMN, Nov. 22, 1941, p. 12; DMN, Dec. 7, 1943, p. 15; DMN, Dec. 9, 1943, p. 1; DMN, Oct. 24, 2012, p. 3B.

3. DMN, Feb. 17, 1942, p. 11; DMN, Apr. 11, 1942, p. 22; Boys' Life, Mar. 1945, p. 35; DMN, Mar. 5, 1942, p. 9.

4. DMN, Mar. 23, 1942, p. 3; DMN, Mar. 29, 1942, p. 8; DMN, Jan. 31, 1943, p. 11.

5. DMN, Mar. 24, 1942, p. 4; DMN, Mar. 25, 1942, p. 3; DMN, Apr. 19, 1942. p. 1; DMN, May 12, 1942, p. 3.

6. DMN, Jun. 14, 1942, p. 11; DMN, Jun. 24, 1942, p. 1; DMN, Jun. 27, 1942, p. 1;DMN, Jun. 28 1942, p. 1; EBM, Aug. 4, 1942, p. 1.

7. DMN, Jun. 29 1942, p. 1; DMN, Aug. 2, 1942, p. 4; DMN, Oct. 8, 1943, p. 15. Eddie Reitz, Interview, May 7, 1912.

8. DMN, Mar. 29, 1943, p. 4; DMN, Jun. 18, 1943, p. 1; EBM, Aug. 4, 1942; 1943 Charter Renewal, CTC.

9. DMN, Jun. 9, 1944, p. 14.

10. DMN, May 5, 1944, p. 5; DMN, May 19, 1944, p. 12; DMN, Aug. 16, 1944, p. 9; DMN, Mar. 2, 1945, p. 12; DMN, Mar. 24, 1945, p. 5; DMN, Mar. 27, 1945, p. 2

11. EBM, 30th Annual Council Ten Meeting, Feb. 9, 1945, p. 1.

12. DMN, Jul. 28, 1946, p. 17; EBM, Apr. 29, 1946, p. 1.

13. DMN, Mar. 11, 1947, p. 5; DMN, Jul. 13, 1947, p. 1

14. DMN, Feb. 15, 1949, p. 1.

15. DMN, Feb. 12, 1949, p. 4; DMN, Mar. 14, 1949, p. 3; DMN, Apr. 30, 1949, p. 1.

16. DMN, May 1, 1949, p. 16; DMN, Jan. 24, 1950, p. 6.

A. DMN, Feb. 18, 1942, p. 1; Donnell Family File, HSM.

B. DMN, Apr. 3, 1944, p. 10.

C. David Pike, Roadside New Mexico: A Guide to Historic Markers, (Albuquerque: University of New Mexico Press, 2004) p. 113, DMN, May 20, 1942, p. 6; DMN, Jun. 3, 1942, p. 14.

D. DMN, Jul. 14, 1942, p. 1, Black History Newspaper, 1977, p. 19, HSM.

E. Black History Newspaper, 1977, p. 19, HSM.

F. EBM, Mar. 27, 1945, p. 1; DMN, Jan. 31, 1946, p. 6; DMN, Feb. 1, 1946, p. 3; www.swt.usace.army.mil.

G. http://www.mannphoto.com; DMN, May 25, 1926, p. 5.

H. EBM, Meeting of Merger Committee of Red River Council and Committee from Circle Ten Council, Oct 15, 1947, p. 1; DMN, Sept. 9, 1940, p. 5; DMN, Dec. 3, 1947, p. 14; EBM, Oct 17, 1947, p. 2.

I. DMN, Jun. 28, 1949, p. 20.

J. DMN, Jul. 22, 1947, p. 3.

CHAPTER 11: THE GOLDEN AGE (1950–1959)

1. DMN, Feb. 18, 1950, p. 3; DMN, Jun. 22, 1950, p. 16.

2. DMN, Jun. 25, 1950, p. 1; DMN, Jun. 27, 1950, p. 4.

3. EBM, Apr. 26, 1950, p. 2. The dedication would be on July 4, 1950.

4. DMN, Jul. 1, 1950, p. 12; DMN, Jul. 5, 1950, p. 1; DMN, Jul. 8, 1950, p. 4.

5. Circle Ten Council Annual Report, 1951, CTC

6. EBM, Apr. 30, 1951.

7. EBM, Apr. 26, 1950, pp. 2–4.

8. DMN, Feb. 1, 1951, p. 14; Dallas Times Herald, Oct 22, 1968, p. 1; EBM, Nov. 14, 1951, p. 2; EBM, Feb. 23, 1971, p. 2.

9. DMN, Nov. 15, 1951, p. 10; DMN, Feb. 25, 1952, p. 3; DMN, May 4, 1952, p. 7.

10. DMN, May 1, 1952, p. 7; DMN, May 2, 1952, p. 3; DMN, May 9, 1952, p. 2; DMN, May 17, 1952, p. 14; EBM, Jun. 5, 1952, p. 3; EBM, Nov. 4, 1952, p. 1.

11. DMN, May 9, 1952, p. 8; DMN, Jul. 12, 1954, p. 1.

12. EBM, Camp Development Subcommittee, Mar. 5, 1953; DMN, Jun. 15, 1953, p. 10; 1953 Charter Renewal, CTC; EBM, Treasurer's Report, Dec. 3, 1956; EBM, Boy Scout Camp Development Fund Memorial Contributions, Camp Construction Committee, Feb. 8, 1954.

13. EBM, May 13, 1958.

14. DMN, Apr. 28, 1960, p. 25.

A. DMN, Aug. 11, 1950, p. 1.

B. DMN, Sept. 23, 1951, p. 11; 1951 Annual Report, CTC; EBM, Jan. 30, 1953.

C. DMN, Mar. 23, 1951, p. 21; DMN, May 13, 1951, p. 1; DMN, May 18, 1951, p. 3; DMN, May 19, 1951, p. 1; DMN, Jun. 3, 1951, p. 12.

D. DMN, Aug. 3, 1955, p. 10; "Silver Beaver Citation,"1960 Circle Ten Council Annual Report, CTC.

E. DMN, Jan. 10, 1954, p. 12; DMN, Feb. 7, 1954, p. 9; DMN, Dec. 15, 1954, p. 15; DMN, Feb. 18, 1955, p. 3; DMN, Feb. 20, 1955, p. 3.

F. DMN, Mar. 23, 1953, p. 11; DMN, Apr. 11, 1953, p. 4; DMN, Apr. 17, 1953, p. 11; DMN, Apr. 18, 1953, p. 1.

G. DMN, May 12, 1940, p. 9; DMN, Mar. 6, 1942, p. 3; DMN, Sept. 23, 1942, p. 7; DMN, Aug. 8, 1948, p. 10; DMN, Oct. 8, 1952, p. 13.

H. DMN, Jan. 4, 1955, p. 5; DMN, Jun. 6, 1955, p. 3; 1956 Charter Renewal, CTC; Kenneth Davis, History of WoodBadge, (New York, NY: Boy Scouts of America) pp. 11–26, 69–70.

I. DMN, Jan. 26, 1956, p. 16.

PART III: SECURING THE FUTURE

1. Written in 1936.

CHAPTER 12: THE COUNTER-COUNTER REVOLUTION (1960–1972)

1. DMN, Apr. 28, 1960 p. 25; EBM, Oct. 4, 1960, p. 4.

2. DMN, Sept. 1, 1961, p. 6; DMN, Oct. 24, 1961, p. 9; DMN, Apr. 25, 1963, p. 12; DMN, Jun. 1, 1964, p. 10; DMN, Jan. 22, 1964, p. 7.

3. 1961 Charter Renewal, CTC; 1965 Charter Renewal, CTC; DMN, Jun. 23, 1964, p. 14; EBM, Feb. 13, 1964; EBM, Apr. 27, 1965, p. 2.

4. DMN, Aug. 3, 1964, p. 10; DMN, Oct. 6, 1964, p. 8; EBM, Mar. 23, 1965.

5. DMN, Sept. 26, 1964, p. 7; DMN, Sept. 30, 1964, p. 9.

6. EBM, Oct. 22, 1968, p. 3.

7. National Annual Report, 1968, BSA.

8. EBM, Nov. 26, 1968, p. 2.

9. BSA, Report to the Nation, Feb. 5, 1970.

10. DMN, Dec. 26, 1970, p. 6; DMN, Dec. 29, 1970, p. 4; DMN, Feb. 26, 1971, p. 2; DMN, Mar. 7, 1971, p. 16; ; DMN, Apr. 5, 1971, p. 11; EBM, May 18, 1971, p. 1; DMN, May 27, 1971, p. 18.

11. "Membership Numbers," BSA.

12. EBM, Oct. 22, 1968.

13. EBM, Oct. 22, 1968, p. 3; EBM, Membership Report, Feb. 22, 1972; EBM, BoyPower Report, Mar. 28, 1972; EBM, Nov. 28, 1972, p. 1; EBM, Membership Report, Jun. 26, 1973.

A. DMN, Jun. 16, 1960, pp. 8, 12; DMN, Jun. 17, 1960, p. 12; DMN, Jul. 19, 1960 p. 4; DMN, Jul. 21, 1960, p. 2; Brad Smith, Interview, Jan. 12, 2012; Harold Smith, Interview, Jan. 12, 2012.

B. DMN, Apr. 8, 2005, Obituaries.

C. Dallas Express, Oct 27, 1962, p. 1; DMN, Oct. 29, 1969, p. 10A.

D. EBM, Feb. 23, 1965, p. 3.

E. EBM, Oct. 27, 1964, p. 1; DMN, Nov. 17, 1964, p. 1; DMN, Aug. 12, 1965, p. 32; EBM, Jun. 25, 1968, p. 1; EBM, Sept. 24, 1968, p. 1.

F. DMN, Feb. 24, 1966, p. 20.

G. EBM, Mar. 23, 1965, p. 1; EBM, May 23, 1965, p. 1; EBM, Jul 26, 1965, p. 1; EBM, Mar. 25, 1969, p. 1; EBM, May 27, 1969, p. 1; EBM, Nov. 25, 1969, p. 1; EBM, Apr. 28, 1970, p. 2; EBM, Finance Committee Report, Nov. 11, 2009.

H. EBM, Apr, 28, 1964, p. 2; DMN, Dec. 21, 1965, p. 6; DMN, Feb. 17, 1966, p. 2; DMN, Feb. 27, 1966, p. 12; DMN, Mar 31, 1966, p. 6; DMN, Apr. 22, 1966, p. 14; DMN, Jun. 23, 1966, p. 18; EBM, Jun. 28, 1966, p. 2; EBM, Oct. 25, 1966, p. 2; "Closing Agreement Between Circle Ten Boy Scout Foundation and Circle Ten Council, Boy Scouts of America, Nov. 30, 1966, CTC; EBM, Mar. 26, 1968, p. 1; William P. Clements Jr. to Circle Ten Council, Oct 20, 1969, CTC; EBM, Oct. 28, 1969; EBM, Apr. 28, 1970, p. 3; DMN, Jun. 2, 1970, p. 4; EBM, Oct. 26, 1971; Agreement between Waymon G. Peavey and Circle Ten Council, Sept. 30 1970, CTC; EBM, Sept. 22, 1970; EBM, May 18, 1971; EBM, Feb. 27, 1973; John Stuart III, Interview, Mar. 8, 2012.

I. EBM, Jun. 25, 1968; EBM, Jun. 24, 1969; DMN, Jul. 7, 1969, p. 7; EBM, Jul. 14, 1969; DMN, Jul. 15, 1969, p. 4; DMN, Jul. 19, 1969, p. 14; EBM, Oct. 28, 1969; Burton L. Scott, Interview, Jan. 14, 2012; George Lankford, Interview, Jan. 11, 2012.

J. DMN, Sept. 24, 1969, p. 1; EBM, Oct. 28, 1969, p. 2; DMN, Jun. 15, 1971, p. 1.

K. DMN, Mar. 15, 1971 p. 4; DMN, Apr. 5, 1971, p. 4.

L. http://shyash765.blogspot.com/2011_03_13_archive.html, (accessed 5/21/12)

M. EBM, Jan. 16, 1971, p. 1; EBM, Feb. 23, 1971, p. 2; DMN, May 16, 1972, p. 1; DMN, Feb. 27, 1973, p. 3–4; DMN, Jun. 26, 1973, p. 2; EBM, Sept. 28, 1971, p. 3.

N. EBM, Apr. 27, 1971 p. 2; EBM, Jun. 22, 1971, p. 1; EBM, Sept. 28, 1971, p. 2; EBM, May 15, 1973, p. 1.

O. DMN, Jan. 30, 1972, p. 18.

CHAPTER 13: STEMMING THE LOSS (1973–1978)

1. Membership Numbers, BSA.

2. Boy Scouts of America, Scout Handbook (New York: Boy Scouts of America, 1972) pp. 90–91.

3. DMN, May 29, 1972, p. 3; DMN, Mar. 19, 1977, p. 2.

4. DMN, Aug. 30, 1973, p. 15; EBM, Oct. 23, 1973, p. 2; DMN, Nov. 20, 1972, p. 7; EBM, Jan. 19, 1974, p. 1, 2.

5. EBM, Apr. 23, 1974, p. 2; EBM, May 21, 1974, p. 1; EBM, Oct. 26, 1974, p. 2.

6. DMN, Apr. 4, 1974, p. 1; DMN, Apr. 6, 1974, p. 1; EBM, Jun. 24, 1975, p. 2.

7. EBM, Jun. 25, 1974, p. 2; EBM, Apr. 22, 1975, p. 4; EBM, Officer's Luncheon, Jul. 14, 1975; EBM, Apr. 25, 1978, p. 1.

8. EBM, Sept. 24, 1974, p. 1; EBM, Mar. 23, 1976, p. 2; EBM, Jun. 22, 1976, p. 3; EBM, Statement on Camp Texoma, Jun. 21, 1978; EBM, Jun. 27, 1978; EBM, Apr. 24, 1979, p. 2.

9. EBM, Report of the Camp Wisdom Committee, Sept. 11, 1974; EBM, Oct. 22, 1974.

10. Membership Numbers, BSA.

11. EBM, Oct. 22, 1968; EBM, Oct. 25, 1977, p. 1; EBM, Membership Update, Apr 25, 1978.

12. How Boys View Scouting, Texas Field Research, Fall 1978, CTC; Scouting: A Parental Perspective, Feb 28, 1978, CTC.

13. EBM, May 23, 1978, p. 1; EBM, Mar. 24, 1981, p. 2.

14. EBM, Sept. 26, 1978, p. 1; EBM, Oct. 24, 1978, p. 2; EBM, Nov. 8, 1978.

A. DMN, Aug. 8, 1973, p. 9; DMN, Aug. 9, 1973, p. 24; William Hemenway II, Interview, Feb. 9, 2012.

B. "Boy Scout Troop No. 167 Visits Governor," Post Tribune, Mar. 1, 1975, p. 1; EBM, Apr. 22, 1975, p. 4.

C. DMN, Jan. 31, 1974, p. 37; DMN, Mar. 15, 1974, p. 9; DMN, May 4, 1974, p. 16; DMN, May 5, 1974, p. 40; Post Tribune, May 18, 1974, p. 13.

D. DMN, Jan. 31, 1976, p. 10.

E. EBM, Apr. 2, 1975, p. 3; EBM, May 25, 1976, p. 2; EBM, Apr. 25, 1978, p. 1; EBM, Jun. 27, 1978, p. 2; EBM, Jun. 26, 1979, p. 3; EBM, Sept. 25, 1979, p. 2.

F. DMN, May 20, 1927 p. 13; Thomas Gervas Beckett Sr., Last Will and Testament, Sept. 19, 1958, BEC; EBM, Sept. 18, 1962, p. 2; EBM, Feb. 14, 1963; EBM, Mar. 12, 1963; EBM, Apr. 30, 1963.

G. DMN, Oct. 8, 1976, p. 4; Black History newspaper clipping, 1977, p. 19, HSM; Mount Vernon Chamber of Commerce Foundation Speakers Bureau, www.mountvernonchamber.com/pdfs/speaker_bureau.pdf, (accessed Mar. 23,2012).

H. DMN, Feb. 16, 1977, p. 20; EBM, Scout Executive's Report, Feb. 22, 1977, p. 3.

I. EBM, Oct. 28, 1975, p. 2; EBM, Gassett to Circle Ten Council, Apr. 25, 1978, p. 1.

J. EBM, Jun. 27, 1978, p. 2; EBM, Sept. 26, 1978, p. 2; EBM, Oct. 24, 1978, p. 2; EBM, Jun. 23, 1981, p. 2; EBM, Sept. 24, 1985, p. 1; EBM, Nov. 26, 1996, p. 1; EBM, Jan. 25, 2000, p. 4.

CHAPTER 14: TURNING TIDES (1979–1992)

1. EBM, Feb. 27, 1979, p. 1, 3; Billy Gamble, Interview, Jul. 9, 2012.

2. EBM, Feb. 27, 1979, p. 2; EBM, Apr. 24, 1979, p. 2, 3; Billy Gamble, email, Jul. 9, 2012.

3. EBM, Jun. 26, 1979, p. 3.

4. EBM, Mar. 25, 1980, p. 1; EBM, Aug. 26, 1980, p. 3; EBM, Oct. 28, 1980, p. 2; EBM, May 27, 1981, p. 2; Billy Gamble, Interview, Jul. 23, 2012 and Jul. 25, 2012.

5. EBM, Oct. 28, 1980, p. 3.

6. EBM, May 25, 1982, p. 1; EBM, Jun. 22, 1982, p. 3.

7. EBM, Feb. 23, 1982, p. 2; EBM, Aug. 31, 1982, p. 3; EBM, Nov. 23, 1982, p. 2; EBM, May 24, 1983, p. 1; EBM, Jun. 28, 1983, p. 1, 2; EBM, Resolution, Oct. 25, 1983; EBM, Oct. 23, 1984, p. 3; EBM, Jan. 22, 1985, p. 2; EBM, Mar. 26, 1985, p. 2; Billy Gamble, Interview, Jul. 23, 2012.

8. EBM, Nov. 26, 1985, p. 3.

9. EBM, Jan. 28, 1986, p. 1; EBM, Feb. 25, 1986, p. 1, 2; EBM, Oct. 27, 1987, p. 2.

10. EBM, May 27, 1986, p. 1; EBM, Jun. 25, 1986, p. 1; EBM, Aug. 26, 1986, p. 1; EBM, Nov. 25, 1986, p. 1.

11. EBM, Jan. 27, 1987, p. 2; EBM, Feb. 24, 1987, p. 3; EBM, Jun. 23, 1987, p.2; EBM, Feb. 23, 1988, p. 3; EBM, Mar. 22, 1988, p. 2; EBM, Sept. 26, 1989 p. 2.

12. EBM, Aug. 29, 1989, p. 3; EBM, Feb. 27, 1990, p. 3; EBM, Mar. 27, 1990, p. 2; EBM, May 22, 1990, p. 1, 2; EBM, Sept. 25, 1990, p. 1; EBM, Oct. 23, 1990, p. 2; EBM, Nov. 27, 1990, p. 2; EBM, May 21, 1991, p. 2; EBM, Mar. 24, 1992, p. 3; EBM, Apr. 28, 1992, p. 3.

13. EBM, Sept. 27, 1988, p. 3; EBM, Feb. 26, 1991, p. 2; EBM, Apr. 23, 1991, p. 4; ; EBM, Mar. 26, 1991, p. 2; EBM, Mar. 23, 1993, p. 3.

14. EBM, Oct. 22, 1991, p. 1, 2; EBM, Oct. 26, 1991, p. 2; EBM, May 15, 1992, p. 1; EBM, May 19, 1992, p. 3; EBM, Oct. 27, 1992, p. 2, 3.

A. EBM, Aug. 28, 1979, p. 2; Robert Higginbotham, Interview, Jan. 30, 2012.

B. EBM, Oct. 26, 1982, p. 1, 2; EBM, Apr. 27, 2004, p. 4; Scott Ferguson, Interview, Jan. 24, 2012.

C. EBM, May 27, 1981, p. 2; EBM, Jun. 23, 1981, p. 1; EBM, Sep. 28, 1982, p. 2; EBM, May 29, 1984, p. 1.

D. EBM, Mar. 23, 1982, p. 2; EBM, May 25, 1982, p. 1; EBM, Aug. 30, 1982, p. 2; EBM, Nov. 23, 1982, p. 2; EBM, Aug. 30, 1983, p. 2; EBM, Apr. 23, 1985, p. 2; EBM, May 28, 1985, p. 2.

E. EBM, Jun. 22, 1982, p. 2; EBM, Jan. 25, 1983, p. 3; EBM, Feb. 22, 1983, p. 3; EBM, Mar. 26, 1985, p. 2; EBM, Nov. 26, 1985, p. 2; EBM, Jan. 28, 1986, p. 1; EBM, Mar. 25, 1986, p. 2; EBM, Jan. 27, 1987, p. 2; EBM, Apr. 23, 1991, p. 3; Nov. 26, 1991, p. 2; DMN, Feb. 13, 1993, p. 1K.

F. EBM, Mar. 23, 1982, p. 1; EBM, Aug. 30, 1983, p. 20; EBM, Jan. 22, 1985, p. 1; EBM, Jun. 18, 1985, p. 2; Billy Gamble, Interview, Jul. 23, 2012.

G. EBM, Jun. 22, 1982, p. 2; EBM, Apr. 26, 1983, p. 2; EBM, Mar. 25, 1986, p. 1; EBM, Apr. 22, 1986, p. 2; EBM, Jan. 27, 1987, p. 2.

H. EBM, Oct. 25, 1983, p. 3.

I. EBM, Jun. 25, 1986, p. 2; EBM, Mar. 27, 1990, p. 1; Billy Gamble, Interview, Jul. 23, 2012.

J. EBM, Aug. 28, 1984, p. 3.

K. EBM, Nov. 27, 1984, p. 3.

L. EBM, Feb. 26, 1985, p. 2; EBM, Sept. 24, 1985, p. 2.

M. DMN, Dec. 10, 1985. p. 19A; Jerry Jordan, Interview, Feb. 25, 2012; Charles Holmes, email, Jun. 25, 2012.

N. EBM, Nov. 25, 1986, p. 3.

O. EBM, Jan. 23, 1990, p. 2; EBM, Oct. 23, 1990, p. 2; EBM, Nov. 27, 1990, p. 1; Gene Smith, Interview, Mar. 7, 2012; Joe Griffis, Interview, Mar. 2, 2012.

P. EBM, Jan. 28, 1986 p. 3.

Q. EBM, Aug. 20, 1991, p. 1; Billy Gamble, Interview, Jul. 23, 2012.

CHAPTER 15: EXPANSION (1993–1999)

1. Karen Klinefelter, "John P. Harbin: Chairman of the Board & CEO, Halliburton Company," Sky Magazine, Sept. 1961.

2. EBM, Nov. 23, 1992, p. 1; EBM, Mar. 23, 1993, p. 1; EBM, Special Circle Ten Council Meeting, Jun. 10, 1993, p. 1.

3. EBM, Special Circle Ten Council Meeting, Jun. 10, 1993, p. 1; EBM, Aug. 31, 1993, p. 3; EBM, Apr. 27, 1994, p. 3; Dick Corcoran, Interview, Feb. 22, 2012.

4. EBM, Sept. 28, 1993, p. 2; EBM, Jan. 25, 1994, p. 3; EBM, Feb. 27, 1996, p. 1; EBM, Aug. 27, 1996, p. 3; EBM, Oct. 28, 1999, p. 2.

5. EBM, Aug. 31, 1993, p. 2, 4; EBM, Sept. 28, 1993, p. 3; EBM, Apr. 27, 1994, p. 1; EBM, Dec. 6, 1994, p. 1.

6. EBM, Jan. 20, 1995, p. 2; EBM, Mar. 28, 1995, p. 2, 3; EBM, Aug. 29, 1995, p. 2; Brian Bennett, Interview, Jun. 4, 2012.

7. EBM, Jun. 20, 1995, p. 2; EBM, May 14, 1996, p. 1; EBM, Jun. 17, 1997, p. 2; EBM, Mar. 24, 1998, p. 2; EBM, Jun. 15, 1999, p. 2.

8. EBM, Mar. 24, 1998, p. 2; EBM, May 19, 1998, p. 2; EBM, Nov. 24, 1998, p. 2; EBM, Mar. 23, 1999, p. 1; EBM, Sept. 28, 1999, p. 2.

9. EBM, Jan. 23, 1996, p. 2; EBM, May 14, 1996, p. 2; EBM, Jan. 28, 1997, p. 3; EBM, Feb. 25, 1997, p. 3; EBM, Sept. 23, 1997, p. 4; Billy Gamble, Interview, Jul. 23, 2012.

10. EBM, Aug. 27, 1996, p. 2; EBM, Sept. 23, 1997, p. 4.

11. EBM, Sept. 23, 1997, p. 4; "Eagle Plaza Dedication Agenda," Oct. 27, 1998, CTC; EBM, Oct. 27, 1998, p. 1.

12. EBM, Jan. 27, 1998, p. 3; EBM, Jun. 16, 1998, p. 1; EBM, Jan. 26, 1999, p. 3; EBM, Feb. 23, 1999 p. 2; EBM, Aug. 17, 1999, p. 3; EBM, Sept. 28, 1999, p. 1; EBM, Apr. 25, 2000, p. 3.

A. Park Cities People, Oct 8, 1998, p. 14.

B. Billy Gamble, Interview, Jul. 23, 2012.

C. EBM, Aug. 19, 1997, p. 3; EBM, Aug. 18, 1998, p. 3; Jack D. Furst, Interview, Mar. 21, 2012.

D. EBM, Mar. 24, 1998, p. 2; EBM, Jun. 15, 1999, p. 2.

E. EBM, Jan. 28, 1997, p. 2; EBM, Sept. 23, 1997, p. 1; EBM, May 19, 1998, p. 1; Jack D. Furst, Interview, Jun. 15, 2012.

F. EBM, Aug. 18, 1998, p. 4.

G. EBM, Feb. 27, 1996, p. 2; EBM, May 14, 1996 p. 1.

H. EBM, Endowment/Development Report, May 17, 2005; EBM, Dec. 13, 2005, p. 2.

I. EBM, May 19, 1998, p. 2; EBM, Sept. 26, 2000, p. 2; EBM, Mar. 27, 2001, p. 3.

J. EBM, Apr. 28, 1981, p. 3; EBM, Jan. 26, 1993, p. 1; EBM, Jan. 25, 2000, p. 1.

K. EBM, Apr. 27, 1999, p. 3; EBM, Nov. 23, 1999, p. 3.

CHAPTER 16: NEW MILLENNIUM, FRESH START (2000–2009)

1. EBM, Apr. 24, 2001, p. 3, 4; EBM, Aug. 28, 2001, p. 2; EBM, Oct. 23, 2001, p. 1, 3.

2. Charles Holmes, email, Jun. 25, 2012; John Stuart, Interview, Mar. 8, 2012.

3. EBM, Apr. 23, 2002, p. 3.

4. EBM, Jun. 28, 2002, p. 2; EBM, Oct. 22, 2002, p. 2; EBM, Membership Report, Jan. 28, 2003; EBM, Commissioners Report, Mar. 25, 2003; EBM, Commissioners Report, Sept. 23, 2003.

5. EBM, Audit & Ethics Committee, Jan. 27, 2004; Scott Ferguson, Interview, Feb. 28, 2012.

6. EBM, Health and Safety Report, Jan. 27, 2004; EBM, Membership Report, Jan. 25, 2005; EBM, Feb. 22, 2005, p. 4.

7. EBM, Aug. 23, 2005, p. 1.

8. EBM, Sept. 27, 2005, p. 1, 2; EBM, Oct. 25, 2005, p. 2; EBM, Dec. 14, 2005, p. 1; EBM, Oct. 24, 2006, p. 1; John Stuart, Interview, Mar. 8, 2012; Ponce Duran email, Jul. 2, 2012.

9. EBM, May 17, 2006, p. 2; EBM, Jan. 23, 2007, p. 2; EBM, Feb. 26, 2007, p. 2; EBM, Aug. 28, 2007, p. 3; EBM, Nov. 13, 2007, p. 1; Jack D. Furst, Interview, Jun. 27, 2012.

10. EBM, Jan. 19, 2007, p. 2; EBM, Mar. 27, 2007, p. 1; Apr. 24, 2007, p. 3; EBM, Jan. 22, 2008, p. 2; EBM, Membership Report, Jan. 22, 2008; EBM, Apr. 22, 2008, p. 4; EBM, Camping Report, May 22, 2008; EBM, Jan. 27, 2009, p. 3; EBM, Mar. 24, 2009, p. 2; EBM, Oct. 25, 2011, p. 2 Craig Hutton, Interview, Feb. 23, 2012; Ponce Duran, email, Jul. 2, 2012.

11. EBM, Jan. 27, 2009, p. 3; EBM, Camping Report, Jan. 27, 2009; EBM, Oct. 27, 2009, p. 3; EBM, Nov. 17, 2009, p. 2; EBM, Dec. 8, 2009, p. 2.

A. EBM, Apr. 24, 2001, p. 1.

B. Don Burke, Interview, Jan. 22, 2012.

C. EBM, May 22, 2001, p. 3; EBM, Nov. 27, 2001, p. 3; EBM, Apr. 23, 2002, p. 3; Daniel Zaccara, Interview, Feb. 23, 2012.

D. EBM, Sept. 24, 2002, p. 2; Stuart, Interview, Mar. 8, 2012.

E. EBM, Camping Report, Sept. 24, 2002; EBM, Mar. 25, 2003.

F. EBM, Membership Report, Mar. 25, 2003; EBM, Jan. 27, 2004; David Klaudt, Interview, Feb. 22, 2012.

G. EBM, Endowment/Development Report, Jan. 27, 2004; EBM, Feb. 24, 2004, p. 3; EBM, Aug. 24, 2004.

H. EBM, Sept. 28, 2004, p. 1; EBM, Oct. 26, 2004, p. 2; EBM, Nov. 16, 2004, p. 2; EBM, Jan. 25, 2005, p. 2

I. EBM, Aug. 23, 2005, p. 1; Jack D. Furst, Interview, Jun. 15, 2012.

J. EBM, Learning for Life Report, May 17, 2005; Karen Thunert, Interview, Mar. 1, 2012

K. DMN, Sep. 2, 2007, p. 1B; "Holiday Magic," Scouting, Nov–Dec 2007; http://www.scouting.org/Media/PressReleases/PreviousYears/2007/20070904.aspx?print=1 (accessed 5/22/12); Michael Ross Interview, Oct. 13, 2012.

L. Wade Graves, Interview, Feb. 11, 2012; Robert Garrett, Interview, Feb. 14, 2012; Kevin Lovett Jr., Interview, Feb. 15, 2012.

M. Bobby Lyle to Jack Furst, Dec 16, 2005, BG; The Full Circle, Apr. 2006, BG Billy Gamble, email, Jul. 22, 2012.

N. EBM, Apr. 25, 2006, p. 2.

O. EBM, Mar. 27, 2007, p. 2.

P. Peter Culver, Interview, Feb. 22, 2012; John Stone, Interview, Feb. 23, 2012; Jack D. Furst, Interview, Mar. 21, 2012.

Q. DMN, Jan. 25, 2010, p. B1; "More Scouts in Action: They Saved Their Friend from a Runaway Rocket!," Boys' Life, Feb. 2011, p. 40.

R. EBM, Jan. 22, 2008, p. 1; EBM, Jan. 27, 2009, p. 2; Matt M. Walker, Interview, Feb. 11, 2012.

S. EBM, Activities Report, Mar. 22, 2005; EBM, May 12, 2009, p. 1; EBM, Endowment Fund Report, Sept. 20, 2011, p. 3.

CHAPTER 17: THE CENTENNIAL (2010–2013)

1. BSA "Words to Live By" National Strategy Report, Jan. 26, 2010, CTC.

2. Pat Currie, Interview, Jul. 12, 2012; Sherwood Blount Jr., Interview, May, 2, 2012.

3. EBM, Apr. 29, 2010, p. 3; Pat Currie, Interview, Mar. 1, 2012; Pat Currie, Interview, Jul. 12, 2012; Circle Ten Council Strategic Plan 2011–2015, CTC.

4. EBM, 100th Anniversary Report, May 12, 2009; EBM, 100th Anniversary Report, Dec. 8, 2009; EBM, Jan. 26, 2010, p. 2; EBM, Aug. 24, 2010, p. 2; Nomination of Jared Lyons, 2010, CTC.

5. EBM, Aug. 24, 2010, p. 2; Thomas Long, email, Feb. 28, 2012; and Feb. 29, 2012.

6. Joey Castleberry, email, Mar. 1, 2012; John Stuart III, Interview, Mar. 8, 2012.

7. EBM, Aug. 24, 2010, p. 3; EBM, Sept. 21, 2010, p. 3; EBM, Nov. 16, 2010, p. 3; EBM, Feb. 22, 2011, p. 2; EBM, Jun. 28, 2011, p. 2; EBM, Nov. 15, 2011, p. 2; Scott Arrington, Interview, Feb. 22, 2012;

8. EBM, Mar. 22, 2011, p. 1; Robert Gates, Transcript, Mar. 3, 2011, CTC; Ernest J. Carey, Interview, Apr. 3, 2012.

9. Laura Bush, Transcript, Mar. 6, 2012, CTC; Condoleezza Rice, Transcript, Mar. 6, 2012, CTC; Don Burke, Interview, Mar. 6, 2012.

10. EBM, Oct. 25, 2011, p. 3; Ernest J. Carey. Interview, Apr. 3, 2012; David M. Williams, Interview, Feb. 22, 2012.

11. Matt M. Walker, Interview, May 9, 2012.

12. "Our Impact"—Circle Ten Council, Dec. 31, 2011; 2011 Circle Ten Council Annual Report, CTC.

13. William J. Bennett, Speech, Orlando, FL, Jun. 1, 2012.

A. EBM, Executive Board Resolution, Jan. 26, 2010; EBM, Oct. 26, 2010, p. 3; DMN, Feb. 22, 2011, p. 2; EBM, Mar. 22, 2011, p. 4; Dick Corcoran, Interview, Feb. 22, 2012; Russell Etzenhouser, Interview, Feb. 22, 2012; Bobby Lyle, Interview, Apr. 9, 2012; Billy Gamble, email, Jul. 13, 2012; Toni Atwell, Interview, Feb. 28, 2012.

B. DMN, Oct. 16, 1938, p. 16; DMN, Jul. 20, 1939, p. 7; DMN, Feb. 9, 1940, p. 7; DMN, Sep. 19, 1941, p. 6.

C. James Alexander, Interview, Feb. 22, 2012.

D. EBM, Oct. 26, 2010, p. 2; EBM, Nov. 16, 2010, p. 1; Don Birdsong, Interview, Feb. 22, 2012; Kip Lankenau, Interview, Feb. 22, 2012; Ange Elliott, Interview, Feb. 22, 2012; Bianca Goolsby, email, Feb. 28, 2012.

E. EBM, Aug. 29, 2000, p. 2; EBM, Urban Scouting Report, May 28, 2002; EBM, Oct. 22, 2002.

F. DMN, Nov. 7, 2010, p. 13B.

G. EBM, Finance Report, Jan. 23, 2007.

H. DMN, Mar. 22, 2011, p. 3; Matt M. Walker, Interview, May 10, 2012.

I. DMN, Apr. 20, 1913, p. 13; DMN, Jul. 9, 1925, p. 16; DMN, Aug. 13, 1928, p. 8; DMN, Mar. 15, 1939, p. 3; DMN, Jul. 4, 1976, HSM; http://www.9key.com/markers/marker_detail.asp?atlas_number=5181012886.

photo credits

NOTE: *All still life photography and image enhancements used on all photographs in this book are ©2013 John K. Shipes*

tl = top left, tr =top right, lr = lower right, ll = lower left
t = top, l=lower, m=middle, ml=middle left, mr=middle right
all= all images on the page

Austin Presbyterian Theological Seminary, 153(tr)
Babcock Library, Springfield University, xvi (lr)
Tom Bohanan, 82(all), 225(tl)
Becket Family Archive, 255(all)
Boy Scouts of America, 327(tr,lr,ll)
Rodney D. Carpenter Archive, 144(photo), 158(tl), 163(t), 169(l), 170(all), 171(t, ll), 172-3(l), 179(l), 181(t), 189(all), 192(t), 195, 202-3, 204(all), 205(all), 212-3(l), 214(lr), 218, 219(ll,lr), 225(mr, ll), 226(lr), 228(tl), 229(t), 232(l), 236(l), 237(ll), 242, 243, 249(all), 256(tl), 259
Shannon Christian, 278
Circle Ten Council Archive, 83(tl,tm,tr), 93(t), 105(all), 131(tr), 133(t), 134(l), 135(all), 138(lmr), 149(lr), 153(lr), 187(l), 190(lr), 192(l), 199(mr), 208, 209(tl), 210(tm), 217(tl), 225(tr), 231(tr,l), 232(tl,m), 233, 234(ll), 235(l), 236(t), 240, 248(ll,lr), 251, 264(all), 265(l), 266, 274(all), 275, 279, 280, 281, 283(r), 285, 286(l), 287(l), 288(all), 289(all), 290(all), 292(lr,program), 293(lr), 301, 302(all), 303(all), 304(photos), 311308(tl,tr,lr), 309(all), 312(tr), 313(all), 314(all), 315(all), 317(tr,lr), 318(all), 319, 324, 328(l), 329, 332(all), 333(all), 335
Nicholas Cobb, 343
Dallas Historical Society xxv (all), 2(t),
Dallas Morning News Archive, xii (all), xiii (t), xix (t), 1, 3(ll), 9(t,m), 13, 14(l), 15(tr), 16(l), 17, 20(all), 23(m), 25, 30(all), 32(t), 33(t), 34(r), 35, 38, 42(lr), 44, 45(l), 46(all), 48, 49(all), 50, 52(r), 55(l), 58(all), 61, 62(r), 63(m), 64(all), 67(t), 69, 70(all), 73, 80, 84(m,l), 85(tl), 87, 89(tl,ll, lr), 90, 91, 102(all), 104(l), 106, 107, 108(ll), 110(r), 112(tr), 115, 131(tl), 138(lml), 139(lr), 143(r), 144(ll), 148(ll), 150(l), 151(l), 152(ll), 164(ll), 166(l), 168(tl, lm), 171(lr), 173(tr), 174, 180(tl), 181(lr), 182(m), 184, 185(ll), 187(tl,m), 190(t,ll), 193, 200(ml,tr), 201(tr), 212™
Dallas Public Library, xiv (t,l), 2(l), 3(tl), 4(tl), 5(l), 9(l), 67(l), 92, 112(ll), 113, 119, 121(l), 126(l) , 131(ll), 134(t), 152-3(m), 217(tr,lr)
David C. Scott Collection, xiii (low), xiv (mid), xv (tr), xvi (tl/tr/lr), xvii, xviii (tr), 6, 8, 11(l), 15(lr), 18(t,m), 28, 34(l), 37, 42(ll),45(r), 47, 51(l), 52(l), 56, 57(all), 59, 62(t,m), 63(l), 65(all), 66(all), 71(t,m), 93(l) , 101(all), 108(lr), 124(tr), 125(tr), 138(ll, tm), 140, 144(handbook), 147(handbook, lr), 148(lr, m), 158(lr), 164(lr), 165(mr, ml), 185(lr), 186(t), 187(tr), 188(t,m), 194, 198, 199(ll), 200(pins, ribbons), 206(all), 212(patches), 214(ll), 215(all), 216(lr), 217(ll), 224(l), 225(lr), 226(mr), 229(ml,ll), 230(tr), 235(tr), 236(m), 237(lr,mr), 239, 246(all), 247(l), 248(tl,ml), 250(tr,lr), 258, 262(tl), 265(t), 268, 273, 283(l), 284, 291, 304(patch), 310(t), 316, 330(m), 339
Ponce Duran Jr., 312(tl)

Wayne Ellis, 330(tr)
Fondren Library, Southern Methodist University, 4(m)
Chris Fox, 305(all)
Joe Griffis Collection, 207(ll), 227(l), 252, 276(all), 277, 330(ll)
Dr. Terry Grove/Mike Roytek, 33(l)
Calvin Grubbs Collection, xviii (ll,lr)
Harbin Scout Museum,   xix (l), 12(all), 15(lr), 21(t,m), 23(t), 24, 31(all), 32(ll,lr), 40, 41, 72, 77, 79, 81, 83(l), 84(tl), 85(tr,m,l), 89(tr), 95, 96(all), 97(l), 98(all), 99(all), 100, 104(t), 109, 110(l), 111, 112(t m), 114, 118, 121(t), 122(ll), 123(all), 124(l,lr), 125(m,ll,lr), 127(all), 128(all), 129(all), 130(all), 132(lr), 133(m,l), 137(r), 141(t), 142(l), 14(patches), 145(tr), 145(ll), 146(all), 147(patch), 148(t), 150(r), 151(t), 154(all), 155, 157, 162, 163(l), 165(ll, lm), 167(all), 169(t), 173(lr), 178(all), 179(t), 181(ll), 182(t,l), 186(l), 207(all photos), 210(l,mr,lr), 211(all), 213(tl,tr), 216(tl,ll), 223(all), 226(tl), 227(tr,lr), 228(mr,lr), 229(mr,lr), 230(tl,l), 231(tl,m), 234(tr), 238(all), 250(ll), 253(all), 254(all), 256(lr), 261, 262(tr), 269(l), 286(r), 287(r), 293(tr), 296-7, 299, 300, 306
William P. Hemenway Collection, 327(tl)
Robert Higginbotham Collection, 263
William "Green Bar Bill" Hillcourt Trust, 197
Charles Holmes Archive, 168(l), 199(t), 209(tr,m,l), 219(tl,tr), 224(tl,tr), 272(all)
Johnsey Family Archive, 126(t)
Dick Johnson, 164(tm)
Library of Congress, xv (tl,l), 3(tr), 14(t), 22, 23(l), 26, 27(all), 39, 42(t), 51(r), 53, 54, 76, 149(ll), 177, 245
Mitch Reis Collection, 139(tm)
Ray H. Marr Archive, 269(t)
Roger Morgan, 310(l), 317(ll)
Tim Olive, 248(br)
Ron Pearlman, 322(tl)
Trevor Rees-Jones, 336(tl)
Eddie Reitz Collection, 138(tr,mr)
Richmond Family Archive, 7(all)
Jamie Schell, 338(t)
Brad Shine Collection, 336(tr)
John K. Shipes, xiii, xxiv, 18, 36, 97(t), 116, 122(r), 141(l), 142-3, 158(tr), 159, 172(l), 180(tr), 183, 191, 201(tl), 216(tr), 220, 292(t,ll), 321, 322, 325(all), 326(ll,lr,mr,tr), 331(t,l), 334, 338(l), 340, 342, 344(tl,l), 347
Stephen Shore, 326(tl), 328(t)
Gene Smith Collection, 112(tl)
Cody Stevenson, 21(l)
Jon Q. Thompson Collection 145(lr, lm)
Scott Thompson, 307(all)
Rex Tillerson, 308(ll)
Troop 70 Archive, 247(lr)
University of Ohio, 137(l),

index

A

A Time to Tell, 273
Ace Medal, 64
Addington, Glen D., 19
Addison, Bob, 31
African American Scouts, 134, 174–175, 184, 185, 186, 227, 231, 232
Eagle Scouts, 335
Age, requirements for Scouts, 194
Akers, Ralph Glenn, 160
Akers, Sambo, 160

Alexander, F.H., 118
Alexander, James, 330
Alexander, Michael, 267
Allen, Arch C., 103
Allen, Austin, 232
Allison, Albert, 209
Allman, Pierce, 233
Allred, James V., 136, 147, 167
Allred, Stanley, 338
Amboree, Durinde, 184
Anderson, Alfred W., 200

Anderson, William M., 107
Angell, George R., 107, 138, 140, 142, 147, 194
Ardinger, Anita, 199
Ardmore (Oklahoma) Council, 106
Ardry, J. Howard, 20
Armstrong, Naomi, 69
Armstrong, Neil, 237
Arnold, F.M., 169
Arnold, L.C., 140
Arrington, Scott, 335

Arrowcorps 5, 318
Ashburn, W.L., 88
Asian Scouts, 228, 279
Atwell, Toni, 324
Atwell, William H., 39, 57
Audit & Ethics Committee, 306
Augsburger, Phil, 280
Avery, Al, 150
Ayers, Clayton, 214
Ayers, Lucretia, 178
Ayers, Norman, 214

B

Babe Ruth, 126, 127
Bachman's Dam campsite, 45-46
Baden-Powell, Robert, 315
Bahnman, 343
Baker, Elmo, 248
Baker, Tom, 103
Ballew, Mike, 237
Ballow, William Chunn, 144, 147
Bankston, Douglas, 160
Barber, Alden, 237
Barcus, Walter Scott, 62, 67, 68, 69, 78, 79, 80, 81
bio of, 69
Barcus, William F. and Katie, 69
Barnes, W.C., 100
Barnett, Rowland, 345
Barnett, W.F., 345
Barnhurst, Douglas, 31
Barrel boxing, 23
Barrow, Clyde, 35, 37
Bartle, H. Roe, 193
Barton, Charles W., 193
Bassett, Wallace, 100
Baxter, Richard, 182
Baylor Medical College, 3
Beard, Daniel Carter, 162–163, 247
Beaupre, Richard, 209
Beckett Place, 254, 255
Beckett, Thomas G., 254, 255
Bee, Phillip, T., 233
Beecherl, Louis, 265
Bell, Claude, 150, 151

Bennett, Brian, 286–287
Benno, Claire, 328
Benno, Louis, 328
Berglund, E.N., 88
Bernet, Harre M., 107, 108
Berry, Hugh, 102
Berry, Jack R., 86, 89, 90
Biegler, David, 336
Billy Sowell Boy Scout Camp, 285–286
Bird-Faulkner College Scholarship, 141
Bird, George Hedden, 140, 141
Bird, John, 141
Birdsong, Don, 96, 97, 331
Bishop, W.L., 41
Bison, Theodore, 102
Bivens, Giroud, 65
Blackburn, Joe, 225
Blackburn, Roger, 225
Blackburn, Thurman, 225
Blackburn, Walter, 225
Blackwell, Pryor, 294, 295
Blackwell, Rebel, 294
Blaffer, Camilla Davis, 258
Blaha, John, 165
Blaine, E.J., 168
Blair, Eliza, 11
Blair, Enoch, 11
Blassingame, W. Doak, 107
Blount, Sherwood, 323
Bobby Lyle and Billy Gamble Scouting Center, 324
Bohanan, Clarence W., 82, 83
Booth, John, 9

Boothman, Mrs. Claude O., 239
Boren, C.C., 162–163
Bouras, Alice, 190
Bowers, Malcolm B., 216
Bowles, Frank R., 105
Bowling, J.S., 41
Bowman, Gus, 223
Boy Scout Farms, 53
Boy Scout Handbook, updated requirements, 245–247
Boy Scout War Service Gardening Medal, 52
Boy Scouting in Oklahoma, 86
Boyd, Houston, 59
Boyle, Allen, 59, 168
Boyles, John Allen, 58
BoyPower membership campaign, 236–238, 241, 245, 255
Boys Cubbook, The, 140, 142
Bradford, Ben, 169
Bradford, R.S., 34
Bradle, Michael, 303
Bradshaw, Eugene, 30
Bradshaw, Lynwood, 30
Brady, David, 267
Breeland, A.W., 206
Brennan, D.J., 106
Bright, D.W., 138, 162–163
Briscoe, Dolph, 249
Brooks, Dick, 295
Brooks, James Albert, 35, 38
Brotherhood of Cheerful Service, 165
Brown, Gene, 226

Brown, Milton, 153, 155, 156, 186
Brown, Ralph, 59
Brown, Ty, 237
Bryan, John Neely, 2–3
BSA membership card, 47
Buchanan, Lex, 110
Buddington, Ralph C., 147
Burget, Ben, 140
Burke, Don, 301, 310, 312, 340–341
Burnett, A.C., 100
Burnett, William G., 128
Burt, Joe, 120, 121
Busch, Adolphus, 59
Bush, Barbara, 339
Bush, George W., 320, 335, 338
Bush, Laura, 338–339
Butler, F.H., 160
Butler, H.M., 47
Butler, Lavinia, 61
Butterfield, Elmer C., 63, 64
Buvens, Jerude, 59
Byers, Maude, 33
Byrd, Richard E., 136

C

Caldwell, D., 49

Cameron, Cecil, 165

Camp 5-Mile Creek, 266

Camp Advancement, 69, 70, 71

Camp Brooklawn, 258

Camp Campbell, addition to Camp Wisdom, 104, 105

Camp Cherokee, 235

Camp Cherokee, 286, 295

Camp Cherokee, renamed, 334, 336

Camp Comanche, 235

Camp Comanche, renaming of, 271

Camp Constantin, 187, 189–192, 206–208, 210, 211, 216, 225, 228, 231, 271, 286, 317

aquatics base and, 288–289

cooking at, 253

gas lease on, 252

Camp Grayson, 186, 188, 283, 286, 295

Camp James Ray, 186, 188, 296

Camp Meisenbach, 271

Camp Murchison, 208, 211

Camp Service, 63, 64

Camp Shuler, 208, 211

Camp Texoma, 186, 188, 206–208, 210, 211, 215, 236–237

constructing monkey bridges, 253

divesting, 252–254

Camp Trinity Trails, 240, 258

Camp Wisdom, 229, 240, 280, 285, 346

adding acres, 270

advertising brochure, 101

craving totem poles, 253

expanding, 294

farm at, 110

Fire Brigade, 96

flag ceremony, 111

Ghost tree at, 123

handicapped facilities at, 267

Honor Camper at, 104, 124

inner city camping and, 254–255

logo for, 100

map showing highway proposal, 233

Owl logo, 130

peaches, 129

renovation of, 206–211, 215

Scoutmaster training at, 99

Winter Camp, 169

Campbell, Clara, 78

Campbell, Claude, 12

Campbell, Mary, 144

Campbell, Payton L., 75, 78, 105

Campbell, T.R., 82

Capers, Kenneth, 12, 17, 31

Carey, Ernest J., 323

Carey, Ernest, J., 339, 341

Carmona, Juan, 162–163

Carnegie, Andrew, 8

Carpenter, C.C., 168

Carpenter, Mary Ann, 107

Castleberry, 329

Catton, John, 105

Cedar Springs, founding of, 2

Centennial Camporee, 331–334

Chambers, Herbert L., 184

Chambers, Miler W., 184

Character Camp, 309

Chickasaw Council, 88

Chitwood, Judy P., 193

Christine, Leah, 145

Christmas Service Projects, 151

Circle Ten Council:

Annual Dinner (1976), 251

merger of, 124

National Jamboree contingency, 162–163

newly renamed, 115

partnership with Dallas Youth Crime Commission, 284–285

Ranch, 120

Strategic Plan 2011–2015, 323

Service badge, 246

technology and, 273

Circle Ten Council Ranch, 120

Clardy, John M. "Don," 115, 182

Clark, Tom C., 20

Clayton, Alison, 182

Clements Scout Ranch, 131, 132, 235, 286

horse program st, 264–265

rebuilding, 265–266, 270

upgrading, 334–335

Clements Scout Reservation, 234–235, 261

gas lease on, 252

Clements, William P. "Bill," 131, 145, 165, 233, 234–235, 238–239, 295

bio of, 132

Cliff Temple's Troop 48 (adult), 138

Clothing, official Scout, 15

Cobb, Nicholas, 343

Cockrell, Alexander, 2

Cockrell, Sarah Horton, 2

Collins, James M., 258–259

Colwell, Joe, 240

Commander, Glenn, 160–161

Computer system, first, 263

Connally, John, 228, 233

Connell, George T., 143

Connor, Ruben Travis, 160

Constantin, Eugene P., 190, 246

Continuing the Legacy Campaign, 312–313, 330

Contreras, Adriana, 311

Contreras, Jose, 311

Contreras, Juan, 311

Coolidge, Calvin, 94, 120, 129

Coolidge, J.R., 21

Cooper, Charles, M., 209

Cooper, S.C., 21

COPES course, 294

Corcoran, C.J., 88

Corcoran, Dick, 284, 324

Corley, Quentin D., 14, 37, 35, 38, 40, 45

Cornelius, Jimmy, 160

Craig, Thomas E., 140

Crate, H.E., 88

Crate, Herbert, L., 168

Crawford, T.A., 168

Crock, Rick, 313

Crocker, Paul, 237

Crocker, Steve, 237

Crofton, Joe, 202

Crook, Tommy, 237

Crosman, Carrie, 251

Cross, J.J., 184

Crow Trammell, 271

Cub Leader Pow Wow training, 264

Cub Scout program:

beginning of, 140, 142–144

uniforms, 146

Cub World Day program, 240

Cub World Space Station, 290

Cub World, 280, 290, 291, 295

Culver, Peter, 315

Cunningham, George, 47

Currie, Pat, 322–323, 330, 341–342

D

Dabbs, Darry, 250

Dallas Council Boy Scout Band:

formation of, 20

performance at Texas State Fair, 23

Dallas Council:

expansion of, 113

first annual meeting, 20

fund-raising for, 88, 90

membership, 91

quarters for, 92

Dallas Scout, The, 73

Dallas skyline:

1914, 26

1918, 43

1920, 77

Dallas Youth Crime Commission, 284–285

Dallas, founding of, 2

Dallas, George Mifflin, 2

Daniel, Price, 225

Danny White Golf Classic, 268

Davis, Clarenton, 55

Davis, Patricia, 258

Davis, T.Z., 227

Davis, Wirt, 258
Dealey, George B., 57
Dealey, Joe, 236
Deffenbach, Charles Levi, 107
Deffenbach, Daniel C., 107
Demases, James, 186
Denison Council, 88, 106
Denning, Leslie B., 138, 147, 152, 174, 328
Denver (Colorado) Council, 130
Diggs, Marshall, 140
Directing traffic, 55
Disabled Scouts, 226, 228, 257, 267
Distinguished Eagle Scout Award, 286

Districts, growth in number of, 55
Dobey, Haron, 38
Donald, L.O., 120
Donnell, Earl R., 178
Dorsey, Henry, 175
Dougherty, Etti, 102
Dougherty, Eugene, 165
Doughty, Walter C., 102
Doughty, Walter F., 102
Drug Awareness Program, 273
Drum & Bugle Corps, 49
Duggan, Orton Lorraine, 129, 130, 131, 138, 142, 147, 151–152, 155, 156
Duke, Spartan, 160
Dumas, J.P., 2

Duncan, William W., 100
Duran, Ponce, 309, 311, 312, 314, 319
Durant Council, 87
Durrett, David D., 301
Dyer, Frank, 88

E
Eagle Palm, 122
Eagle Scout Award kit, 238
Eagle Scout Banquet, 233
Eatmon, Abraham, 227
Echols, W.G., 147
Eckford, J.J., 23
Eckstein, Arnold Carter, 239
Eckstein, Gary, 239
Eckstein, Mary Jane Stevens, 239

Eckstein, Steven, 239
Edson, Carroll A., 168
Eisenhower, Dwight D., 186, 198, 209, 224
Elliott, Ange, 331
Ellison, Dave, 120
Emergency service training, 179
Ernest T. Trigg Award, 240
Etter, Henry, 88
Etzenhouser, Russell, 324
Ewing, Bill, 200
Explorador Scouts, 134
Explorer SOAR Exposition, 239, 241, 247

F

Farmer, Curtis C., 66, 341
Farmers Branch, founding of, 2
Farnsworth, Austin M., 10, 11
Farnsworth, Joseph E., 11, 19, 22, 23, 24, 25, 26, 34, 35, 37
Farrington, Jerry S., 290
Faulkner, Frank V., 140, 141, 208

Federal Reserve Banks, 55
Feed a Soldier gardens, 52
Female Explorers, first, 239
Fenley, George, 170
Ferguson, Scott, 263, 307
Ferris, Carl, 57
Field, Thomas William, 37
Field's Folly, 37
Fisher, C.E., 41

Fitch, James P., 60, 62, 71, 73, 88, 90, 130, 147, 156, 162–163, 179
Fitzpatrick, Ruth, 190
Fletcher, Sandy, 164
Florence, Fred F., 149
Flowers, Bill, 162–163
Folsom, F.V., 170
Folsom, Robert, 257
Ford, Frank, 65
Francis, J.D., 209

Frederich, Ron, 267
Freeman, Don William, 107
French, Lee Hill, 74–75
Frickel, George C., 216
Friends of Scouting Dinner, 339
Furst, Debra, 288–289
Furst, Jack D., 288–289, 290, 295, 304, 308, 312, 314, 315, 324, 329

G

Gamble Law, 262
Gamble, William C., 261–262, 264, 266, 273, 274, 276, 279, 283, 285, 286, 294, 295, 296, 298, 299, 312
Gammon, Bob, 182
Gannon, Edward James, 285
Gannon, Lucille Highes Murchison, 271, 285
Gardner, Clarence, 182
Gardner, Harold Frederick, 103
Garrett, Robert, 310
Garrity, John J., 120
Gas leases, 252
Gassett, Hollis, 258
Gates, Robert, 335, 338, 339

Gatheman, E.F., 169
Gathering of Eagles, 309
Geller, William C., 30
Gender issues, 251, 252
women as scoutmasters, 273
General Eisenhower Waste Paper Medal, 186
George, John W., 50
Gettysburg Reunion, 26, 27
Gibson, G.M., 82
Gifford, P.W., 240
Gilstrap, Noble, 227
Glew, Robert C., 192
Glidewell, James Arthur, 41, 43, 44–45, 50
Glidewell, James H., 44
Godden, Bobby, 170, 182
Gokey, Raymond, 125

Golden Acorn leadership course, 229, 261
Golden Chick/Jay Novacek Celebrity Shoot, 290
Gonzalez, Al, 268
Good Turn Day, 241–242
Goodman, E. Urner, 168
Goodnight, Henry B., 57, 168
Goodson, R.A., 233
Goolsby, Bianca, 331
Gordon, Lee, 91
Gorman, Alice, 34Gorman, Arthur, 17, 20, 30, 34
Gorman, Oscar H., 34
Governor's Trail, 266
Grable, Charles F., 218, 223, 225, 229, 230, 267

Graves, Wade, 310
Gray, Walter S.S., 34
Grayson County Council, 88
Eagle Scouts in, 107
formation, 106
Great American Race, 279
Great Depression, 140
Green, Bart, 263
Green, Wilber, 107
Greene, Forrest, 159
Griffin, James M., 312
Griffin, R.P., 47
Guide to Safe Scouting, 307
Guildart, Jim, 7
Guildart, Richmond, 7
Guion, David Wendell, 149

H

Haas, George M., 78, 125, 127, 145
Haden, Myrtle L., 141
Hall, W.T., 88
Hall, William, 187
Hamilton, George L., 106
Hancock, Curtis, 35, 50
Handbook for Boys, 146, 147
updated requirements, 245–247
Harbin Scout Museum, 287
Harbin, Elijah P., 287
Harbin, John P., "Jack," 282, 287, 290, 295
Hardin, John Alexander, 8
Hardin, Roy H., 8
Hardy, Howard, 209
Hargrave, Norman, 127, 147, 154, 155
Harkey, John, 331
Harris, A.E., 214
Harris, Clinton B., 89, 90
widow of, 120
Harris, Les, 185
Harris, Paul, 20
Harris, Prince, 30
Harvey, Omar, 235

Haseltine, Richard G., 103, 106
Haseltine, Richard S., 103
Hawthorne, Alma, 267
Hawthorne, Douglas D., 280
Hayes, Nat, 168
Haynes, Bill, 165
Haynes, Bonnie, 167
Haynes, Fred E., 165, 167
Haynes, Louise, 167
Head, W.B., 232
Hedgecock, Paul, 301
Heidenreich, Jerry, 242–243
Hemenway, William P., 247
Hendricks, Brian, 345
Hendricks, Earl, 214
Hendricks, O.R., 214, 216
Henning, Charles, 59
Herring, Benjamin O., 29
Hess, Charles, N., 88
Hester, Fred, 110
Hewitt, W.A., 100
Hibbard, Will, 106
Higginbotham, Bobby, 263
Hill, Leslie, 140
Hillary, Eric Eugene, 241
Hillcourt, William, 216, 262

Hillyer, G.B., 138
Hines, Scoutmaster, 103
Hispanic Scouts, 134, 174, 227
Hispanic Together Plan, 268
Hoagland, George S., 105
Hobson, Harry E., 114
Hobson, Harry H., 118, 120
Hodnett, Oscar, 55
Hoffman, Rob, 329
Holland, Frank P., 131
Holland, William M., 14, 15, 16, 23
Holliday, John Henry "Doc," 4
Holman, Mary Ruth, 68
Holmes, Charles, 272
Holt, Gene Allen, 160
Holtmann, C.A., 138
Honor Camper organization, 165
Hoover, Herbert, 129
Hopkins, Granville S., 100
Hord, Thomas Alan, 2, 12, 17, 29, 31, 41, 79, 89, 90, 97, 98, 104, 107, 108, 109, 128, 147, 151, 152, 153, 162–163, 168, 246

Hord, William Henry, 2
Hord's Ridge, founding of, 2
Hotchkiss, Loys L., 155–158, 160, 164, 165, 166, 167, 170, 175, 179, 180, 187, 192, 206, 212, 215, 217–218, 223, 225, 246
Hotchkiss, Martha, 156
House of Eagles, 139
Houston, Sam, 2, 70
Howard, R.G., 128
Howard, Wesley, 209
Hulcy, Dechard A., 192
Hulen, A.M., 160
Hulen, Walter, 160
Humphreys, Albert E., 104, 105–106, 110, 139–140
Hunt, H.L., 296
Hunt, Nancy Ann, 296, 316, 330
Hunt, Ray, 316
Hunt, Ruth Ray, 296
Hunt, W. Herbert, 264–265
Hurricane Katrina projects, 310, 312
Hutton, Craig, 315–316
Hyer, Robert Stewart, 32

I

Ince, James William, 286

Interracial Committee, 134

Irwin, Ivan, 104

Isbell, Christopher C., 122

J

Jack D. Furst Aquatics Base, 288–289, 304
Jacoby, Henry Harris, 38
Jacoby, Henry Hibbler, 38
Jaffe, Morris I., 328
Jennings, Frank, 106
Jester, L.I., 35
Jim Sowell Administration headquarters, 287

John D. Murchison Scouting Center, 291–294
Johnsey, Robert W., 126, 127
Johnson, Dick, 229
Johnson, Hilary, 300
Johnson, J.A., 190
Johnson, J.E., 162–163
Johnson, Jack, 180
Johnson, Lapat, 180

Johnson, Lemuel H., 159, 164, 165, 229
Johnson, Mark, 123
Johnson, Ryan, 96, 97
Jones, George Miller, 139
Jones, Homer C., 166
Jones, Tom, 48
Jonsson Erik, 234
Joor, William, 89

Joplin, Buzzy, 237
Jordan, Jerry, 272
Jordan, Joshua, 304
Jordan, Maple Pearl, 115
Journey to Excellence program, 340–341
Jung, Richard W., 228

K

Kahn, Lawrence, 75
Kalusche, Earl, 168
Kanmacher, Fred, 102
Keeley, George W., 44, 46, 47, 57, 66, 168
Kennedy, Keith, 336
Kerr, C.P., 80
Keyes, Bobby, 180

Kilgore, Bassett, 307
Kimball, Justin Ford, 38, 66, 147
Kimmons, Byron, 33
Kimmons, James M., 33
Kimmons, Richard T., 17, 20, 31, 32, 38
bio of, 33

Kingsbury, Walter E., 83–84, 85, 87
Kitterman, Oscar A., 106, 107, 108, 112, 113, 125, 126, 127, 129
Klaudt, David, 306
Knott, John, 224
Koch, O.H., 86

Krauss, Ron J., 279
Kuhen, Joseph Morris, 78
Kyker, Rob, 312

L

Lake Wozencraft, 83–84, 85, 86
view, 130
Landry, Tom, 248
Lane, Lillian, 107
Lang, Otto (florist), 37, 129
Lang, Otto Henry, 46, 47, 50, 57, 73, 168
Langdon, C.I., 138
Lanier, Red, 165
Lankenau, Kip, 331
Lankford, Harold J., 164
Lankford, Jim, 237

Leachman, Neth, 151, 156
Leaders' Training Continuum, 302
Learning for Life program, 280, 309
Lee, Ingram, 168
Lee, J.E., 66
Lee, Umphrey, 201
Lee, Walter Sanders, 55, 57–58, 59, 61, 62, 64, 66, 67, 68, 69, 82, 168
Lee, William Bell, 61
Lee. Ingram, 55, 59, 67

Leedom, John, 165
Lennon, Howard, 170
Lenoir, Phil, 10
Leslie, J.L., 100
Lewis, Louria F., 57
Lewis, Louria H., 57, 74
Leyendecker, Joseph C., 47
Liberty Loan Bonds, 42, 52, 53, 54, 56, 62, 65
Liberty Loan Medal, 56, 65
Litter Drill, 23
Lively, R.H., 65
Livingstone, Colin R., 67

Long, Thomas, 329
Loper, John, 295
Lopez, Trini, 268
Lovett, Kevin, 310
Lyle, Bobby B., 284, 290–291, 312, 330
Lynn, Andrew, 152
Lynn, Ted Jr., 152-153
Lynn, Theodore E., 152–153
Lyons, Jared, 325

M

Maas, Laura, 11
MacDonald, Anne, 311
Mahoney, Mike, 159, 164
Making of a Scout, The, (movie), 22
Malone, Ralph, 50
Maloney, W.P., 35
Mandrell, Louise, 268
Mantle, Mickey, 268
Marceleno, Troy, 268
Marcus, Stanley, 63
Margolin, Frank P., 48–49
Marr, Ray, 263, 268, 269, 276
Martin, J.A., 138
Marvin, Z,E., 73
Mast, Claude A., 65, 68
Mast, Elfrieda, 65
Mast, Frank A., 65
Matthews, Carl, 160–161
Matthews, Louis Frederick, 91
Matthews, Will, 160
Mazzuca, Robert J., 311, 314, 329
McAdoo Prize, 56
McAdoo, William G., 52, 56
McAnally, D.H., 214

McArthur Garden Award, 187
McClung, Rufus, 131, 162–163, 272
McCord, William C., 285
McCoy, John C., 2
McCoy, John M., 2
McDaniel, Tillman, 107
McDowell, Robert Chester, 42, 48, 51, 52, 56, 57, 59
McDowell, Robert Emmett, 48
McGee, L.E., 50
McGill, Harrison Holman, 59, 63, 64, 65, 67, 168
bio of, 68
McGill, Harrison Hugh, 68
McGill, Maelan, 68
McGregor, Doug, 237
McGregor, George A., 100
McHenry, R.E., 162–163
McKenzie, R. Tate, 291
McKinsey, Jerry, 185
McKnight, Rufus N., 68
McLain, Frank E., 209
McLean, H.L., 106
McNeil, Connor, 317
McNeny, Frank L., 172

Meador, C.J., 140
Meador, Jack, 140
Meador, Joe Mickey, 140
Meisenbach, Kurt K., 120, 128, 271
Meisenbach, Ruby Trim, 271
Mercer, Thomas "Fred," 21
Merit Badge Show, first, 169–171, 173, 174
Merrem, William Elmo, 31
Metrocell Building, 280
Mexican Scout Exchange, 271
Meyers, Walter Howard, 140
Middleton, William A., 12, 35
Mier, John, 165
Mikanakawa Lodge, 165
Service Award, 313
Miller Margaret Cameron, 38
Miller, Bobby, 182
Mitchell-Head Service Center, 232, 270
sell of, 279, 291
Mitchell, Eva Dee, 69
Mitchell, Homer R., 232
Mitchell, John E., 209
Mitchell, John Forbes, 86
Mitchell, Orville, 214

Moffitt, Samuel A., 47–48
Mohrle, Charles, 331
Monson, Arch, 252
Montgomery, T.T., 88
Moody, Daniel J., 120
Moore, H. E., 50
Moore, J.H., 47
Moore, Warren G., 249
Moreno, Sam, 268
Mosher, W.S., 215
Moss, Caleb M., 103
Muire, Forest, 169
Mullaney, Matt, 304
Munger, Roy, 58, 90
Murchison Scouting Center, 279
Murchison, Clint, 234, 285
Murchison, John D., 222, 234, 238–239
Murchison, Lucille Hughes "Lupe," Gannon, 271, 285
Murchison, Virginia, "Ginger," 271
Murray, William D., 8
Muse, E.B., 80

N

Nash, Lloyd, 37
Nash, W.G., 138
National Jamboree (1937), 159, 161-164
National Jamboree, second, 194, 196–199
National Jamboree (1960), 224
National Jamboree (1969), 236–237

National Jamboree (1973), 247
National Jamboree, Centennial (2010), 326–327, 329
National Youth Leadership Training (NYLT), 229
Negro Scout Court of Honor, 174
Neu, Charles T., 47
Newberry, Ben A., 138

Newberry, Ben R., 188
Newell, Charles H., 107, 120, 121
Newhouse, Robert, 339
Newman, Benjamin W., 140
Newton, Conrad, 160–161
Niblo, Grady, 294, 299
Nicholl, James E., 180
Nicholson, Drue Edward, 148
Nicholson, Nadine, 148

Nicodemus, Chester, 6
Nicodemus, John Forrest, 6
Nicols, William, 110, 112
Nino, Jose, 303
Nixon, Pat, 240
Nixon, Richard M., 239, 241
Non-Discrimination Policy, 232
Nunnallee, Rae A., 345

O

O'Donnell, Michael F., 306
O'Dwyer, Thomas A., 260, 261, 262
O'Dwyer, Thomas R., 141
O'Neal, Lloyd, 147
O'Pry, Bill, 280

Oak Cliff Scoutmasters' Association, 100
Oak Cliff Scoutmasters' Club, formation of, 49
Oak Cliff, founding of, 2
Oesterreicher, Jim, 283

On My Honor, I Will, 273–270
Order of the Arrow, 68, 124, 139
  beginnings of, 165, 168
Overbeck, Edward, 159

Owl C patch, 100
Ownby, R.K., 88

P

Pan American World's Fair, 148–150
Parker, Bonnie, 35, 37
Parker, Earl, 147
Parker, Kenneth, 182
Parmerlee, Mark, 290
Parrish, Donnie, 225
Parrish, Leon, 225
Parrish, Ronnie, 225
Patrol Leader's Handbook, 216
Pennington, Fred, 170

Pennington, Randy G., 273–279
Perot, H. Ross, 238, 239, 310, 336
Perrin, T.O., 120
Perry, E. Gordon, 90
Perry, Rick, 329
Perryman, W.A., 100
Peters Colony, 2
Petit, Rafael, 162–163
Peyton, Mae Roger, 145

Phillips, A.R., 37
Phillips, Jerry, 209
Phillips, Waite, 182
Philmont, 224
Philturn Rocky Mountain Scout Camp, 182–183
Pickard, J.M., 206
Pickens, T. Boone, 305
Piercy, Harvey J., 198, 216
Poitt, Joe, 209
Polio Awareness, 157–158

Pollard, Aubrey Wilford, 198
Popcorn sales, fundraiser, 276–277
Porter, Bud, 270
Pote, Harold F., 139
Price, Harvey L., 184, 185, 194
Price, Ray, 268
Project SOAR, 239, 241, 247

Q–R

Raines, Joshua, 317
Ratliff, Hubert E., 81, 84, 86, 88
Ray, James, 296
Reaugh, Frank, 178
Recruiter patch, 225
Red River Valley Council, 88
annexation of, 192
Rees-Jones, Jan, 330, 334, 336
Rees-Jones, Trevor, 251, 330, 334, 336
Rees, William Nelson, 103
Reitz, Eddie, 165, 185
Reitz, Robert, 124, 287, 132, 141, 167, 328

Rice, Condoleezza, 339–340
Richardson, James A., 171
Richmond, Adeline, 7
Richmond, Claude Marion, 2, 3, 5, 6, 8, 9, 10, 15, 16, 17, 19, 24, 28, 31, 34, 43, 82, 88, 106
bio of, 7
fundraising, 20, 35, 38–39
resignation of, 39–40
Richmond, John S., 7
Rigby, Lloyd, 117
Ritchie, Robert, 233
Robb, Dave, 182
Robbins, Ray, 268
Robertson, Duke, 268

Robinett, Dorothy R., 68
Robinson, F.G., 138
Rodriguez, Mike, 174
Rogers, Chris, 317
Roosevelt, Franklin D., 146, 152, 157, 159, 162–163, 174, 177, 328
Rose, Mike, 329
Ross, Michael, 311
Rubio, Raymundo "Tata," 227
Rubio, Raymundo, Jr., 227
Rupard, Edith, 44
Rutherford, P.M., 216
Rutland, Carl J., 208
Ryan, J.W., 16

S

Saam, George W., 10
Sailers, Lon, 199, 224, 272
Sanders, Jimmie, 55
Sanford Aquatic Center, 296
Sanford, Lola, 296
Sanford, Robert F., 296
Sanger, Alex, 13
Sanger, Charles L., 75, 80
Sanger, Eli L., 13, 39, 57, 58, 69, 74, 75
Sanger, Philip, 58
Schlitterbahn, 208
Schoolar, Charles H., 141
Schuck, Arthur A., 147
Schultz, Fred, 170
Scott, Burton L., 237
Scott, Elmer, 110, 114
Scott, Jim, 12
Scout Circus (1958), 201
Scout Circus, 88
attendance, 218
first, 172–174
Scout Commission School, 80
Scout Exposition:
(1949), 194
(1955), 200, 213
Scout Field Day Program, organization of, 49
Scout Handbook, updated requirements, 245–247
Scout Leader's Reserve Corps, 57
Scout Shop, 314

Scout Show:
(1974), 250
(1987), 271, 273, 278
(2007), 314
(2009), 316
last, 330
Scout Stupenda, 62
Scoutfitter, 270, 307
Scouting for Food, 274–275
Scoutmaster Training, first course in, 56
Scoutmaster's Key Award, 131
ScoutReach, 336, 342
Sea Scouting, 181
Seay, Charles, 57
Sedgwick, Dale, 168
Segovia, Felix, 134
Seidenglanz, Charles H., 107
Senior Scout Explorer Programs, 166
Sergeant, George, 151
Service Organizations, 165
Service projects, 158–159, 202-206
Sessions, Loys R., 108, 124, 125
Sessions, Pete, 298, 299
Shaftner, George, 200, 201
Shay, Julia, 141
Shelton, Prior, 254
Shepherd, E.L., 29
Sherman Scout Council, 106
Shivers, Allan, 200, 209

Shoop, Thomas W., 144, 147
Shull, Henry, 150
Shuman, A.L., 106
Silver Beaver Award, 131, 139
Silver Fawn Award, 239
Silver Palm District, 175, 184
Silver Scouters, 294–295
Silvester, Henry R., 23
Siple, Paul Allman, 136–139
Six Flags over Texas, 208
Slaughter, Christopher Columbus, 3
Slayton, John W., 107
Sledge, Edgar, 345
Sliney, Fred L., 30, 35
Sliney, Frederic F., 35
Smile Day, 158, 202–206
Smith, Brad, 224
Smith, Clyde, 30
Smith, Gene, 276, 295
Smith, Harold, 224
Smith, Lee, 141
Smith, McKamy, 214
Smith, Melvin, 215, 216
Smith, Tom E., 214
Sneed, Preston, 100
Snow, Nelda Marie, 145
SOAR Project, 239, 241, 247
Soccer, 303
Sowell, Billy, 285, 286
Sowell, Jim, 267, 285, 286, 287, 291

Sowell, Shirley, 294
Spencer, Perry Holestin, 193
Sports, incorporating, 257
Sprague, George, 168
Stackhouse, Mary Alice, 33
Stark, C.F., 175
State Fair of Texas, 1913, 23
Staubach, Roger, 274
Stellmacher, Herbert, 120, 128
STEM initiative, 341
Stemmons, John M., 270
Stephens, John F., 244
Stevenson, Cody, 21
Stevenson, Coke, 185
Stone, A.L., 128
Stone, Gene, 303, 304, 306, 309
Stone, Glenn E., 298, 300–301
Stone, John, 315
Stowers, Willis L., 140
Stuart, George A., 226
Stuart, George M., 13, 35
Stuart, John, 234, 300, 301, 303, 310, 329
Summer Camp, first, 19
(1950), 207
Summer camps, purchase of, 25, 234
Summerall, Pat, 339

T

Tapp, Robert, 82
Tarr, James L., 230–231, 232, 233, 246, 248, 253, 255, 256, 257, 259, 261, 314, 315
Tarr, Margaret, 315
Taylor, Greg, 263
Taylor, J.H., 168
Taylor, R.H., 102
Taylor, Surce John, 345
Tenderfoot, Tommy, 179
Terrill, Scurry, 19
Texas Centennial Celebration, 149–150
Thomas, Clarence, 284
Thomas, Danny, 268
Thomas, Donald Erick, 335

Thompson, David Henry, 108
Thompson, DeWitt P., 123, 128, 145, 154, 155
Thompson, Hal, 168
Thompson, James W., 108
Thompson, Jesse, 107
Thornton, Robert Lee, 200
Thurber Ranch, 265
Tiger Cubs BSA program, 267
Tillerson, Rex W., 175, 308, 330
Timmons, Mary Nettia, 108
Tipi Huya, 139, 145, 150
Titche, Edward, 12, 13, 35, 38
Toles, Maude, 7

Tree census in Dallas, 80–81
Trevino, Lee, 339
Trevor Rees-Jones Scout Camp, 334–336
Trevor Rees-Jones ScoutReach program, 334–336
Trieller, John, 38
Trigg, Earnest T., 240
Troop 8 (Oak Cliff), history of, 82
Troop 80 (Dallas Gas Company's adult troop), 138
Troop reorganization, 49
Troop Zero, adult troop, 50, 100

Truman, Harry S, 195, 196–198
Tucek, James A., 159, 164
Turner, Winguit A., 30, 38
Tutt, Ernest, 256

U

Uniforms, sellers of, 73

University of Scouting, 147, 264–265

V

Van Slyke, Anson, 162–163
Varsity Program, 270

Venturing program, 300
Victory Book Campaign, 181

Vidler, Jackson W.M., 17
Viglini, John P., 138

W

Waggoner, D.E., 214
Walker, Albert, 168
Walker, Doak, 212
Walker, Matt M., 318, 323, 342
War Service Stamps, 57, 64–65
Ward, Parker, 164
Warner, Laura Jane, 38
Warren, James A., 167
Watkins, Hal, 192
Watkins, Mary Kate, 68
Watson, Bassett, 88
Watson, James, 182
Watts, Albert H., 121, 125
Watts, Bobby R., 170
Webb, Adam, 304
Webb, Hazel Marguerite, 102
Webelos-to-Scout Transition, 306
Webster, C.J., 272
Wells, Ken, 192

West, James E., 51, 52, 71, 83, 122, 145, 159, 162, 174
Wester, Howard W., 90–91, 97, 100, 106, 109
Whitaker, Philip, 312, 313
White Sharks of Tahkodah, 124, 130
White Stag leadership course, 229
White, Andrew, 55
White, Danny, 268, 276
White, Emerson G., 5
White, Otis, 345
White, W.J., 345
Whitney M. Young Service Award, 266–267
Wilderness Camp, 187
Wiles, Major, 88
Wiley, George D., 150
Wilkens, Richmond, 265
Williams, David M., 341
Williams, J.L., 266
Wilson, John B., 3, 90
Wilson, Will R., 150

Wilson, Woodrow, 22, 50–51, 65, 67
Wingren, Harry M., 107
Winn, James, 9
Winn, Steve, 274
Winter Camp, first, 86, 88
Wisdom Guide honor program, 124, 126
Wisdom Honor Camper program, 165
Wisdom Honor Camper, 104, 124
Wisdom Monument, 135
Wisdom, Alfred Henry, 78
Wisdom, Bill, 109
Wisdom, John Shelby, 76–78, 83–84, 85, 86, 94–95, 109, 114, 121, 122, 123, 131, 132, 133, 135, 139, 165
bio of, 78
Wise, Wes, 240
Womack, Hugh Lewis, 160
Wood Badge, 215, 216, 302
Wood, Archie, 140

Woodruff, Elizabeth, 141
Wooldrige, Bob, 306
World Jamboree:
(1937), 159
(1979), Fifteenth, 263, 268, 269
(2007), 314–315
World War II, Scout activities during, 179-181, 184–187
Wortham, A.W., 182
Wozencraft, Frank W., 83–84, 85, 87, 91, 105, 140
Wright, Deran, 294
Wright, Hattie Roberts, 78
Wright, Linus, 295
Wright, Madison "Pink," 76, 78
Wright, Warren, 237
Wynne, Angus G., 13, 208, 209
Wynne, Buck Jim, 13
Wynne, Joanne, 208
Wynne, Toddie Lee, 13

X-Y-Z

Yeager, J.A., 143
Yeager, Y.B., 147
YMCA, influence on Scouting, 6

Young, Clardy, 49
Young, Jay, 31
Young, Towne, 6

Youth Protection Training program, 273
Zaccara, Daniel, 302
Zischang, W.A., 168

DAVID C. SCOTT

Dallas native David C. Scott has been involved with Scouting for over 33 of his 46 years. As a 1981 recipient of the Eagle Scout award that included 5 Eagle palms, Mr. Scott grew-up in the Circle 10 Council and prospered under quality adult tutelage as a Cub Scout as well as a Boy Scout. A Vigil Honor member in the Order of the Arrow and a 2012 Silver Beaver recipient, he graduated Vanderbilt University in 1988 with a B.A. in Psychology. He continued onward to SMU, where he earned a master's degree in Applied Economics in 1993.

In addition to scribing his quarterly column for the International Scouting Collector's Association *Journal* on various topics on Scouting's history,

Dave is the author of two nationally award winning and best-selling books. The first is *The Scouting Party* that recounts the origins of the Scouting movement. The second, titled *We Are Americans, We Are Scouts*, fuses the words and stories of President Theodore Roosevelt within the framework of the ideals of the Boy Scouts of America.

He is a member of the Boy Scouts of America's National Speakers Bank, serves as the Lead of the National Volunteer Training Team assisting BSA's Membership Impact division, and is a member of several National BSA Task Forces.

Dave is a member of numerous lineal and national patriotic societies that include the National Society Sons of the American Revolution, the Sons of the Republic of Texas, the Military Society of the War of 1812, the Jamestowne Society, the Order of the Crown of Charlemagne in the United States of America, the Baronial Order of the Magna Charta, and the Presidential Families of America, being a first cousin (5 generations removed) to President James K. Polk and a second cousin (8 generations removed) to President George Washington.

Dave has been married to his wife of twenty years, Aimee, and they have four children.

JOHN K. SHIPES

"When I was approached by David Scott to work on this book, we spent quite a bit of time discussing the eras that *Where Character Is Caught* would cover. David told a few stories about the early years of Circle Ten and I found them fascinating. We talked about archives of photographs and newspaper articles, and lamented about the vast amount of photographs that do not exist. Important photographs that exist only in microfilm form.

That became the challenge: Create a history of Circle Ten Council with words and images where few images exist.

Thousands of hours were consumed finding and photographing documents, memorabilia, newspaper articles and photographs, then painstakingly restoring and retouch most items. From these stories and images, I am positive you will gain a rich understanding of the challenges and dedication of the people that raised Circle Ten Council into one of the premier Boy Scouts of America councils in the nation."

John K. Shipes is an award-winning photographer, high-end digital consultant and teaching artist. Based in Dallas, Texas during his career, John's work has been published worldwide, including *Better Homes and Gardens, Architectural Digest* and *Gourmet* magazines.

John is an active and dedicated Scouter, since 1996, and has served as Assistant Scoutmaster, Scoutmaster and as District Activities Chair. He is Wood Badge Trained and served on staff at Wood Badge 98.

PenlandScott
PUBLISHERS

PenlandScott Publishers was founded in 2006 for the ambitious purpose of uniting timeless, engaging, and enriching subjects and themes for all ages and interests. Quickly emerging as a resourceful publisher of quality educational, informative, inspirational books and media, PenlandScott also produces award-winning and praiseworthy works for fraternal, faith-based, and service-oriented groups and organizations.